BENJAMIN'S GHOSTS

EDITED BY GERHARD RICHTER

Benjamin's Ghosts

Interventions in Contemporary Literary
and Cultural Theory

STANFORD UNIVERSITY PRESS

STANFORD, CALIFORNIA

2002

Stanford University Press
Stanford, California

© 2002 by the Board of Trustees of the
Leland Stanford Junior University

Printed in the United States of America
On acid-free, archival-quality paper

Library of Congress Cataloging-in-Publication Data

Benjamin's ghosts : interventions in contemporary
literary and cultural theory / edited by Gerhard
Richter.
    p. cm.
  Includes bibliographical references (p.) and index.
  ISBN 0-8047-4125-5 (cloth) —
  ISBN 0-8047-4126-3 (paper)
    1. Benjamin, Walter, 1892–1940.   I. Richter,
Gerhard, 1967–
  B3209.B584 .B45   2002
  838'.91209—dc21

                            2002001134

Original Printing 2002

Last figure below indicates year of this printing:
11 10 09 08 07 06 05 04 03 02

Typeset by Tseng Information Systems, Inc. in
10/14 Janson.

Acknowledgments

Miriam Hansen's essay first appeared in *Critical Inquiry* 25, no. 2 (winter 1999): 306–43; it is here reprinted with permission from the University of Chicago Press. Lutz Koepnick's essay includes material from Chapter 8 of his *Walter Benjamin and the Aesthetics of Power* (Lincoln: University of Nebraska Press, 1999); it appears here with permission from the publisher. Beatrice Hanssen's contribution first appeared in *Modern Language Notes* 114, no. 5 (1999): 991–1013; it is here included courtesy of the Johns Hopkins University Press. German versions of the essays by Eva Geulen, Norbert Bolz, and Bettine Menke appeared, respectively, in *Modern Language Notes* 107, no. 3 (1992): 580–605; *Walter Benjamin: Ästhetik und Geschichtsphilosophie*, ed. Gérard Raulet and Uwe Steiner (Bern: Lang, 1998), 223–31; and *Zeichen zwischen Klartext und Arabeske*, ed. Susi Kotzinger and Gabriele Rippl (Amsterdam: Rodopi, 1993), 307–26. They are included here with permission.

The editor wishes to thank Helen Tartar, as well as Alex Giardino, Amy Jamgochian, Janna Palliser, and Kate Warne, of Stanford University Press, for the scrupulous care they took in seeing the manuscript through the publication process.

Contents

Illustrations

Contributors

NORBERT BOLZ is Professor of Communication and Design at the University of Essen, Germany. Among his recent books are *Weltkommunikation* (2001); *Die Konformisten des Andersseins. Ende der Kritik* (1999); and *Walter Benjamin* (with William van Reijen, 1996).

FRITZ BREITHAUPT teaches in the Department of Germanic Studies at Indiana University, Bloomington. He is the author of *Jenseits der Bilder. Goethes Politik der Wahrnehmung* (2000) and a forthcoming book on the question of why economics became a leading paradigm to explain the world, to be entitled *The Ego Effect of Money*.

STANLEY CORNGOLD is Professor of German and Comparative Literature at Princeton University. Most recently, he is the author of *Complex Pleasure: Forms of Feeling in German Literature* (1998); *The Fate of the Self: German Writers and French Theory* (2d ed. 1994); *Borrowed Lives* (with I. Giersing, 1991); and *Franz Kafka: The Necessity of Form* (1988).

PETER FENVES is Professor of German, Comparative Literature, and Philosophy at Northwestern University and the author of *A Peculiar Fate: Metaphysics and World History in Kant* (1991); *"Chatter": Language and History in Kierkegaard* (1993); *Arresting Language—From Leibniz to Benjamin* (2001); and *Late Kant: An Essay on Failure*. He has also edited *Raising the Tone of Philosophy: Late Essays by Immanuel Kant, Transformative Critique by Jacques Derrida* (1993), and coedited *"The Spirit of Poesy": Essays on Jewish and German Literature and Philosophy in Honor of Géza von Molnár* (2000).

EVA GEULEN is Associate Professor of German at New York University. Among her publications are *Worthörig wider Willen. Darstellungsproblematik und Sprachreflexion in der Prosa Adalbert Stifters* (1992) and *The End of Art: Readings in a Rumour After Hegel*, forthcoming from Stanford University Press.

MIRIAM HANSEN is Ferdinand Schevill Distinguished Service Professor in the Humanities at the University of Chicago, where she teaches in the Department of English and the Committee on Cinema and Media Studies. She has written extensively on German film and film theory and is the author of *Babel and Babylon: Spectatorship in American Silent Film* (1991). She is finishing a book on the Frankfurt School's debates on cinema, mass culture, and modernity.

BEATRICE HANSSEN, a critical theorist and literary critic, was trained in comparative literature at the Humanities Center, Johns Hopkins University, and is Professor of German at the University of Georgia, Athens. She is the author of, among other publications, *Walter Benjamin's Other History: Of Stones, Animals, Human Beings, and Angels* (1998); and *Critique of Violence: Between Poststructuralism and Critical Theory* (2000). In addition, she is the editor of a collection of essays, *The Turn to Ethics* (2000), as well as coeditor of the book series *Walter Benjamin Studies* (Continuum), which will include the volumes *Walter Benjamin and Romanticism* and *Walter Benjamin and the Arcades Project*. She is currently writing a book about the relation between aesthetics and politics from Kant to Adorno and Foucault.

LUTZ KOEPNICK is Associate Professor of German, Film and Media Studies at Washington University in St. Louis. He is the author of *Nothungs Modernität. Wagners Ring und die Poesie der Macht im 19. Jahrhundert* (1994); *Walter Benjamin and the Aesthetics of Power* (1999); and *The Dark Mirror: German Cinema Between Hitler and Hollywood* (2002).

TOM MCCALL is Associate Professor of Humanities at the University of Houston at Clear Lake. He has written extensively on Benjamin and on subjects in diverse fields. His forthcoming book, *Ekpleksis*, juxtaposes ancient Greek and modern European texts on the topic of "the striking" instance.

KEVIN MCLAUGHLIN is Associate Professor of English and Comparative Literature at Brown University. His publications include *Writing in Parts: Imitation and Exchange in Nineteenth-Century Literature* (1995), and the English translation of Benjamin's magnum opus, the *Arcades Project* (1999).

BETTINE MENKE is Professor of Comparative Literature at the University of Erfurt, Germany. Among her many publications are *Sprachfiguren. Name. —Allegorie. —Bild nach Walter Benjamin* (1991) and *Prosopopoiia. Stimme und Text bei Brentano, Hoffmann, Kleist und Kafka* (2000).

RAINER NÄGELE is Professor of German at Johns Hopkins University. His recent books include *Reading After Freud: Essays on Goethe, Hölderlin, Haber-*

mas, Nietzsche, Brecht, Celan, and Freud (1987); *Theater, Theory, Speculation: Walter Benjamin and the Scenes of Modernity* (1991); and *Echoes of Translation* (1997). He is also the editor of *Benjamin's Ground: New Readings of Walter Benjamin* (1988).

GERHARD RICHTER is Associate Professor of German and an Affiliate Professor in the Department of Comparative Literature at the University of Wisconsin, Madison. He is the author of *Walter Benjamin and the Corpus of Autobiography* (2000) and the editor of *Literary Paternity, Literary Friendship* (2002).

LAURENCE RICKELS is Professor of German at the University of California, Santa Barbara. A theorist and psychotherapist, he is the author of *Aberrations of Mourning: Writing on German Crypts* (1988); *Der unbetrauerbare Tod* (1990); *The Case of California* (1991); *The Vampire Lectures* (1999); and a forthcoming study on Nazi psychoanalysis. He also is the editor of *Looking After Nietzsche* (1990); Gottfried Keller's *Jugenddramen* (1990); and *Acting Out in Groups* (1999).

SIGRID WEIGEL, one of Germany's leading feminist literary critics, is director of the Zentrum für Literaturforschung in Berlin. She is the author of, among other recent publications, *Body- and Image-Space: Re-Reading Walter Benjamin* (1996); *Enstelle Ähnlichkeit. Walter Benjamins theoretische Schreibweise* (1997); *Topographien der Geschlechter* (1990); and *Bilder des kulturellen Gedächtnisses. Beiträge zur Gegenwartsliteratur* (1994). She is also the editor of *Flaschenpost und Postkarte. Korrespondenzen zwischen Kritischer Theorie und Poststrukturalismus* (1995), and coeditor of *Gershom Scholem. Literatur und Rhetorik* (2000).

BENJAMIN'S GHOSTS

Benjamin's Ghosts

GERHARD RICHTER

A ghost had appeared to me. I could hardly have described the site of its workings. Yet it resembled somebody I knew, but who was inaccessible to me.

— WALTER BENJAMIN, *"A Ghost," Berlin Childhood Around 1900*

What does it mean to follow a ghost? And what if this came down to being followed by it, always, persecuted perhaps by the very chase we are leading?

— JACQUES DERRIDA, *Specters of Marx*

Today, Benjamin's ghosts are legion. But because they are everywhere, who could speak of them? If we are followers of Benjamin, what does "following" mean? And what would it mean to follow ghosts—Benjamin's ghosts no less—that are always ahead of us and forever lagging behind? How can we tell the difference between following and being haunted? Evoking the many movements of Walter Benjamin's thought and signature today, how could we not feel that his specters speak to us from a time and space—specifically Weimar Berlin, but also Paris, Moscow, and fascist Germany—that is no longer our own but with which we are always seeking to catch up? To speak in the language and in the name of literature and culture today means in some sense to do justice to the ghosts of Benjamin that are always already on board with us. Like Benjamin's image of the past—"The true image of the past *flits* by" (*I* 255; 1:695)—his ghosts make a brief appearance only to vanish again.[1] For Benjamin, the past and the future are always connected through a series of spectral relays because the "dead become ghosts" (*SW* 1:57; 2:136). Before, and in excess of, so many other concerns, learning to read these relays remains our arduous task today.

1

It would be difficult to imagine a theorist of the twentieth century whose oeuvre and its many mutations have more deeply impacted as wide a range of disciplines as Benjamin's. The beauty and rigor of his sentences are matched only by the depth of the enigmatic obscurity from which they so often seem to speak. Benjamin's description of Michelet in the *Arcades Project* as "an author who, no matter where he is quoted, makes the reader forget the book in which the quotation appears" (N 57; 5:584), is equally true of himself. The act of quoting stages a simultaneous presentation and disappearance that has always presented both an opportunity and a predicament for his readers. Because or in spite of the threat of this double movement, Benjamin's texts today inform not only German studies and departments of literary and cultural studies, but also fields such as architecture, the visual arts, art history, film studies, anthropology, communications, sociology, theology, history, political science, and even the more open-minded branches of academic philosophy. A recent international bibliography records some two thousand reviews, articles, and books devoted wholly or in part to Benjamin from 1983 to 1993 alone.[2] Amid a late-capitalist global reordering and the collapse of East European communism—signs that hardly seem to parallel the intensely leftist concerns that sparked the first wave of sustained interest in Benjamin's enigmatic oeuvre in the late 1960s—his writings continue to speak to the theoretical and political commitments of our fin de siècle. In 1997, the newly founded International Walter Benjamin Association convened its first world congress in Amsterdam. In the United States, Harvard University Press has published the long-awaited multivolume standard English translation of a sizable part of his corpus, now making available to English-speaking readers significant aspects of his work with which they were not previously familiar. Yet despite the extensive and ever-growing interest in his work, reading Benjamin's texts continues to be a problem.

On the one hand, Benjamin's powerful sentences remain infinitely appropriatable for this or that cause. He has been championed, for instance, as a New Historicist *avant-la-lettre* and as the modern ur-father—or at least godfather—of the study of popular culture. To be sure, his penetrating analyses of the semiotics of kitsch, snow globes, street lamps, and neon signs, along with his reflections on the city as a text, on the body as a cipher of semiotic struggle, and on the potentially liberating dimensions of mass media such as film and photography, remain classic touchstones for critical cultural studies today. Together with the texts of his friend Sigfried Kracauer, which still await the full attention that they deserve, his analyses of modern popular culture are at least as important as the contemporary ones that have been spawned by such classics as Roland Barthes's *Mythologies* or the more recent work by critics such as Stuart Hall and James Clifford. Indeed, Benjamin's impact on our engagements with popular culture can be measured not only by the wide network of scholarly writing that takes its point of departure in his texts, but also by the ways in which he has become an icon of the popular imagination itself, as demonstrated by the internet sites, comic book, and novel recently devoted to him.[3] Here, Benjamin's suspicion, felt in a heady mixture of all the emancipatory enthusiasm and the sense of mistrust that marked the cultural signs of his Weimar Germany, could not be more relevant: "What, in the end, makes advertisements so superior to criticism? Not what the moving red neon sign says—but the fiery pool reflecting it in the asphalt" (*SW* 1:476; 4:132).

On the other hand, his texts strangely resist assimilation. They work to withdraw from straightforward meaning and transparent expression. The enigmatic truths that they offer must always be sought elsewhere, in a space that his texts perpetually cross and delimit but never fully inhabit. As Benjamin explains in his 1928 avant-garde book of aphorisms, *One-Way Street*: "Nothing is more miserable than a truth expressed as it was thought. Committed to writing in such a case, it is not even a bad photograph. And the truth refuses (like a child or a woman who does not love us), facing the lens of writing while we crouch under the black cloth, to keep still and look amiable" (*SW* 1:480; 4:138). To the extent that any truth can emerge from his writings at all, it is one that the reader must seek in what the text does not say on the surface, not even between the lines, but in an elsewhere that remains open to discussion. Indeed, the truth of his writings *is* this elsewhere. Whether in his early so-called metaphysical writings on language, his engagement with the German and French literary traditions, or his late preoccupation with the politics and technologies of presentation, his concepts are most themselves when they are changing into something else, when their logic can no longer be accounted for by what the texts in which they are embedded seem to be arguing. One can never fully grasp his concepts and sentences, which return to haunt once we turn our back on them. In short, they are ghostly.

This structure of the ghostliness or spectrality is encoded throughout

Benjamin's writings.[4] After all, Benjamin's obsession with ghosts dates back at least as far as his early discussions with Gershom Scholem, when Benjamin tried to break the codes of spectrality, "to formulate the laws . . . of the ghostly" [*des Gespentischen*].[5] On a concrete level, too, there are many figures and motifs of ghosts and phantoms throughout his entire oeuvre, and specters remain with him as a permanent concern from his earliest writings to his last. In this context, it would be necessary to continue and radicalize what Winfried Menninghaus has analyzed as Benjamin's *Schwellenkunde*, a series of meditations on a spectral "in-betweenness" in a world structured by a multitude of thresholds, transitions, and transitory acts and events.[6] This transitory quality of thought and of writing is for Benjamin always both a liberation and a liability.

We could even say that Benjamin's unfinished magnum opus, the *Arcades Project*, is in many ways a ghost book. It presents us with an extensive meditation on the breakdown of concrete empiricity and on the emergence of the ghostly. Benjamin was well aware of the extent to which his project was linked to a whole literary tradition that understood Paris as a city haunted by ghosts.[7] Whether discussing the promise and decay of Paris and the ideological patterns of the nineteenth century, whether circumscribing the ghostly origins and procedures of photography ("This is why old photographs appear ghostly" [5:496]), the haunted nature of technological innovations such as the telephone, street lighting, and railway travel, or the cultural anachronisms of the Baudelairean flâneur and his metropolitan habitats, Benjamin's texts are populated by ghosts and phantoms. Indeed, the whole movement of the *Arcades Projects*, Benjamin's ghost book, can be thought in terms of the specter, as the following passage from "Convolute L" elegantly shows:

> Everyone knows, from dreams, the horror of doors that will not close. More precisely: they are the doors that seem locked without being so. In an intensified way, I made the acquaintance of this phenomenon in a dream in which I, accompanied by a friend, encountered a ghost in the window of the first floor of a house to our right. And, as we proceeded, it accompanied us through the interior of all houses. It walked through walls, always keeping in line abreast with us. I saw this even though I was blind. The stroll we take through the arcades [*Passagen*] is basically, too, such a ghostly path [*Gespensterweg*] in which the doors give way and the walls move. (5:516)

This passage suggests an important dimension of the *Arcades Project*. For the doors that close and do not close—not unlike the Freudian psyche itself—are also the transitory spaces in which images of the past, thought to be gone for good, come back to haunt the present (images of the birth of photography and film, iron construction, advertisements, the metropolis and its ludic drives, concepts that have disappeared yet continue to survive in modernity). There is no absolute closure here. As is so often the case in Benjamin, the specter appears on a windowsill, one of his privileged transitory sites, and hence inscribes itself into the topography of the transitory. The subject's gaze is directed toward the ephemeral ghost that haunts it. It keeps pace with it and even passes through walls, those monuments to changelessness and solidity, massiveness and the empirically given. Indeed, we learn that the entire movement through the arcades of Paris—the traces of the past and the future inscribed in them, the haunting speculations about modernity to which their seemingly endless rows of shopwindows and subterranean catacombs give rise—can be conceptualized as just such an uncanny stroll, a ghostly wandering in which nothing is what it seems.

Benjamin's lesson, if there is one, is that a theoretical emphasis on textual and cultural ghosts is a highly significant form of analysis. The task of the reader who takes this ghostliness seriously is not to undo or exorcise these ghosts—by explaining away difficult textual passages, seen as a provocation or an embarrassment to the hermeneuticist—but rather to learn to think through what they have given us to consider, even when this task cannot find universal ground or metaphysical foundations manifested in transparent language, stable political programs, and factual certainty. The ghostly dimension of his writings helps us to confront the ethical and political implications of the image of those Benjaminian walls that are traversed by phantoms, shaken in their absolute empirical facticity and in their tenacious allegiance to common sense. Sometimes, therefore, in order to assume the responsibility of the real, we may have to read its demands against the grain. As Benjamin teaches us, "Only he who has made his dialectical peace with the world in the moment of deciding can comprehend what is concrete. But to him who wishes to make that decision 'on the basis of the facts,' these facts will refuse to offer themselves" [*werden diese Fakten ihre Hand nicht bieten*] (*R* 97f.; 4:317).

If our ability to read cultural texts is inseparable from our ability to invite the ghostly, then this linkage poses special problems for the writing of cultural history.[8] Indeed, the constant threat of the retreat of culture from the transparent narrative of cultural history and the image of historicism from which it stems preoccupies Benjamin. In a remarkable passage from 1937, he speaks of the difficulty that even dialecticism encounters in the attempt to read culturally. Benjamin writes:

> There is no document of culture that is not at the same time one of barbarism. No history of culture has yet done justice to this fundamental state of affairs, or can well hope to do so.
>
> . . . If the concept of culture is a problematical one for historical materialism, the disintegration of culture into commodities that would turn for human beings into an object of possession is unthinkable for it. The work of the past is not finished and closed off [*abgeschlossen*] within historical materialism. It does not see that work, or any part of it, as falling with convenient quiddity into the lap of any epoch. The concept of culture as an embodiment of forms that are considered independently, if not of the production process in which they arose, then of that in which they continue to survive, is fetishistic. Culture appears reified. Its history would then be nothing but the residue of memorable things and events that never broke the surface of human consciousness because they were never truly, that is politically, experienced. Moreover, one must not neglect that no presentation of history [*Geschichtsdarstellung*] undertaken on the basis of cultural history has ever managed to escape this problematic. . . . To be sure, presenting [*darstellen*] cultural history on the basis of pragmatic historicist narration makes no sense. But the non-sense [*Widersinn*] of a dialectical cultural history as such lies even deeper, since the continuum of history, exploded by the dialectic, suffers in no realm so wide a dispersion [*Streuung*] as in that which is called culture. (F 360; 2:477)

Benjamin's passage suggests, among so many other things, that a productive notion of culture, in order to be effective, must constantly confront various movements of inversion or turnover. In fact, its effectiveness is measured by its ability to think through these internal inversions. For Benjamin, these inversions and transformations include the perpetual movement from culture to barbarism; from a merely problematic notion of culture to the threat of a fully inoperative one; from the citation of a past to the prospect of its perpetual openness; from being embedded in the historical specificity of a cultural situation to the moment that refuses to yield access to its specific materiality; from a cultural object's dependence on its process of production to its independence from the process of its transmission or survival; from a concept of culture as a potentially readable text to its retreat in the form of a fetish, a train of thought that Benjamin shares with Theodor W. Adorno; and, finally, from a concept of cultural history as genuine political consciousness to the reification of the concept. For Benjamin, there can be no productive concept of culture that does not confront its own traversal and inversion of these poles—and not necessarily, as a crude narrative of decline might suggest, unilaterally or in a single direction. Rather, what is proper to a concept of culture *is* this perpetual turnover or inversion. For Benjamin, culture is most fully itself when it is moving toward something else, becoming an other, even an other to culture.

Culture, in Benjamin's signature, is thus another name for the ghostly undoing of the teleology of traditional pragmatic historicism and its modes of presentation. Ultimately, even a dialectical cultural history cannot hope to do justice to the complex notion of culture itself, because the fragmentary, heterogeneous force field of differences that constitute the cultural text suffers from an irreducible dispersion (*Streuung*) and thus poses a threat to readability. One might note, too, that the dispersion of which Benjamin speaks is opposed to the German *lesen*, meaning both to read and to gather. Benjamin was well aware of the double meaning of *lesen*, as becomes clear in "Doctrine of the Similar" when he comments on "the strange double meaning of the word *lesen*" (D 68; 2:209). Undoing the activity of collecting a culture's scattered pieces to prepare a gathering-reading, the dispersive movement of *streuen* remains forever at odds with that of *lesen*. *Lesen* versus *streuen*: this oppositional pair names the aporia that readers of the cultural text must constantly confront, the hermeneutic and ethical predicament to which we must respond. For Benjamin, cultural history is the name of a dispersal to which we must show ourselves responsible in every act of reading.

To learn to read these lessons of Benjamin's ghosts in the climate of contemporary discussions in literary and cultural studies means to revisit a host of issues that bear upon the status and survival of what was once called the humanities. With the transformation of traditional disciplines and the critical challenges that these transformations bring with them into the new millennium, we might begin to ask if and how Benjamin's many ghosts will help us to intervene in these ongoing debates. With this goal in mind, a serious reevaluation of his work could begin—and it could never do anything but begin over and over—with his rearticulations of what it means to read historically; his deconstructions of modernity; his radical problematizations of such concepts as self and subject; his lasting contributions to the theory of technology and the mass media, transposed into the digital age; his questioning of the relationship between a text and its context; his articulations of an ethics of memory; the as yet little examined status of sexuality and gender in his corpus; his notion of perpetual *Umschlag*, or transformation, that exceeds any form of a harmonious dialectics; and his theory of language and presentation that sheds new light on the relays among myth, violence, literary criticism, politics, mourning, aura, allegory, and loss. While Benjamin's corpus of texts will never have yielded to easy systematization or programmatic paraphrase, it invites us to remain faithful to the difficulties that we encounter when we attempt to do justice to the linguistic or textual nature of our objects of literary, institutional, and genealogical analysis.

The essays collected in this volume accept this invitation. In them, internationally renowned voices in Benjamin studies and critical theory struggle again and again with the problematic and inexhaustibly rich texture of his writings. What unites these essays is the underlying assumption that rather than assimilating Benjamin's texts mimetically into this or that ideology—which is then only strengthened, but never challenged, by every act of reading—we may find what is most valuable, most interesting, and most provocative in his oeuvre precisely in those moments that seem to remain obscure and problematic. It is here that Benjamin's texts, perhaps like no other texts, enact for us the most poignant and contested issues of making sense of texts and the world today. While much has been said about Benjamin's texts—and simultaneously so little—the fresh perspectives collected here open up vistas onto his work as if for the first time. These vistas become, like the streets of Benjamin's Berlin, "the space where I read the ghosts for the first time" (6:801f.).

For Benjamin, all literary and historical acts of reading are fundamentally predicated on an engagement with the image. This is the case not only in his famous meditations on technical reproducibility, film, and photography, but also in the most concrete sense of cultural and historical investigation.[9] As readers of Benjamin and of our own visual culture, we are still trying to come to terms with the full range of implications of the *Arcades Project*'s leitmotif, "History breaks down into images, not into stories" (N 67; 5:596). Indeed, a reading of the politics of contemporary culture would have to begin by returning incessantly to this insight. Thus, the readings collected in the first section of this volume, "Cultures of the Image," all take seriously Benjamin's insistence on the imagistic quality of thinking. Placing the Rilkean imperative to "know the image" into a constellation with Benjamin's theory of the dialectical image, Rainer Nägele shows that there can be no reading of Benjamin that does not wrestle with the rhetorical structure of the images and imagistic figures of thought that traverse his entire corpus. Benjamin's notion of the image, Nägele shows, is not the mimetically inflected painterly image, but rather a literalized graphic or rhetorical figure. The image hovers in a spectral sphere because it struggles to name something that is both living and dead. Benjamin's figure of the thought-image (*Denkbild*) cannot be thought in separation from textual points of irruption (*Einbruchstellen*), and Nägele elaborates the theoretical stakes of this problem. Just as there can be nothing that is not found in a space coextensive with language, Nägele suggests, for Benjamin there is no leaving the space that is imprinted with the contours of the thought-image. That Benjamin has given us this image space to read again and again means that any understanding of a self that appears to us in the image of written figures must first traverse the treacherous path of its own historical singularity, one that presents itself only as a constellation of enigmatic images. If Nägele's analyses of Benjamin's figures of thought converge on the contested question regarding the status of the image as a mode of presentation, an image that does not say more than a thousand words but actually less than one, he helps us to understand how the images that Benjamin calls "dialectical" hover in a displaced sphere at the threshold of thought and nonthought, life and death, memory and its historical erasure.

The manifold implications of such a hovering of the image are still to be understood, and Benjamin leaves open whether such a hovering is a promise or a downfall, or both at once. Addressing these questions, Miriam Hansen implicitly takes up Nägele's concern with the variegated Benjaminian image, which she places into the sphere of visual culture. Drawing on examples from recent Hollywood and Hong Kong cinema, Hansen revisits the question of whether in Benjamin's understanding of the image, especially its cinematically mediated forms, experience and sense perception can move beyond the binarism of denigration and celebration. In so doing, her essay speaks to the tension between the alienation of the senses and the promise of undoing this alienation in the sphere of the image. Focusing on the complex category of "innervation" in such Benjaminian texts as *One-Way Street*, Hansen suggests that Benjamin's position on visual culture and mass-mediated modernity more generally cannot be understood in isolation from his concerns with the technologies of presentation that are at the political core of his cultural analyses. In such ambivalent figures as Mickey Mouse, emblematic for a whole trajectory of capitalist modes of image production, Benjamin locates a genuinely antinomic struggle over the image, a struggle whose continued unresolvability signifies what a politics to come, in the cinema and in more recent digital technologies, might entail.

Tom McCall joins Nägele and Hansen in rethinking Benjamin's vexing notion of the dialectical image. But whereas Nägele places Benjamin's image into a constellation with such writers as Rilke, Hölderlin, and Nietzsche, and Hansen offers a consideration of the image in terms of the radical concept of innervation, McCall approaches the image in terms of its relation to silent film comedy and revolutionary messianism. As McCall shows, traditional literary-theoretical discussions have tended to elide the complex phenomenon of comedy in favor of putatively more serious genres such as tragedy. By the same token, the relevance of Benjamin's writings for a conceptual approach to the comedic has been little understood. Working to articulate the potentially messianic or revolutionary dimensions of comedy, McCall brings into syntactical relation Benjamin's dialectical image with such problems as gesture in both silent and sound film comedy. He implicitly shares Nägele's interest in Benjamin's theory of the image as a graphic marker—rather than a pictorial, purely referential mimesis—and Hansen's conviction that the politically explosive aspects of Benjamin's thought can hardly be considered outside of the sphere of the cinematic image. By analyzing such key Benjaminian notions as messianism, translation, gesture, mourning, and montage in the context of both the continental philosophical tradition (from Homer to Hegel and beyond) and film comedies such as Buster Keaton's 1924 *Sherlock Jr.*, the Marx Brothers' 1932 *Horse Feathers*, and Charlie Chaplin's 1936 *Modern Times*, it becomes possible to understand film comedy as a key genre in which the revolutionary demands of Benjamin's antiteleological view of history are made vivid. Like Hansen, McCall locates in contested comedic figures such as Mickey Mouse the graphic space in which the revolutionary moment in Benjamin's understanding of the image assumes it most promising, and therefore most problematic, form.

In learning to think in the wake of Benjamin's images, it is necessary to remain faithful to the shifting fates of their own historical contingencies. After all, as Benjamin tells us in his artwork essay, "The Work of Art in the Age of Its Technical Reproducibility," in the course of "long periods of history, the mode of human sense perception changes with humanity's entire mode of existence. The manner in which human sense perception is organized, the medium in which it is accomplished, is determined not only by nature but by historical circumstances as well" (*I* 222; 1:478). Lutz Koepnick's essay on Benjamin's concept of aura and contemporary visual culture is an attempt to do justice to this demand. Proceeding from the assumption that postmodern culture, with its proliferation of digital images, temporal fragmentations, and spatial expansions, has complicated Benjamin's distinction between auratic and postauratic art to a degree that he could not have foreseen in the 1930s, Koepnick reminds us that the complexly mediated image in which Benjamin hoped to locate a revolutionary impulse in his struggle against fascist politics has become so ubiquitous as to be a primary tool for remainderless globalization and transnational capitalism. Today more than ever, images do not merely reflect—they constitute. In an age of virtual traveling and wrapped political monuments (such as Christo's 1995 wrapping of the Berlin *Reichstag* building), to what extent does Benjamin's thesis linking aestheticization to reactionary, even fascist tendencies remain useful? By analyzing the stakes of postmodern consumer culture and the constellation of technology, identity, memory, and popular culture, Koepnick delineates the ways in which Benjamin's claims concerning the relays between perception and political culture remain actual today, even when the concrete circumstances of the culture of fascism and the culture of postmodern digitalism at the threshold of the twenty-first century differ sharply. To remain faithful to the historical claims of Benjamin's theories of perception and the technologically mediated image is also to break with them, because the stakes and circumstances of our visual culture are constantly shifting into something else. Here, the question of what might still constitute "experience" after Benjamin must be thought through again and again.

The second section of this volume, "Textualities of Experience," addresses itself to possible modes of experience opened up by Benjamin's writings. It is well known that for Benjamin the category of experience is a central concern that groups many of his writings and preoccupations from a variety of phases in his career around a central moment. Whether in his early note on "Experience" (1913), his rearticulations of Kantian notions of experience in "On the Program of the Coming Philosophy" (1918), or his "Experience and Poverty," published shortly after the Nazis' takeover in 1933: experience remains as alluring and elusive a category as any in his writings. The essays in this section therefore attempt to approach the moment of experience in Benjamin's work from a variety of perspectives. In her close rereading of Benjamin's artwork essay, Eva Geulen proposes that we steer clear of the false binarism in terms of which readers have often approached this famous text. Rather than providing either a transparent counterpoint to Adorno's seeming indictment of the culture industry and its products or the incontrovertible proof that Benjamin's unorthodox Marxism was a self-contradictory failure, this essay belongs, Geulen argues, in the context of the theoretical and performative concerns of the *Arcades Project*. She shows how the principal issue of the essay is the experience of representation itself, both in filmic and extrafilmic terms. The form in which Benjamin approaches and represents the issues of reproduction is itself an enactment of reproduction. The technologies of representation that Benjamin attempts to think are thus inconceivable in separation from the gesture that pivots on the reproduction of reproduction itself. This perspective permits Geulen to trace the ways in which "Benjamin's text reproduces the cinematic method of reproduction as representation," a movement that makes it possible for the relays between cinematic and linguistic representation to become thinkable, even as these relays mark both the simultaneity and the distance between the two forms of representation. Reproduction here emerges as the category that names the links and measures the distance between the two.

But the link between reproduction and representation that the artwork essay constructs must be enriched by the more psychoanalytically oriented strains of Benjamin's engagement with experience. In an effort to clarify the relays between psychoanalysis and the Benjaminian corpus, Laurence Rickels's contribution focuses on the constellation of Benjamin and Freud. On the far side of any mimetic or realist theory of influence that, as Rickels argues, was only invented in the orbit of Freud's work, the relays between

Benjamin and Freud can best be traced through the elective affinity of the *Trauerspiel* book and the Freudian case study of Schreber. By placing into a constellation Benjamin's *Trauerspiel* material, his essay "Books by the Insane"—which deals with his collection of texts written by the mentally ill, including Schreber's memoirs—and his review of the psychoanalyst Alexander Mette's work, it is possible to begin to see the contours of a psychoanalytically informed textual process in which patterns of Freudian thought emerge in Benjamin's corpus. What Rickels calls "self-citation or sui-citation" is a mode of experience without which the many ghosts that haunted Benjamin's corpus, and that continue to haunt in its name today, cannot be conceptualized. Thus, while it has become a commonplace for Benjamin's readers to dismiss or to simplify his relationship to Freud, Rickels's essay *performs* what is at stake in the very notion of discussing these two proper names in tandem. In so doing, he also delineates the stakes for any future attempt to come to terms with this uneasy configuration.

The following essay shifts the terms of the discussion of variously mediated experience to writings that belong squarely to Benjamin's celebrated early phase of preoccupation with German literature. Stanley Corngold meditates on Benjamin's exemplary piece of literary criticism, the 1921 essay on Goethe's *Elective Affinities*, setting into sharp relief the complex category of "obscurity," which traverses Benjamin's essay. Obscurity, in Benjamin's tropes, is capable of assuming many different meanings, from delusory deception to a "good" obscurity. In Benjamin's reading of Goethe, Corngold shows, there can be no appearance of beauty that is not touched by a pervasive obscurity. To make comprehensible the treacherous seductions of semblance (*Schein*), for instance, genuine obscurity works to keep alive the productive tension between destruction and revelation, between a systematization of negativity and the lure of transparency. As Corngold demonstrates, the experience of marriage itself—long held to be at the core of Goethe's novel—becomes affected by the movement of obscurity. "Marriage," Corngold writes, "offers the daily opportunity to feel obscurity (or depth) meaningfully, to feel in the banal a certain authenticating obscurity (or depth); indeed, what one marries par excellence is marriage, the marriage par excellence of the banal and the obscure." One could say ultimately that obscurity works both to confirm and to undo a lack of disclosure of which it itself is the cause.

While Corngold focuses on the textual links between obscurity and disclosure, Hanssen argues that the often-neglected category of melancholy allows us to resituate one of Benjamin's prime affects both in the art historical concerns of his time and in his innovative understanding of cultural history. Taking as her point of departure the photographic portrait of Benjamin, Hanssen illuminates the ways in which melancholy helps Benjamin to articulate the historical-critical relation between the Baroque and modernity as well as between presentational and archival concerns. That Benjamin emerges most fully as a philosopher of melancholy when he is read in the context of such scholars of art history as Warburg and Panofsky, and in relation to images by Paul Klee and Albrecht Dürer, means, for Hanssen, that Benjamin's portrait—his image and his legacy—cannot be read in isolation from his dialectical images of the cultural history of modernity.

Benjamin's much debated reconceptualization of history is the theme of the third section of this volume, "Rethinking History." That Benjamin's radical notion of history can be most fruitfully approached from a figurative or allegorical perspective—that is, in the guise of something else—has long been a contested topos among his readers. But Benjamin's rearticulation of history has by no means been restricted to recent genealogical movements such as the New Historicism, which often claims his writings for its own purposes. On the contrary, a rigorous rethinking of Benjamin's concept of history explodes the teleological model of historicism. Always on the way to the figurative space of something else, it ranges from historical materialist approaches (as in Peter Bulthaupt's standard 1975 collection of responses to Benjamin's theses on history) to semiological perspectives (Jeanne-Marie Gagnebin), and from critical cultural histories (as in John McCole and in the recent volume by Michael Steinberg) to an engagement of the relation between history and the language of media such as photography (Eduardo Cadava).[10] In this section, Fritz Breithaupt, Kevin McLaughlin, and Norbert Bolz articulate some of the most significant terms of the discussion mobilized by Benjamin's radically innovative idea of the historical. Breithaupt cautions us that Benjamin's concept of history must be understood in terms of the Benjaminian singularities that often refuse to be related to other, more traditional historicist perspectives. For instance, as Breithaupt shows, Benjamin's explosive notion of the historical does not easily lend itself to the cultural and political systematizations that have recently come under such headings as New Historicism. For Benjamin, history does not simply reveal what is embedded in it. It always struggles with its own status as a mode of disfiguration and transformation. What exposes itself as the historical, Breithaupt demonstrates, is never reducible to the categories of a system of expression or revelation. Learning to read a phenomenon historically in a Benjaminian sense means coming to terms with what it no longer is and with the future perfect tense of what it will have been. Through its encounter with a series of specific events, the subject learns to come to terms with the historical lesson that there is very little to be recognized other than the acts and constraints of recognition themselves. To be prepared to navigate the empty space of what is to come signals the possibility of a future arrival—not in an orthodox theological sense, but as an epistemological affirmation.

To follow Benjamin's complications of the historical in this way, however, is not to foreclose the possibility of naming certain force fields that structure the differentiated core of historicity. On the contrary, Benjamin invites us to become ever more sensitive readers of the historical in a way that avoids the many mimetic temptations in calls for realism and the return to the "way things really were." In this vein, McLaughlin suggests that issues of translation in Benjamin necessarily open up onto issues of history. To understand the specific challenges that Benjamin poses to standard or traditional ways of approaching culture and history requires a close examination of certain key words and phrases that become problematic not only in and of themselves but especially in the act of translation. Tracing such concepts as *Gehalt*, or content, and virtuality through German aesthetic theory since the eighteenth century allows McLaughlin to juxtapose their traditional meanings with the radically new ones that Benjamin assigns them—in an act of conceptual, if not morphological translation, as it were. This procedure leads McLaughlin to suggest that in Benjamin's *Arcades Project* the central cipher for modernity—Paris itself—comes to be invested with the logic of Benjaminian virtuality and content, precisely in the ways that the virtual possibilities of modernity open up for us. Like the flaneur wandering through the streets of Paris, Benjamin's translator shares a force field of historical insight that unfolds in separation from realist conceptions of history, even when our responsibility toward a very real history is at stake. What withdraws from the flaneur's gaze is what withdraws from the pen of the translator; it returns as a ghost in the experience of a passing itself.

There can hardly be a reading of Benjamin's notion of history that does not address the messianic or theological element in his writings. Jacques Derrida has recently suggested that we think of Benjamin's theology as naming something "messianic without messianism," as a structure that wishes to hold on to a historical promise without remaining confined by the logic of any religion.[11] The difficulty and actuality of this double structure remains open to debate. In a double gesture of inscription and erasure, Benjamin once wrote, "My thinking relates to theology the way the blotting paper does to ink. It is soaked through with it. If one were to go by the blotting paper, though, nothing of what has been written would remain" (N 61; 5:588). Here, Norbert Bolz's essay returns us directly to the problem of theology in Benjamin's unconventional reading of historical materialism. The underlying principles of Benjamin's late work, Bolz claims, are drawn neither from a philosophy of history nor from a repoliticized concept of the aesthetic, but rather from the messianism of an inverse theology. Bolz suggests that we picture Benjamin's thinking as moving in elliptical lines around the poles of theology and media theory. If Benjamin teaches us to hold on to difference and the capacity to differentiate, he does so on the basis of a religious structure of thought that refuses to remain religious. We can thus conceptualize his rethinking of the historical in terms of the unorthodox messianism with which his thinking about cultural phenomena is suffused.

The fourth and final section of this volume comes under the heading "Figures of Finitude." There can be no thinking in Benjamin's wake that does not take into account that whatever his thought touches is touched by a consideration of its immanent absence. As Benjamin writes in the *Arcades Project*, his main interest belongs to the ghostly moment when things are about to become something else or even vanish, "things in the moment of the being-no-longer" [*Dinge im Augenblick des Nicht-mehr-seins*] (5:1001). In this context, Peter Fenves addresses the far-reaching problem of tragedy as it arises in Benjamin's study of the baroque *Trauerspiel*. Fenves traces the ways in which Benjamin's understanding of tragedy not only seeks to counter the prevailing triumphalist discourses of his contemporary Weimar culture in which a new Germanic tragic artwork is said to emerge, but also how the notion of the tragic becomes a figure for a multitude of political and theoretical issues that are central to his larger corpus of writings. Revisiting the famous distinction that Benjamin makes between tragedy and mourning play, Fenves shows that his interest in the tragic can be understood in terms of his pre-occupation with messianic time, a temporal structure that is absorbed fully into the movements of natural history. Through the figures of silence and echo, Benjamin's theory of tragedy is structured by the unresolved question of how tragedy relates to prophecy. Here, Fenves argues, Benjamin enacts a break both with the notion of tragedy as a return (rather than as a singularity to come) and with the notion of a stable community or German *Volksgemeinschaft* to whose ideological stability the tragic could be returned in the first place. For Benjamin, tragedy is always radically pluralized, traversing or reverberating in the empty space once called the self.

While Fenves organizes his discussion of tragedy around such figures as silence and echo, Bettine Menke traces a different set of Benjaminian figures: ornament, constellation, and flurries. She demonstrates how writing for Benjamin is always a performance that sets into motion the movement of a series of lines, signs, and marks on the surface of the text. By placing writing into the textual margins that these marks and figures name, Benjamin negotiates the ways in which these signs are always on the verge of becoming something else, that is, of entering the *Gestöber*, or flurry, of letters in which they may no longer be recognizable. Taking her point of departure in the theoretical claims that Benjamin outlines in "The Doctrine of the Similar," Menke's close readings demonstrate that what enables Benjamin's figurative language to become effective is always also the danger that threatens to undo its transparency at any given moment. Such central Benjaminian figures as the ornament, the constellation, and flurries thus become visible as the ciphers that encrypt the treacherous movement of all of Benjamin's sentences: they name simultaneously the beginning and the finitude of sense.

The final essay returns to one of the most significant and least understood texts in Benjamin's corpus, his 1931 essay on the writer Karl Kraus. It is here, Sigrid Weigel proposes, that an examination of the status of sexuality in Benjamin's thought could find its point of departure. Usually cited only for its passage on the politics of quotation, the essay on Kraus contains both open and concealed traces of a thinking that places into relation language and sexuality. While discussions of Benjamin's readings of sexuality are often anchored in a discussion of the whores that traverse his writings on Baudelaire, Weigel suggests that the Kraus essay embodies Benjamin's attempt at a systematic consideration of the constellation of sexuality and intellectual production, mediated by his theory of language. Tracing the relays between this essay on other passages in Benjamin's work that have a direct relevance to his understanding of sexuality—such as aphorisms from *One-Way Street* and thought-images such as "After Completion"—Weigel follows the ways in which Benjamin's reading of language and of eros intersect. The Kraus essay is characterized by an irresolvable tension: on the one hand, it hopes to systematize the many links between sexuality and intellectual production in the sphere of the linguistic; on the other hand, in taking seriously the results of this pursuit, it hopes to inaugurate a new and antisystemic mode of writing that no longer relies on the rhetorically produced effects of full transparency and the programmatic concerns of writing as a sexually and intellectually fruit-bearing act of male convincing. In this irresolvable tension, the Kraus essay points forward to the theoretical and cultural concerns of the late Benjamin, and especially the *Arcades Project*.

Taken together, the reading performances of these essays suggest that what Benjamin's many ghosts leave behind for us today, at the dawn of a new millennium, is neither an "approach" nor a unified Benjaminian "thought" that could simply be applied in an analysis of a particular cultural text. Rather, as these essays aim to clarify, the explosive and performative potential of his texts resides precisely in the specific ways in which they refuse themselves to particular versions of instrumentality and to the economy of use value that have so thoroughly gripped our disciplines and institutions. Here, Benjamin's ghosts share an elective affinity with Adorno's. "For it is one thing to believe in ghosts," Adorno tells us, "and another to tell ghost stories. One is almost tempted to concede true pleasure in these stories only to the person who does not believe in them but rather gets involved in them precisely in order to enjoy his freedom from myth." [12] Today, the dangers inherent in the myths perpetuated by a postmodern model of institutional knowledge that works in a corporate mode of globalized productivity, along with its late-capitalist demands of businesslike instrumentality and commercial exchange value, needs to be confronted by the double movement of disruptive and myth-dispelling ghosts. This urgency has recently been made vivid for us by such critics as Bill Readings and J. Hillis Miller. [13] By contrast and perhaps on the far side of instrumental reason, Benjamin's ghosts may point to some possible ways in which we can begin to come to terms with an engagement with texts, and the histories and cultures to which they belong, that touches us in and as something other than mimesis. His specters may help us to resist the seductions of what Fredric Jameson has recently called an "anti-theoretical, which is to say an anti-intellectual time," a time that relies on the treacherous comforts of "local positivisms and empiricisms."[14] These often work to reinforce, rather than place out of joint, the logic and economy of the system that produced them.

Yet, by contrast, as Paul de Man reminds us, "Nothing can overcome the resistance to theory since theory *is* itself this resistance."[15] The task of critical theory would thus be not to undo the resistance against it but to realize—in the sense of understanding, but also of activating and actualizing to the highest degree—what it is that within it determines the modes of the resistance that it both calls forth and contains. Perhaps more than anything, Benjamin's texts teach us that the aporias of presentation and historical understanding, if we engage them rigorously without falsely undoing them, may position us politically on the brink of a perpetual transformation. His ghosts invite us to stay clear of programmatic empiricism and a notion of "history that showed things 'as they really were'" (N 51; 5:578). Instead, to help us become readers and historians, Benjamin wishes us to "brush history against the grain" (*I* 257; 1:697) so that other histories and other ghosts might emerge. In so doing, he returns us again and again to the notion that the "image that is read, that is, the image of the Now of recognizability, bears to the highest degree the stamp of that critical, dangerous moment that lies at the ground of all reading" (N 50f.; 5:578). That we cannot decide whether our inability fully to come to terms with this dangerous moment is a victory or a defeat names the promise of Benjamin's ghosts. The following essays will not cease to engage this dangerous moment.

PART I

Cultures of the Image

ONE

Thinking Images

RAINER NÄGELE

Wisse das Bild

—RILKE

Es ist Alles Bilderrede

—NIETZSCHE

Wisse das Bild: Know the image. The curious imperative of Rilke's ninth sonnet to Orpheus can be read as a slight transformation of the Apollonian-Delphic imperative: *gnothi sauthon*: know yourself. As the *gnothi sauthon* formed the inscription over the entrance to the Delphic oracle, one might say, that this Rilkean-orphic command, *Wisse das Bild*, could be the inscription over the gate to Benjamin's work.

This at least seems to be Benjamin's concept of the dialectical image as an image that is not a painterly representation, but rather a figure and constellation to be read, as he explains in a letter to Gretel Adorno in 1935:

> The dialectical image does not copy the dream in a painterly representation [*Das dialektische Bild malt den Traum nicht nach*]—it was never my intention to say that. But it seems to me to contain the instances, the place of the irruption of awakening [*die Einbruchsstelle des Erwachens*] and to produce [*herzustellen*] out of these places [*aus diesen Stellen*] its figure, like a star-constellation [is formed] by the sparkling dots.[1]

This image, then, although called a *Sternbild*, is not a picture or a painting, but instead a figure: it belongs to a graphic sphere in contrast to the sphere of painting. The difference between the two spheres is marked by the categorical spatial difference of horizontal and vertical surface: painterly representation appears on the vertical surface (as the shape of a tree that has been cut vertically), the graphic sign or design appears on the horizontal surface (as the rings of the tree on the horizontal surface of the trunk). Condensed to the opposition of *Zeichen* (sign) and *Mal* (mark, stigma, birthmark, from which is derived *malen* = to paint), Benjamin emphasizes again the categorical spatial difference in a letter to Scholem in January 1918: "The plain of the sign [*Zeichen*] is—seen from the perspective of man—horizontal, that of the mark [*Mal*] vertical."[2]

The spatial setting of image and graphic figure is further underlined in the emphatic repetition of *Stelle* and *stellen* that marks the production of the dialectical image. Already the *Instanzen* (instances or agencies) in the dialectical image point at a position: at a stand or stance, but also at something that insists. These instances are characterized, in the singular, as an *Einbruchsstelle*: a place, a spot where something breaks in, irrupts and interrupts. This *Stelle* is then multiplied again in the *Stellen* out of which the figure emerges, or rather is produced, brought forth, put there, as Benjamin's use of the verb *herzustellen* suggests.

The instance of the dialectical image as a *Stelle* places it in German in an overdetermined space of epistemological operations and productions circling around the words *vorstellen* (to represent, to imagine; in English, the image returns here) and *darstellen* (to present, to perform theatrically). A *Stelle* in a text could also be translated as a passage. Where the English, following the French, emphasizes the moment of a passing, the German word marks the interruption: *Stelle* as *Stillstand*, dialectic in standstill, as Benjamin defines it. Benjamin remarked on exactly the same shift from movement to its interruption in another French-German pair of words to which we will return later.

At this point we merely remark and insist on the *Stelle*, where the dialectical image is to be produced (*herzustellen*), as an *Einbruchsstelle*: a place where something interrupts, breaks in, intervenes, like a thief in the night; although the thief here is the awakening in the morning. It is the moment of a caesura where the intervention of the breaking in (*einbrechen*) allows perhaps for a new departure into the open (*aufbrechen*), as Hölderlin's elegy "Bread and Wine" announces it: "Göttliches Feuer auch treibet, bei Tag und bei Nacht,/Aufzubrechen. So komm! daß wir das Offene schauen" [Divine fire also drives us, day and night, to depart. Come then, that we envision the open] (vv. 40–41). The same poem also invokes the moment of an Einbruch, calling for it as a desired moment full of bliss, but not without danger: "wo brichts, allgegenwärtigen Glücks voll / Donnernd aus heiterer Luft über die Augen herein?" [Where does it break in, full of omnipresent bliss, thundering out of clear air over the eyes?] (vv. 63–64). The breaking in, the thundering intervention out of the blue that accompanies the lightning bolt (which characterizes the dialectical image according to Benjamin) also bears the implication of a blinding.

It did break in over the eyes of Oedipus at a time when Delphi was awake and did not slumber as in the present, where, according to Hölderlin, *Delphi schlummert* (v. 62). The Sophoclean tragedy would thus be the instance and the staging of an *Einbruchsstelle des Erwachens*. Indeed, Jokasta tells her son and husband Oedipus that everything will be fine if he just goes on dreaming: "As far as marrying your mother is concerned, don't worry," she says to him, "many men have been dreaming of sleeping with their mother. But he who pays no attention to it, will live most easily" (vv. 980–83). But Oedipus, the famous riddle solver, wants to know: and thus it breaks in over his eyes.

In Hölderlin's poem the breaking-in occurs in the blissful (dis)solution of the shared word that flies from tongue to tongue. What differentiates the first solving of the riddle of the sphinx, which made Oedipus famous, from his later solving of his own riddle is, partly at least, the shared, public word: the fact that the word is publicly spoken. That things and words be expressed, uttered, "spoken out" is the repeated request of Oedipus. He himself will "speak out": *exerô* (v. 219); and in anger he reproaches Tiresias: "You won't speak out?" [*ouk . . . exereis pote*] (v. 334–35). While the first riddle is solved face-to-face with the sphinx, the second riddle enters the public discourse to the detriment of the one who cannot bear it. "Es ertrug keiner das Leben allein" [No one could bear life alone]; "Ausgetheilet erfreut solch Gut" [distributed such good gives joy] ("Bread and Wine," v. 66–67). As "Oedipus in Colonos" suggests, the word that destroyed Oedipus enters the community as a mysterious blessing.

A cryptic remark of Benjamin's seems to point in a similar direction: "Lösen ließen sich daher viele Rätsel durch das bloße Bild, erlösen aber nur durch das Wort" [Many riddles might be solved by the mere image, but redeemed only through the word] (6:18). And like the word in Hölderlin's poem, Benjamin's redeeming word is an *einbrechen*, a breaking-in: the situation that constitutes the riddle and poses the question can be solved only in the word "breaking-in in all its immediacy" [*in seiner ganzen Unmittelbarkeit hereinbrechend*] (6:18).

The passage from Benjamin's text has become the threshold for the passage of several other texts. The text about the *Einbruchsstelle* has become the *Einbruchsstelle* for other texts and the place of a constellation of texts and of signifiers in which the German *Stelle* intersects with the Latin *stella* in the figure of a transfiguration and translation.

It is first and predominantly a constellation of passages signed by Hölderlin and Benjamin, projected onto the starry sky of Greek tragedy and its translations of mythic imagination. It is a constellation that is close and yet distinctly different from the dreamy nostalgic opening of Georg Lukács's *Theory of the Novel* (1920), which invokes the blissful times of the Greeks "for whom the starry sky is the map for the passable and necessary paths."[3] Lukács's projection of this Greek transcendental topography is explicitly the projection from the situation of a "transcendental homelessness."[4] At about the same time Benjamin began to write his essay on "The Task of the Translator" with its emphatic references to Hölderlin's translations of Sophocles; and in the following years Benjamin begins his own project on modernity that finds its first major articulation in the incisive difference of the baroque *Trauerspiel* from Greek tragedy.

The articulation of this difference as an allegory of modernity finds its most condensed model in Hölderlin's translations of the two Sophoclean tragedies *Oedipus* and *Antigone* and the accompanying notes. Both the translations and the notes are an attempt at a reading that wants to know the images of the Greeks: "die Mythe . . . beweisbarer darstellen" [to present the myth in a more provable, demonstrable way] (*FA* 16:415).[5] This does not exclude the recognition that the Greek tragedies are themselves already readings of the mythic images, readings of the dreams in the form of a *Darstellung*, and thus already moments of awakening: *Einbruchsstellen*. But because the awakening is always a momentary one in a given time and space, and the rest is sleep and dream for the beings that are of such stuff as dreams are made of, it is our fate and task, as Benjamin says at the beginning of the treatise on the German *Trauerspiel*, "to stand with every turn anew before the question of presentation" [*mit jeder Wendung von neuem vor der Frage der Darstel-*

lung zu stehen] (1:207). The question before which we stand, before which we are posited and posed, is itself posed by the *Darstellung* to us more than we pose it.

Hölderlin's notes on both *Oedipus* and *Antigone* begin with remarks concerning an *Einbruchsstelle* in the Greek tragedies: the function of the caesura as the constitutive mark of the tragic process and its *Darstellung*. In Hölderlin's system of poetics, tragedy is not just one presentation among others: its structure is the law of poetic (re)presentation itself. Two general laws of poetic representation intersect in Hölderlin's conception of tragedy: the law of succession and sequence, already articulated in Lessing's *Laokoon*, coincides with Hölderlin's structure of poetic representation as the inversion of a ground (conceived as a musical tone or tuning) in the manifest artistic form (*Kunstcharakter*). This fundamental structure of all poetic (re)presentation appears in tragedy as the metaphor and inversion of an "ideal" tone, that is, of an original unity and totality, into a "heroic" form, that is, into dissonance and separation. Tragedy, in other words, is the enactment of the general poetic necessity to disperse and disseminate all unity and totality into successive and sequential moments. Thus Hölderlin characterizes Empedocles, the hero of his first attempt at tragedy, as one who is dissatisfied and suffering even in the best of circumstances, simply because, as soon as his heart and thought embrace the totality of existence, "he is tied to the law of succession" (*FA* 13:544).

The notes on the Sophoclean tragedies begin again with the law of succession as the law of poetics. The human being is now conceived as a sensory system or apparatus (*ein Empfindungssystem*). The poetic law is the calculable law that governs the various sequences and successions of the elements of this sensory apparatus, the way in which "imagination [*Vorstellung*] and sensation [*Empfindung*] and reasoning [*Räsonnement*] emerge one after another" (*FA* 16:250).

At this point, one short sentence, set off as a separate paragraph, intervenes and gives the tragic (re)presentation and its process a new turn: "Der tragische Transport ist nemlich eigentlich leer, und der ungebundenste" [The tragic Transport namely is actually empty, and the most unrestrained].

The sequence of elements in tragedy is now called a "transport," a carrying-over. The word *Transport* can be read as an overdetermined translation. It is first a variant of the word "translation" itself; it is also the Latinized form of metaphor. Metaphor is, in Hölderlin's poetics, the name for all poetic processes: the lyrical a "metaphor of One feeling," the epic a "metaphor of great strivings," the tragic a "metaphor of an intellectual intuition" (*FA* 14:369). The seventeenth-century *Dictionnaire Furetière* gives further testimony for this connection: "La metaphore est un transport d'un mot propre à un sens figuré." The word has an additional important significance in the *tragédie classique*: it is virtually synonymous with passion. It is not only the word for something being carried over, transmitted, but also of someone being carried away, on all levels: from the violent passions of the soul ("l'agitation de l'âme par la violence des passions") to the medical delirium of the brain seized by violent fevers ("Quand le fièvre est violente, on apprehende le transport au cerveau qui cause le delire").

It is precisely this violence of a transport threatening to carry us away that emerges now in Hölderlin's text in the form of a violent transport of changing imaginations or representations (*Vorstellungen*). Hölderlin calls it a "reißenden Wechsel der Vorstellungen." *Reißend* has the connotation of torrential rapids, of the violent flow of a river that irresistibly carries everything away in its rush. The first section of the notes on *Oedipus* ends with the word *reißt*, referring to a violence and power that pulls the human "into the eccentric sphere of the dead" [*in die excentrische Sphäre der Todten reißt*] (*FA* 16:251).

In a first little caesura, we might remark at this point that the imperative of the Rilkean sonnet, "Wisse das Bild," finds its place in the double sphere of the living and dead, in a kind of circulation between the spheres where the images, rather than being violent and torrential, become "ewig und mild." But we are not ready yet to read this constellation.

Hölderlin's juxtaposition of the emptiness of the unrestrained tragic transport and the torrential change and sequence of imaginations indicates a paradigmatic structure of representation as a structure of inversion: the fuller the passion, the emptier its representation. Something must intervene, interrupt, must stop the torrential transport. Hölderlin calls it, in explicit reference to metrics, the caesura, but also "the pure word—*das reine Wort*." The pure word as a pure interruption and break of a sequence places it in the position of a pure signifier: a pure differential like the phoneme. Or, to use a Benjaminian figure, the pure word is the inexpressive that intervenes in the flow of expression.

The result of this caesura is the transformation of a movement into a static balance. Tragedy is therefore according to Hölderlin more balance than sequence. Instead of the sequence of images and representations what appears is what Hölderlin calls "die Vorstellung selber," or "the representation itself" (*FA* 16:250). It is tempting to read this "Vorstellung selber" in the most literal sense as a theatrical performance, which can be called a *Vorstellung* in German. But since this "Vorstellung selber" has the caesura as its condition, it cannot be simply any theatrical performance but rather one that opens up in its interruption to the condition and production of the *Vorstellung*. The *Vorstellung* comes to a standstill at the *Stelle*, the place of its interruption; the rushing images, ideas, sensations coalesce in a figure to be read.

If this reading echoes with resonances from Benjamin as well as from Brecht's epic theater, it is yet an echo that is rigorously determined by Hölderlin's text and its Kantian echoes. The notes on *Oedipus* that begin with the caesura as the condition for the "Vorstellung selber" end with an interpretation of tragic suffering as the reduction to the pure conditions of time and space: "At the extreme limit of suffering namely there exists nothing anymore but the conditions of time or of space."[6] Tragic *Darstellung* would thus be literally the *Darstellung* of the conditions of *Vorstellung*.

This seemingly purely formalist Kantian reading of tragedy assumes intense historico-political resonances in the notes on *Antigone*. Hölderlin reads this tragedy as an explosion of the formless in the all-too-formal ("das unförmliche entzündet sich an allzuförmlichem" [*FA* 16:420]). We are dealing here with the drama of the formal itself on all levels: from the formalization of the dramatis personae as mere representatives of social classes "daß sie als Personen im engeren Sinne, als Standespersonen gegeneinander stehen, daß sie sich formalisieren" (*FA* 16:420) to a concept of revolution as the revolution and inversion of all modes and forms of representation and imagination ("die Umkehrung aller Vorstellungsarten und Formen" [*FA* 16:419]). It is precisely the radical Kantian formalism of Hölderlin's argument that goes beyond any idealist displacement of the revolution into a mere reform of ideas. For Hölderlin is not writing of a change or a revolution of ideas, but rather of the revolution of *all modes and forms* that constitute the conditions for the production of *Vorstellungen*.

It is time to interrupt this eccentric excursion into Hölderlin's notes in order to return to the image of Benjamin and its *Einbruchsstellen*. Returning to the point of irruption is, however, also a return to the point of departure of the eccentric course. Benjamin's writing returns to and takes off from a task and vision that had been articulated most concisely and programmatically in a fragmentary text published only in 1917 by Franz Rosenzweig under the title *Das älteste Systemprogramm des deutschen Idealismus*.[7] The manuscript, written in Hegel's handwriting, is generally considered the joint product of Hegel, Hölderlin, and Schelling. The questions addressed in this text are certainly crucial in the writing of the three authors. The very possibility of philosophy and aesthetics, and their interrelation after Kant are at stake. Kant's philosophy has produced a turn in philosophy that cannot be undone and from which all philosophy has to begin. At the same time, the fragment insists, Kant's philosophy has "exhausted nothing" [*nichts erschöpft*] yet, thus leaving room for a new philosophical creation, even a creation out of nothing (*Schöpfung aus Nichts*).[8] The two terms that most emphatically characterize this new philosophical creation are the "idea of beauty" [*Idee der Schönheit*] and "mythology of reason" [*Mythologie der Vernunft*], an idea of which the text claims that it has never before occurred to any man's mind.[9]

Whereas Benjamin's writing clearly excludes the exuberant inversion of the "nichts erschöpft" into the "Schöpfung aus Nichts," his writing all the more emphatically takes up the program of a philosophy after Kant and its search for a necessary complement without betraying the rigorous foundation of Kant's critique. As if in direct response to the publication of the *Systemprogramm* in 1917, Benjamin writes his own "Program of the Coming Philosophy" (Über das Programm der kommmenden Philosophie) (2:157ff.) in late 1917.[10] But there is a significant shift in the central term that describes the complementary extension in Benjamin's text: instead of beauty and mythology Benjamin invokes the necessity of thinking "experience" [*Erfahrung*], and more precisely experience as a "singular temporal" experience that is evanescent in contrast to the "universal philosophical interest" directed at a form of knowledge of atemporal value.

The philosophy that finds itself before the question of singular and evanescent temporal experience is the same one that finds itself "with every turn anew before the question of presentation" [*mit jeder Wendung von neuem vor der Frage der Darstellung*] (1:207). It is here, facing the question of presentation, that Benjamin's writing takes up the program not only in content but also in the modes and forms of his writing. And it is here that the question and task of thinking the image has and takes its place as a thinking image: as a *Denkbild*.

Standing before the question of *Darstellung* at the juncture of timeless epistemological certainty and the temporal-historical singularity of experience, facing it with every new turn, places philosophical writing in a precise constellation with Hölderlin's reading of tragedy as the exemplary form of presentation and as the manifestation of the conditions of time and space. In such a moment, Hölderlin says, time takes a categorical turn: "weil sie in solchem Momente sich kategorisch wendet" (*FA* 16:258).

One of Benjamin's earliest literary essays presents a remarkable, intense reading of two Hölderlin poems, or rather two versions of a poem whose diversity turns them into two categorically different poems. The turn is already indicated by Hölderlin's own categorical change and inversion of the title from *Dichtermuth* (The poet's courage) to *Blödigkeit*, which one could translate as timidity, shyness, or unworldliness. Benjamin's comparative reading presents the second poem as the fulfillment of a poetic task that the first one was not yet able to achieve. In a move that seems almost conventional at first glance, Benjamin criticizes the first poem as the presentation of an abstract knowledge that does not become tangible, or literally "feelable" (*fühlbar*): "We know this thought . . . we know it" [*Wir wissen diesen Gedanken . . . , wissen ihn*], but it is not "feelable" (2:109). It seems here that to "know" is precisely the failure.

Benjamin is not imposing popular sentimental aesthetic values on Hölderlin's poem. *Fühlbar* is a key term of Hölderlin's poetics, particularly in his most extensive poetological essay, known from its opening phrase: "Wenn der Dichter einmal des Geistes mächtig . . ." (*FA* 14:180ff.). *Fühlbar* and *Fühlbarkeit* are not terms for the expression of feelings, but rather for a possibility and condition produced by a poetic language as the product of a process and labor working through the antinomies and oppositions of reflection. It is the work of a *Darstellung* that stands under the law of sequence and succession and thus of separation and differentiation of all totality in order to produce its echo as a product of language. Through separation and opposition coherence and connection become tangible ("fühlbaren Zusammenhang und Identität im Wechsel der Gegensätze" [*FA* 14:311]).

Benjamin's contrasting use of Hölderlin's *fühlbar* to *wissen* has its place in his own philosophy of language. It is less an opposition to *Wissen* per se than to a particular and conventional concept of the relationship between knowledge and practice. In a fragmentary text on various modes of knowledge (*Arten des Wissens*), Benjamin defines the possibility of a determining influence of knowledge on praxis as a determination that can only work through the structure of language, not through "motivation."[11] It is thus opposed to a Socratic belief in the causal motivational force of knowledge. In this opposition, Benjamin is close to both Nietzsche and Freud.[12] The difference of the *Fühlbarkeit* of a psychoanalytic effect is precisely the difference of an effect of language as the product of "working through" in contrast to the completely ineffectual communication of knowledge.

Benjamin locates the *Fühlbarkeit* or the absence thereof in the conditions of time and space, in a spatio-temporal unity (2:110) as the conditions for the poetic image. The central term of Benjamin's poetics, *das Gedichtete* as that which produces the *Fühlbarkeit* is defined as "the spatio-temporal penetration of all figures" [*die raumzeitliche Durchdringung aller Gestalten*] (2:112). The intensity of the poetic force is one that produces space at every spot ("an jeder Stelle Raum schaffen" [2:113]). The poetic world is emphatically a world of spatial extension: "the extension of space, the expanded plain" [*die Erstreckung des Raums, der gebreitete Plan*] (2:113). Extension, *Erstreckung*, constitutes the very existence of language according to Benjamin's essay "On Language as such and Human Language." "The existence of language," Benjamin writes, "extends not only over all the regions of human intellectual expression, which in some sense are inhabited by language, but it extends essentially over everything."[13] Language, one might say, is *res extensa*, not only one-dimensional in its syntagmatic linear extension but also in its vertical paradigmatic architecture. It is coextensive with space itself, the condition of all possible positions and prepositions, condition for all *Vorstellungen* and *Darstellungen* and thus also for that other space invoked in Benjamin's essay on surrealism as *Bildraum* (image-space) and *Leibraum* (corporeal space) (2:309). In this sense Benjamin's conception of language allows for no *hors-langue*, no outside of language, to use a parallel formulation of Derrida's that there is no *hors-texte*.[14] Neither formula says that everything is language or text, but both insist on the impossibility of stepping outside of a space that is coextensive with language.

The irreducibly spatial character of language also extends to the concept of truth that, for Benjamin, is constituted by the structure of language.[15]

Again, Benjamin's philosophy of language intersects precisely with Hölderlin's text and thus can take it literally by its word. When Hölderlin's poem asks rhetorically and reassuringly, "Geht auf Wahrem dein Fuß nicht, wie auf Teppichen?" [Does not your foot walk on the true as on carpets?], Benjamin speaks accordingly of the *Lage der Wahrheit* (the situation [or: situatedness, layer] of truths) (2:114).[16] It is literally the layer where, for Benjamin, "the spatial and intellectual order turn out to be connected in an identity of the determining and the determined" (2:114). The spatial principle is that which makes this identity tangible or visible: "Es erfüllt in der Anschauung die Identität des Bestimmenden mit dem Bestimmten" (2:115). In another literal echo of Hölderlin's poem, space becomes *Identität von Lage und Gelegnem* (identity of situation/layer and situated/opportune). The *Gelegne* echoes Hölderlin's verse: "Was geschiehet, es sei alles gelegen dir!" [Whatever happens, may it all be opportune to you]. The *Gelegne* is the opportunity offered by the *Lage*, the gift of the situation, as it were, and as such already marked by a certain timeliness. This temporal moment is indicated in Hölderlin's poem as a layer across which the poet walks, step after step, word after word, tone after tone in the sequence of the poem's extension. And Benjamin takes up this step and walk in order to establish in the extension of the walk "the intensive activity of the walk as inner plastic temporal form" [*die intensive Aktivität des Ganges als innere plastisch zeitliche Form*] (2:115). Extension of space and "intension" of time intersect in the linguistic layer of truth constituted by the poem. And it is in this specific, singular form of the intersection, in the singularity of the web of this text, that something becomes *fühlbar* (2:116) that was not yet *fühlbar* (2:109) in the first version.

Yet this *Fühlbarkeit* is also the result of a curious displacement: the figures of life—the poet and the people—are completely displaced (*versetzt*) into the circle of song (*in den Kreis des Gesangs*). In this displacement they are flattened out into a surface, into a *flächenhafte Einheit* (2:116). The layer of truth appears now as a flat surface onto which the figures are projected. According to some notes of Benjamin, the projection onto a surface is the condition that something becomes readable and thus perceptible: "Wahrnehmung ist Lesen / Lesbar ist nur in der Fläche Erscheinendes" [Perception is reading / Readable is only what appears in the surface] (6:32).[17] Configurations and constellations, two central terms for Benjamin, are precisely such projections onto a surface.

The projection onto the surface can also be read as a geographical and historical displacement: from the occident to the orient, and from the post-Renaissance, "modern" perspectival image with its dominance of painterly, "realistic" representation, to the aperspectival representation of earlier times and other cultures. Benjamin brings this double displacement together in the comparison with "byzantine mosaics" (2:116). Throughout the essay, Benjamin underlines the "oriental" quality of the later version of Hölderlin's poem. This emphasis is a remarkable testimony to Benjamin's power of reading. At a time when many of Hölderlin's late texts were not yet available, Benjamin reads in this one text of Hölderlin the oriental hidden layer that Hölderlin himself reads as the ground-layer of Greek culture and which he attempts to present in the form of his translation of *Antigone*. This "oriental" displacement will reemerge again in Benjamin's reading of Kafka as a mode of writing in modernity that unsettles the traditional occidental literary forms and the conventional differences of artistic and didactic writing. Kafka's "parables" represent a form of writing on the literary side that finds itself confronted with the same question of presentation as the contemporary philosophical writing that does not simply repress its irreducible involvement in the figures of language. On both sides, if one can still call them "sides," the borderlines that were supposed to separate clearly literary and philosophical presentation, figural language and conceptual language, are blurred.

It is, however, not a simple "leveling of the generic differences between literature and philosophy," as Habermas would like to make us believe.[18] It is rather a kind of writing that, in the most rigorous pursuit of its own laws of genre, explores with unrelenting patience the demarcations of the borders and the seams. It is a mode of writing that lingers as it were in a kind of *Saumseligkeit*, to use a Benjaminian pun.[19] Such exploration easily gives the impression of the unseemly to the Puritan eye and its censorships.

The conventional differentiation between literary writing as a metaphorical writing in "images" and philosophical writing as denotative and conceptual is put into question by Benjamin's rethinking of the image as figure and construction. This rethinking passes through the invocation of the mosaic as an image type different from the "realistic," secular painterly image.

The brief and tentative invocation of the byzantine mosaic in the Hölderlin essay returns emphatically in the preface to the book on the German mourning play. It appears as the epiphany of philosophical *Darstellung*, its image, so to speak, and its thought, the thinking image *kat' exochen* with all the constitutive marks of the thinking image. The first constitutive mark of philosophical *Darstellung* is the "renunciation of the uninterrupted course of intention" (1:208). It opens up to the caesura, to the *Einbruchsstelle*: every paragraph, every sentence not only an *Absatz* and *Satz*, but an *Absetzen*, an interruption and sitting down in order to lift off (*hebt an*) again and again, and to return again and again in patient endurance to the object itself (*die Sache selbst*). The movement that thus intends the object and the matter at hand assumes itself the figure of breath at the borderline of matter and dematerialization. At the same time the figure of the breath is called the "most proper form of existence of contemplation": figurality is its property.

Under the incessant impact of the pneumatics, metrics, and rhythmical caesuras of this figural breath, the sameness of the *Sache selbst* is unfolded and transfigured in a differentiated scale of sense, into layers and levels of meaning (*Sinnstufen*). The *Sache selbst* is, as it were, broken to pieces, and the pieces enter into the figural constellations that are the condition of readability. Here, the image appears as a mosaic that not only does not lose but owes its majesty to the destruction of the *Sache selbst* into pieces and fragments. The impact that shatters the matter into capricious particles is the condition for the construction of an image that gives testimony to "the transcendental impact and weight" [*die transzendentale Wucht*] of truth (1:208).

Benjamin's emphasis that the image is the assembly of "disparate" pieces indicates already that the mosaic is a construction and not a reconstruction. The construction is as different from the shattered phenomena as the dream interpretation is different from the dream. The analogy is precise: in Freud's technique of dream interpretation the dream images are shattered into their smallest elements, which enter through the chain of association into new constellations and contexts in which the dream-thoughts are constructed. The radical difference of construction and reconstruction marks in Benjamin's later work the difference between historicism and historical materialism: "It is important for the materialist historian to differentiate most rigorously the construction of a historical state of affairs [*Sachverhalt*] from that which one usually calls its reconstruction. The reconstruction in the mode of empathy [*Einfühlung*] is one-dimensional. Construction presupposes destruction" (5:587). The image that emerges from this destruction/construction is no longer pure image, certainly not a picture, but the construction "of an image-forming and intellectual whole" [*des bildnerischen und intellektuellen Ganzen*] (1:208). The German word *Bild* resonates now with the etymological cognates that are still prevalent in its derivatives (*Bildung* = formation, and *bilden* = to form); as a construction, this *Bild* is also a building, an architecture and a figurative formation.

Benjamin's formula of the "image-forming and intellectual whole" [*des bildnerischen und intellektuellen Ganzen*] resonates with Hölderlin's formula for a sphere that can neither be grasped purely conceptually nor purely in terms of events, facts, or phenomena, but, in Hölderlin's words, only "intellectually historically" [*intellectuell historisch*] (FA 14:48). The shift from Hölderlin's "historical" to Benjamin's image-forming (*bildnerisch*) remains fully within the logic of Benjamin's philosophy of history and memory. For, as Hölderlin already perceives the post-Kantian task as an integration of experience in thought in a sphere that encompasses memory (*Gedächtniß*) and thought (*Gedanke*) (FA 14:47), Benjamin's work on the same task (explicitly formulated in the early essay "On the Coming Philosophy") culminates in a philosophy of history and memory that finds its sphere in the construction of the dialectical image.

Yet, as always in Benjamin, the concept of the "dialectical" shifts ground. Not only is it a "dialectic in standstill," but also there remains this residue, this insistence on a duality and opposition that resists full resolution. Thus, while in the mosaic and in the dialectical image thought and experience enter into the sphere of the true, Benjamin returns to a moment of opposition that seems to question the possibility of a fulfillment of the imperative to know the image.

In a diary entry of 13 May 1931, he poses the question, "Whether the pleasure in the world of images is not nourished by a somber spitefulness against knowledge?" He illustrates this resistance of the image against knowledge in a scene:

> I look out into the landscape: there lies the sea smooth like a mirror in the bay; forests extend [*ziehen*] as an immobile mass up to the top of the mountain; up there, the decayed walls of a castle as they stood there already centuries ago; the sky radiates without clouds, in "eternal blueness," as one says. That is the way the dreamer, immersing himself into the landscape, wants it.[20]

This image of calmness and immobility is contrasted with a knowledge of an incessant movement: "that this sea rises and falls at every moment in millions and millions of waves, that the forests tremble anew at every moment from the roots to the last leaf, that there is an incessant tumbling and rippling in the stones of the castle ruin."

Image and knowledge are contrasted here in terms of an opposition of immobility and movement. But the language of the description already inscribes the movement into the immobility: "die Wälder ziehen als unbeweg-liche. . . . Masse" [the forests extend (literally: move, pull, draw) as an immobile mass]. The opposition reverses the constellation of the dialectical image, which is a dialectic in standstill and, like Hölderlin's *Vorstellung selber*, the result of a caesura that interrupts the incessant flow of images and representations. The image of this landscape is a dream image, not a dialectical image. It is the image before the *Einbruchsstelle* of waking up.

In order to wake up, in order to invert this inversion, another stop, another kind of interruption and stopping is necessary. Benjamin differentiates two ways of stopping the movement: one he calls "Einhalt gebieten," to command nature to come to a halt in the serene images of the landscape, which is also the landscape of the aura with its branches and mountain lines. This auratic image is the result of "the black magic of sentimentality" (6:428). But there is another image invoked, also the result of a stopping of movement, one apparently more somber than the serene auratic landscape: a petrification under the call of the poet: *Sie unter neuem Anruf erstarren zu machen*. Petrification, *erstarren*, is for Benjamin the effect of the intervention of the inexpressive into expression, the condition of the emergence of something true that is neither pure image nor pure thought, but rather is dialectical image.

There is another dialectic at work here, or rather a return to that which is constitutive of all dialectic. The word *erstarren* invokes connotations of death, and yet it is the *erstarren* that is invoked here against the mute and silent power of death in the serene auratic image. As a dream image this auratic landscape is also an image of desire: this is the way the dreamer wants it, and he does everything to forget, to deny the knowledge. This desire makes the apparent serene image so somber in its spitefulness against knowledge; for it is a desire of death: the dreamer wants to give himself up to images in which he finds "peace, eternity, rest" (6:428). This desire of death consists in the refusal of a knowledge of death. For what the dreamer does not want to know is the movement of death, the "incessant tumbling and rippling" of decay.

Death as the dialectical force enters the text most concretely where the writing hovers on the threshold of the autobiographical. Benjamin's diary entries of May and June 1931 in Juan les Pins bear in more than one sense the signature of death whose lines are intertwined with the curve of life to form the monogram of writing. The "bow of life" is an old Greek, Heracleitean pun, *biós* and *bíos*, "bow, arc, curve" and "life"; Hölderlin recalls it as *Bogen des Lebens*. The first word of the diary invokes *Die Bogen*, but in another curve of the semantic shift they now refer to sheets of paper, as the ground on which the following entries will be written: "Die Bogen, die mir von diesem Papier noch bleiben, will ich einem Tagebuch vorbehalten" [The sheets that still remain of this paper I will reserve for a diary] (6:422). The *Bogen*, the last remainder of a certain amount of paper, are reserved for another remainder, for what remains, precariously, of the *Bogen*, the curve of Benjamin's life whose traces are to mark these sheets. This other *Bogen*, the curve of life, is bent toward its end by an intense fatigue that marks life's condition as a whole: "Most important of all: I am tired" (6:422), as well as individual moments of it: "Later at night, deadly tired on the bus" (6:425). It is a fatigue imbued with the peace (*Friede*) (6:422) that the dreamer of the serene landscape-image wants to preserve ("Frieden haben will" [6:428]).

Benjamin wants to preserve instead the last remaining sheets for what might be his last notations, in any case: for writing. This preservation introduces a kind of anticipatory stopping or interruption, indicated in the German word *halt*, that appears in Benjamin's verb *vorbehalten* (to reserve, to retain). The word appears a little bit later as a noun and with a somber semantic shift as "Der universale Vorbehalt de[r] eignen Lebensweise gegenüber" [The universal reservation concerning [my] own mode of life] (6:422), which goes hand in hand with the readiness for the ultimate stop and interruption, "the increasing readiness to take my own life" (6:423). The *vorbehalten* of the sheets of paper for the written traits of life is thus intertwined with the *Vorbehalt* that is both the last stop and the last hold of life, its *Einbruchsstelle*: forming the monogram that writes the image of Benjamin in that sense in which Benjamin wrote of and toward the "image of Proust."

Indeed Benjamin's reflections on the writing of the *Berlin Chronicle* indicate that *Vorbehalt* might be the fundamental condition for the writing of memory and autobiography and for memory and autobiography to become writing: "Soll ich es mit einem Wort sagen, was ich Paris für diese Betrachtungen verdanke, so ist es: der Vorbehalt" [To say in word what I owe Paris for these contemplations, it is: *Vorbehalt*] (6:467). It is difficult to translate the term at this point, because "reservation" does not quite render the constitutive line drawn by this a priori hold and rupture as a precondition before any writing can begin.

Once this *Vorbehalt* is acknowledged it inscribes its *halt* into all movement. Dead tired on the bus on the night of 5 May 1931, Benjamin notes this constellation as that of two languages: "The French say *allure*, we: *Haltung*. Both words are derived from 'walking.' But in order to say the same—but this remark indicates in what limited sense it is the same—the French speak of the walk itself—*allure*—the Germans of its interruption—*Haltung*."[21]

Allure could also be translated as "gait," the gait of a horse for example as the unmistakable physiognomic signature that can be read by the experienced reader even when Alexander's horse Bucephalus has become a lawyer in Kafka's story, walking up the steps, stepping toward the gate of the law. But in order for the gait to approach that gate, to step over its threshold, it needs a stop, a *Halt* that arrests it at the threshold. It is the threshold of an *Einbruchsstelle* of diverse spheres: of life and death and death in life; of autobiography and writing in the two directions of autobiography as writing and writing as autobiography; of image and knowledge in the two directions of image as knowledge and knowledge as image, forming the monograms of writing as dialectical image that performs the imperative: *Wisse das Bild*, knowing it only and over and over again and anew in the *Doppelbereich* of the living and the dead. It is the curve of a life drawn and determined "by the proportion of the number of the living to that of the dead whom one has known."[22]

The imperative *Wisse das Bild* is thus indeed also the Delphic imperative "know yourself," but knowing yourself in the monogram and in the polygram of the figures of writing. For this image is both: polygram as the result of many disparate writings and palimpsests, monogram as the historical singularity of the image. Reading this image of a self in its written figures means also passing through it, stepping over its gates as Benjamin comments on Brecht's autobiographical poem "Vom armen B.B.": "He who has read this poem has passed through the poet as through a gate on which one can read the weather-worn letters B.B." The place of the gate, its *Stelle* and its standing there, allows the passage of the gait. The gate is of course not Bertolt Brecht; it has stood there perhaps for centuries.[23] But it bears his initials, and as a gate, a *Tor* in German, it signals the author, the *Au-tor*. Perhaps, if the letters are read, and not only the letters but also their weather-wornness, the tumbling and rippling of decay, that includes the author, his image might become readable again in the singularity of a historical constellation, as we are trying to read here, and again and again, the image of Benjamin.

TWO

Benjamin and Cinema

Not a One-Way Street

M I R I A M   H A N S E N

More than any other contemporary film practice, Hong Kong cinema seems to resonate with Benjamin's efforts to theorize mass-mediated modernity, with its twin etiologies of technical reproduction and capitalist consumption. To paraphrase Benjamin in the most general terms, these efforts concern the impact of the industrially altered environment on the human sensorium, the epochal restructuring of subjectivity and collectivity, the crisis of the aesthetic, and the conditions of possibility for postauratic forms of experience and memory, intersubjectivity and agency. Hong Kong films of the last decade, with the clock ticking toward the 1997 handover, reformulate these concerns for an age of digital, gene, and transplant technologies; of accelerated speed, escalated violence, and refined mechanisms of power; of globalized economies and new, at once local and transnational, media publics.

A recent instance of such cinematic inquiry, *Face/Off*, a Hollywood production directed by emigrant director John Woo, raises the question of the fate of sense perception and personal identity to splendidly nightmarish proportions. The FBI agent originally played by John Travolta, having lost his face and voice, by way of a transplant scheme that misfired, to the terrorist who killed his son, ends up in a fascistic top-security prison without evidence of his "true" identity, while his nemesis, the terrorist originally played by Nicholas Cage, walks free wearing Travolta's face and voice, is about to take over the FBI, sleeps with Travolta's wife, and covets his daughter. Whatever you may think of this plot device, it effectively dramatizes the question of what it means to "trust your senses" in a world in which fundamental parameters of human appearance and character can be altered and simulated, in which experience (in Benjamin's emphatic sense) not only has lost its currency but, more importantly, is deployed to deceive—a world in which people are no longer capable, in Benjamin's words, "of telling . . . proven friend . . . from mortal enemy."[1]

Although we might expect such concerns in a sci-fi-inflected version of the gangster/killer film or, for that matter, in so many versions of the transnational action genre, they emerge more surprisingly in the supposedly softer genre of romantic comedy. The most successful Hong Kong film of 1997, *Comrades: Almost a Love Story* (*Tianmimi*, directed by Peter Chan), is an epic romance about two immigrants from the mainland, played by Maggie Cheung and local pop star Leon Lai. The process of acculturation, in particular the young man's, is staged through the old comic trope of the country rube encountering technological modernity—in this case, an advanced-capitalist late modernity that is no longer centered in the West (in fact, New York, where both characters have emigrated by 1993, is marked as backward and uncivilized compared to Hong Kong). The high-tech accoutrements of daily life, such as pagers, TV monitors, and video and audio cassettes are ubiquitous, as are automatic-teller machines, and economic activities range from the neighborhood food business through McDonald's to the stock market ("stocks and shares are the national products of Hong Kong, just like oil in the Middle East," the heroine explains to the marveling comrade).[2] The overt catalyst for the formation of the romantic couple is Taiwanese pop singer Teresa Tang, with her eponymous song "Tianmimi," who is herself emblematic of the vicissitudes of an emerging pan-Asian culture industry.

The catastrophic downside of romantic and economic success, however, is embodied by a star of a different medium and period: Mickey Mouse.[3] Reduced by the 1987 stock market collapse to earning her living as a massage girl, Qiao (Cheung), the female protagonist, confronts a particularly intimidating client, gangster boss Pao (Eric Tsang). Since she is not afraid of anything—"only rats," as she replies to his taunts—he returns for the next session "with a friend," as he puts it, "heard you're afraid of him," and we get a close-up of a Mickey Mouse design tattooed on his already densely ornamented back. She refuses to laugh—except for an extra tip, as she explains in good Brechtian style—but Mickey becomes the mascot of her subsequent life with the gangster, who is further aligned with the Disney figure by way of his squat shape, violent energy, robustness, and basic kindness. The affinity of laughter and fear, as of laughter and horror (which Benjamin had pinpointed in the figures of Mickey Mouse and Chaplin), is reinforced toward the end of the film, after Pao has been killed in a scuffle with street kids in New York. Taken to the morgue to identify him, Qiao asks that he be turned over; the viewer, unlike the coroner, knows what she sees and why she smiles, even chuckles, only to break into violent sobbing, exacerbated by a slow zoom into her face. The reverse shot closing in on the tattoo may be redundant and excessive by Western (art-film) standards, but the emphatic gesture condenses in the figure of Mickey both the shock of real loss and the possibility of a happy ending. The inscribed skin that identifies the gangster's body, his corpse, becomes a screen for the recovery of sensory affect, suggesting in turn a film practice that might pierce the scar tissue formed in the adaptation to the regime of capitalist technology. "In the cinema," to quote Benjamin not quite out of context, "people whom nothing moves or touches any longer learn to cry again."[4] *Comrades* ends happily, if barely so, moving us by a "sentimentality restored to health" of the kind that Benjamin perceived in 1920s commercial cinema and advertising, and it does not shy away from kitsch (in Benjamin's rather than Clement Greenberg's sense).[5]

In this chapter I hope not only to restore Mickey Mouse to Benjamin's theory of cinema (which I've done in greater detail elsewhere), but also, more generally, to reactivate a trajectory, suggested by my two examples, between the alienation of the senses that preoccupied the later Benjamin and the possibility of undoing this alienation that he began to theorize as early as *One-Way Street* (1928), particularly through the concept of "innervation."[6] I am not trying to offer a Benjaminian reading of Hong Kong films (and do not claim expertise in that area), nor do I intend to impose a theoretical framework developed in relation to Western modernity onto cultural phenomena that are incommensurate. What I want to suggest, however, is that Benjamin's speculations speak to the concerns of these films, and vice versa, because the problems he articulated vis-à-vis film and mass culture, and the antinomies in which his thinking moved, persist today—in different forms and on a different scale, to be sure, but with no less urgency and no more hope for easy solutions. In this regard I share the emphasis on the antinomic structures in Benjamin's work that critics have discerned in various ways, following Benjamin's own observation that his thinking, like his life, "moved by way of extreme positions."[7] But this "radical ambivalence" (John McCole) or "*ontology* of extremes" (Irving Wohlfarth) was not just a matter of his temperament or his friendships, nor even of a strategic self-positioning within the contemporary "intellectual field" at a time of major upheaval and crisis.[8] Rather, Benjamin's imperative to "actuality" compels us to realize that the structure of his thinking, in particular with regard to the technical media, corresponds to irresolvable contradictions in media culture itself, in the very fact of mass-mediated culture, now more so than ever.

Let me try to define this particular antinomy in Benjamin's thinking as succinctly as possible, at the risk of being reductive. Position A, developed under the traumatic impact of World War I, welcomes the technical media— photography, film, gramophone, radio—because they promote the "liquidation" of the cultural heritage, of bourgeois-humanist notions of art, personality, and experience that have proved bankrupt in, if not complicit with, the military catastrophe and the economic one that followed, inadequate to the social and political reality of the proletarianized masses. At this historic crossing, Benjamin turns his back on the decaying "aura," which cannot be salvaged anyway, and tries to promote "a new, positive concept of barbarism" whose outlines he finds in the contemporary "culture of glass" (Loos, Le Corbusier, Klee, Brecht, Scheerbart).[9] This presentist, collectivist, "liquidationist" position (McCole), which is commonly taken to be the message of his famous essay, "The Artwork in the Age of Its Technical Reproducibility" (1935-1936), has by and large dominated Benjamin's reception in cinema and media studies, from Brechtian film theory of the 1970s to more recent cultural studies.

Position B, formulated under the shadow of the rise of fascism and the "coming war" (which Benjamin foresaw in 1933) and largely to be found in his essays on Baudelaire, Proust, and Leskov, laments the decline of experience, synonymous with "the disintegration of the aura in the experience of shock" (*I* 194). The decline of experience, "Erfahrung" in Benjamin's emphatic sense, is inseparable from that of memory, the faculty that connects sense perceptions of the present with those of the past and thus enables us to remember both past sufferings and forgotten futures.[10] In this account, the media of visual and acoustic recording merely consummate the process inflicted on the human sensorium by the relentless proliferation of shock in Taylorized labor, city traffic, finance capital, and industrial warfare, by thickening the defensive shield with which the organism protects itself against an excess of stimuli. Furthermore, by vastly expanding the archive of voluntary memory or conscious recollection, the technical media restrict the play of involuntary memory or remembrance. What is lost in this process is not merely the peculiar structure of auratic experience, that of investing the phenomenon we experience with the ability to return the gaze, a potentially destabilizing encounter with otherness; what is also lost is the element of *temporal disjunction* in this experience, the intrusion of a forgotten past that disrupts the fictitious progress of chronological time.

But Benjamin's positions on film and mass-mediated modernity cannot be reduced to the antinomy of "liquidationist" versus "culturally conservative" (McCole), nor to the antinomic opposition of "distraction" and "destruction" (Gillian Rose).[11] Both positions hook into each other in ways that may generate a dialectic, but may just as well turn into a *mise-en-abîme*. The problem Benjamin recognized is that each position contains within itself another antinomic structure whose elements combine with those of its opposite in more or, hopefully, less destructive ways. The most destructive combination was currently pioneered by fascism, while the alternative possibilities were increasingly eroded in the polarization of liberal capitalist media and the cultural politics of Stalinism.

Let me elaborate this point by way of the logic of "aesthetics and anaesthetics," which Susan Buck-Morss has pinpointed as the linchpin of what Benjamin means by "politics" in the artwork essay. Specifically, Buck-Morss links Benjamin's pessimistic adaptation of Freud's concept of shock in his 1939 essay on Baudelaire, with its emphasis on the defensive numbing of the sensorium, to his polemics against "the aestheticization of politics" in the artwork essay, his somewhat curious assertion that the fascist spectacularization of the masses and of war consummates the tradition of "l'art pour l'art."[12] What makes this link compelling, according to Buck-Morss, is a dialectical relation between *anaesthetization*, the numbing that splits momentary perception from experience (synaesthetics, memory), and *phantasmagoria*, the deployment of ever more powerful aesthetic techniques, ever more spectacular thrills and sensations, to pierce the protective shield of consciousness, yet only momentarily and on isolated occasions that distill auratic effects into a kind of false sublime (world fairs, wax museums, Wagner). As a result of such overstimulation, experiential numbing is aggravated to a degree of "self-alienation" that makes humanity "experience its own destruction as an aes-

thetic pleasure of the first order" (7:384). In terms of the antinomic structure of Benjamin's thinking, this means that in the fascist mass spectacles
and glorification of war, the negative poles of both positions outlined above,
the anachronistic perpetuation of the aura in position A and the anaesthetizing effects of technology in position B, combine to enter into the most fatal,
violent, and destructive constellation.

The key to the politics of the artwork essay, in Buck-Morss's analysis,
is that Benjamin casts his critique of the aesthetic tradition, the aesthetic
narrowly understood as pertaining to the bourgeois institution of art, the
ideal of "beautiful semblance," within the larger project of the aesthetic more
broadly understood as the "theory [*Lehre*] of perception that the Greeks
called aesthetics" (7:381), which pertains to the entire domain of human perception and sensation. At this point in history, Benjamin warns fellow intellectuals, the aesthetic can no longer be defended in terms of the idealist values
of the few that make it complicit with the suffering of the many, nor even
in terms of style and artistic *technique*; rather, the political crisis demands an
understanding of the aesthetic that takes into account the social reception of
technology, the effects of sensory alienation on the conditions of experience
and agency. At this juncture Benjamin locates the historic function of film:
"to establish a balance between humans and technology" (7:375), "to make
the vast technical apparatus of our time an object of human innervation"
(1:445). The cinema emerges as the foremost battleground of contemporary
art and aesthetics, not because of a futurist or constructivist enthusiasm for
technology, but because film is the only medium that might yet counter the
catastrophic effects of humanity's (already) "miscarried [*verunglückte*] reception of technology" that had come to a head with World War I.[13]

In Buck-Morss's reading of Benjamin, however, the historical trajectory
of shock-anaesthetics-aestheticization appears less like a dialectic than an
accelerating spiral or vortex of decline, culminating in a catastrophe that
only the revolution or the Messiah could stop. The crucial issue is therefore
whether there can be an imbrication of technology and the human senses
that is not swallowed into this vortex of decline; whether Benjamin's egalitarian, techno-utopian politics could be conjoined with his emphatic notion
of experience/memory; whether and how the "profane illumination" he discerned in the project of the surrealists could be generalized into a "collective bodily innervation," the universal and public integration of body- and

image-space (*Leib- und Bildraum*) that had become structurally possible with technology.[14] If that possibility amounts to nothing less than the revolution, troped in at once messianic and anthropological-materialist terms, its weak version is the more pragmatic option of a "general and mild politics of distraction" (Rose), which Benjamin appears to endorse in the artwork essay. This second option, however, willingly puts up with the loss of experience/ memory entailed by the technological media and thus risks underwriting its anaesthetizing opposite, that is, a "new barbarism" that, as Adorno cautioned Benjamin more than once, comes close to identifying with the aggressor.[15]

If there is a key term in Benjamin's efforts to imagine an alternative reception of technology, then it is the concept of "innervation." Related to the notion of an "optical unconscious" familiar from the artwork essay, innervation refers, broadly, to a neurophysiological process that mediates between internal and external, psychic and motoric, human and mechanical registers. The term still appears in the second and in the third (French) version of the artwork essay, but is missing in the essay's fourth, dubiously canonic version.[16]

The concept of innervation emerged with a new "cycle of production" that Benjamin inaugurated with *One-Way Street* and that, as he told Gershom Scholem in a letter of January 1928, he hoped to complete the following year with his "very curious and extremely precarious project" on the Paris arcades. The latter project was to bring the new cycle of work to a close "in much the same way in which the *Trauerspiel* book concluded the German cycle."[17] Benjamin never completed his *Arcades Project* and did not return to it until 1934; but during the hiatus of the late 1920s and early 1930s he wrote a number of texts that are more important to film and media theory today than even the most thorough reading of the artwork essay.[18] In addition to *One-Way Street* (and the few articles specifically devoted to film and photography), these texts include essays on surrealism and on Proust and Kafka, speculations on the mimetic faculty, texts on (Berlin) childhood, "Hashish in Marseille" and other *Denkbilder*, and the programmatic piece "Experience and Poverty," as well as the early layers of the *Passagen-Werk*.[19] If the Germanist cycle of production remained largely within the genres of literary history and criticism, shot through with metaphysical and theological concerns, the new cycle took on the question of modernity in its profane actuality, having to do with the impact of industrial-capitalist technology and commodity production, with the emergence of mass society and the resulting political crisis.

One-Way Street is commonly understood as documenting Benjamin's turn to Marxism, under the influence of Asja Lacis, the "engineer" who, as he puts it in his dedication to her, "cut it [the street] through the author" (*SW* 1:444). But the book is also part of a more general turn, around 1925, among critical intellectuals as strongly influenced by Jewish messianism and gnosticism as Benjamin, from lapsarian critiques of modernity to a more curious and less anxious look at contemporary realities, in particular the marginalized, ephemeral phenomena of everyday life and leisure culture. "Access to truth is now in the profane," was Siegfried Kracauer's parting shot in his 1926 polemics against Martin Buber and Franz Rosenzweig's translation of the Bible.[20] The concern with "actuality," shared, although understood differently, by Benjamin, Kracauer, and Ernst Bloch, shaped their reception of Marx in idiosyncratic ways.[21] More than either of his interlocutors, however, Benjamin focused on the question of technology; and, more than they, he sharpened his approach to modernity with recourse to psychoanalysis, including the neurological, anthropological, and surrealist fringes of Freud. This twin orientation marks *One-Way Street* not only in its thematic and analytic concerns but also in its avant-garde mode of presentation (which Bloch somewhat glibly heralded as the "revue form in philosophy"), in textual strategies that articulate—or, as it were, innervate—the political, erotic, and aesthetic implications of the *Bahnung*, or pathway, cut by modernity, the street that entwines technological and psychic registers in the book's title trope.[22]

If Jean Laplanche and J.-B. Pontalis feel compelled to say that "the term 'innervation' may pose a problem for the reader of Freud," one can only wonder what they would say about Benjamin's use of the term. According to Laplanche and Pontalis, in Freud's earliest writings the term refers to a "physiological process: the transmission, generally in an efferent direction, of energy along a nerve-pathway."[23] This definition by and large tallies with the term's usage in the discourse of physiology since the 1830s, where it denotes the process by which "nerve-force" is supplied to organs and muscles, or the "stimulation of some organ by its nerves."[24] In his (and Breuer's) work on hysteria, however, Freud uses innervation more specifically to describe the phenomenon of "conversion," the transformation of an unbearable, incompatible psychic excitation into "something somatic." As in physiological discourse, this process is assumed to be unidirectional, which for Freud means an energy transfer from the psychic to the somatic. But instead of effecting a normal functioning of the organism, innervation in the hysteric facilitates a pathway related to the "traumatic experience" (which itself is repressed); excitation is "forced into a wrong channel (into somatic innervation)," which, as a "mnemic symbol," remains other and strange, lodged "in consciousness, like a sort of parasite."[25]

In *The Interpretation of Dreams* (1900), innervation appears in the more general, "structural" sense, although with a significant twist. In his discussion of the "psychical apparatus" as a composite instrument comparable to various systems of lenses used in optical devices, Freud again asserts that the psychic apparatus has a definite direction:

> All our psychical activity starts from stimuli (*whether internal or external*) and ends in innervations. Accordingly, we shall ascribe a sensory and a motor end to the apparatus. At the sensory end there lies a system which receives perceptions; at the motor end there lies another, which opens the gateway to motor activity. Psychical processes advance in general from the perceptual end to the motor end.[26]

Although in the context of the studies on hysteria innervation represents a response to an *internal* excitation (whatever traumatic experience may have caused the excitation), here the sources of stimulation also include *external* ones. Freud resumes this distinction, along with the model of the psychic apparatus, in *Beyond the Pleasure Principle* (1920), when he discusses the case of traumatic neurosis caused by sensory overstimulation through mechanical violence (most acutely, in the recent war)—which returns us to Benjamin's account of the decay of experience under the urban-industrial-military proliferation of shock. In Freud's speculation, traumatic neurosis does not simply result from a thickening of the protective shield against excessive stimuli (*Reizschutz*), but from an "extensive breach being made in the protective shield," to which the psyche responds by summoning massive amounts of "cathectic energy" around the area of the breach: "An 'anticathexis' [*Gegenbesetzung*] on a grand scale is set up, for whose benefit all the other psychical systems are impoverished, so that the remaining psychical functions are extensively paralysed or reduced."[27] The term innervation does *not* appear in this context, and for good reason, because it refers to the very process that is *blocked* in the configuration of shock-breach-anticathexis, the discharge that alone could undo and counteract the anaesthetizing effects pinpointed by Benjamin.

Whether Benjamin borrowed the term from Freud or from the neuro-physiological and psychological discourse of the period, innervation comes to function as an antidote—and counterconcept—to technologically multi-plied shock and its anaesthetizing economy. In Buck-Morss's words, "'Inner-vation' is Benjamin's term for a mimetic reception of the external world, one that is empowering, in contrast to a defensive mimetic adaptation that protects at the price of paralyzing the organism, robbing it of its capacity of imagination, and therefore of active response."[28] To imagine such an en-abling reception of technology, it is essential that Benjamin, unlike Freud, understood innervation as a *two-way* process, that is, not only a conversion of mental, affective energy into somatic, motoric form but also the possi-bility of reconverting, and recovering, split-off psychic energy through mo-toric stimulation (as distinct from the "talking cure" advocated by Freud and Breuer).[29] This possibility would make the protective shield against stimuli, the precarious boundary or rind of the bodily ego, a bit less of a carapace or armor and a bit more of a matrix or medium—a porous interface between the organism and the world that would allow for a greater mobility and cir-culation of psychic energies.

Imagined as a two-way process, Benjamin's concept of innervation may have less in common with Freudian psychoanalysis than with contemporary perceptual psychology, reception aesthetics, and acting theory, in particu-lar the Soviet avant-garde discourse of biomechanics that must have reached Benjamin through Lacis. A major reference point in this regard is Sergei Eisenstein who, drawing on and revising William James and the conserva-tive philosopher Ludwig Klages (the latter an important influence/irritant for Benjamin), sought to theorize the conditions of transmitting or, more precisely, producing emotion in the beholder through bodily movement.[30] Seeking to adapt Klages's (metaphysically grounded) concept of expressive movement for a materialist theory of signification and reception, Eisenstein, like his teacher Vsevolod Meyerhold, returned to James's axiom that "emo-tion follows upon the bodily expression" ("we feel sorry because we cry"), although Eisenstein modified James by insisting on the two-way character and indivisible unity of movement and emotion.[31] Without going into distinctions here, what seems important to me regarding Benjamin's concept of innervation and its implications for film theory is the notion of a physiologically "contagious" or "infectious" movement that would trigger emotional effects in the viewer, a form of mimetic identification based in the phenomenon known as the Carpenter Effect.[32] The recourse to neurophysiological, mechanistic, and reflex psychology may not be as sophisticated as the insights of psychoanalysis; yet it may have been more in tune with new, technically mediated forms of aesthetic experience, predicated on mass production, unprecedented circulation and mobility, and collective, public reception.

In *One-Way Street*, the term innervation appears only twice, but the concept pervades the text in a series of variations, culminating in the grand finale of the book, "To the Planetarium." In the two places where the term is used explicitly it involves two distinct senses of *Technik*—technique and technology—in one case referring to the practice of yoga meditation, in the other to the tools of writing. In the section labeled "Antiques," under the subheading "Prayer Wheel," Benjamin states axiomatically: "No imagination without innervation" (4:116–17; *SW* 1:466). The preceding sentences, alluding to both Aristotle and Schopenhauer, assert that "exact pictorial imagination" [*genaue bildliche Vorstellung*] is essential to the vitality of "the will," in contrast with the "mere word," which at best inflames the will and leaves it "smouldering, blasted." The following sentences exemplify the connection between imagination and innervation in terms of an at once bodily and spiritual practice: the discipline of breathing in yoga meditation. "Now breathing," Benjamin states just as tersely, is "[innervation's] most delicate regulator." And the sound of the formulas, he goes on, is "a canon of such breathing."[33] Inverting the traditional Western cliché that associates the Buddhist prayer wheel with mindless mechanicity, Benjamin sees in the ascetic integration of external rhythm, physical posture, and mental processes a source of the imagination and, therefore, of power. "Hence [the yogis'] omnipotence [*Allmacht*]," he concludes—which, like a prayer wheel, returns the reader to the initial sentence on the vitalness of the pictorial imagination to the force of the will.

If yoga meditation provides a model of imaginative innervation, it can only do so under the heading of "Antiques."[34] Its imbrication of physical and mental energy harks back to a ritualistic, premechanical conception of the technical that Benjamin sought to theorize, in the early versions of the artwork essay, with his distinction between a first and second technology (*erste und zweite Technik*), as part of his effort to redefine the relationship between aesthetic technique and industrial technology.[35] This distinction revolves around the human body and the degree of its implication: "The first technology involves the human being as much, the second as little as possible." The second technology originates as "man attempts, with unconscious cunning, to gain distance from nature" (a motif that Max Horkheimer and Adorno were to elaborate in their historico-philosophical reading of the *Odyssey*, but that also recalls Ernst Jünger's reflections in his famous essay on pain).[36] As Benjamin explains, "The greatest feat of the first technology is, in a manner of speaking, the human sacrifice; that of the second is in the line of remote-controlled airplanes that do not even require a crew." Yet, where a contemporary reader might prolong this line into the Gulf War, Benjamin makes an amazing turn: "in other words," he continues the speculation on the second technology's constitution through distance, "[its origin] lies in play [*im Spiel*]" (7:359).

Unlike Frankfurt school critiques of technology from *Dialectic of Enlightenment* through Habermas, Benjamin does not assume an instrumentalist trajectory from mythical cunning to capitalist-industrialist modernity. The telos of *Naturbeherrschung*, or "domination of nature," defines the second, modern technology only "from the position of the first," which sought to master nature in existential seriousness, out of harsh necessity. By contrast, Benjamin asserts, "The second technology rather aims at the interplay [*Zusammenspiel*] between nature and humanity."[37] Benjamin pinpoints the training, practicing, or rehearsal (*Einübung*) of this interplay as the decisive function of contemporary art, in particular film. Film assumes this task not simply by way of a behaviorist adaptation of human perceptions and reactions to the regime of the apparatus (which seems to be the tenor of parts of the artwork essay), but because film has the potential to reverse, in the form of *play*, the catastrophic consequences of an *already failed* reception of technology. For instead of providing humans with a "key to happiness," technology, in its capitalist-imperialist usage, had become a tool for the domination of nature and thus of humanity's (self-)destruction; bourgeois culture had been complicit with that process by disavowing the political implications of technology, treating it as "second nature," while fetishizing an ostensibly pure and primary nature as object of individual contemplation.[38] Because of the medium's technicity, as well as its collective mode of reception, film offers a chance—a second chance, a last chance—to bring the apparatus to social consciousness, to make it public. "To make the technical apparatus of our time, which is a second nature for the individual, into a first nature for the collective, is the historic task of film" (7:688).

Innervation as a mode of regulating the interplay between humans and (second) technology can only succeed (that is, escape the destructive vortex of defensive, numbing adaptation), if it reconnects with the discarded powers of the first, with mimetic practices that involve the body, as the "preeminent instrument" of sensory perception and (moral, political) differentiation.[39] Where Jünger turns his equally astute observations on the impact of technology into a paean to anaesthetization, self-alienation, and discipline (celebrating a "second and colder consciousness" capable of seeing its own body as object), Benjamin seeks to reactivate the abilities of the body as a medium in the service of imagining new forms of subjectivity.[40] For Benjamin, negotiating the historical confrontation between human sensorium and technology as an alien, and alienating, regime requires learning from forms of bodily innervation that are no less technical but to a greater extent self-regulated (which ties in with Benjamin's autoexperiments with hashish, gambling, running downhill, eroticism). Hence, when (in the second version of the artwork essay) he speaks of revolutions as "innervations of the collective," he specifies, "more precisely, efforts of innervation on the part of a new, historically unprecedented collective which has its *organs* in second technology" (7:360, my emphasis). He goes on to illustrate the utopian excess of such innervation with recourse to developmental psychology: the child learns to grasp "by reaching for the moon the same way she or he reaches for a ball" (7:360).[41] This crossing of political history and the history of the human physis defines a key concern of Benjamin's anthropological-materialist politics that he sought to elaborate in the *Passagen-Werk*, in particular the sections on Fourier and Saint-Simon, but that no less informs the artwork essay, at least its early versions. What breaks through—and is as soon marginalized—in modern revolutions, he observes in a footnote, is a "double utopian will": alongside the "utopias of second nature," concerning society and technology (the Soviet experiment), there emerge the "utopias of the first," concerning in particular the "bodily organism of the human individual" and its repressed "existential questions [*Lebensfragen*]," "love and death" (Fourier, de Sade) (7:360, 665f.).

The concept of innervation, then, has to be seen in the context of Benjamin's speculations on "natural history" [*Naturgeschichte*], as bridging not only aspects of the first and the second technology but also the gap between human history and a history that encompasses all of creation (*Kreatur*) in its transience and contingency, including mutations of the physis caused/enabled by technology.[42] In Benjamin's messianically inflected science-fiction scenario, technology not only transforms but also has the capacity to redress the discrepancies of human existence in (to some extent, Western) history. These discrepancies include, in particular, the perceptual limitations constitutive of the human being qua individual body (such as the old Machian problem that we cannot view our own body as an integral shape); the anthropocentrism that maintains the hierarchic polarization of humans over the rest of creation; and capitalist society's perpetuation of the self-identical individual against the realities of modern mass experience.[43]

It is from the perspective of this "negative" or "refracted anthropology" (Gertrud Koch), that Benjamin's utopian—and by the 1930s largely contrafactual—overestimation of the radical potential of film has to be understood. As Koch compellingly argues, film appeared as the one medium capable of overcoming the physiological, historical, and ideological limitations of the human body. As a prosthetic extension of our perception that gives us a more complete vision of ourselves (through variable framing and editing), the camera, for Benjamin, assumes "Messianic-prophetic power," making the cinema a "technical apparatus which permits one to forget anthropological lack."[44] Furthermore, the cinema has spawned creations, like Mickey Mouse, that unhinge experience and agency from anthropomorphic identity, and thus enact Fourier's project of "cracking the teleology of nature."[45] Finally, the cinema provides a structural equivalent to the radical integration of "image space" and "body space," which Benjamin discerned in the experiments of the surrealists, projecting a "world of universal and integral actuality," but one that, in the case of cinema, is institutionally, qua mode of reception, predicated on the sensorium of a collective.

Benjamin is well aware that the "leap into the apparatus," effected by the collapsing of "body- and image-space,"[46] is itself an image, just as the lap dissolve from human physiognomy to alarm clock (at the end of the surrealism essay) remains a metaphor, albeit a surrealist one; the tension in the relation between human physis and the technical persists, even if recast as interplay. To a degree, therefore, innervation is necessarily based on miscognition, constituted within the register of the imaginary (in Lacan's sense): the child will never succeed in grasping the moon. But from this miscognition arise creative and transformative energies (different from the Lacanian scenario), in art as well as politics.

Whether the relation with technology will be transformative and cooperative (or, at the very least, benign) or whether it will continue on its destructive course turns on the classical polarity of "semblance and play" [*Schein und Spiel*] that Benjamin traces back, past Goethe and Schiller, to ancient practices of mimesis.[47] Since the oldest forms of imitation, "language and dance," knew only one material of creation, the imitator's body, semblance and play were two sides of the same process, still folded into one another: "The person imitating makes a thing apparent [*macht eine Sache scheinbar*]. One could also say, he plays [or performs] the thing [*er spielt die Sache*]: Thus one touches on the polarity that rests at the basis of mimesis" (6:666). In Benjamin's genealogy of art, this polarity has been tipped toward semblance, autonomized in the Western tradition of "beautiful semblance" [*schöner Schein*], which has dead-ended in aestheticism (illusion, phantasmagoria, aura in the narrow sense). Play, by contrast, is linked to repetition and iterability, as both an internal principle and the modality of imagining a second chance, the hope of sidetracking a catastrophic history. This is why Benjamin conceives of second technology not only in terms of its destructive, anaesthetic trajectory but also, and significantly, as grounded in a ludic and performative impulse. A mimetic innervation of technology would counter the perpetuation of illusion promoted by fascism with an aesthetics of play, an imagination that plays games—but also, to invoke Kracauer, gambles—with technology's otherness.[48]

As my excursion into Benjamin's speculations on first and second technology should have made clear, these speculations cannot be easily assimilated to contemporary media theory, certainly not the teleological variant (for example, Paul Virilio, Friedrich Kittler, Norbert Bolz) that marshals a vast number of sources to demonstrate—celebrate or decry—the subject's inevitable abdication to the a priori regime of the apparatus.[49] Although Benjamin no doubt participates in the critique of Western bourgeois conceptions of the subject since Nietzsche, he would hardly have reduced "the subjective factor" to an element in a loop that processes information and sensory signals. On the contrary, the very impulse to theorize technology is part of his project *to reimagine the aesthetic*—in response to the technically changed sensorium, to be sure, but in a desperate effort to reassess, and redefine, the conditions of experience, affectivity, memory, and the imagination. By the same token, however, we should guard against reading Benjamin too optimistically as assuming that the anaesthetization and alienation wreaked by technology on the human sensorium could be overcome, that "*the instinctual power of the human bodily senses*" could be "*restore[d]*" "*for the sake of humanity's self-preservation*," and that this could be done, "not by avoiding the new technologies, but by *passing through* them."⁵⁰ For Benjamin there is no beyond or outside of technology, neither in immanent political practice, nor even in his visions of messianic reconstitution. There is no way he would conceive of a restoration of the instinctual power of the senses and their integrity that would not take into account the extent to which the apparatus has already become part of human subjectivity, and there is no strategy for preventing humanity's self-destruction in which technology would not play an essential role. *Because* Benjamin so clearly recognizes the irreversibility of the historical process, the second fall that is modernity, he pursues a "politicization of art" in terms of a "collective innervation of technology," rather than a "restoration" of the sensorium to an instinctually intact, natural state: the issue is not how to reverse the historical process but how to mobilize, recirculate, and rechannel its effects.

To return to *One-Way Street*, the philosophy of technology that subtends the artwork essay emerges, in outline, in the trajectory from reflections on techniques of the individual body, particularly in the section "Madame Ariane: Second Courtyard on the Left," to the book's concluding piece, "To the Planetarium." If the former suggests a productive recourse to first technology through the category of a "bodily presence of mind," the latter presents a short-circuiting of bodies and (second) technology on a grand scale, on the battlefields of World War I. Generically another "antique," "Madame Ariane" contrasts modern forms of prophecy and superstition with ancient practices that had in the naked body their "most reliable instrument of divination" (Benjamin's often quoted example here is Scipio's gesture of throwing himself on the Carthaginian soil and exclaiming, "teneo te, terra Africana!").[51] What makes this example appear more relevant to the contemporary crisis than that of the "Prayer Wheel" is that it defines "presence of mind" as the key to averting danger, "to turn the threatening future into a fulfilled 'now'"; in other words, it reminds us that "precise awareness of the present moment" is the very condition of possibility of effective agency.

The other proleptic strand in "Madame Ariane" is thrown into relief at the end of the book, with Benjamin's disturbing mise-en-scène of World War I as an ecstatic, collective communion with the cosmos, "an attempt at new and unprecedented mating [*Vermählung*] with the cosmic powers" (*SW* 1:486, trans. mod.). The provocative link between these two kinds of bodily communion is his implicit invocation of Klages, whose treatise *On the Cosmogonic Eros* (1918) ostensibly dealt with erotic, ecstatic, and mystical practices of antiquity but strongly resonated with the ideologies that had fueled German (intellectuals') enthusiasm for the war.[52] In a language barely less pornographic than Klages's, Benjamin takes up the cosmic mating fantasy but radicalizes and detonates it through the very term that Klages, like other proponents of *Lebensphilosophie*, had disavowed and opposed: technology.

> Human multitudes, gases, electrical forces were hurled into the open country, high-frequency currents coursed through the landscape, new constellations rose in the sky, aerial space and ocean depths thundered with propellers, and everywhere sacrificial shafts were dug into Mother Earth. This immense wooing of the cosmos was enacted for the first time on a planetary scale—that is, in the spirit of technology. (*SW* 1:486f.)

Instead of scapegoating technology as such, Benjamin shifts his critique to the capitalist and imperialist harnessing of technology for the purpose of mastering nature. Here he begins to sketch an alternative relationship with both nature and technology predicated on pedagogy (as a discipline ordering intergenerational relations rather than one of mastering children), which points to the politics/aesthetics of interplay and innervation developed in the artwork essay.

As in the later text, Benjamin's critique of capitalist-imperialist technology by and large elaborates the Marxian axiom that the productive relations that keep the productive forces fettered also, by propelling the development of those forces, produce the conditions for their own abolition.[53] The subject of this process would be a collective that organizes its relations with both nature and technology in different ways than through "nations and families." What is more astounding, however, is that Benjamin phrases even the alternative reception of technology in the language of ecstasy, cosmic communion, and orgasmic convulsion, an affective terrain more typically occupied by the right. The "moderns" who dismiss this kind of experience as individual rapture commit a "dangerous error," he argues, because the desire for ecstatic communion with the cosmos is not only real and powerful but also, above all, communal and ultimately therapeutic. "The 'Lunaparks' are a prefiguration of sanatoria" (*SW* 1:487). Bringing the new collective physis enabled/projected by technology under control may demand as violent a "paroxysm of genuine cosmic experience" as the mass destruction that brought it into recognition in all its negativity, that is, as the historic failure of innervation whose repetition has to be prevented at all cost. Having opened the Pandora's box of therapeutic violence, Benjamin tries to close it again by handing the key to the proletariat, whose power is "the measure of [the new body's] convalescence." It is no coincidence, then, that the proletarian "discipline," which has to "grip" the new physis "to the very marrow," is cast in phallic, heterosexual terms: "Living substance [*Lebendiges*] conquers the frenzy of destruction only in the ecstasy of procreation" (*SW* 1:487).

It is hard to think of a smooth transition from this scene of Theweleitian male fantasy to the cultural politics of the late Weimar Republic. It is not surprising that Benjamin pursues the question of collective innervation by turning to surrealism, a movement whose publications and activities he sums up as revolving around the project of " '[winning] the energies of intoxication [or ecstatic trance, *Rausch*] for the revolution' " (2:307; *SW* 2:215). (In fact, where "To the Planetarium" goes beyond the vitalistic bombast reminiscent of Klages—as in its reference to Lunaparks, or in phrases such as "In the nights of annihilation of the last war, the frame of mankind was shaken by a feeling that resembled the bliss of the epileptic"—the language seems closer to the archive of surrealism, in particular Bataille and Artaud.) To imagine a collective innervation of technology in the German context, and not as a "last," or latest, "snapshot of the European intelligentsia" (the subtitle of the surrealism essay) but on a wider social basis, was likely to be a more problematic enterprise for Benjamin; there was no clear and direct path from that utopian snapshot to the cinema. As he himself knew, the collective assembled in the movie theaters was hardly that of the heroic proletariat (not an empirical category to begin with); rather, the cinema audience was in tendency part of "the mass," the blind, instinctual, insensible, self-destructive formation that Benjamin had denounced in an earlier, more pessimistic, section of *One-Way Street*.[54]

But perhaps the question of how the cinema figures in Benjamin's effort to theorize an alternative reception of technology requires opening up the framework of his philosophy of natural history and anthropological materialism to include economic and social processes not entirely synchronized with the logics of technology. For the leap into the apparatus, enabled by and rehearsed in the cinema, also entailed a leap into the capitalist market, into the world of commodities, into mass consumption. It is significant that Benjamin did not reserve the concept of innervation for Soviet film, although Eisenstein and Dziga Vertov no doubt helped him confront, to some extent, the problem of reconciling utopian claims with the actual possibilities —and limitations—of contemporary film culture. Rather, he discerned specifically cinematic forms of innervation in two highly popular figures of American provenance: Chaplin and Mickey Mouse. I now take up the concept of innervation as it relates to industrial-capitalist commodity production and mass/market culture, in particular the experience of a new relationship with "things" and with it the possibility of new forms of mimetic practice. This perspective not only foregrounds specifically modern forms of sensory perception, affectivity, and temporality, but also brings into view new modes of writing, reading, and reflexivity. Complicating Benjamin's focus on technology with his equally intense interest in the collective phenomenology of commodity culture will allow us to bring the concept of innervation to bear on the more familiar, although highly elusive and underexplored, notion of the "optical unconscious."

As already suggested, the possibility of collective innervation is bound up with the fate of the "mimetic faculty," the capacity to relate to the external world through patterns of similitude, affinity, reciprocity, and interplay. Like other writers reviving the concept of mimesis (such as Roger Caillois and Adorno), Benjamin takes up the anthropological, paleontological, zoological, and language-theoretical strands in the tradition, rather than the aesthetic strand more narrowly understood, as pertaining to works of art and standards of verisimilitude.[55] (In fact, as we saw with his speculations on the polarity of "semblance and play," it is the very dissociation of these strands, the monumentalization of the aesthetic and its isolation from social experience, that motivates Benjamin's recourse to a more comprehensive concept of mimesis in the first place.) Beyond naturalist or realist norms of representation and a particular relation (copy, mirror reflection, semblance) of the representation to reality, the mimetic is invoked as a form of practice that transcends the traditional subject-object dichotomy and its technologically exacerbated splittings of experience and agency—a process, activity, or procedure, whether ritual, performance, or play, of "producing similitudes"; a mode of cognition involving sensuous, somatic, and tactile forms of perception; a noncoercive engagement with the other that opens the self to experience, but also, in a darker vein, "a rudiment of the formerly powerful compulsion to become and behave like something else."[56]

Like the concept of the aura, equally central to Benjamin's theory of experience, the mimetic faculty is a category that comes into view only at the moment of decay; one might say that its conceptualization depends on the withering away of that which it purports to capture. Benjamin seems, for the most part, well aware of the concept's historicity and resists idealizing mimetic experience as a kind of Edenic merging. More important, his inquiry is framed by the possibility of a resurgence of mimetic powers *within* the disenchanted modern world: "The question is whether we are concerned with the decay of this faculty or with its transformation" (*SW* 2:721). One major area in which this question poses itself is language, in particular written language, which he calls an archive, "our most complete archive," of "nonsensuous similarities, of nonsensuous correspondences" (*SW* 2:722); that is, the mimetic qualities of script and reading are not obvious or commonplace, but hidden, encrypted, hinging (as in astrology) on a past conjuncture, a lost indexical bond. With the emergence of new technologies of inscription such as photography and film, however, this archive not only is vastly expanded but the new *modes* of inscription have significantly altered the terms under which mimetic relations can be actualized—possibilities Benjamin elsewhere designates with the shorthand of the optical unconscious.

The other area in which Benjamin discerns at once a persistence, albeit diminishing, and a historical transformation of the mimetic faculty is childhood—the ways in which children perceive, organize, and interact with their environment. "The child plays at being not only a shopkeeper or teacher, but also a windmill and a train" (*SW* 2:720). The physis thus engaged is not that of an immutable organic nature, but the historically formed, constantly changing nature of urban-industrial capitalism, with its growing heap of ever-new commodities, gadgets, masks, and images. Children practice an inventive reception of this new world of things in their games and modes of collecting and organizing objects, producing a host of bewildering similitudes and hidden correspondences, tropes of creative miscognition.[57] What interests Benjamin in such mimetic explorations is not the discovery of a Heideggerian "thingness" of things, but the index of a *temporality* that he considered key to capitalist modernity: the return of archaic, cyclical, mythical time in the accelerated succession of the new (fashion, technology), the mingling of the recently obsolescent "with what has been forgotten of the prehistoric world"—the same temporal slippage that attracted him to the surrealists' visions of Paris, their efforts to turn the mythical energies activated by capitalism into revolutionary ones.[58] Where adult society naturalizes the new as "merely" fashionable, children have the capacity to "discover the new anew," that is, in both its otherness and its utopian promise, and thus to incorporate it into the collective archive of images and symbols.[59] In other words, children pioneer a model of innervation on a par with modernity's destructive and liberating effects.

It is in *One-Way Street* that Benjamin begins to think more systematically about the possibility of the mimetic in modernity, by juxtaposing various sites, forms, and models of mimetic innervation—writing, childhood, dreaming, eros, politics. In most of these cases, the process of mimetic innervation entails dynamics that move in opposite, yet complementary directions: (1) a decentering and extension of the human sensorium beyond the limits of the individual body/subject, into the world that stimulates and attracts perception; and (2) an introjection, ingestion, or incorporation of the object or device, be it an external rhythm, a familiar madeleine, or an alien-(ating) apparatus. The prototype of the former is the lover's gaze at the wrinkles in the beloved's face, an affectively charged perception or sensation that is anything but the critically distanced, testing look of the Brechtian observer: "If the theory is correct that sensory perception [*Empfindung*] does not reside in the head, that we perceive a window, a cloud, a tree not in our brains but rather in the place where we see them, then we are, in looking at our beloved, too, *outside* ourselves."[60] I'd like to think that Benjamin recognized something of this affectively charged, eccentric perception at work as well in the dispersed subjectivity of the cinema experience.

The prototypical figures of the *incorporative* dynamic, on the other hand, are the child, the cannibal, the screen actor, the clown: "Suspension of inner impulses and the bodily center. New unity of dress, tattoo, and body. . . . Logical choice of deep expressivity: the man sitting on a chair will remain seated even after the chair has been removed."[61] In this image of extreme concentration the apparatus becomes part of the body; that is, the performance enacts, in an expressive, imaginative form, a process more commonly—and destructively—imposed upon people in everyday life. Both aspects of mimetic innervation are personified in the figure of the "eccentric," a precursor to Chaplin who, by "chopping up human expressive movement [*Ausdrucksbewegung*] into a sequence of minute innervations," internalizes the law of the apparatus, whether conveyor belt or filmic montage, thus giving the encounter with technology an expression in the "image world."[62] One might say that Benjamin finds in Chaplin an allegory, one allegory, for the very concept of innervation in and through film.

As mentioned above, the grounding of innervation in the mimetic faculty entails a link between innervation and written language. While in his speculations on the mimetic faculty Benjamin stresses the practice of *reading* (invoking graphology and physiognomy, as well as Hugo von Hofmannsthal's phrase "to read what was never written"), in *One-Way Street* he is rather concerned with the activity of *writing*. In a number of variations on his own craft, Benjamin sketches the principles, conditions, and rituals of successful writerly innervation, including the correct use of writing tools (see, for instance, "The Writer's Technique in Thirteen Theses"). This is the other context, besides "Prayer Wheel," in which the term innervation appears verbatim, significantly in a reflection on the future—and to some extent already outdatedness—of the typewriter.

> The typewriter will alienate the hand of the man of letters from the fountain pen only when the precision of typographic forms will enter directly into the conception of his books. This will likely require new systems of more variable typefaces. They will replace the pliancy of the hand with the innervation of the commanding fingers. (*SW* 1:457, trans. mod.)

What Benjamin would like, obviously, is a computer, and a word-processing program that operates in the graphic mode. Better yet, he wants to be wired —provided the new systems of writing are precise, flexible, and variable enough to play a productively mimetic role in the conception of his books. Only then will he give up the beloved fountain pen, with its more intimate, habitual relation to the writer's hand, a traditional mimetic bond that makes the old-fashioned writing tool superior to the typewriter in its present form.

As new technologies of inscription emerge, there are indications that "the book in [its] traditional form is nearing its end" (*SW* 1:456). For Benjamin, the passing of the Gutenberg era is signaled by poetic texts like Mallarmé's *Un Coup de dés*, which was "the first to incorporate the graphic tensions of the advertisement" into the "script-image" [*Schriftbild*] of the printed page. The models of poetic experiment are the more profane formations of film and advertisement ("a blizzard of changing, colorful, conflicting letters"), which have forced script from its refuge, the book, into the street and into the "dictatorial perpendicular," just as the card index has expanded it into three-dimensionality. Thus writing "advances ever more deeply into the graphic regions of its new eccentric figurativeness" or pictoriality (*Bildlichkeit*). And if poets are farsighted enough to collaborate in the development of this "picture-writing" [*Bilderschrift*], which includes learning from statistical and technical diagrams, they will renew their cultural authority in and through the medium of an international "Wandelschrift" (4:104). More than simply a "moving script" (*SW* 1:457), *Wandelschrift* implies two senses in which writing has become at once more moving and more mobile: a new mutability and plasticity of script (*Wandel* in the sense of change), which heralds a resurgence of writing's imagistic, sensuous, mimetic qualities; and the connotation of the verb *wandeln* (to walk, amble, wander), which suggests writing's migration into three-dimensional, public space and which makes reading a more tactile, distracted experience.

The new graphicity that evolves with modern media and advertising not only hybridizes pictorial and scriptural qualities, but also makes writing part of a new economy of *things*, a changed phenomenology of nearness and distance, a different kind of sensory, aesthetic experience.[63] In *One-Way Street*, Benjamin articulates this new relationship with things most strikingly in "This Space for Rent" (*SW* 1:476), a piece that anticipates key concerns of the artwork essay. The terms of opposition here are not art and technical reproducibility, but rather criticism (*Kritik*) and advertisement (*Reklame*), which, in Benjamin's words, is today "the most real, mercantile gaze into the heart of things." While criticism used to be defined by a stable vantage point and "correct distancing" (just as art, as he says elsewhere, used to begin "at a distance of two meters from the body"), advertising tears into the liberal space of contemplation and "all but hits us between the eyes with things," in the same way that "a car, growing to gigantic proportions, careens at us out of a film screen."[64] And as the cinema renders furniture and facades sensational by means of their insistent, jerky nearness, advertising "hurls things at us with the tempo of a good film." In other words, advertising, like film, is a thing that both depicts the new world of things and, in its tactile, visceral appeal, significantly redramatizes our relation to things.[65]

The emphasis on physicality, speed, and directness aligns Benjamin with the enthusiasm for Hollywood films and all things American that was pervasive among avant-garde artists and intellectuals of the period, whether French, German, Soviet, Chinese, or Japanese. What is less common, however, certainly among German proponents of Americanism, in particular the technophile modernists of Neue Sachlichkeit, is the way Benjamin entwines this new relation to things with dimensions of affect and sentimentality, even kitsch.[66] Here we encounter the quotation I used in connection with the Hong Kong films at the beginning of this essay:

> Thereby [with advertisement's foreshortening of space and time in relation to things] "matter-of-factness" [*Sachlichkeit*] is finally dismissed, and in the face of the huge images spread across the walls of buildings, where toothpaste and cosmetics [*"Chlorodont" und "Sleipnir"*] lie handy for giants, sentimentality is restored to health and liberated American style, just as people whom nothing moves or touches any longer are taught to cry again in the cinema.[67]

Skirting the critical cliché about moving the masses with clichés, Benjamin envisions a regeneration of affect by means of technically produced images, that is, the possibility of countering the alienation of the human sensorium with the same means and media that are part of the technological proliferation of shock-anaesthetics-aestheticization. The chance to engage the senses differently lies in the epochal reconfiguration of "body- and image-space," in the emergence of new modes of imaging that refract the given organization of space, its forms and proportions, and articulate a new relation with the material world.

Corresponding to this new image world Benjamin observes a mode of reception that combines sensational affect with reflexivity and, conversely, reflexivity with sensory immediacy. For it is not the message of the advertisement that moves people, even if they are moved to buy. Benjamin never loses sight of the fact that it is money that "effects [this] close contact with things," that the means of innervation are subject to "the brutal heteronomies of economic chaos" (*SW* 1:456) (which should make us hesitate, pace Kittler and Bolz, to turn Benjamin into a McLuhanite *avant-la-lettre*).[68] But his primary concern here seems to be neither message nor medium (nor the priority of the latter over the former). Rather, he is fascinated, at a more phenomenological level, with the sensory-aesthetic effects of advertising, in particular a new imagination of color that blurs the fixed lines of objects, spaces, and institutions: "What, in the end, makes advertisement so superior to criticism? Not what the moving red neon sign says—but the fiery red pool reflecting it in the asphalt."[69]

Profane illumination, indeed: The trope of commercial lighting, literalized and refigured in the manner of Kracauer's vignettes on the same theme, suggests an excess of sensation over the capitalist design, a mimetic connection with the afterlife of things.[70] At the same time, the red pool becomes a medium of reflection, albeit an ephemeral one, exemplifying a type of reflexivity that inheres in the material.[71] This reflexivity is anything but contemplative, assuming a safe distance between observer and object; on the contrary, it implies a momentary fusion of vision and object, of body- and image-space, related to the curious condition that Benjamin refers to in the surrealism essay as a "nearness that looks out of its own eyes" [*wo die Nähe sich selbst aus den Augen sieht*] (2:309). If we agree that Benjamin sought the equivalents of auratic experience (in the sense of investing the other with the ability to return the gaze) through and in the rubble of modern history, we should also heed what he insisted upon concerning the psychopoetic experiments of the surrealists: that they were on the trail—track, trace, *Spur*—"less of the soul than of things" (2:621). In other words, they (like Benjamin) were less interested in things as a means for experiencing "structures of frail intersubjectivity" (as Habermas would have it) than in innervating the "secret life of things," their different temporality, their nexus with an "other" history.[72]

How does one make things look out of their own eyes, as it were, from inside out?[73] At this point the concept of innervation intersects with the notion of an optical unconscious. This juncture should help us understand more systematically why Benjamin needed the cinema to think both of these concepts—and why the cinema, like other technical media but more so, was central to his effort to both articulate and mobilize the antinomies of modernity. The answer, tentatively, will turn on the double mediation involved in the cinematic process, that between the film and the depicted world and that between the projected film and the audience, that is, distinct yet mutually interdependent mediations both at the level of film as a technology of *inscription* and at the level of cinema as the social, collective, public space/time of *reception*.

When Benjamin first uses the term in his "Little History of Photography" (1931), the optical unconscious refers primarily to the level of inscription, specifically the ability of the apparatus and particular photographic techniques to register aspects of material reality that are invisible to the unarmed human eye—the microtexture of plants, the way people walk. The mimetic, cognitive capacity of photographic inscription rests, almost paradoxically, with the element of chance or contingency inherent in mechanical vision, however constructed and manipulated; the camera's otherness, one might say its track with the look of the other, translates into an affinity with the unseen, the overly familiar, the repressed—with anything that eludes conscious, intentional perception: "For it is another nature [*eine andere Natur*] which speaks to the camera rather than to the eye: 'other' above all in the sense that a space informed by human consciousness gives way to a space informed by the unconscious" (*SW* 2:510).

Since the element of contingency pertains to the *indexical* dimension of photographic representation, that is, the material bond with the world depicted (the camera having been there at a particular point in time, light rays having linked the object with the photochemical emulsion for fractions of a second), the notion of the optical unconscious involves a distinct and heightened temporality—a temporality that inevitably implies and implicates the beholder. Looking at the wedding picture of the photographer Dauthendey and his wife, who committed suicide after the birth of their sixth child, Benjamin observes:

> No matter how artful the photographer, no matter how carefully posed his subject, the beholder feels an irresistible urge to search such a picture for the tiny spark of contingency [*Zufall*], of the here and now, with which reality has (so to speak) seared the character of the image, to find the inconspicuous spot where in the thusness [*Sosein*] of that long-forgotten moment the future nests so eloquently that we, looking back, may rediscover it. (*SW* 2:510, trans. mod.)

The eruption of the uncanny into representational space/time is experienced—and provoked—by the beholder, but the forgotten future that answers to the searching gaze is assumed to be deposited, seared, encrypted in the photographic image. This unconscious archive makes photography, early photography at least, a mnemotechnical device capable of compensating for the historical loss of "all natural, physiological aids of memory," which Benjamin saw as the precondition of the "Copernican turn" in both remembrance and historiography (5:490). This is to say that, pace Proust and contrary to Benjamin's own pessimistic analysis (in the Baudelaire essay) of photography's erosion of the *mémoire involontaire*, the optical unconscious marks a spot that readmits dimensions of temporality and memory via, and into, the very technologies capable of eliminating them. Like the images of involuntary memory ("developed in the darkroom of the lived moment"), the optical unconscious does not just reactualize a lost prior vision: rather, it makes us see "images that we have never seen before we remember them" (2:1064).[74] Unlike Proust's elegiac, personal quest, however, photography's mobilization of an unconscious past points toward a form of memory that is transindividual and potentially collective—both in spite and because of its technically mediated character.

"The possibility of creating an openness to the future," which Howard Caygill locates as the gist of the optical unconscious, assumes a more overt political significance in relation to film.[75] It is no coincidence that Benjamin begins to develop the notion of an optical unconscious (without naming it) in his defense of Eisenstein's *Battleship Potemkin*, around the time he was completing *One-Way Street*. In a polemical exchange over "collectivist art," he speaks of the "conspiratorial relationship between film technique and milieu" as the "most intrinsic project [*Vorwurf*]" of film, arguing that this aesthetic affinity advances an irrefutable class perspective.[76] In language that anticipates the famous passage on the optical unconscious in the art-work essay, Benjamin outlines the functions of film vis-à-vis the "prison-world" of urban-industrial modernity as simultaneously revelatory, mne-monic, and transformative. The mimetic capacity for capturing traces of social experience in the ostensibly dead world of things draws on both the representational qualities of photography (including indexically grounded contingency) and procedures specific to film (such as slow motion, variable framing, and editing). Thanks to these fracturing, alienating techniques film does not merely depict a given world, but makes that world visible for the first time, produces it for the sensoria of a spectating collective. Hence Benjamin underscores that film in fact opens up "a new region of consciousness"; it provides a "prism" that transforms the past forgotten in the hopeless present into the possibility of a future:

> To put it in a nutshell, film is the only prism in which the spaces of the immediate environment—the spaces in which people live, go about their business, and enjoy their leisure—are laid open before their eyes in a com-prehensible, meaningful, and passionate way. In themselves these offices, furnished rooms, bars, city streets, train stations, and factories are ugly, in-comprehensible, and hopelessly sad. *Or rather, they were and seemed to be until the advent of film.* The cinema then exploded this entire prison-world with the dynamite of its fractions of a second, so that now we can take extended journeys of adventure among its scattered ruins. (*SW* 2:17; trans. mod., emphasis mine)

The dynamic temporality suggested in this passage is one of historical tran-sition and social transformation. For the adventurous spaces Benjamin ex-plores in his defense of *Potemkin* are spaces of the collective, and they apprise the bourgeois intellectual of the passing of his own class: "The proletariat is the hero of those spaces to whose adventures, heart pounding, the bourgeois gives himself over in the cinema, because he must enjoy the 'beautiful' pre-cisely where it speaks to him of the destruction of his own class" (*SW* 2:18; trans. mod.).

But the cinema's most important collective space is, or at least used to be, the cinema itself—the movie theater as a public space of exhibition and reception, moviegoing as a specifically modern, technically mediated form of collective sensory experience that most clearly distinguishes the reception of a film from that of literature and the fine arts, including the stage. The moviegoing experience would therefore seem to be the logical site for thinking through the possibility of a "bodily collective innervation," as the condition of an alternative interaction with technology and the commodity world. For the optical unconscious, as the medium of a transformed mimetic capacity, to become effective as/in collective innervation, the level of inscription would have to be hinged into that of reception, that is, the psychoanalytically inflected temporality of the former would have to mesh with the collective subjectivity of the latter. Only then would the technically enabled extension and decentering of the sensorium (at the level of the filmic text) translate into an imaginative, empowering incorporation of the apparatus on the part of the audience. Benjamin seems to suggest as much when he asserts that it is only with the "human collective that film can complete the prismatic work that it began with milieu," although he subsequently limits his discussion to the moving masses depicted in Eisenstein's film, the collectivity on, rather than in front of, the screen.

It is this step, the extension of the optical unconscious to the spectating collective, which Benjamin attempted in the early versions of the artwork essay, specifically in his remarks on the "globe-orbiting" Mickey Mouse (whose name headed the entire section on the optical unconscious in the first, handwritten version). As I have elaborated elsewhere, Benjamin's reading of Mickey Mouse as a "figure of the collective dream" maintains a sense of disjunctive temporality, the mnemonic/psychoanalytic slant that marks the optical unconscious at the level of filmic inscription (leaving aside for the moment that Benjamin makes his case with an animated creature rather than a figure from photographic live-action film; he could have chosen Chaplin). The dream memory that Mickey innervates, however, is inseparable from that of nightmares, in particular modern nightmares induced by industrial and military technology. The early Disney films function as a form of "psychic inoculation," Benjamin argues, because they effect a "premature and therapeutic detonation" of mass psychoses, of sadistic fantasies and masochistic delusions in the audience, by allowing them to erupt in the collective laughter (7:377). The films provoke this laughter not only with their "grotesque" actions, their metamorphic games with animate and inanimate, human and mechanical traits, but also with their precise rhythmic matching of acoustic and visual movement—through a series of staged shocks or, rather, countershocks that effect a transfer between film and audience and, hopefully, a reconversion of neurotic energy into sensory affect.[77]

The politics of innervation I have tried to delineate in Benjamin involves an understanding of the cinema as a form of sensory, psychosomatic, aesthetic experience that includes but does not reduce to poststructuralist notions of writing and reading, however psychoanalytically inflected. For the promise the cinema held out was that it might give the technologically altered sensorium access to a contemporary, materially based, and collective form of reflexivity that would not have to surrender the mimetic and temporal dimensions of (historically individualized) experience. At this juncture, the cinema appeared as the only institution capable of linking the antinomic trajectories of modernity and thus wresting them from their catastrophic course; that is, the cinema, rather than thriving on and exacerbating the spiral of shock, anaesthetics and aestheticization could work to diffuse the deadly violence unleashed by capitalist technology, could yet be revolutionary in the sense of "a purely preventive measure intended to avert the worst."[78] If the Medusan gaze of the camera is affiliated with the backward-flying angel of history, then Mickey Mouse embodies the possibility of meeting that gaze and countering it—with apotropaic games of innervation.

But Mickey disappeared from the final version of the artwork essay, and with him the term innervation. In that version, the section on the optical unconscious opens with a reference to Freud's *Psychopathology of Everyday Life*, which Benjamin invokes to illustrate the enrichment of our perceptual world with the advent of film. Just as this book has "isolated and made analyzable things which had heretofore floated along unnoticed in the broad stream of perception," film has brought about a "similar deepening of apperception" for the entire spectrum of optical, and now also acoustical, phenomena (*I* 235). Benjamin introduces the comparison with an example from the sphere of language, "a slip of the tongue," but then retreats, on the side of film, to the discourse of surgery (introduced in a previous section), as he extols the filmic representation of a scene or situation for its ability to "isolate" a performance or behavior "like a muscle of a body," which illustrates the importance of film's "tendency to promote the mutual penetration of art and science" (*I* 236). In either case, the optical unconscious is lodged at the level of inscription; its actualization remains a matter of individual analysis, whether conceived as reading, deciphering, or dissecting. What drops out of the concept is the specificity of the cinema experience, in particular its sensory-somatic immediacy, anonymous collectivity, and unpredictability. Accordingly, collective reception is segregated into the following section, subsumed under the notion of distraction, which in turn is reduced to a Brechtian attitude of critical testing and thus robbed of its mimetic, eccentric, as well as mnemotechnical dimensions.

Why did Benjamin give up on innervation? It is easy to blame Adorno for the mutilation of the artwork essay, but we should not overlook Benjamin's own ambivalence, not least regarding the figure of Mickey. In a note accompanying the early drafts of the essay he remarks on the "usability of the Disney method for fascism" (1:1045) and in a footnote to the second version he expands this remark to suggest that the most recent Disney films manifest a tendency already implicit in the earlier ones: "the cozy acceptance of bestiality and brutality as corollaries of existence" (7:377). Nor can we ignore the problems that Benjamin might have had with the actual collective assembled in urban movie theaters, a collective whose demographic profile was not predominantly and simply working class, let alone consciously proletarian. The heterogeneous mass public that congregated in, and was catalyzed by, the cinema of the Weimar period consisted largely of people who bore the brunt of modernization—women, white-collar workers of both sexes; its demographically most salient feature was gender rather than class.[79] And as a new social formation this mass public was just as unpredictable and politically volatile as German society at large. It would have been conceivable to think of the moviegoing collective as being made up of individual viewers, with the kinds of mimetic engagement Benjamin found in the surrealists, the child, the beholder of old photographs, or, for that matter, Proust. But it is also historically understandable why Benjamin, unlike Kracauer, did not make that leap of faith—why he submerged the imaginative, mnemotechnical possibilities of the medium into a presentist politics of distraction, renouncing the cinematic play with otherness in view of the increasingly threatening otherness of actual mass publics.

Collective innervation as an alternative to anaesthetics, the apotropaic game with technology, seems to have failed, at least in Benjamin's lifetime; the cosmic mating fantasy in the spirit of technology as which he pictured the First World War at the end of *One-Way Street* returned in the Second as a bloodbath of exponentially vaster scope and efficiency. But we have to admire Benjamin for having taken on the gamble, the "*vabanque* game" with technology. For if anything was *not* an antinomy for Benjamin, nor even cause for ambivalence, it was the connection between aesthetics and politics: the insight that the fate of the "beautiful" was inseparable from the transformation of the human sensorium; and that the fate of the human senses, pertaining to the very conditions of social experience, the ecology of public life, was a political question of utmost urgency. This is why his turn to a profane, materialist understanding of "actuality" involved recognizing the centrality of the question of technology, as the medium in which the decisive confrontations over humanity's future were taking place.

This is also why taking Benjamin's imperative to actuality seriously today means recognizing that the cinema, once celebrated for articulating the secret affinities among things in an age of accelerated obsolescence, may itself have become a thing of the past. As video and digital technologies are replacing the medium of photographic film (with its indexical dimensions of temporality and contingency) and as the cinema, as an institution of public, collective reception, has ceased to be the primary venue in which films are consumed, Benjamin's reflections on film and media culture may likewise have lost their actuality and may stand, as Bolz has recently proclaimed, as nothing more than "beautiful ruins in the philosophical landscape."[80] But reconstructing these reflections in their complexity and extremity is not just a philological endeavor, nor a matter of "getting Benjamin right" versus oversimplifying readings and appropriations. Rather, understanding the issues he struggled with as genuine antinomies, and the limitations of his argument as limits posed by historical and political realities, should help us not only to guard against idealizations of either individualized or collective subjectivities and identities but also to discern similar antinomies in today's media culture—that culture which, whether we like it or not, is the framing condition of any cultural practice today. Whether the cinema, having lost its economic, social, and epistemic centrality, will remain open to the future depends in part on whether the electronic and digital media that have displaced and transformed it will allow for new forms of innervation, different possibilities of mimetic experience, temporal disjunction, and reflexivity. It also depends on whether the cinema can remain open to its own forgotten futures in other than merely nostalgic ways. If Mickey Mouse confronted Benjamin from the elsewhere of America and in the mode of cel animation, then we confront Mickey Mouse today from the elsewhere of Hong Kong, as part of a film practice that engages with technologies of incorporation and embodiment that indeed make the cinema a memory, in more than one sense.

THREE

"The Dynamite of a Tenth of a Second"

Benjamin's Revolutionary Messianism
in Silent Film Comedy

TOM MCCALL

The image is a characteristic exhibition of modern life. If twentieth-century electronic media have eclipsed in sheer mass impact the earlier forms of public culture, in large part that impact has been delivered through pictorial (photographic and cinematic) images, which make up something like a base unit of modern history. Yet *images* are not always as easy to recognize as one might think. Mixed up with other media, with printed word or synchronized sound (also called *images*), the legibility of the image is complicated by its multimediality. There is no such thing as a pure image for the reason that there is no single pure medium, no unmixed Edenic medium that could name or picture the constitutive units of its own articulation. Media are not self-contained, rigorously separate from other media—which makes translating across them far from simple. This problem, central to Benjamin and to the contemporary evaluation of his critical writings, may be stated simply as the problem of identifying images and reading history in their medial mix. From early to late in Benjamin's career, history exhibits itself in "images" [*Bilder*]. While varying across contexts and not always easy to pin down, *images* seem associated with high-stakes criticism or crucial (yet difficult) distinctions. Images have the power to seduce (this is their special power), but also to wake up (their special power). The critical intelligence becomes melancholic when it can neither fall asleep (be completely seduced) nor wake up (locate itself with its images). Image may best be understood as this limbo state, this wakeful somnolence.[1]

The strange homunculi on the silent screen flash images, those often memorable but mutely self-abolishing disjunctive images called "moving pictures": "the past held like an image flashing in the moment of recognition."[2] The reference here is to the "dialectical image," an enigmatic yet suggestive critical articulation of the later Benjamin. The dialectical image does not so much represent a determinate content, a close-up of a face, for instance, as it marks out a limit or blind spot in the visual field of the present. Graphically yoking "the past and the now" in a striking constellation that "leaps out" at us (*GS* 5:577) from the homogeneous present, the "dialectical image" points out limits or fields of abstraction within the present (rather than within the past or future, which can only be projections from the present). For viewers of today, with years of cinematic history in a collective viewing experience, silent films represent aspects of their own medium that become visible in the form of a technological and historical alienation. In the same way that baroque allegory had staged the incompatibility of the spoken to the written word, silent films foreground gestures that tend to be conjured away or naturalized in synchronized sound films.[3] Most narrative films produced by Hollywood continuity editing make heavy use of sound as a way to naturalize and synchronize the actor's gestures into the generic worlds-within-the-film. By contrast, the gestures of silent films (accompanied by music, these were mute or silent in regard to on-screen or diegetic sound) come to signify eccentrically what Benjamin in the artwork essay calls "the unconsciously penetrated space" of lived experience.

The blockbusters of today are proleptically the "silent films" of tomorrow. To the extent that modern identities are interwoven by the massive and pervasive apparatus of media cultures and mass entertainment, we ourselves are the ghosts of a time seventy years into the future. Today, a life span after the shift to talkies (1928–1929), silent-film images offer dialectical images of our own times—outmoded and out of kilter with the rapidly changing technologies of the future.[4] The images of late-twentieth and early-twenty-first-century vintage will soon begin to "flash," to "leap out," to gesticulate, as in the oldest silent films, to appear faded, strangely textured, pixilated, antique, a ruin in future.

In Benjamin's thought, the modern image is characterized by its ability to shock; indeed, to have a (modern) experience is to have a "shock-experience" [*Schock-Erlebnis*], the experience of viewers caught within the image's proleptic knowledge of its own looming status as yesterday's news. What makes images shocking in part stems from tensions of their basic mode, their "transitoriness and reproducibility." In the accelerated exchange economies of advanced capitalist consumer technology, the image must shock—must get its point across—before it flashes off the screen (or flashes back on). In this it would exhibit the built-in, more-than-human wisdom of media that Benjamin was so apt at finding in other media—for example, in early photography, the baroque theater of the seventeenth century, or the language of translation.

I. Splitting Images

With these hints we are in a position to examine the Benjaminian image through a larger collateral structure: silent film comedy—like the image, a hybrid of technology and traditional genres. This triple frame (of *film*, *silent* film, silent film *comedy*) enhances a reading of *image* in Benjaminian text—and, through it, to critical image theory in the twentieth century and after. The features of the (silent) film comedies to be isolated below are no more stable than those of "dialectical images"; but the instability of singular moribund images is, so to speak, potentiated in the cinematic spaces of comedy, where their shock waves proliferate beyond the frames in multiple institutions.

The "dialectical image" passes easily into a theory of film comedy. Take the sight gag, a structural unit of film comedy (both silent and sound), which isolates and stages "the norm" in telling images. That is, the cinematic comedy image performs the unremarkable and usually automatically processed shot (or the action within it, an object or gesture or situation) in another context where it is out of place. In the same way that giving someone the finger—a violent totalizing gesture—crystallizes a microstructure of interactive systemic violence, the sight gag in the following example may be taken as a "pictorial image . . . of dialectics."[5] A three-shot sequence from *Horse Feathers* (Marx Brothers, 1932) serves as a quick example, one of countless that distill a constant structure. Zeppo (the fourth, or "straight," character to the other three Marx Brothers) gives flowers to a woman he is courting in her boudoir; the next shot shifts to Harpo (the silent clown), sitting on a street curb and also giving a bunch of flowers to someone (a woman?) off screen. But (as the subsequent shot reveals) the object of romance is a horse who "accepts" the gift, masticating it. Harpo, a mute hologram walking among the speaking dead, fragments the customary sense into two pieces or places, into two realms whose simultaneity suggests a messianic text: "of origin and destruction," as Benjamin writes of "quotation" in the Karl Kraus essay.[6] As if sensing the dirty secret of authority (namely, that its homogeneous worlds of reiterated behavior depend upon everyone's largely unreflected complicity), Harpo (a light-bearer, a Lucifer) presents the viewer with dialectical—that is, with split—images: a traditional signifier of romance is "hollowed out" and placed into an alien framework (flowers given as "friendship-offering" to horses). In the sight gag, a different image is spliced off from a first (established, "reified") image, opening up a difference from the same; but this difference is then abolished in the next moment—it was just a fleeting image, a joke. The "love interest" serves as a paradigm of social attachment, which understandably provides much material for disruptive comedic gestural quotation. In order to thrive and endure, institutions must engender (or enforce) a broad-based attachment, most often to people and things, to forms of labor and property. But comedies undercut such loyal attachment to institutions (and instituted people) by "quoting"—detaching—the gestures of care.

In the example, Harpo diverts the traditional signifieds-for-exchange of courtship and true love into a momentary connection with a very large (and already domesticated, already "courted") animal, who acts out (drooling) the beloved's acceptance of gifts. Harpo and horse are uninvested in and unattached to "the schemata of imposed identification" (Adorno). A well-established association of ritualized erotic invitation is succinctly re-presented in a first frame (the flowers given to the woman in a courtship routine), but this conventional scenario suddenly shifts into a new frame (now occupied by a huge animal). It is not as if the second sense (horse) "corrects" the first; it merely negates it—but uses the viewer's automatic processing of the customary image as the impetus into the filmic sight gag, a critical demonstration of "phantasmagoria," which emerges here in a mildly shocking recognition marked by the laugh, a kind of grunt, an inarticulate sound of throat-clearing.

Dialectical images are forceful critical instances of their own (mostly hidden) force (as quotable gesture, performable ritual, representable organization). Received meanings are detached from their established contexts of customary operation and framed as organizational patterns, as the (picto)-graphic designs and the telling (highly invested) gestures they are. The "dialectical image" re-presents a first-order mythic force in a second-order pictorialization (or verbalization, schematization, gesturalization), which makes legible that force in a framed organization (image). The comedic image does not show us another world that would go beyond the customary, but only the customary usage in a closely related image (in a kind of double exposure), which implies the first as limit. The "flowers placed into the horse's mouth" is an image that (as discrete image) happens to open up upon a kind of world (supplied by just one image, which, however, implies a world of sense), but this world is nothing more than a counterposition to the customary image, whose gestures now reappear as "transitory and reproducible," those characteristics of the cinematic image singled out in the artwork essay.

Criticism has traditionally been an anxious and melancholic genre allied more to "tragedy and philosophy" than to comedy. Overall, literary-theoretical criticism has privileged the genres of tragedy (ancient, classical, postclassical) as the most telling narratives to expose the abstract "gravity" of sociomythic orders and their textual-referential claims. For Benjamin, myth names deeply entrenched power structures that weigh upon the living (and the dead), to fix objects and objectified people into its heavy atmospheres. (In the words of Karl Marx, "The tradition of all the dead generations weighs like a nightmare on the brain of the living.") To such "mythical violence" Benjamin opposes countermythical genres or technological modes such as ancient tragedy, baroque allegory, early photography or film, surrealism and other avant-garde movements, epic theater, or "awakening" modes of critical writing, such as the historiographical montage of the *Arcades Project*. Yet much of Benjamin's critical project could be aligned with comedic critique—whether named as such (as in the early essay "Fate and Character") or not (in many texts that play into comedy, such as the essays on Kafka, surrealism, or "Experience and Poverty," featuring Mickey Mouse). Could one speak of a comedic critique—a critical levity running above gravity-laden tragedic critique—which also cuts into the mythical order just as sharply as serious genres with higher critical authority, but at a different register, with far greater impact, but far less effect?

II. Sight Gag

"Image" may be conceived as a critical bifurcation within a "myth" or mythological fusion, an enduring target of Benjamin's criticism. The critical problem, here as elsewhere, is that of making dialectic operation more noticeable, of framing its operations with more impact, in a moment of relative "waking up" that would be "the dissolution of mythology into the space of history" (*GS* 5:571–72). If the split image illustrates an instance of the dialectical image, that image would be "unsplit" in myth time, the "empty, homogeneous time" of critical naïveté. In the inbred violence of the mythic scene, bodies are seized when words are spoken (read): word, scene, and body are fused. In myth, "thoroughgoing meaning" never exhibits itself as "hollowed out" (*GS* 5:582), never shows itself as image. "Dialectical images are constellations of alienated things and thoroughgoing meaning, pausing a moment in the balance of death and meaning . . . in the nineteenth century, the number of 'hollowed out' things increases at a pace previously unknown, because technical progress is continually putting more utensils out of circulation" (*GS* 5:582, emphasis mine). In an age of incessant technological refashioning and accelerating consumption of ever-new commodities, the "dialectical image" anticipates and freeze-frames the passage of "thoroughgoing meaning" into "hollowed out things." It stands to reason that the dialectical image will itself be preeminently a "fetish commodity" (a Marx Brothers or Chaplin film, a Mickey Mouse cartoon). What other means would be available for critique in an age saturated with the ephemeral commodities of consumer capitalism? This gives a principle of materialist criticism: only that which happens to flow into the present historically and materially (into the present, as a fluctuating series of public fashions) may be used as the instruments to critique that present. As I discuss below, the critical moment of this "pausing" (a moment that elsewhere has been called "stillstand" or even "caesura"), becomes a key articulation of dialectical images.

Images are thoughtful pauses. This "pausing of the image," which is not an assimilation, is not a dialectical appropriation in the Hegelian sense. Hegel's dialectic is a two-step process in which an other, an "in-itself," is found out to be one's own, a "for-itself," at which stage another other (to be owned) would then pop up in subsequent narrative dialectic. Diverging from Hegel's model, Benjamin's dialectical image comes closer to a singular, localized deconstruction than to a speculative dialectic that labors incrementally toward increasing self-reflexivity. The "image is the caesura in the movement of thought . . . [that] is to be found wherever the tension between dialectical oppositions is greatest" (*GS* 5:595). The comedic image operates as a topical negation, an evanescent disruption or momentary caesura whose effects cannot be compacted together in a phenomenological narrative. Benjaminian "dialectics" shows criticism its impossible task: that task of accounting for—separating out and itemizing, delimiting—the myriad entwinements and stratifications that constitute "the everyday" and make it "impenetrable." The more it is scrutinized, the more a given quoted gesture threatens to unravel into a regressive series—further gestures and gestures within them. The process of unraveling has no stop. Such is the caesura of thought.[7]

The critical potential of film comedy (bringing the case now into the cinematic instance) may be seen in its ability to symbolize the "customary" in pointed instances that themselves do not form integral parts of the plotline. Unlike noncomedic genres (sentimental, serious, [melo]dramatic), the disjunctive episodes of comedy are linked only arbitrarily and loosely into overall plots. Mack Sennett's World War I-era slapstick (for example, the Keystone Cops) established the principle of later film comedy sequences: "A gag had to begin, develop, and finish off within a hundred seconds."[8] This narrative looseness assures the comedy of keeping its point, which would be blunted if it needed to support an overarching story line.

The historical materialist aims to detach an epoch (or the epochal) from its reified historical continuity in order to "set to work an engagement with history original to every new present" which would be the sign of "a messianic stillstanding of occurrence" [*messianische Stillstellung des Geschehens*].[9] This breaking out, this "unique engagement" with the present, may be illustrated in a four-shot clip from Chaplin's *The Adventurer* (1917), in which the rigid frameworks of class and social division are dialectically presented and comedically "recited" through a series of visual puns. Chaplin is an escaped convict who passes out on a pier after heroically rescuing several drowning aristocrats. The first shot of this sequence shows Chaplin as he wakes up in bed. Throughout this (long take) shot and the next, Chaplin's gaze dominates the viewer's attention—we watch him watching, implicitly adopting the disoriented escapee/hero's viewpoint as he wakes up in bed (which, in a medium shot with camera placed at the foot of the bed, reveals only his upper body and head, framed by the bed and its iron bedstead). Not quite awake, he looks at three objects nearby: the coverlet on the bed, the pajama top he's wearing, and the iron bars of the bedstead above his head. His bemused expression suggests a ghost of a thought: "Silk covers in prison? . . . Where am I?" He then sees his pajamas, striped like the inmate's prison garb, yet curiously silky. The black steel bars come into view; these are part of the bedstead, a fact that he does not grasp, as his facial expression gives to understand, "No, I'm still in prison." In the next (second) shot, the camera has moved back and (now in a medium long shot) can include much more of the room/cell—the bed in its spatial configuration with walls, ceiling, furniture, and the door (just offscreen). The shot merely records a brief action: a man walks in, leaves towels, nods at Chaplin, and exits. Still in bed, the (ex?)con nods back, as if this were perfectly ordinary—while being all too cognizant on other levels that inmates don't get this kind of room service. A third shot brings attention to what Hollywood continuity editing (to which Chaplin himself contributed much) is so adept at concealing, the arbitrariness of shot sequencing: a close-up of a couple (an aristocrat and a young woman), a romantic interest subplot that (among other subplots) loosely strings the comic incidents together. The fourth shot, which ends the sequence and clarifies "the riddle of the bars," cuts to Chaplin, who has by now realized that he has in fact "broken out" of prison: dressed in tuxedo and immediately assuming his new position, he descends a staircase in palatial settings—to command a drink from a waiting servant.

In a vertiginous transition between antipodal social extremes, he has been catapulted from escaping convict to sleeping aristocrat, the two "ends" of the common system that creates their respective subject positions. The high and the low are linked by the vertical stripes of their respective uniforms (pajamas, prison garb), this pattern reinforced by the vertical bars of their respective habitations (wrought-iron bed, cell window) that (among many others) work as signifiers of property division and status.[10] In this episode, the iron bars of the convict's cell and the wrought-iron bars of the aristocrat's bed (such rigidities make up what Benjamin, in the artwork essay, calls "the traditional system of property") are mosaically "montaged" across objects and appear as the stage props of a cleverly constructed mise-en-scène. The bars that have one "locked up hopelessly" (WA 236) are reinscribed and quoted at a moment of "waking up" (literally, in this scene). Although such a shift would not itself qualify as "Now-Time" [*Jetzt-Zeit*], it would still comprise something like an aborted portal into it—something like an "iris in/iris out" of the Now-Time.

This sequence illustrates what Benjamin calls (in the essay on surrealism) "a dialectical optic"; in the latter, "the everyday [*das Alltägliche*] is recognized as impenetrable [*undurchdringlich*], the impenetrable [*das Undurchdringliche*] as everyday."[11] This neat chiasmus conveys a messy (and, in fact, messianic) scenario, in which "the real" is a kinetic constellation of tensions whose motions are imaged in the fixations or fixed points (for example, the vertical and horizontal bars) of the reified world. A number of specific constellations (undifferentiated and overlapping, material fragments fused with incorporeal residuals) come together to produce the specific institutions and social practices of "the everyday." The example in *The Adventurer* presents a dialectical optic: one image (the bars of a bedstead; or an aristocrat's pajamas) projects another image (the bars of a cell; or a prison's uniform), which is in fact the same image, recontextualized in changed historico-material circumstances or lifetimes. Framed as dialectical image, the contents of the image—although indispensable to the gag itself—are upstaged by the critical power released in that work. Again, in dialectical-critical overview, the point of the comedy is not so much that one of these image-projections is correct and the other simply a mistake, but rather that, implicit within any given image, there lie other potential material trajectories impacted mutely into the same image. This is less a romantic glimpse of possibilities than a dead end of the present, when its own contradictions, momentarily focused, jab back at it in the form of two simultaneous yet mutually exclusive possibilities.[12] Of course, dead ends (even those suggested by powerful representations) can never bring the whole to a grinding halt (that happens only in myth, in mythic apocalypse or network news); "it" never stops, but it may be said (metaphorically) to "pause." Even if a few splinters of itself have been thus detached or chipped off in comedic representation, the conglomerate—so huge as it is, so endlessly splinterable—does not falter, but may emit a grunt, guffaw, snort, or hiccup. In the darkened theater, the moment of pausing or stillstand is audibly marked as a collective hiccup. From the perspective of dialectical materialism, this reaction (of rising and falling laughter, of throat-clearance) resembles the existential and political scenarios of "Now-Time," less a time than an oscillation of two (nearly simultaneous) movements—of an opening up to and a closing off from. Rather than merely canceling each other out, the swerves into/away from "Now-Time" enact what Benjamin, in the Theses, refers to as a "weak messianic force," that is, an attunement to revolutionary potentialities in a self-determining and collective body politic. Briefly stated, whatever opening (whatever closure) takes place is always only incipient. This makes the sight gag (or any dialectical image) not itself "dialectics," but only a simile for it (a resemblance, an image). In its sheer everydayness and impenetrability, dialectics could not be reduced to a gag, nor to given abiding images (which would be too determinate, too simple), but it could legitimately be said to resemble the oscillation between two sights given through one image.

This sight gag plays out ambiguization, a swerve (or the intimation of one) toward different simultaneously given places (or image spaces). This notion appears to lie at the heart of Benjamin's intriguing point that film opens up (and also closes off, one might add) the "unconsciously penetrated space" in the cultic "space consciously explored by man": "The camera introduces us to unconscious optics as does psychoanalysis to unconscious impulses" (WA 236–37). This critical complex of the "unconsciously penetrated" spaces in "dialectic optics" finds another articulation as an "image of ambiguity": "Ambiguity is the pictorial image of dialectics, the law of dialectics seen at a standstill."[13] Chaplin, puzzled by the interference of the two image-tracks (the two "trajectories" of the mutually exclusive images: rich man or convict?) expressively displays "a pictorial image of ambiguity." This gag would not so much present "dialectics itself" (or a "Now-Time") but would provide images—models, analogues, exemplary stillstands: openings and (simultaneous) closings.

Charlie and Harpo's sight gags join to exemplify a further strata of Benjaminian thought (where we note in passing that the "example" is a stillstand par excellence). "When thinking reaches a standstill in a constellation saturated with tensions, the dialectical image appears." A "constellation" exists as an intensive but semiarticulated dynamic of tensional points that for the most part go unremarked or unnoticed as tensional movements; in the different (overlapping and interlocking) constellations that guide it, thought has to break down (get jammed into images) before it starts thinking, but it cannot materialize (wake up to) the tensions of its thought unless it breaks down (and so stops thinking). Thought, here, is "thinking": less a fixed product than an activity, one commensurable with (resembling, working as simile for) the "swirl" of tensions.[14] Briefly, in the intense environments of a constellation, "thinking" stops—in broken reflections called dialectical images. Tension is a differential movement that both sustains and overruns meanings. Images, considered critically (as dialectical images), show thinking where it is not— and this is a way to begin thinking, by thinking images. This paradox determines thinking as an incipient enactment, always just a beginning—even if, in the heavy, guilty world, particular kinds of insufficiently self-critical thinking always seem to have been installed as the final form or as the real itself. A well-known aphorism suggests an ambiguous pause of thought in these words: "The very heart of the allegorical attitude," writes Benjamin, is where "every image is only a form of writing" [*Jedes Bild als Schrift*].[15]

If "thinking" in the Benjaminian context shows itself in images (especially in images that evanesce), thinking would seem to be comical or comedic. Chaplin, the first star of the Hollywood studio system, presents dialectical "images of ambiguity" in the familiar screen image of the Tramp. In the homeless urban man with the sensibility, manners, and gestures of the fastidious aristocrat, Chaplin conflates the two extremes of the socioeconomic ladder into one ambiguous persona, the Tramp. The existential situation is incessantly gesturalized—as in an extended eating sight gag of *The Gold Rush* (for example, starving Chaplin wraps the shoelaces of a boiled boot around his fork and enjoys this spaghetti). This particular mix of the materially "low" with the attitudinally "high" no doubt helped to make him a cult figure of the middle class; his ambiguity calls to the viewers from both ends of the spectrum, to fix them somewhere "in between." If Chaplin's fame helped reinforce the status quo, if his impact could seem in the end to regress from revolutionary openings, this conservative aspect of his stardom mattered far less to Benjamin (and Brecht) than his status as star. "In his films, Chaplin has appealed to the most international and at the same time most revolutionary sentiments of the masses: laughter. 'In any case,' says Soupault, 'Chaplin brings us to laughter. But apart from the fact that this is the hardest to do, it is also, in the social sense, the most important.'"[16] "The star" may mesmerize the masses (keeping them even more hopelessly out of touch with themselves, unwittingly entrenched as they are in the power hierarchies of the social pyramid), but the fact of stardom—this possibility of a daemonic screen face and figure that could galvanize and focus mass energies—gave evidence of the cinema's revolutionary potential.

In the essay on the mechanical work of art, Benjamin notes that the very same public that would have a "regressive" relation to a Picasso painting could have "the most progressive" [*fortschrittlichste*] relation to a Chaplin film. ("Regressive" [*rückständig*, "backwards," outmoded] also hints at "disengaged," standing back.) By comparison with pop culture megastar Chaplin, even that "most progressive" of painters, Picasso, would become fully regressive; the crowds are driven back by the high-culture auras that still emanate even from the revolutionary artwork (*GS* 1:496–97; WA 234). "Progressively," not through contemplation but, more directly through physiology, in a reactive-assimilative exchange of impulse and image. Part of Benjamin's thesis in the artwork essay is that the automatic character of thought can be made legible with a new emphasis in the age of mechanical reproduction. Cinema, which helps to create this automatism, also helps to expose its workings. The key point is that the productive and consumptive capacities of anonymous urban masses, hanging suspended or abstracted in established power, might now, with the advent of the new technology, develop a less alienated relation to their *Umwelt*: "The adjustment of reality to the masses and of the masses to reality," writes Benjamin in the 1936 "Work of Art in the Age of Mechanical Reproduction" essay, "is a process of unlimited scope." Images from the first reel of Chaplin's *Modern Times* (1936), released in the same year, suggestively play across Benjamin's formulations. The first part portrays historical process as a full-scale intermeshing of human-gestural and cybernetic mechanisms, to create (through Chaplin, the generic assembly line bolt-tightener) a historico-philosophical novum, the twentieth-century laborer as an ecstatic cyborg who dances out the repetitive movements of his factory "career." Less than one day on the assembly line, the Tramp snaps; whatever looks like a bolt he gives a good twist of his wrench, including the buttons on a woman's dress, symmetrically displayed around erogenous zones. (The episode ends when the lunatic dancer is carted off to a special factory, a circular assembly line for nonproductive workers called "the insane asylum.") The interpenetration or rewiring of physiological impulses and cybernetic structures is a characteristic theme in Benjamin's criticism and does not have to represent an alienated state. Question: Is the driving force behind Chaplin's ballet libidinal or mechanical? Answer: this distinction, which can no longer be drawn, is in any case just academic.

That this scene from *Modern Times* inverts Benjamin's positive valorization of technology into a comedic nightmare is less important than the way in which this film engages and reenacts signal images in the surrealism essay (conceived and written in the final years of the silent film, 1925–1929). Take the formulation of the "image-space" [*Bildraum*], where "body and image so interpenetrate that all revolutionary tension becomes bodily innervation, and all bodily innervations of the collective become revolutionary discharge," whereby "reality transcends itself, as in the Communist Manifesto."[17] Such a transcendence would be realized when the masses become a "collective body" in relation to the evolving technological apparatus; the (mass) body is wedded "one hundred percent" to its image-spaces—as if glowing with transformative potentialities.

In conjunction with the sight gags discussed, the passage (above) on the "progressive" Chaplin points to a gnomic statement that sums up both surrealism and comedy in Benjamin's articulation: "Surrealism is the death of the last century through comedy" (*GS* 5:572). Deciphering this formula requires a few words on quotation as "montage." Notebook N of the *Arcades Project* presents the critical writing of history in cinematographic terms explicitly linked to montage and imagistic quotation. As a strategy to explode the continuist abstractions of previous historiographies—master narratives told over and over from the standpoint of "the victors," which tend merely to reconfigure past formulas to make their own 'on-the-way-to-us' narratives—material history would "carry the montage principle over into history" (*GS* 5:572). The *Arcades Project* (Passagen-Werk) advocates raising to "the very highest level the art of quoting without quotation marks. Its theory is intimately linked to that of montage" (*GS* 5:572). As we know, "montage," the structural principle of the cinema, is the calculated serial arrangement of shots whose unreeling is the movie. This "art of quoting without quotation marks" is a finely attuned awareness that given meanings and constituted texts are the (potentially) recycled phrases and recomposed miniformulas of previous and future texts. Any text (written or read) may be thus "quoted," critically signaled, as if it were an aura-destroying cinematic image, the cinematic image as the citation par excellence, the citation in its "transitoriness and reproducibility." The elements of the "quoted" text would be critically processed—as if their meaningful passage had been nothing but quotations, pasted together, one after the other (cf. "montage"), lined up horizontally (in the written text) rather than vertically (as the frames of a film strip).

To miss seeing the quotation (which wouldn't be signaled by quotation marks) within the texts one reads is to invite catastrophe, the ongoing "catastrophe" that is "to have missed the opportunity; the critical moment—the status quo threatens to hold firm" and that therefore would make up the "homogeneous, empty time" of the present: "That it 'continues thus' [*Daß es 'so weiter' geht*] is the catastrophe."[18] Film comedy re-presents this "art of quoting without quotation" in the graphic silent comic gestures of the Harpo or Chaplin sequences. In the artwork essay, Benjamin describes montage in terms that would just as well apply to comic actions: in montage, "the camera intervenes with the resources of its lowerings and liftings; its interruptions and isolations; its extensions and accelerations; its enlargements and reductions" (WA 237). The languages of cinema thus come to give critical writing its efficacious form: asyndeton, the deletion of formal linkages as a way to bombard viewers with critical objects unreeling in a montage of rapidly shifting camera angles, distances, and graphic relations.

III. Comedy and Inceptive Understanding

Benjamin's thought is guided, explicitly and implicitly, by a theory of genres and generic media—tragedy, the baroque mourning play (*Trauerspiel*), historiography, "phantasmagoria," surrealism, photography, film—which are significant in the way they operate as technico-historico-critical paradigms able to give criticism its contemporary episteme or structural formation. Although they are crisscrossed by its formal operations, his critical strategies have little to say about comedy; as in literary theory and criticism generally, comedy in Benjamin's text has remained at the stage of beginnings only—incipient critique. Yet to read Benjamin (but not only him) is to begin to read comedy; for when the latter term appears in Benjamin's text, it is linked to important adjuncts such as surrealism, Kafka, Marx (Karl, not Harpo), or "the messianic"—a "pure violence" that cuts into human historical time and condemns it, too, to become "just a start." This incipience, this "always-having-to-start-it-up-again," could be aligned with other topics in Benjamin's criticism (the gambler, for example, or fashion cycles).

In the Benjaminian theorization, comedy shares a nexus common to the baroque mourning play and to ancient tragedy but also diverges from the latter in distinctive ways. Like ancient tragedy and *Trauerspiel*, comedy is a negative critical operation upon established meanings; the exemplary critical gestures of comic silent film comedy are graphic and pointed—without anxiety but also seemingly without gravity. In contrast to the brief, highly structured comedic incident, lasting affective states (such as dread or sentimentality) seem much closer to one another. Film comics generally float through the dense atmospheres of guilty (dreadful, sentimentalized) life in a state of permanent attention-deficit disorder; they characteristically experience the world as if it were a kind of montage—a place of flitting images that could never be woven into lasting horizons (whether "grave" or even light-hearted). The atmospheric melancholia of the baroque would not penetrate into the comedic consciousness of, say, the Marx Brothers, even if they were to "go baroque."

To allegorize is to reduce a signification (a single word, a nexus, an empire) to cliché. "The one brooding [*der Grübler*], whose shocked glance falls on the fragment in his hand, becomes the one who allegorizes [*wird zum Allegoriker*]."[19] "Cupid," for instance, would be allegorized when his nexus of qualities is brought down to those attendant and mildly idiotic "rosy cheeks."[20] In the gesture of allegory (and allegory is itself a rhetorical gesture), a customary or "universal" attitude is repeated, alienated in a way that makes it appear (from a detached view) as a singular instance. This critical detachment qualifies as a "rescue," yet—in view of the pervasiveness and extensiveness of entrenched power—a detachment can only be a "small spring"—without hopes for an actual transformation. For hope, one of the most vicious forms of sentimentality, is antiallegorical. "Within the ongoing catastrophe, rescue aims at the small jump."[21] Both allegory and comedy offer limited critical "small jumps" within the "continuum" of establishment.

Every jump has a spin. The courtly figures of the mourning play spin into the spiritual atmospheres surrounding them, trapped as they are in the black intelligence of the fallen world (*Naturverfallenheit*). Melancholy, the characterological and psychological component of allegory in the baroque mourning play, is a visionary energy that incessantly sacrifices its own signi-fications to the unsignifiable otherness of redemption. "Melancholy betrays [*verrät*] the world for the sake of knowledge"—but this knowledge is forever delayed, promised but postponed.[22] In the baroque drama, allegory gener-ates residual attachments called guilt. In the critical allegory that Benjamin finds in the seventeenth-century baroque theater, the unredeemed objects of the world generate in the baroque character an abyssal interiority, a wound of guilt that cuts as deeply as the desire for redemption. "Guilt" names a psychosocial force of normalization that binds individuals into fateful ever-similar institutions of sense. This may be thought as an Oedipal memory or as a "religious" tie, something that binds "again and again"—a re-ligio. In the Benjaminian text, the category of the religious takes place both within the earthly continuum and in the messianic discontinuity; deciding just where or how to draw the line between them is for Benjamin both a melancholy undertaking—and a comedic one.[23] In the baroque *Trauerspiel*, to know is to be guilty, and to be guilty is to remember. Guilty life is an inbred, ineradi-cable constituent of the world; since it always enters into the cognition of objects, it cannot be detached.

As a rule the comedic consciousness is not driven by such melancholic fixations or guiltiness. Even when they themselves do great violence to them-selves and others, the Marx Brothers, Laurel and Hardy, Buster Keaton, or the Three Stooges stand outside of the "guilt-relation" and interact with the things of their world in a guiltless (undaemonic, unfated) way. To the one who laughs, violence boomerangs back in the mode of the in-nocent (in-nocens, "not-injuring"). Terror, the anticipation of a force to come, is the antithesis of comedy; or rather, terror is comedy, affectively registered as levity, "gravity" (a force pushing down) felt as levity (a force pushing up).[24] Freud writes that jokes provide "relief from psychical expenditure that is al-ready there."[25] If one might use this quote to draw a general distinction: the brooding figures of the baroque are attuned to "the expenditure that is al-ready there." In a few cryptic pages of *The Origin of the Mourning Play*, Ben-jamin writes, "Comedy—or more precisely: the pure joke—is the essential inner side of mourning, which from time to time, like the lining of a dress at the hem or lapel, makes its presence felt." He extols Calderón and Shake-speare for insights into the interactive nexus of *Trauerspiel* and *Lustspiel* (for example, *Hamlet*). The German practitioners of the baroque drama were actually held back by their lack of insight into the relation between comedy and mourning play: never quite understanding that the comedic play was the obverse or "internal lining" of the mourning play, they "never progressed beyond the rigidly orthodox type."[26]

As with seventeenth-century baroque tragedy, so with ancient Greek tragedy: beginning from a common point, the comic also diverges from the ancient tragedic counterpart in distinctive ways that help to support the claims of the present essay. In an early work ("Fate and Character"), the comic character is said to dwell outside of "fate" [*Schicksal*, or destiny] and "the natural life." The latter is a "mist of guilt" or "sky" of highly charged, "colored," totalized immanent meanings "far more deeply interfused" (to borrow from Wordsworth) with the natural element or the guilty life. Benjamin's theorization suggests that what goes into the unspeakable "immanence" as "arbitrary signs" comes out as natural objects (the colored, the misty, the fateful, or guilty). In order to condemn an object to "fate," to nature and fallen existence, all the "clairvoyante" (*OWS* 128) need do is locate or name what, within the object, seems assignable to a given "natural life," which will then be seen to absorb and mark (or "color") that object as its own. "Fate" is a sky of singular traits (colors), powerful abstractions (streaks) that are all too easily personalized or universalized: whoever dwells in this sky (and "the homogeneous, empty time," may be seen as a later variant of colorful sky) ends up avowing something like "I am part of it [fate, *Schicksal*]; it means (colors) me." This is opposed to the comic and tragic genius, who operate in a "colorless (anonymous) sky." Those noncomedic and nontragedic souls might have found more distance had they an inkling of a guiltless (untouched, uncolored, anonymous comic) part of their body, an "invisible" and "best part" (*OWS* 128), not penetrated by "the immense complexity of the guilty person." To the "mystical enslavement of the person to the guilt context," both comedy and tragedy give "the answer of genius" (*OWS* 130). The "genius" may be viewed as a discoloration, a consciousness that swerves from a colored, guilty, fated sky toward a "colorless" and "anonymous" one. Although this can only be a piecemeal motion, this genial swerve is linked to "freedom."[27] Coming under another sky unseen (unnamed, uncolored, anonymous), this "best part" has no language, conception, or ritual ("sky"). That is, the comedic and tragic character emerge in the possibility of a conditional release from immanence, from the "deep" or "natural" fusions of unthinking correspondence, which, having no language, have little or no thought. The tragic hero raises his "head of genius" above the fog of guilty life condemned. Yet only the head, the visionary or genial part of tragedy, rises above the mists; its mythic body, still installed in the past, weighs it down. As the slightly emphasized word "Haupt" (*das Haupt des Genius*) suggests, the divide between guilty and nonguilty life acts as a guillotine that nearly decapitates the tragic hero, weighted down by the mythic Oedipal body. Comedy, so Benjamin's understated conceptual metaphors would give to understand, has no Oedipus, or at least no Oedipus with a complex. The implication is that, in comedy, there is not just a head—but a whole body that rises (or begins rising), as a levity above the mists, in the "colorless, anonymous sky."

The standard black and white (orthochromatic) film of the 1920s registers brightness of hue rather than color; when projected on the screen, the blue sky of the original filmed scene has turned into an ashy white in which clouds (those traditional emblems of the messianic) disappear into a "colorless," "anonymous" sky.

Yet complete anonymity—as the "colorless, anonymous sky" of the comic character—could perhaps be realized in a climate of complete citability, as this notion emerges in one of the "Theses on the Philosophy of History": "Only for a redeemed humanity has its past become citable in all its moments."[28] In the citable moments of the redeemed world, everything and anything would be completely legible as a part of that sphere, as planned and proper, as an intrinsic part of its agenda ("citation a l'ordre du jour"). In Benjamin's critical vision, what is hidden (embedded) does great violence both to the living and the dead. As Benjamin puts it in the "Theological-Political Fragment," "Only the Messiah himself consummates all historical occurrence, in the sense that he alone redeems, completes, creates its relation to the Messianic. Therefore nothing historical can, of itself, wish to relate itself to the messianic" (*OWS* 155). In the messianically redeemed world, there is no history—which is to say, there is nothing hidden: no images. There is also no need of criticism whose task is to sensitize one to the repositories of sociosymbolic violence hidden within official histories. If "the past" were "citable in all its moments," the new scenes (senses) conjured up through the comedic (mis)quotation would be commensurate and "plastic" with one another. From the divine point of view, words posit the worlds they imply. Any quotation would generate "light" rather than the "ashes" Benjamin finds in comedy. All the scenarios projected through quotation would always already be integrated with the quotation. Puns could not exist. Nor sight gags.

From the angle of redemption, the sight gag or the joke would be profane parodies of messianic citation. For this point we turn to Groucho Marx, whose disconnected, attention-deficit-disordered discourse constantly fragments the stable contexts of dignity (the "empty, homogeneous world," in Benjamin's phrase). At a fancy dress ball on a steamship (in *A Night at the Opera*), he asks a woman "Do you rumba?" Rising to the occasion, she is left standing, slain by his quip: "Well, take a rumba from one to ten." In context this juvenile pun enacts comically (and negative-critically) a kind of redemption, as suggested in the citation quoted above: "Only for a redeemed humanity has its past become citable in all its moments."

Groucho (and one could make this point with Buster Keaton) acts as if "the past" were "citable in all its moments." This Luciferic comic acts as if everything were redeemed already (in this he is "proleptic," leaping ahead just a bit). He acts as if everything he does or says had been fully commensurate or interchangeable with the normal response, without excess or misalignment; as if the accidents of language—"rumbah" and "numbah," this phonemic similarity—could have been sufficient to overcome the contingencies of historical usage, as if canceling out heterogeneous modes. At the critical limit, the messianic may best be (re)presented when it appears only as a minor glitch (like a joke). Its cutting violence may be purest when it is imperceptible—but this, of course, would be an impossible, nonrefundable critical thesis.

In the messianic mode of an Edenic language, the name for a dance could shift seamlessly from one situational context (asking someone to dance) into another (asking someone to pick a number "from one to ten"); merely on the basis of phonemic similarity, a dance could morph into a verbal guessing game, the leap between these different contexts not felt in the least as an interruption (as it is in the joke). In the redeemed atmosphere, all the social forms of love would work transitively across species, so that there would be nothing odd about horses (or women) who eat the signifiers of ritualized courtship, whether flowers or chocolates. By shifting the context from a polite dance invitation to a mathematical guessing game, Groucho's joke would exemplify one small step toward an infinitely delayed redemption or profane illumination, insofar as a piece of language or an image is lifted out of its gravity-laden existential context and "blasted," or "quoted" as a fleeting—and self-consciously staged—repetition of a sense that usually "captivates" its auditors in the (conventionally) right way, but that here and now, and for this comedic moment, does not. In Benjamin's writings, the critical is the comedic, both revolving around this notion of detaching pieces from—or having oneself detached in pieces from—contexts of embeddedness and deep gravity.

In Thesis IV, the historical materialist in the class war is not marked by spoils won but by "humor" (along with "cunning," "courage" and "impassivity" [*Unentwegtheit*]). The comedic act could serve as a microevent in what Thesis V formulates as a great task, the "wresting tradition away from a conformism that is about to overpower it." In the artwork essay, Benjamin had stated this hope for the revolutionary cinema in hyperbolic terms: "Our taverns and our metropolitan streets, our offices and furnished rooms, our railroad stations and our factories appeared to us locked up hopelessly. Then came the film and burst this prison-world asunder by the dynamite of a tenth of a second, so that now, in the midst of its far-flung ruins and debris, we calmly and adventurously go traveling" (WA 236). The long-standing institutions of the "barred" social space are blasted apart "in the dynamite of a tenth of a second."[29] That this "dynamite" may always only be cartoon dynamite (a graphic representation that blasts apart on-screen spaces only) need not detract from the point. With its energies coming from the dominant, comedy takes back in the next moment (sometimes marked by the laugh, which of course need not accompany comedy as a structural occasion) what it postulated and what it thereby ends up in a sense reaffirming, as a (for the moment) ineradicable part of the status quo.[30] That repressive regimes may sometimes tolerate a popular comic derision of their own authorities may be explained by the fact that comedy tends to cancel out whatever "revolutionary sentiments" it may have opened up. Comedy is a conservative genre in many ways: what works in comedic representation fails as revolutionary praxis. And yet: even if it may be only cartoon dynamite, behind the operation of the "dynamite of a tenth of a second" lie rudimentary materials for materialist philosophy. The "far-flung ruins and debris" of the passage cited recalls the desublimated debris left behind in the baroque mourning play, with its "scene of existence" turned into "a rubbish heap of partial, inauthentic actions."[31] If baroque tragedy leaves a rubbish heap, comedy would melt it down to "ashes," a Benjaminian trope of comedic operation associated with "a divine enterprise of unmasking": "Only by becoming humor can language become critique. The magic of true critique appears precisely when all counterfeit comes into contact with the light and melts away. What remains is the authentic: it is ashes. We laugh at it. Whoever emits light in great profusion ends up by initiating these divine enterprises of unmasking that we call criticism."[32] A profane image for these "divine enterprises of unmasking" comes to mind: an usher, before the picture starts, who points out the exits in a packed movie theater, but so swiftly that no one even looks. "For every second of time was the strait gate through which the Messiah might enter."[33]

FOUR

Aura Reconsidered

Benjamin and Contemporary Visual Culture

LUTZ KOEPNICK

In our present era of global media networks and ever-more inclusive technologies of space contraction, visual culture seems to have gone far beyond the task Walter Benjamin envisaged as the utopian charge of film and photography. In an explosive passage of the artwork essay, Benjamin wrote in 1936:

> Our taverns and our metropolitan streets, our offices and furnished rooms, our railroad stations and our factories appeared to have us locked up hopelessly. Then came the film and burst this prison-world asunder by the dynamite of the tenth of a second, so that now, in the midst of its far-flung ruins and debris, we calmly and adventurously go traveling.[1]

More than half a century later, film's once astonishing displacement of time and place has become the order of the day. What Benjamin analyzed in terms of the figure of shock, for contemporary couch potatoes constitutes a daily living-room routine. Individuals as much as nations today articulate their agendas, memories, and identities in response to values and passions that are increasingly formed through far-traveled images: images from TV and advertising to cinema and the Internet.

Anne Friedberg has introduced the concept of a "mobilized virtual gaze" in order to theorize the effects of postmodern media culture on our modes of perception, our strategies of cultural consumption, and our construction of individual and collective identities. Rooted in precinematic activities such as walking and traveling, on the one hand, and in all forms of visual representation, including cave painting, on the other, the compound term is meant to describe forms of scopic pleasure that travel "in an imaginary *flâ-nerie* through an imaginary elsewhere and an imaginary 'elsewhen.'"[2] According to Friedberg, virtual mobility today is inseparable from scenarios of transnational commodity consumption; it may be found in shopping malls, multiplex cinemas, or in front of the home multimedia station. Virtual traveling seems to bring to full fruition what Benjamin described as the explosive thrust of mechanical reproduction. It caters with unprecedented means to the desire "to get a hold of an object at very close range by way of its likeness, its reproduction."[3] The irony of Benjamin's 1936 argument, then, as seen from today's perspective, is that the mode of experience Benjamin associated with emancipatory and communist cultural practices has transformed into standard fare for audiences in a world ruled by the hegemony of transnational capitalism.

The centrality of visual experiences and virtual gazes in contemporary culture indicates that images can no longer be seen as simply reflecting the world in which we live. Instead, images and scopic experiences are now as much a material force of shaping history as social or economic forces; they intimately contribute to the making of the world. What is important to emphasize, however, is that postmodern culture produces not only despatialized and detemporalized viewing subjects but also a field of visual images that appears intrinsically heterogeneous and hybrid. No longer do we simply experience a film at the movie theater; we also experience it as video, through posters and advertisements, trailers and TV clips, newspaper reviews and Internet sites. Indicative of a profound change in the ways we make use of symbolic materials in order to negotiate meanings and construct identities, visual culture today issues an ever-more accelerated multiplication of hardly ever consistent viewing position. In doing so, it progressively undermines what Victor Burgin calls the "integrity of the semantic object."[4] Under the aegis of remote controls, fast-forward buttons, and other technologically mediated modes of cultural consumption, traditional models of hermeneutic understanding—models that locate meaning primarily in an artifact's peculiar registers of representation or address—no longer will do. Seemingly stripped of all auratic authority, contemporary technoculture takes the expression of a construction site, one at which meaning is produced in competing, highly selective, and often unpredictable gestures of posthermeneutic appropriation, in the kind of cultural practices that incorporate symbolic material through various media channels.

But does this kaleidoscopic gestalt of our age of digital reproduction really conclude the elimination of aura that Benjamin attributed already to film and photography? Don't we observe ubiquitous attempts to resurrect auratic sentiments, to resurrect—in Hans Jürgen Syberberg's words—"with the means of contemporary technology a new aura, in particular in film and photography"?[5] Can we continuously rely on Benjamin's dichotomy of auratic and postauratic art when postmodern culture, while emphatically endorsing technologies of temporal fragmentation and spatial stretching, is obsessed with the de- and recontextualization of auratic art in megaexhibitions and digitally remastered CD collections? Does the popular success of events such as the "Three Tenor" concerts, commercially promoted and circulated through various media channels, indicate an ironic and belated triumph of aura over distraction, of Adorno over Benjamin?

It is not difficult to see that these questions address issues much more complex than the concern with proper classification and periodization. According to Benjamin, the resuscitation of auratic values through postauratic means of reproduction brought with it the aestheticization of politics, that is, fascism. Benjamin, in the famous epilogue of the artwork essay, in fact generically defines fascism as the attempt to recycle auratic modes of perception in the context of a postauratic culture: fascism reinscribes aura in order to masquerade hierarchy and power as spectacle. How useful, then, we must ask, is Benjamin's conceptual apparatus when discussing the spectacular elements of contemporary media societies and their massive reproduction of auratic values? What seems clear at the outset is that given the ubiquitous perseverance of auratic elements, any political evaluation of the postmodern imaginary in mutually exclusive, normative concepts of auratic and postauratic art, of contemplation and diversion, appear way off the mark.

Christo's 1995 wrapping of the Berlin Reichstag building, a supreme exercise in mingling auratic and postauratic elements, is a good case in point.[6] In contrast to nineteenth-century monuments and their function to shape a homogeneous national community, Christo's spectacle constituted the focal point of eminently decentered practices of consumption.[7] While emerging as the object of Christo's own sketches, as the source of abundant allusion within the domain of advertising, as the center of discussion groups on the World Wide Web, or as the point of contention in the ardent debates in the German Parliament, *Wrapped Reichstag* ended up inviting multidiscursive and highly unstable strategies of appropriation. Significantly, the speechless awe in front of the final product was as much a part of the spectatorial response to *Wrapped Reichstag* as the nervous distraction of those who waited for the latest reproduction on the official Web site. Auratic through and through, Christo's shiny propylene fabric, one might therefore argue, literally served as a silver screen upon which to project competing agendas, ideologies, and tactics of diversion. Auratic elements in the context of *Wrapped Reichstag* allowed for the temporary emergence of a multilingual vernacular whose specific manifestations were highly dependent on the viewing situation, that is to say, the ways in which situated viewers made use of the various and overlapping interfaces that mark cultural consumption today.

It is important to note that many of Christo's opponents resorted to Benjamin's critical apparatus in order to debunk the project as an exercise in monumental seduction. Accordingly, *Wrapped Reichstag* was understood as a refeudalization of the public sphere reproducing the introduction of aesthetics to politics so prominent in Nazi Germany. Like the Nazi spectacle, Christo's project, it was argued, replaces rational communication with scopic politics; it solicits affective identification and auratic contemplation in order to subdue the viewer and to obscure the complexity of procedural politics.[8] But to consider Christo's viewers as duped by the auratic power of the project fails to recognize what must be understood as the altered role of aura in a post-Fordist information society. The aura of Christo's *Wrapped Reichstag* was at the core of cultural practices that in often seemingly contradictory ways could have it both ways at once, depending on the viewers' ability to surf the various channels of reception offered by our contemporary media society. *Wrapped Reichstag* did not situate its viewers—whether they gathered in front of the "real thing," confronted its iconography in the news media, or checked it out on the Internet—solely on only one side of the putative fault line between the auratic and postauratic. Instead, contradicting Benjamin's account of the elimination of aura in the modern age, the spectacular success of Christo's project points to the fact that aura not only outlived mechanical reproduction but also, as Jim Collins has argued in a different context, no longer designates a mode of textual address and enunciation. Rather, aura becomes a matter of personal projection and appropriation that ironically cannot be realized *without* technological mediation and exists as one tactic beside many others that make use of cultural material. Representative of an age in which high art has been thoroughly incorporated into the circuits of the popular, Christo's project belies any attempt to ground accounts of the politics of today's culture in facile juxtapositions of aura and mechanical reproduction, high art and popular entertainment. If the spectacle *Wrapped Reichstag* has one dominant meaning at all, then it is to convey to us that "rather than being *eliminated* by ever more sophisticated forms of distribution and access, the production of 'aura' has only *proliferated* as it has been dispersed through the multiplication of information technologies and agents responsible for determining value."[9]

Systematically blurring the lines between the idioms of high art and the expressions of popular culture, *Wrapped Reichstag* neither resulted in a mere Hollywoodization of avant-gardist practices nor did it reproduce the postauratic aura of fascist strategies of aestheticization. As Andreas Huyssen has argued, *Wrapped Reichstag*, to the extent to which it rearticulated aura as a process, product, and catalyst of historical memory in postauratic times, "stood as a monument to a democratic culture rather than a demonstration of state power."[10] The event's popular success consequently urges us to rethink Benjamin's dialectics of aura in twentieth-century culture and politics. Does the present resurgence of aura as a critical and intrinsically heterogeneous corrective to accelerated global stretching and amnesia relegate Benjamin's modernist critique of auratic revivals to the dustbins of intellectual history? To what extent does Christo's rearticulation of aura render Benjamin's aestheticization thesis a typical expression of a modernist and Fordist discourse, a discourse that neither provides adequate answers to nor asks the right questions about the cultural politics of postmodernity? Is it possible at all continuously to identify, with the help of Benjamin, strategies of aestheticization today without classifying them as "fascist"? The following pages seek to give some answers to these questions, thereby thinking through what the veritable industry surrounding Benjamin today mostly takes for granted: the actuality of the aestheticization thesis for the analysis of postmodern consumer culture. In order to do so, I first recapitulate Benjamin's theory of auratic and postauratic experience in light of the arguments of some of his most insightful critics, in particular Theodor W. Adorno, Patrice

Petro, and Miriam Hansen. Second, I examine postmodern interfaces between technology, identity, memory, and the popular dimension in order to better understand the altered function of auratic sentiments in contemporary public and private spheres. Finally, I rephrase the question of Benjamin's actuality, arguing emphatically that contemporary criticism can still learn from Benjamin's aestheticization thesis even if the imbrication of politics, perception, and culture at the threshold of the twenty-first century fundamentally differs from the peculiar configuration Benjamin sought to identify during the 1930s.

A term only inappropriately captured by the English "experience," the category of *Erfahrung* is at the heart of Benjamin's entire critical program. It unifies in various configurations his overall work from the 1910s to his final theology of history of 1940. Explicitly opposed to scientific or positivistic definitions of experience, Benjamin unfolds his concept along spatial and temporal vectors at once. Experience mediates individual modes of perception with collective patterns of cognition and material modalities of production, transportation, and information; experience articulates conflicting temporalities, including those of utopian promises and historical memory, of conscious and unconscious acts of recollection and remembrance. Let us recall that Benjamin in the artwork essay and his studies on Baudelaire claims that the fundamental restructuring of temporal and spatial relations in modernity undermines the possibility of auratic experience. Defined as a quasi-magic perception of an object invested "with the capability of returning the gaze," aura withers in modernity.[11] Taylorism, industrial mass production, and urbanization render obsolete any enchantment with a unique phenomenon however close it may be; they displace auratic experience with distraction. Film, for Benjamin, is both symptom and agent of this transformation. It extends the thrust of social changes to the arenas of cultural exchange and aesthetic expression. Accordingly, the shock of cinematic montage emancipates cultural practices not only from auratic sentiments but also from aesthetic experience altogether; it links cultural formulations—for better (communism) or worse (fascism)—directly to political projects. As a postaesthetic counterpart to the shifting grounds of collective perception, Benjamin's cinema seems no longer to allow for moments of profane illumination, for the magic spell of the mimetic faculty, or for a reciprocal interaction between humanity and nature. Unless it subscribes to a false resurrection of aura, cinema—as conceived in the artwork essay—does not return the viewer's gaze. Instead, it circumscribes a site of rational insight and critical debate, of scientific examination and egalitarian self-representation. A training ground for distracted modes of reception and cultural appropriation, mechanical reproduction thus emancipates modern society from ritual, tradition, and the bourgeois cult of art at the cost of severing the individual from the resources of memory, nonintentionality, and playful mimesis, of the ecstasy of retrieving an unknown past, of forgetting oneself and becoming Other.

It has often been pointed out not only that Benjamin overestimated the liberatory potential of postauratic visuality but also that his political appropriation of cinema remained pseudoradical in that it assumed all-too-close affinities between the modes of rationalized industrial production and the peculiar principles of mass cultural reception.[12] A modality of experience after the end of experience proper, Benjamin's category of distraction, as a consequence, "elides—and all too readily surrenders—the regressive aspects of the cinema, its mobilizing of pre-rational mental processes, and thus unwittingly joins the long tradition of bourgeois rationality that asserts itself in the containment and exclusion of the other, of sensuality and femininity."[13] Benjamin's theory of modern disenchantment and visuality undermines the very position it seeks to emphasize. To the extent to which the category of distraction glosses over potential gaps between ideological uses of cinema from above and the often unpredictable ways in which actual viewers—positioned in historically contingent viewing situations—make use of the specific viewing event, Benjamin inhibits any thorough understanding of how a film makes its entry into the spectator's head, and how films might be consumed according to divergent needs and agendas. Benjamin's celebratory use of the category of distraction, in other words, obstructs the possibility to understand cinema as a public horizon that helps organize human experience across dominant demarcations of public and private. Although meant to offer a site of critical exchange and cultural empowerment, Benjamin's postauratic auditorium is populated by spectators who have nothing left to see or say anymore.

Given such critical blind spots in Benjamin's expulsion of aura from the topographies of mechanical reproduction, it should come as no surprise that even some of Benjamin's closest intellectual allies saw reason enough to challenge the conceptual centerpiece of Benjamin's interlaced theory of film and the aesthetics of politics. Rigorously questioning Benjamin's dismissal of aura and aesthetic experience, Adorno insisted that auratic and contemplative elements clearly survived the arrival of a full-fledged culture of mechanical reproduction in the twentieth century. According to Adorno, aura not only persisted in the riddles of enigmatic modernism but also—in however perverted form—in the culture industry's attempt to reconcile the fault lines of modern culture "by absorbing light into serious art, or vice versa."[14] For Adorno, Benjamin's category of postauratic distraction falsely heroized commodity fetishism as strategies of cultural empowerment and subversion. Benjamin's distracted poachers, Adorno believed, simply reproduce the culture industry's ideology of pseudoindividualization, defined as the "halo of free choice" on the basis of standardization.[15] Read against the backdrop of what is clearly missing in Benjamin's account of film—namely a critical theory of the commodification of cultural practices—postauratic inattentiveness in Adorno's view disintegrates the ability to conceive of semantic unity as a repository of determined negation and resistance. Far from liberating humankind from the authority of tradition and ritual, distraction transforms disconnected parts into fetishes in front of which "consumers become temple slaves."[16]

Adorno defended aesthetic figurations of aura against Benjamin's artwork essay because he sensed a precarious complicity between the philosophical denigration of auratic experience, on the one hand, and the industrial transformation of perception as well as the logic of commodity fetishism, on the other. Played out in the hermetically sealed environment of autonomous art, mimetic experience, subjectivity, and art's quasi-magic sense for sameness, similarity, and correspondence were to voice Adorno's desperate protest against the leveling of critical meaning and the disciplining of pleasure administered by twentieth-century mass culture. In her recent *Joyless Streets*, Patrice Petro has added provocatively to this critique of Benjamin's account of postauratic visuality, suggesting that we understand the demolition of aura through cinema not as an effect of cinematic technology per se but of the peculiar and historically contingent formation of dominant film practices and the systematic marginalization of alternative forms of spectatorship.[17] Petro argues that by reconstructing the course of spectatorship in terms of a general paradigm shift from aura to distraction, Benjamin explains away the factual heterogeneity of spectatorial practices in particular in early cinema. Most importantly, he completely elides the gender-specificity of early cinematic forms of address and consumption, the parallel existence of distracted and concentrated, industrialized and emotionally attentive modes of looking. Although Benjamin's category of distraction might indeed encode the experience of those permitted to participate in the processes of social and cultural modernization since the middle of the nineteenth century, it obscures the structures of experience of those, in particular women, who owing to given landscapes of power remained at the margins of these processes. Female spectatorship, especially during the 1920s, was often at odds with the kind of principles Benjamin presented as a universal ontology of cinematic communication. Highly popular in Weimar cinema as a "female" genre, the melodrama according to Petro bears testimony to the existence of modes of spectatorship different from those described by Benjamin under the rubric of distraction and inattentive, detached appropriation. In the context of the 1920s melodrama, mechanical reproduction addresses those for whom distraction has not become the norm, those whose "concentrated gaze involves a perceptual activity that is neither passive nor entirely distracted," and who therefore desire what Benjamin would label the aura of contemplative identification and emotional intensity.[18] Although increasingly obliterated by the industry's attempt to shape a unified spectatorial subject, the "woman's film" evidences the historical possibility of an empowering survival of aura on the grounds of mass culture itself, a nonantagonistic coexistence of mechanical reproduction and auratic perception.

Both Adorno and Petro agree that Benjamin's theory of experiential exhaustion in modernity cannot account for the survival or discontinuous return of aura in twentieth-century art and popular culture. Benjamin not only undermines the very kind of categories that energize his overall criticism of modern culture, including his studies of surrealism, nineteenth-century *flânerie*, Baudelaire, and Kafka. As he mixes theoretical, historical, and normative lines of argumentation, Benjamin also implies all-too-facile and misleading links between the persistence of aura and the aestheticization of politics, between fascism and the resurgence of aesthetic experience in mass culture. Instead of understanding modernity in terms of a differentiation of competing modes of looking and cultural consumption, Benjamin forges the complexity of modern spectatorship into a rather monolithic cast himself. In so doing, he renders the effects of historical contingencies as "natural" facts; it mistakes a peculiar formation of visual culture and spectatorship for the ontology of the media.

Given these blind spots in Benjamin's reasoning on film, it appears timely to recapitulate the argument of the artwork essay and search for less monolithic accounts of auratic and postauratic visuality. After all, it is unlikely that Benjamin could have so drastically forfeited his self-proclaimed aim of dialectical thought without leaving behind numerous traces of containment or repression. Reading Benjamin against the grain of his iconoclastic posture, Miriam Hansen has shown that the artwork essay indeed contains a number of allusions to mimetic experience and auratic figuration "suggesting that the cinema's role in relation to experiential impoverishment could go beyond merely promoting and consummating the historical process."[19] Hansen proposes that what are often seen as the essay's most pseudoscientific pronouncements contain building blocks for an alternative theory of vision in the age of mechanical reproduction. Particularly Benjamin's comments about the tactile, ballistic, and hence, anti-illusionary thrust of film, on the one hand, and about the photographic image's "optical unconscious," on the other, allow Hansen to reconsider Benjamin's wholesale denigration of aura. Hansen's formula will allow us to disentangle Benjamin's imprudent conceptual approximation of postauratic aura and fascist aesthetics.

First of all, there is good reason to conceive of what Benjamin understands as the tactile dimension of film as a mimetic figuration of the atomized structure of modern existence and not simply as a catalyst of discursive insight and truth. "Being based on changes of place and focus which periodically assail the spectator," cinema literally allows us to touch upon what can be seen in the image.[20] A source of visual attractions and visceral astonishments, film results in a radical displacement of self in sentience; it takes us outside of ourselves in likeness to the ways in which a child "not only plays at being a grocer or teacher, but also at being a windmill or a train."[21] In the same way Kracauer endorses distraction as a sensuous "reflection of the uncontrolled anarchy of our world," Benjamin valorizes the ballistic qualities of film because they involve a mimetic component that clearly exceeds the bounds of a Brechtian aesthetics of cognitive distantiation and discursive truth.[22] Although hostile to the spatial dimension of auratic distance, Benjamin's cinematic image retains something of aura's temporality; it is powerful enough to actualize a prehistoric stratum of human practice. Film bestows upon the viewer the experience of quasi-magic contact, a preconceptual and sensory form of knowing that resembles the infant's attempt to know an object by eating it.

Secondly, residues of auratic experience may also enter into postauratic film practice through the backdoor of what Benjamin calls the optical unconscious. With the help of the optical unconscious Benjamin admits dimensions into his theory of postauratic representation and spectatorship that clearly contradict his overall emphasis on presence, tracelessness, expertdom, and radical distraction. Far from solely indicating an utterly disenchanting rationalization of vision, Benjamin's equation of camera work and Freudian psychoanalysis hints at film's capacity to authorize an unprecedented mimesis of technology and nature, "a thoroughgoing permeation of reality with mechanical equipment."[23] On the one hand, the camera pierces quotidian surfaces with its peculiar technologies of representation; yet on the other, it tends to make its own work invisible. Film, then, is capable of ushering the spectator into the realms of profane illumination, into an arena of flash-like, nonintentional, and sensuous cognition similar to the one Benjamin unearthed in the works of the surrealists, of Baudelaire, and in the context of his own experiments with drugs and intoxication. Cinema may after all allow for forms of reciprocity reminiscent of the experience of auratic phenomena: the optical unconscious rearticulates for the era of mechanical reproduction what in Romantic philosophy empowered nature to return the gaze.

All things considered, Benjamin's thesis about the tactile nature of modern vision is more ambiguous and "dialectical" than it may seem at first. Not only does the advent of the filmic image far from condemn *all* auratic experience as complicit with authority and traditionalism. Understood as an unsettling counterpoint to dominant film practices, a cinema that returns the gaze could also provide an antidote to the very kind of instrumental rationality and temporal fragmentation Benjamin's endorses all too quickly and homogeneously as the signatures of modern life. While the surgical devices of film clearly participate in the destruction of the aura of first nature, of the halo that surrounds natural presences and wonders, film's mimetic powers, its physiognomical mode of signification, and its indebtedness to what Tom Gunning calls the "cinema of attraction," may at the same time map second nature as a dimension of profane illumination and, in so doing, empower modes of spectatorship that escape the grasp of reification Adorno saw at the bottom of Benjamin's theory of film.[24] "If the mimetic capacities of film were put to such use, it would not only fulfill a critical function but also a redemptive one, registering sediments of experience that are no longer or not yet claimed by social and economic rationality, making them readable as emblems of a 'forgotten future.'"[25]

To thus bring into focus the artwork essay's discontinuous reinscription of aura in and through film allows us to link Benjamin's account of postauratic visuality to critical concepts of modern mass culture, that is, theories that map the popular dimension as an ambiguous domain circulating often archaic utopias of meaningful collectivity while simultaneously perpetuating the opposite. Moreover, rectifying what both Adorno and Petro, from different perspectives indeed, vehemently oppose in Benjamin, the revised notion of auratic experience makes it possible to demystify Benjamin's mysterious concept of aura itself and to free it from the all-too-facile suspicion that any return of auratic moments necessarily coincides with (fascist) strategies of aestheticization. If even Benjamin himself observes the survival of mimetic elements within postauratic visual practices, then it would be more than foolish to construe all rearticulations of aura as a replay of fascist media politics. Surely, fascism elicits auratic experiences through postauratic means in order to relocate decadent aesthetic values to the arena of political action, to entertain the masses with the imagery of autonomous politics, and to provide a unifying product image for a heterogeneous ideological commodity; fascist mass culture appeals to utopian elements in auratic experiences in order to channel them into a project of national rebirth and racial purification through imperial warfare. But inasmuch as that which Benjamin calls the optical unconscious of mechanical reproduction itself offers valuable residues of auratic experiences, there is no conceptual reason why aura could not play a role in critical visual practices as well.

Aura, its decay, and its return, are fundamentally ambivalent categories even in Benjamin's highly overdetermined philosophy of history and media aesthetics. Their political value is a matter of historical contingencies; it cannot be understood by means of universalizing theoretical or formalistic arguments. To suspect, therefore, that any postauratic return of aura today may yield directly regressive political effects clearly misses the point. It would fall prey to the same kind of formalism and aestheticism Benjamin was so eager to overthrow. Neither today's politics of commodification nor its commodification of politics today directly duplicate what Benjamin sought to expose as the origin of fascist aestheticization. To discuss crucial differences, and thus to open up a framework in which it becomes possible to talk in a meaningful and differentiated way about the political uses and abuses of aura and experience under the condition of postmodernity, will be the task of the final two sections of this chapter.

David Harvey has suggested that the postmodern condition by and large reflects a political, social, and cultural response to a fundamentally new way of how capitalism works in the late twentieth century. The postmodern represents a break with the regime of Fordist modes of standardized mass production and mass consumption, and a foray into an era of "flexible accumulation" as the hegemonic principle of capitalist reproduction, an era "characterized by more flexible labour processes and markets, of geographical mobility and rapid shifts in consumption practices."[26] Inaugurated circa 1970, this new post-Fordist phase of capitalist accumulation brings forth the emergence of highly diversified sectors of production, of unstable, heterogeneous markets, and of heated cycles of innovations. It also involves a new round of space-time compressions that shrink the temporal and spatial horizons and, in so doing, spread decision-making processes over an ever-more global, variegated, and accelerated space. Flexible accumulation disperses traditional capitalist relations and the concentration of capital; it displaces large production plants and surrounding cities in favor of diversified small-batch manufacturing sites, subcontracting firms at peripheral places, and a decentering of the urban lifeworld.[27] In response, post-Fordist societies observe the advent of new modalities of individualized and highly diversified commodity consumption. However ambiguous in nature, flexible accumulation cannot succeed without equipping individual consumers with a new kind of market authority that supersedes the standardized practices of Fordist mass consumption.

Fordist mass culture offered little choice between different media channels or offerings and thereby produced a relatively homogeneous community of however atomized viewers or consumers. One of the reasons for the immediate success of TV was that it was able to offer private pleasures of seemingly public relevance. Situated in the homely shelter of the living room, everyone pretty much watched the same show at the same time, and hence was able to experience isolated acts of cultural consumption as a quasi-communal affair. Fordist consumerism carried the burden of providing an always precarious mythology of social integration and democratic egality. It offered the image of a unified population pursuing the same goals and hunting for the same objects of desire.

Post-Fordist culture, by way of contrast, is characterized by the workings of hybrid multimedia aggregates and diversified and hardly ever consistent identities. Confronted with technologically mediated processes of temporal and spatial stretching, the relatively predictable consumer of Fordist mass culture converts into a symbolic poacher who seizes heterogeneous materials from different times and spaces, takes position in multiple temporalities at once, and assumes ever-shifting positionalities. Post-Fordist technoculture grafts the principle of flexible accumulation onto the exchange and acquisition of symbolic materials. In doing so, it nullifies what allowed the individual to experience Fordist consumer societies as imagined communities. Cultural technologies such as VCRs or Walkmans, fast-forward buttons or digital cameras, discharge the assumptions about homogeneous time and space so central to the ideological effects of Fordist mass media: "One can literally rent another space and time when one borrows a videotape to watch on a VCR."[28] The integration of PC, telephone, TV, and video, the emergence of PC banking and shopping, the direct access to Internet archives and databanks, and the dazzle of new video games and virtual reality simulations, all point toward the arrival of a new kind of consumer whose continual selections result in a highly individualized (and commodified) use of an eminently diverse media landscape.

Benjamin understood mechanical reproduction as a stimulus for new forms of cultural authority: the newspaper boy who discussed the outcome of a bicycle race, for Benjamin, indicated the advent of a culture of experts thriving on the fact that Fordist mass media satisfy "modern man's legitimate claim to being reproduced."[29] In the age of digital information, Benjamin's participatory utopia of cultural empowerment seems to have come to full fruition. Not only do we find ourselves as objects of visual or digital reproduction, but also we seem to be in relative control over the very means and technologies that allow us to shape our identities and self-representations.

In order to exhaust the multiplicity of opportunities and warrant the most effective accumulation of pleasure and leisure, postmodern consumers need to know much more than simply how to consume. Expertdom in fact has become a prerequisite of cultural survival today. Consumers need to know how to manipulate sophisticated technologies and traverse various media channels at once. Furthermore, they also need to know how to handle mounting pressures to reduce complexity, to make distinctions, to forget about alternative offerings while consuming a specific option, and to meet a dynamic inflation of demands and expectations.[30]

Yet even if postmodern culture seems to require us to become experts in Benjamin's sense, it is not difficult to see that our contemporary life on-screen fundamentally differs from the kind of images and identities Benjamin hoped to see expertly circulated on the screens of Fordist mass culture. On the World Wide Web, for example, we construct a network identity by composing and pasting words, images, and sounds drawn from perplexingly global and inconsistent sources.[31] Experts surfing the Web furnish their homes by fusing diverse materials, genres, styles, and idioms of expression into one intrinsically decentered and infinite hypertext. Postmodern technoculture thus couples its new forms of cultural authority to a multiplication of identities and viewing positions that supersede the unified identity of Benjamin's proletarian newspaper boy fascinated with proletarian spectator sports. Needless to say, this diversification of cultural identities extends to the realm of the political as well. Helmut Dubiel's "Mercedes-worker from Baden-Württemberg, who is unionized yet also—as a member of an action group—protests against a nearby Mercedes test course and who votes for the Christian Democratic Party because it promises lower taxation on factory cars" is a good case in point here.[32] He not only indicates the accelerating refractions of the postmodern political consciousness but also the fact that—under the rule of flexible accumulation—political identities result from an increasingly complex and by no means stable combination of various parameters and elements—parameters and elements that reflect competing and hardly predictable compounds of social, economic, and cultural positionalities.

Fordist concepts of cultural production, consumption, and reception, then, no longer will do in order to theorize the ways in which individuals today make use of media channels and the pluralization of modes of expression. "Consumers in the classical sense appear antiquated in the face of the new offerings."[33] If the concept of postmodernism is meant to signify more than simply a cultural fashion or a new aesthetic paradigm, then it ought to bring into view precisely what is different about the conditions of individual experience and the institutions of cultural consumption today, that is, to conceptualize the relationship between the emergence of highly strategic practices of symbolic appropriation, the progressive decentering and multiplication of identity, and the changes in the global economic system that make us live in a permanent elsewhere and elsewhen. Rarely meeting this complex task, however, and often eliding necessary institutional analysis, much postmodern criticism tends to overlook possible complicities between today's flexible accumulation of hybrid identities, nonhierarchical differences, and heterogeneous forms of agency, on the one hand, and the ways in which Western capitalism works on a global and local scale in the late twentieth century, on the other. Instead, it uncritically heroizes the centrifugal force of post-Fordist societies as part of a

> fantastic unbinding of cultures, forms of life, styles, and world perspectives that today no longer simply encounter each other, but mutually open up to one another, penetrate each other in the medium of mutual interpretation, mix with one another, enter into hybrid and creative relationships, and produce an overwhelming pluralism, a decentered, hence obscure multiplicity, indeed a chaos of linked but contingent, nearly undecipherable sounds and texts.[34]

As a result, particularly in its poststructuralist inflections, this form of criticism often all too quickly assigns subversive meanings to the fracturing of identity and the present roamings of cultural poachers, glossing over the fact that local acts of cultural empowerment do not necessarily result in inclusive articulations of resistance or opposition. What is important to keep in mind is that no carnivalistic unbinding of fixed traditions, unified identities, or Fordist media practices per se will yield the emancipatory effects many theorists attest to technoculture's bursting asunder of prepostmodern space, experience, and meaning. If the multiplication of cultural identities should not lead to a cacophony of highly fragmented image bits and sound bytes, but rather help enable politically relevant processes of collective will-formation, then what is needed instead is the formation of public and counterpublic spheres that mediate between the global and the local, between the by no means synchronized forces of cultural, political, and economic stretching. Only if, in other words, the post-Fordist refraction of culture and its scenarios of virtual travel are linked to a successful institutionalization of infrastructures that calibrate the conflicting dimensions of globalization, only then will it be possible to safeguard forms of solidarity that empower individual and collective agents to make effective use of the logic of spatio-temporal displacement so pertinent to our kaleidoscopic age of digital information.[35]

In many instances the contemporary desire for auratic experiences expresses nothing other than the hope for structures of mediation that negotiate the global and the local, restore meaningful spaces to the exploded topographies of postmodern culture, secure forms of individual agency and mimetic nonintentionality, and thus find remedies for the loss of memory in our fantastically unbound culture of channel surfers. Whether cultivated in contemporary museum practices, the digital airlifting of nineteenth-century opera, or the wrapping of political monuments, postmodern aura indicates that the anarchic freedom of global poachers remains imaginary if they fail to develop an ethos of significance, that is, individual and collective structures of valorization that allow situated subjects to distinguish between narratives, images, sounds, and symbols of lesser and of greater importance. Although having been thoroughly incorporated into the circuits of commodified culture and digital information, aura today therefore often also signifies the however paradoxical and quixotic quest for a return of the real, a critical outcry against ever-more inclusive spectacles of simulation.[36] As it aims at a transitory reenchantment of human perception and object relations, a discontinuous reinscription of aura can remind us of our need for experience in its most emphatic sense. It probes the economic and cultural hegemony of flexible accumulation, vocalizing residues of opposition to the universal dominance of exchange values, to the devaluation of objects under the rule of global commodification. At a time when post-Fordist capitalist relations simultaneously shrink and expand the spatio-temporal dimensions of our lifeworlds in an unprecedented manner, the reinvention of auratic experiences offers a "testing ground for reflections on temporality and subjectivity, identity and alterity."[37] Aura today brings into focus that a life without memory and without the thick materiality of sentient experience is not a life at all.

It opens our eyes to the fact that armchair voyages through hyperspace and along electronic information superhighways—in spite of all their liberatory potentials—may ironically imprison meaning and freedom in an iron cage of false empowerment, of pseudoindividualization. As one among multiple other modes of mass cultural experience, the return of aura demonstrates the fact that contemporary popular culture itself contains correctives to its own ideologies and practices, to the vanishing of history and memory into "terminal" perceptions that are endlessly replayed as film and video. Objecting to the dematerialization and detemporalization of experience in postmodernity, aura reminds us that any collision of heterogeneous spaces and conflicting temporalities may release us from oppressive traditions and monolithic identities only if we succeed in relating the symbolic material of diverse cultures to the experiential trajectories of sentient bodies and the materiality of everyday practice.

The syncretic blend of auratic charisma and mass appeal in Christo's *Wrapped Reichstag*—to return to the opening discussion of this chapter—is a good example. A local event with global reverberations, Christo's *Wrapped Reichstag* evoked the charm of auratic and mimetic experiences in order to constitute what I would like to call a hybrid visual public sphere, one in which—unlike Habermas's classical model of the bourgeois public sphere—the body and its pleasures played an undeniable role. *Wrapped Reichstag*'s transitory aura opened up cultural spaces in which it became possible not only to negotiate past and present, the local and the global, but also the diverse itineraries of sensuality and cognition, corporeal experience and discursive intervention. *Wrapped Reichstag* appealed to auratic desires in order to transform a monument into a literal projection screen; the project's aura called forth competing images of past and present, bringing into focus the constructedness of history, truth, and identity. In a time in which motion pictures make history return forever as mechanical reproduction, Christo's *Wrapped Reichstag* evidenced that a nation's imaginary today is highly heterogeneous, that visual culture and experience only exist in the plural, are internally diversified, and coexist with many other cultures and modes of experience in what one might call the multilingual plurality of competing public spheres. Instead of rearticulating notions of unified spectatorship or mapping the visual as a force of emotional synthesis, the aura of *Wrapped Reichstag* turned our attention to processes of representation and conflict themselves, illustrating how post-Fordist visual culture is implicated in the workings of political legitimation, the organization of private and public spaces, and the construction of shifting and often contradictory identities.

Christo's intervention reminded us that visual culture in the age of flexible accumulation—even as global spectacle and mass diversion—can delimit a site of division, difference, and contestation. To consider Christo's viewers with the help of Benjamin as duped by the auratic power of the project therefore fails to recognize the altered landscapes of experience, communication, and commodification in a post-Fordist information society. In the tradition of a long-standing Western ocularphobia, it also grossly underestimates the potential virtues of the visual today to articulate experience, insight, and knowledge across given boundaries of public and private.[38] In readmitting auratic experiences through the backdoor of postauratic culture *Wrapped Reichstag* exposed the very inadequacy of evaluating the intentional fabrication of aura today within a Benjaminian framework, to equate the workings of postmodern visual culture with the Nazi spectacle. In a time of accelerated amnesia and spatial displacement, the transitory aura of *Wrapped Reichstag* energized the formation of an ethos of significance. Far from resulting in a retrogressive aestheticization of politics, the project's aura made it possible for Germans to rethink what it means to be German in a globalized culture, to reevaluate critically the legacy of their past, and to reinsert the body and its pleasures into postnationalist negotiations of culture and the construction of a hybrid and intrinsically heterogeneous community.

Given these fundamental changes in the nature of visual culture today, did Adorno, when polemically defending aura against Benjamin, get it right after all? Does the persistence of aura today evidence a posthumous victory of Adorno over Benjamin? Does post-Fordist aura relegate Benjamin's artwork essay, the philosophy of mechanical reproduction, and the concomitant critique of the aestheticization of politics to the dustbins of intellectual history?

There are good reasons to believe that Benjamin's critique of aura and the aestheticization of politics no longer provides what it originally was meant to offer: a critical yardstick that measures the political instrumentality of modern cultural expressions and practices. Surely, Benjamin's analysis of twentieth-century visual culture is still useful in order to conceptualize the ways in which contemporary culture endorses and commodifies the postmodern regime of mobile virtual looking. At the same time, however, we cannot overlook radical changes in the organization of experience separating us from Benjamin's time and reasoning. Whether they concern transformations in the production and social function of auratic perception, in the bearing of today's media channels on the formation of cultural authority, or in global capitalism's strategies of commodification, these historical differences, I would argue, should caution us not to draw any facile parallels between the media spectacles of the 1990s and what Benjamin called the aestheticization of politics, that is, fascism. Reckoning with fundamentally different modes of how we look and how we assume subject positions in the fields of visual culture, any postauratic refurbishing of aura today must result in quite different political effects than under the rule of fascism. As indicated by the critical success of Christo's *Wrapped Reichstag*, auratic experience in the 1990s may in fact articulate and reclaim spaces of self-reflexivity in mass culture itself. Contrary to Benjamin's assumption, aura, in other words, survived the gestalt of a full-fledged culture of mechanical reproduction, but it did so under conditions that also run counter to Adorno's philosophy of art, namely under the condition of a full integration of economics and culture and the concomitant abolition of a radically separate sphere of the aesthetic. Neither Adorno's virulent critique of Fordist mass culture and his heroization of the negativity of autonomous modernist art, nor Benjamin's one-sided valorization of postauratic art and his ambivalent charge against aesthetic experience, therefore, will do in order to provide keywords for a critical theory of postmodern consumption and amnesia. Each in its own way fusing historical-descriptive and normative lines of argumentation, the paradigmatic categories of Adorno and Benjamin respectively are progressively consumed by the very historical process they were meant to theorize. The point, therefore, is not to speculate about who may have won over whom, or—like Collins—check Benjamin and Adorno into the Grand Hotel Abyss of modernist theory, but rather to investigate what can be redeemed of Benjamin (and Adorno) for our own times, that is to say, how we can see ourselves in his critique of modern culture, and how we can envision his role under the postmodern conditions of flexible accumulation.[39]

It is not difficult to see that there has never been a greater need to take critical issue with the nexus of cultural expressions, media technologies, and modes of political legitimation. Postmodern culture has bundled the various dimensions of representation—semiotic, aesthetic, and political—into a global grammar of commodity consumption, prioritizing the image over reality and promoting fun and diversion to the primary glue of what might hold society together. An unmediated Benjaminian perspective, however, will hardly help us reflect about the agendas and effects of current spectacles. Although the stage-managing and commodification of the political might have become the norm today, it would be foolish to argue that any fusion of politics and consumption in the age of TV campaigns continues the project of fascist aestheticization. Media spectacles such as the Gulf War clearly re-play under postmodern conditions aspects of what Benjamin meant when speaking of the aestheticization of politics. But we would level all historical distinctions if we rendered the antiseptic and strangely auratic presentation of warfare on CNN itself in a Benjaminian mode as the one and only telos of postmodern politics.

According to Benjamin's peculiar understanding, historical materialism—as applied to the realm of aesthetic theory—inquires into the technical and economic conditions motivating our attitudes toward beauty.[40] What we consider beautiful is a matter of historical contingencies. It reflects changing structures of experience, of the modes in which technologies of reproduc-tion and exchange inflect our ways of seeing, feeling, remembering, knowing, and dreaming. Benjamin's artwork essay theorized individual and collective perceptions of beauty in a Fordist age of standardized mass production and mass consumption. The aestheticization thesis was meant to think through the political instrumentality of nineteenth-century conceptions of beauty as a means of integrating the Fordist mass into the social system of fascism. It hoped to conceptualize how fascism feeds on changing attitudes toward auratic and mimetic experience in order to carry out its counterrevolutionary projects of warfare and national rebirth.

Benjamin's materialist insistence on the historicity of aesthetic experience should alert us not to apply his critical terminology in an unmediated fash-ion to the political managing of the visual in our post-Fordist age of digi-tal information and flexible accumulation. Neither contemporary structures of sensual perception nor those of individual and collective recollection are identical with those that Benjamin believed to be at the center of the fascist spectacle. To be sure, as I have argued earlier, Benjamin's notion of experi-ence is clearly too narrow (and too gender biased) itself to remain fully valid even for the period he himself sought to examine. His thesis about the decay of aura is too monolithic to explicate the diverse and competing registers of seeing and experience that mark the modern condition. But in spite of such conceptual bottlenecks, it is precisely his emphasis on the historically specific organization of individual pleasure and collective perception that provides us with a strong argument to counter both revisionist reconstructions of fascist aesthetics as mere style and iconography, and impetuous portrayals of contemporary visual culture as an uncanny relative of the fascist public sphere.[41] In many respects much more of a critical historicist than he was willing to admit, Benjamin himself urges us to understand notions such as fascist aesthetics and political aestheticization in their historical context. Instead of mindlessly inflating Benjamin's conceptual apparatus and speculating about what else might be fascist besides fascism, we fare much better if we employ his tools of criticism for the purpose of better understanding what exactly was considered beautiful under fascism—and by whom.

Such cautionary use, however, is by no means meant to strip Benjamin of his actuality and make his aestheticization thesis join the pantheon of intellectual history. Even if our structures of experience have undergone crucial changes since the 1930s, in Benjamin's emphatic insistence on experience we may find what is still burningly actual about his reflections. If we want to follow Benjamin's lead indeed, then any meaningful analysis of the nexus of power and the aesthetic, of aura and domination, today needs to meet strong intellectual and methodological demands. In critiquing the aestheticization of politics, Benjamin's aim was to show how political presentation interacts with historically contingent patterns of perception, and how imperatives of power and money may colonize the specific ways of what and how we see. Any theory of the postmodern spectacle learning from Benjamin, therefore, cannot do without a strong ethnographic component, one which is able to map from a phenomenological perspective the symbolic spaces and cultural practices of everyday life. Contrary to Adorno, who was unwilling to see the everyday as a site of meaningful action, Benjamin encourages us to understand the everyday as a site of continuing negotiations and interventions, of struggle and articulation. Unlike Adorno, Benjamin did not lose hope vis-à-vis what has become the inescapable norm today: the commodification of all cultural practices. Instead, he was eager to read the popular dimension against the grain and find those moments of rupture where commodity culture turned against its own ideologies and generated footholds of a better life. In light of the postmodern demise of any meaningful notion of autonomous, noncommodified art, Benjamin's pragmatism remains a highly viable intellectual strategy. It teaches us that no talk about the aesthetic moment of the political can assume any validity today if it fails to account for how the postmodern proliferation of images interacts with the historically specific topography of experience, how sentient bodies today maneuver their ways through the endlessly refracted and progressively virtual spaces of culture in order to assume shifting positionalities and try to make and mark history.

PART 2

Textualities of Experience

FIVE

Under Construction

*Walter Benjamin's "The Work of Art
in the Age of Mechanical Reproduction"*

EVA GEULEN

Of Walter Benjamin's works, none is as often quoted, none has to the same
extent the character of required reading as the essay, "The Work of Art in
the Age of Mechanical Reproduction," written in exile in Paris in 1935–1936.[1]
Even those who otherwise know nothing about Benjamin will at least be
familiar with the famous conclusion to the fifteen theses: aestheticization of
politics versus politicization of art. But the meaning of these catchy formulations is by no means evident. Nonetheless (or perhaps therefore), this brief
work continues to spark controversies and discussions.

As is apparent from even the earliest discussions between Benjamin and
Adorno or Horkheimer (the editor of the "Zeitschrift für Sozialforschung,"
where the oft-revised text first appeared in French translation), the questions Benjamin opened up were considered to have principal significance for
the problems of constructing a materialistic theory in the age of modernism. This continues to be the case. Consequently, an impartial approach to
this overburdened text, which has been a perpetual source of intellectual dis-
putes, is hardly possible any longer, nor is it desirable. However, there has
been a tendency in Benjamin research and reception to reproduce only those
readings and interpretive models that favor the further entrenchment of already entrenched positions. On the one hand, the essay has become a key
text for all those in search of a theoretical counterposition to Adorno's strict
verdict on the "culture industry."[2] On the other hand, Benjamin's attempt to
think in Marxist terms is a hopeless failure, and his theory of film is untenable.[3]

Ironically, this of all texts, with its extraordinarily problematic historical and editorial genesis, has managed to achieve canonical status. Its programmatic character also speaks against this, for nothing becomes obsolete more quickly and more thoroughly than manifestos. The novelty of technical innovation cannot account for its urgency—Benjamin's text arrives relatively late in the history of the theory of film—nor can considerations of a principally theoretical nature have been the sole decisive factor. The text is clearly marked by traces of the conditions of its production; it attempts to formulate an ad hoc response to the political situation of 1935. Its topical circumstances do not, however, exclude concerns of a more principled kind. Indeed, Benjamin's own claims were far from modest. He was, as one reads in his correspondence, "the first to discover several fundamental theorems of a materialist theory of art" (1:984). He left no doubt as to the programmatic manifesto-character of his "polemic theses" (1:473; *Ill.* 218). The catchy character of certain formulations, especially the sloganlike concluding thesis, is dependent as much on its time as its genre.[4] In the notes to the *Arcades Project*, for example, Benjamin repeatedly emphasized that a "blunt conclusion" is preferable to a refined one in materialist works (5:592). But this does not mean that exclusively tactical considerations were decisive in determining the form of the essay. It is more likely that questions of means and ends, conceptions such as tactics and strategy, method and goal, are themselves at issue in this text. This suggests that problems of representation play a particularly important role in this essay and therefore need to be considered in its interpretation.

The context also indicates as much, for the essay on the work of art belongs to the immediate historical and thematic setting of the fragmentary *Arcades Project*. In a letter to Adorno, Benjamin explained the temporary interruption of his work on the *Arcades* with reference to problems of representation; in particular, he found problematic the "forbidden 'literary'" form of his drafts (5:1138). It is possible that the essay on the work of art—about which Benjamin had said in a letter that, with regard to the *Arcades Project*, it stood in "no material relation, methodically however in the most intimate" (1:984)— is an attempt to experiment with a different mode of representation. Adorno noted the stylistic inconsistency between this text and earlier as well as later texts: "A certain simplification of the linguistic means is unmistakable."[5] This is a question of perspective. Adorno's formulations are implicitly based on an instrumental concept of representation, the critique of which Benjamin's essay carries out. It has rightfully been claimed that the text is the "arena of a crisis."[6] Benjamin was aware of this—so much so that one ought to view the text less as the *description* than as the *production* of a crisis in art. The essay on the work of art is not a descriptive text, not an analysis of the status quo. Rather, its theses are themselves the result of that which, in a purely thematic perspective, appears to be its program. The form of the text is the result of a method that has made the laws of cinematic production its own. Just as the film sequence stands in an asymmetrical or nonsimultaneous relationship to its production, so too does the historical continuum that Benjamin constructs originate in discontinuity: "In the studio the mechanical equipment has penetrated so deeply into reality that its pure aspect freed from the foreign substance of equipment is the result of a special procedure, namely the shooting by the specially adjusted camera and the mounting of the shot together with other similar ones" (1:495; *Ill.* 233). In contrast to film, where this constitutive discrepancy generally goes unnoticed, the process of reading reveals it in the contradictions, breaks, and inconsistencies of the unfolding text. To strive to reconstruct the artistic character, the structural artifice of this essay, does not entail its depoliticization.[7] Its mode of representation contains impulses that are decisive for the method of materialist critique. Indeed, there is a continuity between this text and the early works with respect to the ruling affinity of art and critique. But if the early work, as Steiner claims, is characterized by the "birth of critique from the spirit of art," then what is at stake here is, conversely, the birth of art from the spirit of critique.[8]

Benjamin's critical thought is so intimately bound up with its object that one might rightly say that the objects themselves dictate to him the method of their critical representation. Where object and method converge in the process of representation, the concept of method, first of all, loses its conventional meaning, insofar as method is never just method, never a means in relation to ends or a path toward a goal. Secondly, the process of the object's constitution takes precedence over its concept and substance. In the final analysis, the exclusivity with which Benjamin's thought attends to the primacy of representation leads to a form of objectlessness. His thought is, to use one of Adorno's music-theoretical concepts, as "athematic" as it is concrete.[9]

Benjamin's engagement with the question of the relationship between object and method, content and form, goes back as far as his earliest works. One can view the problematic of representation in the epistemological and aesthetic domain as one of the constants of his thought. As early as his commentary on Hölderlin's "Dichtermut" and "Blödigkeit," Benjamin derives the standard of his critical judgment from the formal violence that characterizes the second version of the poem: "The structure of the poem is proof of the insightfulness of Schiller's dictum: 'The real artistic secret of the master craftsman consists in the annihilation of the content through the form'" (2:125). But the problem of representation is not a concern exclusive to art.[10] Rather, representation becomes the essence of the concept of critique, taking the place of the system that was still envisioned in "On the Coming Program of Philosophy." Since the quality of a critique is measured by its capacity for methodological and objective legitimization, questions of method are constantly described and reflected on together with the object of critique.[11] This attests to Benjamin's affinity with the Romantics and with Hegel's speculative method. But the decisive question is how, in any given case of critical representation, the annihilation of the content by the form is to be achieved. Although Benjamin turns against Schlegel in the end, he arrives at his own concept of critique through an engagement with the Romantic conception.[12] The most difficult but also the most rigorous articulation of this concept is worked out in the epistemological-critical preface to the mourning play study. Its object, the *Trauerspiel* (mourning play), is neither an object, nor an empirical fact, but rather an idea, the representation of which is nonetheless realized through empirical means. It takes the extremes as its point of departure: "For the philosophy of art, the extremes become necessary, historical development virtual. Conversely, the extreme of a form or genre is the idea that, as such, is inaccessible to literary history" (1:218). It is well known that this text is one of the most difficult in Benjamin's oeuvre, and by no means does it lend itself to being directly related to the essay on the work of art. But one could rightly say that all of Benjamin's texts have their "epistemological-critical prefaces," and the essay on the work of art, despite its apparent singularity, is no exception.

With film, Benjamin approaches an object that technologically realizes a fundamental principle of his notion of representation: objects are not in themselves given, but rather arise first in their representation. But the affinities between film and its theoretical representation in Benjamin's text are not based on simple analogies. The essay on the work of art is not constructed like a film. We are not dealing with direct references between film and text, but rather with a similarity that determines the relation between object and method, in the text as in film.

Benjamin's relegation of the task of object-constitution to representation is, contrary to popular opinion, not necessarily incompatible with materialist thought. Nonetheless, it is accepted as a fact that Benjamin's attempts to define his method as dialectical-materialist led either to inconsistencies in his thought, or compelled him to abandon earlier ideas in favor of materialism. The second thesis—based on an extremely limited notion of materialism— is nowhere contradicted more decisively than in the essay "On Some Motifs in Baudelaire," written in the first half of 1939. Benjamin has nothing to say about the theoretical and methodological difficulties of a motif-analysis, and yet his essay represents perhaps its only valid model. Although there is no explicit formulation of a relation between his procedure and its object, one can say of Benjamin's method of investigation what he himself establishes as the essential characteristic of the motif of the crowd in Baudelaire: "The masses had become so much a part of Baudelaire *that it is rare to find a description of them in his works*" (1:621; *Ill.* 167, emphasis mine). The crowd motif is not a theme; it is nothing external, but rather a "deeply submerged figure" (1:623) in the work. The motif of the crowd in Benjamin (and in Baudelaire) opens up a dimension that oversteps the bounds of the psychological and intentional domain and is therefore *stricto sensu* a motivating factor. The motif *carries* the work: "This very crowd brings to the city dweller the figure that fascinates" (1:623; *Ill.* 169). What Benjamin reads in Baudelaire anticipates and underscores his own investigation, for methodological reflection unfolds entirely from within the object: the invisible crowd is not just any old motif, but rather a depiction of how the object provides Benjamin with his mode of procedure. Accordingly, his studies have a claim to exemplarity precisely insofar as no binding norms for motif-analytical studies in general may be deduced from them.

In the epistemological notes to the *Arcades Project* Benjamin maintained that this procedure—which must always unfold and legitimate itself anew, thus ensuring in principle its own versatility—was understood by him also, and precisely, as materialist: "Scientific method is characterized by its capacity to lead to new insights and to develop new methods" (5:591). The same formulation, with the addition of "dialectical method," returns at a later point (5:593). If there is a relationship between the *Arcades* and the essay on the work of art, then the latter work would also have to live up to the standard of articulating a new method that corresponds to its objects in such a way that both object and method are developed in mutual reference to one another.

Of course, the work of art essay is quite different from, for example, a work such as the study on Baudelaire. One notices little of the elegance characteristic of Benjamin's mode of procedure in other texts. His method amounts to little more than harsh contrasts, seemingly arbitrary analogies, and interpretations of historical events and dates that border on recklessness in their exclusive reference to film: for example, we read that Dadaism had already worked toward the realization of effects that were to become effortlessly available only with the advent of the new technologies of film. Or we learn that the task of art has always already been to create demands that can be fulfilled only in coming times (1:500; *Ill.* 237). To point out that historiography for Benjamin is always aligned with the "Now-Time" [*Jetzt-Zeit*]—as though it were already clear what the "now" at any give moment is—will hardly suffice to legitimate such apodictic maxims. The meaning of the urgency of the present moment—in Benjamin's emphatic usage of this word, its *topicality* ("Aktualität")—must first be shown. Only then will it be possible to understand the remark that the point of the work of art essay is "to determine the precise place in the present to which my historical construction relates as to its vanishing point" (1:983). The place of the Now-Time is itself not given, but rather is yet to be indicated. If it were otherwise, his historical construction would lapse into arbitrariness. How then does Benjamin justify and how does he answer for his rather immodest claim to view the problem of reproduction "from the perspective of world history" (1:474; *Ill.* 219)? The substance of the theses contributes little in the way of an answer.

In fifteen sections, Benjamin diagnoses the decay of the aura as a symptom of modernity. The receptive stance corresponding to the auratic work of art is that of contemplation. Both are based on the concept of cult-value, which is opposed to the exhibition-value of the work of art that is not only re-producible, but is from the start conceived with reproduction in mind. From the standpoint of reception, film demands and promotes the stance of dis-tracted attention, the structural characteristics of which Benjamin develops with reference to architecture as an ideal type. The other central theme is the modern masses, the advent of which Benjamin relates in temporal and mutually causal terms to the new technologies of reproduction. Fascism and reactionary politics aim to repress the revolutionary character of the new media, in which the masses look themselves in the eye for the first time. The cult of stars testifies to the politically motivated and inherently anachronistic attempt to reanimate the aura of former times. "This is the situation of poli-tics which Fascism is rendering aesthetic. Communism responds by politi-cizing art" (1:508; *Ill.* 242).

So much for the theses. They are not lacking in clarity. But one cannot in-fer from these statements why it is that Benjamin, in the addenda to the essay concerning the "characterization of the particular structure of the work," writes: "It [the work of art essay] does not impose the method of material-ist dialectics on *any old* object, but rather unfolds the method along side that object—in the domain of the arts—that is *coeval* with the method" (1:1049). Since the advent of film is indeed by no means contemporaneous with the "discovery" of the materialist method, it is the task of representation to cre-ate this simultaneity in the first place. Under the condition that simultaneity can be only an effect of representation, Benjamin's text takes on performa-tive characteristics. His procedure demands that the objects and material—texts, historical dates, and so on—first be placed in a position of simultaneity qua representation. This leitmotif of simultaneity, present in the text as the telos of all technological developments, appears in the note quoted above as a precondition, but it is at the same time also the result of a procedure that is alone constituted through representation, and it is only there that it can be sought.

This is already stated in the first sentence of the work: "When Marx undertook his critique of the capitalistic mode of production, this mode was only just beginning. Marx *directed his efforts in such a way* as to give them prog-nostic value. He went *back* to the basic conditions underlying capitalistic pro-duction and *through his representations* showed what could be expected of capi-talism in the future" (1:473; *Ill.* 217, emphasis mine). The opening reference to the work's methodological horizon also contains a program of representation; more specifically, the mode of procedure consists alone in representation, for Marx *"directed his efforts in such a way . . . through his representations."* It was thus a specific mode of representation that enabled Marx to make his prognoses. But Benjamin's commentary on this procedure is contradictory. Since the capitalistic mode of production "was only just beginning," it seems puzzling that Marx was able to "go back" to something that had, in its "fundamental relations," only just begun to establish itself.[13] This tiny gap in the opening sentences is apparently intended to draw attention to the temporal distance that separates Marx from Benjamin. Accordingly, in the following section Benjamin says of the slower transformation of the superstructure in the course of the nineteenth century: *"Only today* can it be indicated what form this has taken" (1:473; *Ill.* 218, emphasis mine). Consequently, it is only when we realize that this characteristic of the Marxist mode of procedure becomes manifest *only today* that the apparent nonsense of these sentences begins to make sense. What Benjamin says of film is applicable to the event that the passage both describes and performs. It "presents a process in which it is impossible to assign to the spectator a viewpoint which would exclude from the actual scene such extraneous accessories as camera equipment" (1:495; *Ill.* 232–33). The spatio-temporal discontinuity noted here serves to indicate that the past, for Benjamin, is always a constructed, represented, and thus distorted past, that history becomes history in the first place only by virtue of its representation. The specific form of the methodological requirement that Benjamin secures in this sentence shows it to be an application, an already executed practical instance of the procedure.

The procedure introduced in an exemplary manner in the first sentence is characteristic of the overall structure of the essay: it describes no "facts" whatsoever, but rather constitutes them in the act of representation.[14] Although Benjamin—with one exception—systematically avoids the future tense, using the descriptive present with regard to film and the historical imperfect with regard to the prehistory of film, he refers to his theses in the foreword as "prognoses": "theses about the developmental tendencies of art under present conditions of production" (1:473; *Ill.* 218). He emphatically stresses that "the concern of our present study" is not based on a concrete "revolutionary criticism of social conditions" (1:473; *Ill.* 231, altered). In a letter written at the time of the essay's conception, Benjamin also insists on this dimension of futureness in his work: "As far as things go with me, I am trying to direct my telescope, through the fog of blood, at an aerial view of the nineteenth century, which I am trying to paint in colors that will appear in a *future state* of the world, liberated from magic" (1:984, emphasis mine). History is to be written from the perspective of a future that does not yet exist. The glaring contradiction between the prognostic intention and the tenses of the verbs used is rendered meaningful when Benjamin's own text is read as an example, as it were, of precisely those tendencies it describes. The text is its own prophecy in a twofold sense. The manner in which film is represented here, the narration of its history—and not film as such—provides a model of future (critical) art. But this prognostic character of the text results from the position it assumes, from the virtual point of a possible future.

That the text was written from the standpoint of a future that had yet to be decided is indicated by certain textual markers. In the afterword, for example, there are two contrary interpretations of the relationship between man and technology juxtaposed in one and the same sentence. Here, the war provides (in the present tense) the proof "that society *was* not mature enough to incorporate technology as its organ, that technology *was* not sufficiently developed to cope with the elemental forces of society" (1:507; *Ill.* 242, emphasis mine). The shift in tense refers to the temporal origin of the text: only from the future can the present be described as the past. On the level of semantics, Benjamin omits the "either/or" construction that might have linked the two sides of the alternative. In the mute undecidedness between these two possibilities, there speaks a future that eludes design, that might turn out thus or otherwise, that is still to come.

Benjamin's epistemological stance is thus not a fixed point, not a critical position, but rather the mark of a virtual point. The fixed position is undone, dissolved in the movement of anticipation of the future and intervention into the past. The legitimization, indeed necessity, of this "positionless" thought even increases with the advent of film. Like Benjamin's text, film demonstrates "a process in which it is impossible to assign one single viewpoint to a spectator" (1:495; *Ill.* 232, altered). Film can and must no longer be approached with the categories and methods of traditional art history. The standpoint of the older discourse was predetermined by the "standpoint of the original" (1:476; *Ill.* 230), which constituted the point of departure for the pursuit of a given tradition. But with the discovery of photography, this standpoint gave way to a "crime scene" (1:485; *Ill.* 226). This is how Atget's photographs of empty streets appear to Benjamin. One can take the forensic-juridical term to mean that theoretical standpoints are, from now on, also crime scenes, characterized by an efficacious anticipation of the future and concomitant intervention into the past.[15]

Benjamin's anticipation of the future and its intertwinement with a re-visionary intervention into the past is made possible and legitimate through the principle of representation: the simultaneity of method and object. Si-multaneity is thus not itself a temporal category, but instead is constitutive of temporality. History, conceived as the intertwinement of the future with the past, is determined by neither of these temporal dimensions. Surely, all the developments *represented* by Benjamin strive toward the telos of simulta-neity, which provides the standard of the correspondence of the represented object and the representational method in film: graphic art "began to keep pace with printing" (1:475; *Ill.* 219). Shortly thereafter, "the process of picto-rial reproduction was accelerated so enormously that it could keep pace with speech" (1:475; *Ill.* 219). Finally, with the advent of film, the decisive tem-poral discrepancy in the development of superstructure and the conditions of production also disappears. But these phenomena owe their simultaneity alone to the simultaneity that is the product of *representation*.

The recognition that the forward-looking character of the past presents itself first in the process of representation leads in this text repeatedly back to the question of film. Benjamin emphasizes that temporally and logically ante-cedent events can be inserted after the fact and even filmed at a later point. "After a knock at the door, one might direct the actor to give a start. Perhaps this jolt did not turn out as desired. Then, the director can resort to an expe-dient: when the actor happens to be at the studio again he has a shot fired be-hind him without being forewarned of it" (1:491; *Ill.* 230, altered). As is well known, Benjamin views modern experience as characterized by the category of shock.[16] But Benjamin does not choose this of all examples only because of the extremity of its character. The "shot" designates in the language of film a cinematic sequence taken from a particular camera-perspective. The lit-eral coinciding of the (gun-)shot and the (film-)shot is an indication that this example is also not merely an example, but rather the very thing itself. It is characteristic that the sentence not only describes the effect of a technologically produced "hysteron proteron," but rather also rhetorically produces it: "*After* a knock at the door, one might direct the actor to give a start" (1:491; *Ill.* 230, emphasis mine). The stage direction for the actor to give a start is logically antecedent to the knocking.

The motif of the shot acquires additional significance in light of a later passage, in which the experience of shock is likewise contained in the image of the shot: "From an alluring appearance or persuasive structure of sound the work of art of the Dadaists became an instrument of ballistics. It hits the spectator like a bullet" (1:502; *Ill.* 238). The Dadaist work of art is a shot only in a metaphorical sense, but in film, the metaphor acquires unmediated physical reality: "By means of its technical structure, film has taken the physical shock effect out of the wrappers in which Dadaism had, as it were, kept it inside the moral shock effect" (1:503; *Ill.* 238). In the word and the substance of the cinematic shot, the figural meaning and its physical instantiation achieve a state of simultaneity.

To the extent that simultaneity of this kind is first produced in the act of representation or reading, it is the product of a temporal sequence of events. But in accordance with its essence, simultaneity is also the condition of possibility of time, in the form, for example, of the intertwinement of the present with the future. Simultaneity is at once precondition as well as result; in other words: the difference between the precondition and the result of the procedure is absorbed by the procedure itself. This simultaneity is not time and has no time.[17]

Scholars have repeatedly referred to Benjamin's philosophy as a "dialectic at a standstill," thinking of his predilection for holding fast, immobilizing, and captivating.[18] The expression is justified, but primarily due to its ambiguity. As a dialectic of representation, Benjamin's dialectic is not just a dialectic that has been brought to a standstill, a dialectic in a state of immobility; rather, the dialectical movement is extended to include even that which is seemingly firm and immobile. More specifically, in its most extreme form—namely, at that point at which everything external has become form and form, object—the movement and the standstill of the dialectic are simultaneous, just as the two mutually exclusive readings of the preposition "*at* a standstill" are *simultaneously possible* and, since they are mutually exclusive, *impossible at the same time*.

One final example will serve to verify that the simultaneity of method and object is only secondarily a question of time. Benjamin repeatedly refers in his essay to the gradual erosion and eventual flattening of traditional distinctions brought about by film; among these, the disintegration of criteria according to which reception and production were held apart. For a long time, a small flock of producers stood before the broad masses of moviegoers. This began to change with the advent of the modern news media, which increasingly enabled readers to participate as authors. With film, this quantitative shift suddenly turns into a qualitative one. The loss of the difference between theory and practice, between the production and critical reception of works of art, rests on the same logic. Benjamin has hopes that the "greater accessibility to analysis" of film will "promote its tendency toward the mutual penetration of art and science" (1:499; *Ill.* 236, altered).[19] This hope is legitimated through the interpretive turn to the past. In section XIII, Benjamin refers to Freud to illustrate, with the help of an analogy between film and psychoanalysis, how "man . . . can represent his environment with the help of mechanical equipment": "*Film* has enriched our field of perception with *methods* which can be *illustrated* by those of Freudian *theory*" (1:498; *Ill.* 235, altered; emphasis mine). Benjamin thus grants the status of method to the images of film, while Freud's psychoanalytical method diminishes to the status of an image, in that it "illustrates" that which is true method only in film. It is true method because the cinematic image is a representation in which method and object stand in a relationship of simultaneity. Freud's methods have enabled an analysis of the realm of memory, but only film has succeeded in deriving a methodological structure from the realm of memory. In other words, film has enabled "entirely new structural formations of the subject matter" (1:500; *Ill.* 236, altered). With the advent of reproduction as representational technique, matter has finally become what it was supposed to be in Benjamin's philosophy all along: representation. This is radical materialism, emancipated from the assumption that matter or material is somehow purely given in itself. But matter is representation only to the extent that representation is more than a passive medium and film more than empirical fact. Rather, its representation must be seen as essential to the respective object of representation. Benjamin sees this ideal, worked out in his own theory of representation—often enough dismissed as esoteric—as potentially realized in film: "In the Soviet Union work itself is given a chance to speak. And its representation in words makes up a part of the skill necessary for its execution" (1:493; *Ill.*

232, altered). In this case, representation has become so essential to its object that it constitutes a "part" of the object.

If it is the technique of cinematic representation that dictates to Benjamin his method—or to put it differently, if Benjamin has elevated film *as* the principle of representation *to* the principle of representation of his own text—then the question remains why this is nowhere explicitly stated in the text, but discloses itself only in its interpretation. Again, the answer to this question—and this is the *circulus vitiosis* of the text, the representation of which is so immanent to the object that a term such as self-referential would be inaccurate—is provided by film. In the cinema, there is no object apart from its representation: "What is really jeopardized . . . is the authority of the object" (1:477; *Ill.* 221). The thing, the object, hands its authority over to its representation. The dialectic of this process, and that of Benjamin's text, consists in the fact that there is no longer any mediation, neither one between method and object, nor one that might fall to representation, for representation is itself the object (and the method), and film is accordingly pure mediation.[20] By the same token, technological reproduction "is directly founded on the technology of production" and is thus immediately inherent to the mediation.[21] Benjamin discusses the role of props and actors in film as opposed to the stage in the nineteenth footnote, quoting "Pudovkin's statement that 'the performance of an actor which is connected with an object and is built around it . . . is always one of the strongest methods of cinematic construction'" (1:490; *Ill.* 247, altered). Film is indeed the star *performer* ("Haupt*darsteller*") of this text. Benjamin continues, "Film is thus the first art form capable of demonstrating how matter plays tricks on man" (1:490; *Ill.* 247). In Benjamin's representation of film as representation, matter becomes palpable. The terms "Handgriff" (grasp), "Handhabe" (handling) and "Handgreiflich" (palpable, also manhandling) form a semantic field of their own in the text: "The liquidation of the traditional value of the cultural heritage . . . is most palpable in the great historical films" (1:478; *Ill.* 221, altered). And in another passage: "Thus it becomes palpable that the nature that speaks to the camera is different from that which speaks to the naked eye" (1:500; *Ill.* 236, altered). For the time being, we should defer the problem of the latent violence inherent in the expression "Handgreiflich." More important still is the question—to which we must also defer for the moment—whether and in what manner this violence is different from that of early film theory, in which cult elements were read into film with "blind violence" (1:485) and "unprecedented ruthlessness" (1:487; *Ill.* 227, altered). What is to be understood by "Handgreiflichkeit" is initially indicated by the beautiful and succinct comparison of the magician and the surgeon (1:495f.; *Ill.* 233f.). The latter manhandles when he feels about with his hand among the organs without looking the person as a whole in the eye. His nearness to the organs is coeval with his distance to the totality of the person. The precise and resolute, but also strangely violent, manner in which Benjamin's text deals with its material derives its justification once again from the material. Film accommodates the needs of the crowd "to *get hold* of an object at very close range" (1:479; *Ill.* 223, emphasis mine). Accordingly, Benjamin names photography and film the "most handy procedures" (1:484; *Ill.* 225, altered) for acquiring insight into current changes. But such handling takes place "under the hand" (1:503), like the tactile reception of architecture: the hand is not the means, but rather the unmediated medium.

To write history means: to quote history

—*Arcades Project*

Thus far, I have restricted my reading of the work of art essay with regard to the problematic of representation to examples and cases that do not touch on the core of the argument, the decay of the aura. But precisely the theory of the aura—on which the entire essay rests—is also subject to the conditions sketched out here. The aura differs, however, from the other examples in that it is not an historical "fact," but rather an historico-philosophical concept. The thesis of the primacy of representation must not only prove its value with reference to the concept and theory of the aura; rather, the reference to the aura will serve to substantiate and more precisely state the thesis.

The oft-noted ambivalence characteristic of Benjamin's attitude toward the loss of the aura, which comes to light as though involuntarily in the sullen descriptions of the melancholic beauty of early photographic portraits, is, in any case, not a question of subjective positions, but rather is based on the object itself, that is, representation. The theory of the aura is distinguished above all by its dual character. It is just as much a theory of history as it is an historical marker of the theoretical incision that serves as the point of departure for Benjamin's remarks.

In light of the futile discussions about whether the loss of the aura is to be welcomed or regretted, it is important to emphasize that the aura, ephemeral and anything but concrete, is less a concept than a performative intervention. The theory of the aura articulated in sections II–IV stands clearly under the sign and under the title of the last sentence of the first section. Nothing is more revealing for the analysis of modern technologies of reproduction, Benjamin writes, "than the influence these two different manifestations—the reproduction of works of art and the art of the film—have had on art in its traditional form" (1:475; *Ill.* 220, altered). The theory of the aura is an attempt to circumscribe history, not only practically but also theoretically, from a standpoint that has no factual basis. That is, the concept of the aura must mark and localize itself from within the essay. The aura belongs to the vocabulary of a virtual, future historiography. As an anticipation of the future, it brings about an intervention into history, thereby indicating what the present is. The aura, as the distinguishing feature of traditional art, becomes visible only to the extent that art has lost this character. The manifestation of the aura arises out of its loss.

This is clarified by the remarks on the concept of authenticity, or of the original, which precede the detailed exposition of the aura: "At the time of its origin a medieval picture of the Madonna could not yet be said to be 'authentic.' It became 'authentic' only during the succeeding centuries and perhaps most strikingly so during the last one" (1:476; *Ill.* 243). Authenticity is a belated effect. In the beginning was not the original, but rather the reproduction, which makes the concept of authenticity possible in the first place. Authenticity becomes "authentic" only against the background of reproducibility. That means, however, that authenticity is compromised from the start, inauthentic from the start, for its origin lies not in itself, but rather in its opposite, reproduction.[22]

Like authenticity, the aura is essentially determined through its loss. The decline does not happen to, but rather constitutes the aura. The content and contours of the definition of the aura are determined by the fact that it appears only as it is disappearing. The distance Benjamin takes from any definitive explanation finds direct expression in the definition: "the unique phenomenon of a distance, however close it may be" (1:479; *Ill.* 222). One can apparently get hold of a definition of the aura as little as one can get hold of the aura itself.

The explication of the aura does not proceed from a pregiven point of departure, but rather is constituted in a series of steps and under a variety of perspectives.[23] In the second section, the aura is conceived in relation to the category of authenticity with regard to works of art. In the third section, by contrast, Benjamin introduces the aura as a dimension of historically variable perceptions and illustrates its concept with reference to natural objects. At one point, the aura is defined as a fragile temporal core (1:477; *Ill.* 221) that characterizes the work of art. At another, Benjamin explains that the perception of the aura "withers" (1:477; *Ill.* 221) like an atavistic organ. And finally: "The peeling away of an object's cover, the smashing of its aura" (1:479; *Ill.* 223, altered). Peeling away—an operation reminiscent of the liberation of the shock effect from its moral packaging—is apparently not the same as smashing, where one is more likely to think of a kernel than a peel. But it is precisely the unmediated juxtaposition of both formulations, which are indeed secretly linked by the affinity between kernel and peel, that refers to the objective ambivalence of the operation in question.

Jürgen Habermas has claimed, "Benjamin does not explain this deritualization of art."[24] For lack of a better alternative, Habermas makes do with Max Weber's concept of disenchantment, which could not be more wrong, for the problem of reproduction is not the loss of enchantment, but rather the fact that it perennially returns in the "stale enchantment of the commodity" (1:492; *Ill.* 231, altered). However, the loss of the aura requires no further explanation, for the aura itself is the explanation. To the extent that Benjamin attempts to circumscribe history "in its name," the aura is just as much the result of a shattered tradition as the act, the deed of shattering. That is why the aura is not a concept in the classical sense, but rather in the Hegelian one: act and result at once. That a concept such as the aura has at all become conceivable is thus a sign that art is no longer auratic. But the fact that Benjamin describes the history of art from the perspective of its aura, and the manner in which he describes this, gives the concept performative qualities. The theory of the aura itself actively contributes to the "the liquidation of the traditional value of the cultural heritage" (1:478).

This form of conceptual intervention has its model in Hegel's *Lectures on*

Aesthetics. The function and conception of the decline of the aura are comparable to what Hegel articulates under the rubric of "the end of art": "The peculiar mode to which artistic production and works of art belong no longer satisfies our supreme need. We are above the level at which works of art can be venerated as divine, and actually worshipped."[25] Benjamin quotes a similar passage verbatim in the tenth footnote. The references to Hegel's text are intended to support the thesis that the polarity between the exhibition-value and the cult-value, which has no place in the idealist system, was nonetheless able to "to announce itself as clearly as possible within the limits of Idealism" (1:482; *Ill.* 244–45). To substantiate this, Benjamin refers to Hegel's remark that "fine art has arisen . . . in the church . . . , although it has already gone beyond its principle as art" (1:482; *Ill.* 244–45). The analogue to this in Benjamin's essay is that authenticity appears at that point in the course of its development where the authentic ceases to exist.

In Hegel's aesthetics, the end of art is not a fact, but rather an event. Art comes to an end in Hegel's lectures: "Thought and reflection have taken their flight above fine art."[26] Only as it has come to its end, sublated in its philosophical exposition and determination of the beautiful, does art become what it truly is (has been): the sensual appearance of the idea. That is why Hegel calls the beautiful in art an ideal. The *recognition* that art enables the sensual intuition of the general and the particular in their mediation cannot be achieved by art itself. It occupies its privileged position by virtue of the decree of philosophy. Art cannot recognize what it is in reality, for it is "only" the idea of intuition. It is only through philosophy that art comes to its truth, thanks to the fact that art was already a product of spirit, which comes to itself, as Hegel puts it, in the philosophical system. In the introduction to the lectures on Aesthetics, Hegel writes: "The beauty of art is the beauty that is born—and born again, that is—of the mind."[27] Art is reborn in philosophy, which brings forth the concept of the beautiful of art. This rebirth presupposes the end of art as the highest form of the self-representation of spirit: "In all these respects art is, and remains for us, on the side of its highest destiny, a thing of the past."[28] Accordingly, it is not the case that art ceased at some point to exist, and that philosophy thereafter suddenly found itself confronted with the question of its end. It is precisely the opposite: philosophical reflection put an end to art. The real problem that is thus bequeathed to all post-Hegelian aesthetic reflection is not the end of the production of art, but rather the end of the possibility of a form of aesthetic reflection that *does not* bring about the end of art.[29]

Benjamin's concept of the aura and his comments on authenticity participate in this Hegelian tradition. That the decline of the aura is "traditional" in the substantive rather than any merely nominal sense only goes to show once again that the liquidation of the value of tradition is possible not from any external perspective, but only through recourse to a tradition.

Everything now depends on whether and how Benjamin's staging of the decline of the aura differs from Hegel's end of art. While art, in its philosophical exposition, has de facto come to an end in Hegel's eyes, Benjamin maintains the preliminary character of his constructions. That is, they remain at the level of construction and sketch.

Hegel's Owl of Minerva commences her flight at dusk. For Benjamin, it is not dusk but midday that is the moment of knowledge. In a letter to Kitty Steinschneider-Marx, Benjamin writes, "It is almost as if these considerations [concerning the work of art essay], which concealed themselves in the early morning of the dawning day, have become accessible to my grasp only at being brought out into the light of noon" (1:984). Noon is the time of simultaneity, the time of decision and of stillness. While Hegel attempts to overtake history and art through philosophical representation, Benjamin is concerned with the opening up and fragmentation of representation under the rule of simultaneity: "Then came film and burst this prison-world asunder by the dynamite of the tenth of a second, so that now, in the midst of its far-flung ruins and debris, we calmly and adventurously go traveling" (1:499f.; *Ill.* 236f.). The purpose of representation is not to catch up with the past, but rather to free it and to open it up. Or, to use one of the central concepts of the historico-political theses and of the *Arcades Project*: the past is to become citable. Tradition wants to preserve its objects, in order to preserve their self-identity, while citation preserves as well as destroys, because no citation remains the same from context to context. The citation preserves tradition in that it destroys it ever anew, because the citation puts the new and the old in a relation of simultaneity. In this sense Benjamin demands of his *Arcades Project*, "The work must take the art of quoting without quotation marks to the highest level" (5:572). The omission of quotation marks indicates that the difference between text and commentary, interpretation and its object, and above all the difference between the original and the cited reproduction, disappears. In the laws of cinematic production, it becomes obvious what quotation without original is supposed to mean.

This form of activation and topicalization in the act of representation is of decisive significance, not only for the representation of the aura but for the essay as a whole. The relationship of his procedure to the procedure of film becomes apparent in one of the most difficult and enigmatic passages of this text: "The technique of reproduction detaches the reproduced object from the domain of tradition. By making many reproductions it substitutes a plurality of copies for a unique existence. And in permitting the reproduction to meet the beholder or listener in his own particular situation, it reactivates the object reproduced" (1:477; *Ill.* 221). The grammatical subject of the sentence is the technique of reproduction, so that one must take it to mean: the technique of reproduction reproduces the reproduction. This reproduction to the second power enables the inclusion of the process that is the object of Benjamin's interest. By enabling "the reproduction to meet the beholder or listener in his own particular situation," reproduction "*reactivates* the object reproduced" (1:477; *Ill.* 221, emphasis mine). Radicalized reproduction, what Benjamin refers to here as the reproduction of reproduction, makes possible its topicalization. In the relationship of the various definitions of the aura to one another, but also in the relationship of film to text, a process plays itself out that Benjamin speaks of as a consequence of the technology of reproduction, and in fact speaks in such a way that the object of speech is created in the act of speaking.

It is difficult to determine exactly what Benjamin means by the reproduction of reproduction.[30] But for the text and its method—and this alone is at issue here—a decisive insight concerning the relationship between representation (in film) and representation (in text) lies hidden within the formulation. What has been referred to thus far as the simultaneity of method and object in representation can be stated now with greater precision. Benjamin's text reproduces the cinematic method of reproduction as representation. Only by virtue of the representation to the second power achieved in Benjamin's text can film claim for itself the topicality that Benjamin grants it. The reproduction of reproduction is what enables cinematic representation and its linguistic representation to appear simultaneously in the first place. The reproduction of reproduction determines in the final instance not only the relationship of the text to its object, but also it marks the limits of its simultaneity. The reproduction of reproduction is achieved not by film per se, but rather by its representation in Benjamin's text. The difference between the technology of reproduction in film and its specific representation in Benjamin's text is thereby given its due. This difference marks the text as a program not yet fulfilled.

The circumstances under which Benjamin wrote the essay on the work of art were characterized by dictatorship and violence. This had left behind not only thematic but also stylistic traces. That to become "palpable" (*Handgreiflich*) can also mean to become violent is only one of a series of examples of truly militant formulations in this text. The exhibition value begins to "*drive back* [cult value] *all along the line*. But cult value does not give way without resistance. It takes up position in a final *entrenchment*" (1: 485; *Ill*. 225, altered; emphasis mine). The shot and the bullet also contribute to this gesture, and the proximity between tactical and tactile may in like fashion be taken as less than entirely accidental. After all, the essay is, in Benjamin's words, a "weapon" (1:473; *Ill*. 218).

The final sentences of the essay not only attest to violence but also are themselves not free of violence: "The imperialistic war is a rebellion of technology, a technology that realizes, in the form of 'human material,' those claims which society has stripped of their natural material" (1:507; *Ill*. 242, altered). This sentence is just as problematic as the notion that technology can be "raped" (1:507; *Ill*. 242). The difference between this war and the violence of Benjamin's formulations is decisive. What separates the one from the other form of violence is identical with what separates cinematic representation from Benjamin's representation of cinematic representation: war is a revolt of technology, the revolutionary demands of which have gone unfulfilled. That is, this form of technology is mere reproduction, for it has been prevented from becoming what it is able to become in Benjamin's text. Instead of the reproduction of reproduction, which brings about a topicalization, the technology of reproduction has been put at the service of production, enslaved as a means and violently subjugated to the ends of production.

The problem of ends and means in the domain of violence had occupied Benjamin for some time. In the early essay "Toward a Critique of Violence," he differentiates between a law-positing and a law-preserving authority. This differentiation can be applied to the work of art essay: just as fascism tries violently to preserve the old laws—the outmoded order of private property—so did the ruthlessly interpretive film theory violently seek to hold fast to outdated aesthetic standards. Benjamin's essay, one could say, attempts to place the new law in its right. But in the absence of the final, divine authority, which is never "a means of divine enforcement" (2:203) (Benjamin calls this the "sovereign" [*waltende*] authority), a final decision cannot be made, either about the success of this attempt or about its authority. In this ambivalence lies also an autolegitimization of this text, as much a demonstration of its topicality as of its historicity.

What is specifically inhuman in Benjamin's thought is that it threatens to annihilate the very objects to which its representation is dedicated. Benjamin himself emphasized the "cannibalistic urbanity" (1:990f.) of the work of art essay. But this alone, claims Benjamin, pays tribute to the object, preserving its integrity by destroying it. When Benjamin commended the cannibalistic qualities of his essay to Adorno, he added that it was precisely this that attested to his love of the objects. Of Baudelaire's poetry he said that what falls prey to it is by no means destined to be cast aside (1:666). It could be that Benjamin's inhumanity is the very essence of humanity—or could at some point have been, if his thought were under way.

Translated by Eric Baker

SIX

Suicitation

Benjamin and Freud

LAURENCE A. RICKELS

Questions of influence tend to fall in line behind a certain couples therapy or theory that works out the proper settlement between two distinct persona or bodies. One corpus has lent another corpus the helping and. But this *UND*, in German, is also just a breath away from *HUND*, the dog Benjamin designated in *Der Ursprung des deutschen Trauerspiels* (The origin of the German mourning play) as mascot for the melancholic sensibility (1:329).[1] From Freud's side of this "shaking and" story, influence was always strapped across parallel tracks, stuck in alternation and alteration between parallel universals, the separate words or worlds of transference and of telepathy.

While copyright versus copy-writing, plagiarism or improper burial has been our concern throughout the datable history of that unconscious Freud elaborated in its working relationship to repression, resistance, transference —the era Adorno and Horkheimer referred to as the "dialectic of enlightenment"—a certain anxiety of influence is really no older than the real time of appearance of Freud's thought. Psychoanalysis was the first and remains the only science of influence. But whenever psychoanalysis makes an intervention, a spectacular form of misunderstanding or resistance emerges right out of the interpersonal columns. The so-called psychologizing moment in psychoanalysis is really the sociologizing or interpersonalizing moment of resistance to Freud's intrapsychic model. Where everything gets taken so interpersonally, what is overlooked are the inside-out—now transferential, now telepathic—relations between self and other that move forward what we can think about as influence only since Freud. The issue of influence thus always goes back to Freud, his science, and the resistance to that science, in all its aspects, including its history and its influence.

That is why influence can't be measured by standards of sameness. Only what has been mutated, digested in part—part object, part objection—resisted, disavowed, and displaced can count as influence on the sliding scale from transference to telepathy. Plagiarism, the ancient direct hit of theft and improper burial, was in turn diversified to include, just the same, an influence that is out of context, one that is never to be, bearing the status of foreign body, but including therefore a kind of uncanny or outer-corpus experience of transmission, thought transference, or projective identification bearing unholy resemblance, in both parts, to the unread.

The Origin of the German Mourning Play and Freud's Schreber study are the same book. Same in the sense, for example, that Freud's *Civilization and its Discontents* and Nietzsche's *On the Genealogy of Morals* are the same book. Same, as in Eternal Return of the Same, as in an almost telepathic compatibility between two bodies even or especially when few missing links can be discovered or constructed between them.

The struggle for acceptance of *The Origin of the German Mourning Play* as Benjamin's initiation writing into a university career began already in 1919. The main period of composition, generally considered a turning point in Benjamin's writing, fell somewhere between 1924 and 1925, and the publication of the completed work waited out three more years of diplomatic negotiation after Benjamin had withdrawn it from its immediate context of academic intrigue. Nevertheless, Benjamin could also date the beginning of the *Origin* book back to 1916, in time for his first essays on the distinction between tragedy and mourning play and on language as such. That places the origin of the *Origin* book one full year prior to the first undeniable contact with Freud's thought in seminars Benjamin attended at the University of Bern; these seminars were taught by Haeberlin, who was given to consider Freud's ideas among psychologies of suggestion and of the occult. Before Freud's datable influence, therefore, there were original works by Benjamin that Benjamin self-cited in the later book. We are already familiar with the passing thought that any work of collection refers always also to a melancholic fantasy of self-collection. In Benjamin's corpus there is a related endeavor, a work of citation that implies throughout and is practiced in large part as a mode of self-citation or *sui*-citation. Benjamin's earliest writing makes a ghost appearance in the *Origin* book, while the *Arcades Project* was a vast recycler that began at home base, all along running beside or inside

Benjamin's other writing projects. Benjamin's obscure relationship to Freud represents the gap that kept the corpus, for the time being, from performing the complete act of suicide. What fell by the wayside of this gap, increasing the range of detour, were the out-of-corpus experiences that began preceding all the origins of self-citation.

The earliest date Benjamin gives Freud inside his own thought is a threesome that counts in Schreber's *Memoirs of My Nervous Illness*. In 1928 Benjamin published a short illustrated piece entitled "Books by the Insane: From My Collection." He begins by recalling what difficulties he had giving the works of the insane their respective generic brandings as autobiography or philosophy, for instance. It turned out there was nothing extraneous about the deranged sensibilities of their authors. By default or displacement the books found themselves collected together as their own subsection or genre. In 1918, Benjamin recalls, the Schreber book came into his collection. "Had I already heard about the book back then? Or did I only discover the study a few weeks later, the one by Freud in the third volume of his *Short Writings on the Theory of Neurosis*? (Leipzig, 1913). It's all the same. The book immediately grabbed me."[2] While the discovery of the Schreber book and his knowledge of Freud's study are all the same, Benjamin shows an acute awareness of Freud in the context of language speculation, the zone of his own work's original origin. He points to the connection between the primal language Schreber elaborates in his mad memoirs and Freud's examination of the opposite meanings simultaneously contained within so-called primal words. When he summarizes some of the highlights of Schreber's book he throws the high beam on what is so comparable about Schreber's divine zone of legibility inhabited only by corpses to the focus on the empty world of the melancholic state and its allegorical perspective given in his *Origin* book: "The sense of destruction of the world, not uncommon in paranoia, governs the afflicted to such an extent that the existence of other human beings can be understood by him only as deception and simulation, and, in order to come to terms with them, he refers to 'quickly made up men,' 'wonder dolls,' 'miraculated people' etc." (1:616).

One year later, in 1929, Benjamin reviewed psychoanalyst Alexander Mette's book *On Relations Between Language Peculiarities in Schizophrenic and Poetic Productions*. This was more than some stray assignment. That an exchange of understanding between psychoanalysis and Benjamin on the narcissistic neuroses or the psychoses (including melancholia) had transpired seemed confirmed, and without reservation, when Mette went on in 1931 to review Benjamin's *Origin* book for *Imago*.[3] This just goes to show that even bad press is better than a good repression. Benjamin makes Mette's interpretation of mad language and poetry part of the problem, not the resolution: there is "something desperate," in other words, about Mette's "play with symptoms, this conjoining of schizophrenic and lyrical texts."[4] He charges Mette with psychologizing or interpersonalizing conflict and thus getting lost in overextensions of his analyses to a psychology of the lyrical poet or in boundary constructions or blendings between schizo versus poetic production or insanity versus normalcy. Mette, who never cites Freud in this study, and thus not even the Schreber analysis, should have followed Freud, Benjamin implies, by addressing it all on a theory's own terms as mental illness. Finally Benjamin overcharges Mette, on the other and, with overlooking the original context or contest of schizo conflict inside another's provenance, language as such. If only Mette had recognized schizophrenia as a "movement in the medium of language and thus as a phenomenon that can be understood only in its vital contrast to the language community." While both dive down into language's primal time, the poet goes ahead in "the diving bell of artistic form and with full responsibility and for a set duration," the schizo goes it all alone down there "with the treasures he is unable to lift up."[5] But if the schizophrenic is worse off than the poet, it is not because he lacks the foundation, formation, infrastructure, metabolism to take it in and then put it back out there in the mode of objectification, but rather because the objectification has already been accomplished collectively by language itself. The schizo thus struggles to put his own calling into a process of language that already took all calls, and just holds them, holds them together.[6]

The melancholic, according to Benjamin's *Origin* book, holds a different degree of conflict or psychosis than the schizo poet. He doesn't dive down beyond the world or words of psychoanalytic understanding. The melancholic betrays the world to knowledge. But his submergence takes the dead things back up within their contemplation, and thus rescues them.[7] According to Mette's 1931 review, Benjamin has assembled his *Origin* book along lines recognizable to the analytically oriented reader, ranging from the psychological features of melancholia, madness, and mourning, to their unique language characteristics.[8] The symptoms of melancholia and mania link and separate the tyrant and the martyr as two phases of one psychopathological continuum. The intriguer lies somewhere between that sliding scale and a functionalism that takes the counterpart. He has a humorous side that lines him up with future transformations of the mourning play.[9] Just like the intriguer, Mette won't let go of his designs on the desperate scenario of reading. After recapping the dynamics of the baroque language medium in Benjamin's terms, Mette concludes with a renewed attempt to get close with his understanding of the unique linguistic characteristics of schizophrenia.[10] Mette concludes, however, with a Freud-on-Schreber-compatible diagnosis: "From another perspective, the peculiar juxtaposition of melancholia and mania and the strange agreement with schizophrenic phenomena point to a severe conflict around recognition from the superego, in other words, around the maintenance of object cathexes."[11]

It is not about a direct correspondence between the materials of psychotic discourse and Benjamin's insights into the linguistic character of the baroque mourning play. That would mean, for example, taking for granted (and leaving to the side) Mette's own intriguing transference on the one hand and, on the other, that allegorical dimension or dementia Freud admits, even if by another name, via the concept of endopsychic perception. At this point of excess of self-reflection, which in turn allows access to psychoanalysis on allegorical terms, the delusional formations, which indeed could be reformulated in terms of persecution, martyrdom, and rescue, wash up onto the outer limits of Freud's own theorization. Freud's inside view of Schreber's delusions catches rays belonging at the same time to an endopsychic perception, one that already reflects back the same view and even the theory of these paranoid views within views. Freud thus reaches the limit concept of endopsychic or paranoid reading, which borders on the same suicitational impulse that drives Benjamin's allegorical project onward.

What is, at least materially, most compelling, however, about the sameness of the two books is the way both reintroduce Goethe's *Faust* to the setting of the paranoid or melancholic world, where one world's destruction is another world's reprojection or allegorical resurrection out of a libido of self-absorption. Schreber's delusional system, so recognizable to the allegorical reader of the melancholic state, represents an act of recovery. Freud's guess is already another man's ghost: at the time Schreber was writing his memoirs, his older brother was already deceased; he had skipped the class of delusional patients and gone down the one-way street of suicide. Not only suicide, however, but recovery too is already equally implicated in the world that empties out in the mode of catastrophe: "The delusion-formation, which we take to be a pathological product, is in reality an attempt at recovery, a process of reconstruction. Such a reconstruction after the catastrophe is more or less successful, but never wholly so." [12] This surprising turn away from the downbeat of psychotic shutdown and fadeout to the positive thinking that is delusion was introduced with Freud's quotation from *Faust*. A chorus mourns the world Faust has destroyed inside and out only then to pick up where that left off and enjoin him, the overman, the over-and-out man, to build it all up brand new from within himself. Between the lines of both Freud's and Benjamin's silent readings, one cannot but recall that Faustian striving is itself constituted as the deferral of a suicidal impulse that overtakes Faust in the setting of his academic world and almost compels him to cut off his life to spite his fate or father. The motor of his recovery is his splitting image, Mephistopheles, the spirit of negativity. Recovery, according to Freud's analysis of Schreber's case, can often only run for the cover of negativity. His persecution or selection by God at least—at last!—recaptures some relation to the world. For Schreber the limit concept of this recovery, up there with big brother, was suicidal withdrawal into a dead world, the world of the dead, inside him. But one need not develop the psychotic's closure or delusions as a result of these detachments of our libidinal connection. It happens in "normal mental life," Freud reassures us and adds, "and not only in periods of mourning." [13] The potentially suicidal detachment, therefore, in its alternation with projection from out of our narcissistic libido of a whole culture of recovery (some call it California), offers another way to get around losses that is not the one-way consumer choice between mourning or melancholia.

While fascinated by and clearly familiar with "psychiatric" interpretation, Benjamin in his 1928 review of his own mad book collection declines attempting such a clinical retelling of the Schreber case, in particular of all that led to the mechanism or state that he finds most compelling, namely, "the stations this illness passed through all the way to this remarkably strict and happy encapsulation of the delusional world." [14] Benjamin closes the review with a guarded, tongue-in-check, update on difficulties attending acceptance of insane works for publication. Our tolerance and interest must have risen by now. "And yet I've known for a few months now about a manuscript that in

terms of human and literary value at least equals Schreber's book, and sur-
passes it in accessibility, and which nevertheless seems as hard as ever to sell
to a reputable press." [15] How could Benjamin not be referring, at least at the
same time, to his own book, *The Origin of the German Mourning Play*, as the
other mad book with a Freudian reception already in place? Although by 1928
it had at last survived its submitted manuscript status, his *Origin* book would
for Benjamin never shake its martyr role on the stage of intrigue.

As summarized by Benjamin in 1928, Schreber's delusional system, which
also extends divine understanding from ray ways to the railways, looks forward to Benjamin's mediatic translation of his earlier work on mourning
and melancholia into the terms and resettings of "The Work of Art in the
Age of its Mechanical Reproducibility." That work appeared in 1936, after
Adorno had pressed for a revision that left out one moment of recognizable Freud-compatibility, Benjamin's reading of Mickey Mouse's relationship to the psychotic structure of mass psychology as a control-releasing
"inoculation," another form of "encapsulation," one that this time doubled
and contained the violence and mass mutuality of identification. [16] In 1939,
in time for Freud's passing, Benjamin's Baudelaire essay admitted psychoanalysis into the foreground of his thought around references to trauma,
repetition, anxiety defense, and, in sum, the nonoriginal origin of the ego. [17]
At this time Freud's name enters Benjamin's corpus together with the concepts of repetition compulsion and death drive. Freud's own development of
this kernel form of his drive theory, one that he had received from Sabina
Spielrein in the performatively fast-forwarded form of her 1912 monograph,
"Destruction as the Cause of Becoming," was articulated with delay, in turn
performing the alternations between eros and thanatos within the big picture of his theory. In 1912, the time of his composition of *Totem and Taboo*,
Freud still resided in an earlier time zone, that of the death wish, mourning,
and haunting. Before there could be, for Freud, the jump cut to the ultimate
drive theory, there had to be mourning and melancholia, death-wish projection and funereal identification, the Schreber case for paranoia, and all
the vestigial pointers toward an interpretation of the technologization and
trauma-internalization that crowds these moments. That a shock of recognition and repetition should accompany Freud's acceptance within the public
corpus of Benjamin's name is also fitting, in the uncanny mode.

In 1936, the year that saw completion of the transition from the *Origin* book to the mass-mediatically framed syndication of that work, Benjamin corrects and protects, in his letter to Werner Kraft of January 30, his theory of language, which overlaps with the origin of the *Origin* book, the origin of that death-driven part of his corpus pressing toward sui-citation. He wants to give the theory as a whole a shot at continuity, continuity with all that is postmetaphysical about his work, a post Benjamin scholars tend to see being addressed for the first time around 1925, usually, by association, in Marx's name:

> As for your comment on my essay on the theory of language, whose limits were prescribed by its form: it does not anticipate anything about a "metaphysics" of language. And I have structured the essay, albeit not at all manifestly, so that it leads precisely to the place where my own theory of language begins. I put this in writing in a very short programmatic note several years ago on Ibiza. I was very surprised to find significant correlations between this theory and Freud's essay "Telepathy and Psychoanalysis," which you can find in the 1935 Almanach of psychoanalysis.

Just as Benjamin leads us to the end of a work where his theory begins, we get a completely phantasmatic reference to Freud's parallel work. At least I couldn't find it. An essay "Psychoanalysis and Telepathy," which was published posthumously in the 1940s, but which was presented to Freud's close circle of disciples in the early 1920s, and may thus have been transmitted and paraphrased by work of mouth, elaborates various cases of wish and deathwish fulfillment that become legible as such between the lines of books that can't but then cannot but be remembered.

Adorno, the first philosopher to accept psychoanalysis as a major part of his own thought's formation, nevertheless sought to straighten out a metaphorical tendency in Benjamin's materialist reading of mass-media society by demanding implicitly that Benjamin sacrifice Freud compatibility to compatibility with Marx's dialectic. This exchange took place, however, according to the terms of Adorno and Benjamin's couples therapy, which, in Marx's name, linked and limited their "and" to an interpersonal or sociological alliance.

Benjamin (like Kafka) admired Freud from the distance of total following, the displacement of telepathic syndication or translation. It was like the long-distance love affair with the name Benjamin elaborated on several occasions. And yet, at the same time, in the pileup of textual bodies and names that

Benjamin collected, cited, libidinized up front, Freud seems just about the only name in history that, at least in name, doesn't come under the allegorist's contemplation. Adorno for his part, his astute and daring readings of or with psychoanalysis notwithstanding, could stumble over a piece of literalmindedness he brought to the task, the one that is always around anyway, a cornerstone in fact of a task not of translation but of application. In particular, the prospect of and prospects for homosexuality in the psychology of groups and within perverse and psychotic structures was decontextualized by Adorno in the literalizing mode. This literalization of the psychoanalytic complex of homosexuality, which is where Freud's speculations on mourning, melancholia, sublimation, and technologization always begin and return to, contributes even to Adorno's sponsorship of psychoanalysis a kind of monumentalism that transferentially distorts in a manner resembling idealization many of Freud's concepts and contexts. Adorno's entire relationship with psychoanalysis breaks down at the point of his projection onto homosexuality of a certain cold rigor and reductive same-differencing that he suddenly was all along picking up from orthodox analysis. These same cluster projections blast psychoanalysis with an equal share in one homopathologization. The couples context for this breakdown of relations with Freud, for Adorno's social snubs and social studies, which is all so interpersonal, belongs, already on the upbeat, to the ideal marriage Adorno proposed between psychoanalysis and Marxism. How long could Adorno maintain the balancing acts between Freud's science and Marxism as though their division of labor represented equal partnership in the development of his and Benjamin's understanding of mass culture? In the case of Schreber Adorno, while still on the good side of his unexamined relations with Freud, saw the study as a cautionary fable about reactionary political formations that is where all the degrees of repressed homosexuality start fitting into psychohistories (which are really sociologies) of totalitarianism, directly in Canetti for example, under cover of displacement in *Anti-Oedipus*, and I understand still to this day. On a bad day Adorno and company could see forever that the psychoanalytic reading of paranoia was a paranoid reading of psychoanalysis, the one that gave it all away.

There may be a model here for the reconstruction of psychoanalytic influence on contemporary thought around two resistance obstacles: Freud's inclusions of the death wish (together with haunting and techno-projection) and of homosexuality (which in turn includes as part of its complex of associations the other worlds of the group, the pervert, the psychotic, the gadget lover). One line of defense lies in the literalization and expulsion of homosexuality always in the context of another couples theory; the other, which is closely related, lies in the forced marriage between psychoanalysis and Marxism, which similarly serves to straighten something out in Freud through splitting or division of labor. The necessity of resistance and delay in the reception of Freud's thought—because the station break guarantees, if only by default, although by no default of its own, that there will be time left for the good works of transference and mourning (in which such concepts as the death wish must be metabolized in fact)—finds one kind of confirmation in Benjamin's complicated or paradoxical case and the other kind in Adorno's unexamined and demonic or demonizing ambiguity or ambivalence with regard to, with best regards to Freud. Benjamin left Freud out of his all-out work of citation, as though it alone could stand proof against his original project's totalization. Thus he turned up all the volumes of a silent reading between his project or projection and Freud.

Around the issue of intrigue, emptied-out worlds, and allegorical rescue, Benjamin just had to recognize the address to his thought in works of and on madness. Persecution doesn't just keep happening to you. In "The Uncanny," Freud's companion piece to *Beyond the Pleasure Principle*, reference to the eternal return of the same is made above the woman in love who was always surviving her husbands. Repetition is a structure not an intention, not an exchange conducted between two persons or partners.

Benjamin was drawn to two scenes as different, according to Freud's Schreber study, as the repression mechanism that led to Schreber's derangement and the formation of his symptoms. He was there, at yet another scene of persecution by and martyrdom to intrigue. But in drop scenes he could also assert a tyrant's or an intriguing court official's mastery of the situation, for the time being. He was courtier, wit, follower, and reader of intrigue. But Benjamin was also surrounded by a suicide scene, one dedicated to so many others who were close to him and who made this scene, but which also did overlaps with his own suicide attempts. In the circle of family and friends it is striking how many suicides there were for him to know firsthand. When the scene of suicide proved too compelling, there was always a scene of intrigue waiting in the wings where martyrdom took turns with rescue. Intrigue alone, Benjamin concludes, can organize the allegorical show so that mourning has application and exit at once (1:409).

When everyone is his own clone running on empty there are no more ghosts: there is only live or life's transmission. Within the legible sensurround of intrigue, tyranny, or martyrdom, there can still be, on the way to the completion of the system, for both the figures of the mourning play and for the Schrebers, haunting by ghosts. Like withdrawal of connections, these ghosts of the deceased are readily available to your everyday everyman, not only to the psychotic or rather precisely not to the psychotic. But then there is Benjamin's question: What about the ghosts of living people entering the stage of mourning they never left? Death, whatever that is, is thus manifested. This lines up these surprising ghosts with the suicidal perspective of the primal model of the martyr figure, Socrates, who looked forward to a death at the hands of his persecutors that he accepted willingly. Death remains unimaginable, even or especially to this figure who resides in the Before and After and remains without any connection to death, in other words, to a dead person with whom he has identified.

When Freud hits the outer limit of his study of paranoia and doubles over with a wounding that is also all wonder and amazement that there could be so much truth in Schreber's delusions and so much delusion in his own theory, he calls on a witness, thus bringing all acts of overreading full circle within a court setting, the opening frame Benjamin sets up for the mourning play. What comes rushing in on us, including on Freud, stands guard at the beginning of Benjamin's *Origin* book, in the introductory section that puts the reader on trial for philosophy. Basically, that is, in the *Grundsprache*, or in those primal words he really had to hand to Freud, Benjamin says that the world of ideas grows stronger the more real world gets projected and introjected by the system. But the interpretations that ideas deliver of phenomena are not the incorporation of the phenomena. At the same time, on the other side of one limit, ideas do not withdraw into hypotheses about phenomena (which would represent the manic or journalistic metabolic counterpart to what goes down on the melancholic side with incorporation). Because ideas are thus in their own world, they can't offer the criteria for what they contain, for what they're about. There isn't a pregiven fit, like between a concept of genre and what it organizes and subsections off. The mourning play is an idea. Like the self-collection of mad books, it represents at best its own genre, a clearing where thinking or reading can remain nonphobic about any juxtaposition that comes its way. Ideas take us down, with Goethe's *Faust*, to the realm of the "mothers" where representation and recovery are at the same time what's happening. Only the name is a match for the force of empirical attachment. The name, which is always in shorthand, gives ideas as given, not so much in a primal language as in a primal interrogation, the interview that opens up arrest to the proceedings of the court. This new span of attention that Benjamin prescribes for the reception of his treatise refers at the same time to the allegorical space of tension in which we all find ourselves, beginning with Benjamin, after Freud: there is a tension, for one, between the closed system that cannot generate all its terms out of itself and that narcissistic system's introjection and projection of current events; then, for seconds, there is also the tension of interpretation, which is always also the interpretation of influence, one that pushes and pulls between the shorthand of psychoanalytic theory and the slow time, the in-session materiality, of the transference.

SEVEN

Genuine Obscurity Shadows the Semblance Whose Obliteration Promises Redemption

Reflections on Benjamin's "Goethe's Elective Affinities"

STANLEY CORNGOLD

But Passion most dissembles, yet betrays
  Even by its darkness; as the blackest sky
Foretells the heaviest tempest, it displays
  Its workings through the vainly guarded eye, . . .

—LORD BYRON, *Don Juan*

Visionary power
  Attends the motion of the viewless winds,
  Embodied in the mystery of words:
  There, darkness makes abode, and all the host
  Of shadowy things work endless changes . . .

—WORDSWORTH, *The Prelude*

I shall begin with a reminiscence.

In the spring of 1966, during my last year of graduate school, I spent a term at the University of Zurich, attending the lectures of Emil Staiger, Georges Poulet, and Paul de Man—and eating my *Wähen* (which are quiches of sorts) in the classisistic Mensa. It was the last year in which I was to eat my *Wähen* in such exalted surroundings.

Staiger spoke on Thomas Mann's *Doktor Faustus*—with understandably intense dislike. Georges Poulet spoke, with athletic ease, on French pre-

Romantic writers, like Rousseau, Senancour, and Constant, whom he tire-lessly excerpted. The subject of de Man's lectures was Rousseau and Goethe —in particular, the likenesses and differences between Rousseau's great, lim-pid novel *La nouvelle Héloïse* and Goethe's difficult and uncanny *Die Wahl-verwandtschaften* (Elective affinities). In a moment unusual for him, de Man referred with apparent hesitation to a piece of secondary literature he had been reading, saying, impromptu: there are two sorts of essays that German writers write. One kind is excruciating for its banality; the other, excruciat-ing for its obscurity.[1] And then, in a gesture I'd not seen him make before, he shook his head, with impatience—and also a sort of wonder, an incomprehen-sion, and also a readiness, perhaps, still to believe that, although Hegel was dead in both senses, there was still someone left to learn from. The second sort of essay, he said, is Walter Benjamin's essay on Goethe's *Elective Affinities* (1921).[2]

I bother with this reminiscence because it has lately dawned on me that the distinction de Man was making between the banal and the obscure is in fact a distinction found in Benjamin's own essay; it is a distinction that his work develops. To begin with, Benjamin spends a good deal of time and lin-guistic energy deriding the banal essayists on *Elective Affinities* whom he has consulted: Bielschowsky, for example, and Hebbel, too, and Gundolf above all; and Gundolf gets the brunt of it (keywords: "platt" [flat], "hausbacken" [homemade], and so on). Gundolf, let us note right at the outset, gets the brunt of Benjamin's sarcasm because Gundolf, the good disciple of Stefan George and the author of a celebrated triumphalist biography of Goethe, holds the Goethean art impulse as such to be sacred; and because Gundolf's morality, especially as that of the habilitated professor, is a sturdy everyday morality of piety toward the commonplace. Benjamin means to explode the notion both of a sacred artistic creativity and of an ethics of commonplace experience, so he must destroy Gundolf in doing so.

So much, for the moment, on banality, according to Benjamin. Now for obscurity. This is a much more delicate matter; and it is far less a dimen-sion that Benjamin discovers in other essayists than a dimension in play in Goethe's *Elective Affinities* itself.

Benjamin speaks of "obscurity" (of "ein Dunkles," of what is "verdun-kelt") in a number of places in his essay, assigning different degrees of value to it. First, a defective obscurity informs what Benjamin all throughout the first part calls "the mythic world" of *Elective Affinities*—a particularly seductive, delectable form of the ominous, a dark, natural intelligibility, nature saturated with the mood of meaning. Captivation by mythic obscurity is the great obstacle to redemption—for myth, with its seeming coherence and seeming inevitability (its sense of doom), offers an only deceptive semblance (*Schein*) of a truth or essence. Mythic thinking (stress on "mythic") valorizes obscurity as the mode in which appearance and truth might coincide; it is the mode of existence of the natural symbol, of the banal at its most interesting.

Goethe himself, according to Benjamin, was to become a slave of this interest. Benjamin thought that Goethe—in the words of Benjamin's American editor Michael Jennings—"saw manifestations of truth in every conceivable natural phenomenon," with the result that Goethe was soon thereafter "trapped (in what Benjamin calls) 'the chaos of symbols.'"[3] That is, he could no longer see "le forêt des symboles" for the chaos.

Goethe, however, also fought against this captivation, and traces of this struggle are inscribed in *Elective Affinities*. This, in rude outline, is Benjamin's thesis.

Recall that we are discussing the "myth" of natural signification in Benjamin's essay, as one mention of the category "obscurity." In another passage, obscurity is literally named—and defined more subtly. Regarding the character Ottilie, who in the novel grows mute, Benjamin writes, "All speechless clarity of action is semblance-like, and in truth the inner life of those who in this way preserve themselves is no less obscure [*verdunkelt*] to them than to others" (337). Here we have obscurity wrapped in the apparent clarity of action. Still, obscurity might be valued as the condition of a certain intactness of spirit—the intactness of those who keep themselves pure by silent action, like Ottilie. (According to Benjamin's recollection of the plot, she starves silently.)[4]

The inner mantle of obscurity is, therefore, not merely deceptive or delusory. But, from what we must conclude from Benjamin's praise of naming, elsewhere in this essay, and his caveat against silence, the intactness of spirit that needs obscurity becomes in its own way a semblance. ("Doch konnten wir nicht/hinüberdunkeln zu dir: es herrschte Lichtzwang" [Celan]). Benjamin continues, "No moral decision can enter into life without verbal form and, strictly speaking, without thus becoming an object of communication"

(336). And so, in Ottilie's silence, the morality of her desire to die becomes critical.

Last of all, in another place, Benjamin writes importantly of obscurity as the feature of a poetics: "Yet it is unmistakable that those Goethean figures [in *Elective Affinities*] can appear to be not created [*geschaffen*] or purely constructed [*gebildet*], but conjured [*gebannt*]. Precisely from this stems the kind of obscurity [*Dunkel*] that is foreign to works of art" (345). Here, then, *Elective Affinities*, and especially the entire figure of Ottilie, come mantled in the kind of obscurity *not* normally found in literary works of art—"the kind of obscurity," Benjamin continues, "that can be fathomed only by someone who recognizes its essence in the semblance" [*dem allein, der dessen Wesen in dem Schein kennt, zu ergründen ist*] (345). Obscurity now seems to be the necessary condition of that spellbound Goethean semblance—Ottilie, most importantly—in and through which beauty appears; it becomes the condition in which the beautiful of the spellbound in the work of art appears, the condition in which the truth of conjured beauty is veiled and sheltered.[5] By now it should be evident that in his essay Benjamin distinguishes plainly enough between the banal (or the false-obscure) and a kind of genuine obscure—the veil of beauty ("For semblance belongs to the essentially beautiful as the veil" [350]).

Now what does Zurich, 1966, add to Benjamin's distinction between the banal and the obscure? When de Man turned away from Benjamin's essay because it was so obscure—turning us, his audience, away with him—he was simultaneously turning himself toward the essay as one who, *in the world of this essay*, turns away from Ottilie as the figure of obscurity. (Compare Goethe's lines: "Passionate, then, is also the disapproval with which the friends turn away from the novella" recited to them in the novel [344]). De Man's aversion could constitute a position, a rejection of a certain traditional "discourse," of the Idealist philosophy of beauty, which thinks beauty as the mediation of an essence by a phenomenal appearance, either emphasizing the realism of the incarnation implied in this moment (Hegel and Solger) or struggling to diminish the realism of the incarnation implied in this moment (Schopenhauer and Benjamin himself). Benjamin's impossible formulation reads: they are not separate (the essence and the material envelope), but they do not mingle.

Interestingly, de Man's turning away from the Idealist discourse on beauty has its own complicated afterlife, in which, I suppose, this very chapter you are reading plays a part. For when, a year later, in 1967, de Man delivered a lecture called "The Crisis of Contemporary Criticism," which was to re-appear in 1971 as the first chapter of *Blindness and Insight*, he had evidently found in Benjamin a form of the thesis on the obscurity of beauty clear enough to shape his own thought. In this essay, de Man composes an unac-knowledged paraphrase of Benjamin's thesis on obscurity: "[The] outward appearance [of the *schöne Seele*]," he writes, "receives its beauty from an inner glow (or *feu sacré*) to which it is so finely attuned that, far from hiding it from sight, it gives it just the right balance of opacity and transparency, thus allow-ing the holy fire to shine without burning."[6] Certainly this is a fine moment of paraphrase of Benjamin's view on beauty, with our word "genuine obscu-rity" standing in for de Man's "right balance of opacity and transparency." The inspiration to this formulation is doubtless Benjaminian, especially as de Man also calls the *schöne Seele* the figure of a privileged kind of language; and in the *Elective Affinities* essay, Benjamin writes, exactly apropos of Ottilie in death as the sign of beauty: "Truth is discovered in the essence of language" (353).

This latter point requires some explanation. I shall quote Benjamin and attempt to explain things as I go along. "Thus nothing mortal," Benjamin writes, "is incapable of being unveiled," which means: everything mortal is capable of being unveiled—hence, of becoming dead. "When, therefore, the *Maxims and Reflections* duly characterize the most extreme degree of such incapacity to unveil"—that is, a certain negativity adhering to what is im-mortal—"with the profound words, 'Beauty can never become lucid about itself,' God still remains, in whose presence there is no secret and everything is life."

Readers of Benjamin's essay will have encountered the trope "the bliss-ful vision of the divine name" earlier as the moment of coincidence between the material content (*Sachgehalt*) associated with the semblance (or veil) and the truth content (*Wahrheitsgehalt*) associated with beauty (300). Life is a moment of coincidence of material content and truth content, constituting, too, the work of art at its beginning (they are "united at the beginning of the work's history" [297]). Thereafter the life of the work is extant—but hidden: extant, in principle, because perceptible to "the blissful vision of the word of the divine name" (300) and hidden—in language hidden in what Benjamin will call, in "The Task of the Translator," the original's "way of meaning" [*die Art des Meinens*] (260). In the *Elective Affinities* essay Benjamin continues, "The human being appears to us as a corpse and his life as love, when they are in the presence of God." Love and death are here put together, and yet not surprisingly, since "love by nature seeks continuance sooner in death than in life" (301). "Thus, death has the power to lay bare"—to *unveil* what is mortal—"like love. Only nature cannot be unveiled, for it preserves a mystery as long as God lets it exist." We cannot discover the truth of nature. Whereupon Benjamin makes the powerful leap I have anticipated: "Truth is discovered in the essence of language. The human body lays itself bare, a *sign* that the human being itself stands before God" (353, emphasis mine).

Here, I want to return directly to the Benjaminian reference in de Man, which is further confirmed by an *occultatio* when de Man says about the "romantic imagination" described above:

> It embodies this figure [of the *schöne Seele*] at times in the shape of a person, feminine, masculine, or hermaphrodite, and seems to suggest that it exists as an actual, empirical subject: one thinks, for instance, of Rousseau's Julie, of Hölderlin's Diotima, or of the beautiful soul that appears in Hegel's *Phenomenology of the Spirit* and in Goethe's . . . *Wilhelm Meister*. (!) [*Occultatio!* Right church, wrong pew.][7]

De Man's appropriation must by the same token qualify as a deeper instance of blindness and insight; for Benjamin also makes clear that even turning toward Ottilie (as the reader of Benjamin's essay is turned toward her) inevitably means also turning away from her, not now because she is a figure of defective obscurity but because she is in principle *always* vanishing (*entrückt*) (338). There is no approach to her, let alone one guided by the shining fire. Neither turning away from nor toward her brings one further away from understanding her or closer to understanding her—at least for as long as she lives. Her obscurity is in the deeper sense without expression. This moment of hindered apprehension has the rhythm of petrified life connected with what Benjamin calls "the expressionless" [*das Ausdruckslose*]:

> The life undulating in it [the work of art] must appear petrified and as if spellbound in a single moment. That which in it has being is mere beauty,

mere harmony, which floods through the chaos (and, in truth, through this only and not the world) but, in this flooding-through, seems only to enliven it. What arrests this semblance, spellbinds the movement, and interrupts the harmony is the expressionless. This life grounds the mystery; this petrification grounds the content in the work. (340)

One could say, following Benjamin, that this opacity can be rendered transparent as the condition of beauty only with Ottilie's death.

Yet the irony of Zurich, 1966, continues to glow. In the moment in which de Man was saying in his lecture that he could not or would not follow Benjamin, he was making his point by means of the distinction (between banality and obscurity) that organizes Benjamin's essay—and which, more importantly, is the distinction that Benjamin elaborates at almost every point in his essay. For banality (as I have suggested) is not only the preserve of morally obtuse essayists holding university chairs; it is the form of all appearance as such *outside the work of art*; it is the dimension of which Benjamin speaks ruthlessly under the head of *Mythos* (myth), *Moral* (morality), and even *Sache* (material thing or material sign).[8]

What banality chiefly amounts to is the (delusory) absence of obscurity—or, equally, the presence of an obscurity that seems penetrable. Banality is the negative, in the fallen world, of divine transparency. I do not know of any twentieth-century writer (Kafka included) who so enlarges the scope of the finally banal, uselessly obscure, merely significant (but not for that reason truthful) as does Benjamin, relentlessly Gnostic in 1921. And in like measure, no one so much as Benjamin, in the essay on Goethe's *Elective Affinities*, makes obscurity the beginning of truth—and here I make my turn, with Benjamin—in such phantoms as the obscure beauty of fictional beings conjured and spellbound; the obscure prospect of pure language; the obscurity of starlight; and the obscurity of hope, which is given to us "only for the sake of the hopeless ones" (356).

But I shall put aside for the moment such truth-terms—terms invoking the category of a good obscurity—to return to the key topological formulation of the moment in Zurich that has detained us. This point concerns the place of the difference (between banality and obscurity) that de Man put forward as outside Benjamin but one that is better grasped as inside him—inside him, and internally divided. This state of affairs could be interpreted in a more general and perhaps forceful way, with respect to this essay, as follows: At points of felt obscurity, there appear the very things of saving importance one can speak of (in chapters like these), even while one remains quite unable to grasp the measure of their truth. At such moments, one's resistance concerns what one does not want to understand about what one nevertheless must write down. This point might be illustrated by means of a crux occurring early in the Benjamin essay—one that I have never before seen addressed. Here Benjamin writes:

> If, therefore, the works that prove enduring are precisely those whose truth is most deeply sunken in their material content, then, in the course of this duration, the concrete realities rise up before the eyes of the beholder all the more distinctly the more they die out in the world. With this, however, to judge by appearances [or "to judge phenomenologically," *der Erscheinung nach*], the material content and the truth content, united at the beginning of a work's history, set themselves apart from each other in the course of its duration, because the truth content always remains to the same extent hidden as the material content comes to the fore. (296)

I shall leave aside the disturbing question of why the phrase "united at the beginning of a work's history" is not "mythical thinking."

The crux is the phrase "der Erscheinung nach," which obscures the claim that the material content and the truth content grow ever more distinct during the lifetime of the work of art, since we cannot know whether this claim is true according to a legitimate phenomenological standpoint or—quite the opposite!—whether it only seems to be true. The entire passage raises at least two fundamental questions: the first concerns the literal meaning of what Benjamin is saying; the second concerns the aspect under which this meaning is to be understood—as true or only ostensibly true and therefore illusory and semblance-like.

The possibility of making sense of this passage depends, I think, on allowing the material content, at the beginning of the work's history, to be found in two places at once. The material content is found in the world, and it is found in the work. In both places it is laden with its truth. In this sense, the material content of the work of art is at the beginning "united" with the truth that dwells within the concrete realities of the world.

In the course of the duration of the life of the work, two things happen in parallel. First, the truth-laden material content that was once visible in the world disappears from sight. To this extent a certain truth has vanished. At the same time, the material content of the work of art grows more and more conspicuous, and to this extent the truth has not vanished because it shelters in this material content. But it is not for this reason visible. It is visible neither in the concrete realities in the world, since their vanishing from sight is the very condition of the growing conspicuousness of the material contents of the work of art; nor is it visible in these contents, since in them the truth is "deeply sunken," that is, hidden.

The point about aspect now concerns how we are to understand this argument in light of the phrase "der Erscheinung nach." The material contents in the work of art become more and more eye-catching as they die out in the world. But here a doubt arises. Either a genuine distinction and separation occurs between these contents and the truth, or their distinction and separation is only apparent. In the latter case, we are forced to at least one unwonted conclusion: since the fate of the material content remains united with the truth content, then, as the truth-laden material contents die out in the world, so does the truth vanish from the material contents of the work of art. These material contents become more and more mere semblances of the truth. They live an only specious "verging and bordering on life," and yet this may be all the life that they possess (350). They have only the luster of truth (indeed, they engender this luster).

It is *only* in the perspective of such a doubt that it makes perfect sense for Benjamin to ask in the passage immediately following "whether the semblance/luster [*Schein*] of the truth content is due to the material content or whether the life of the material content is due to the truth content" (298). Here, the second alternative is being put forward as a mere hypothesis when, to judge from what was said at the beginning of the passage, it ought to be true and necessary, for the truth content allegedly informs the material content in the work of art. But now it appears to be the correct answer only if the material content in the work of art does indeed catch up the truth that is said to have vanished, along with concrete realities, from the world. But if this is only apparently the case—"der Erscheinung nach"—then the truth content of the work exists as mere semblance, due entirely to the material content;

and the posited "setting themselves apart" of the material content (in the work) and the ill-fated truth content (in the world) would itself be a myth. It may be true, as Benjamin continues, that "as they [the material content and the truth content] come apart from each other in the work, they decide on its immortality" (298), but do they indeed come apart "phenomenologically" or in an only semblance-like manner?

There is another obscurity in this matter of aspect. The passage claims at the outset that a judgment made according to appearances could distinguish the relative locations of the material content and the truth content, so that one might say that in the beginning they are united and that thereafter they are separate. Yet, supposing they have thus set themselves apart, in what way could they be perceived? To hold that the truth content could be "beheld" as an essence abstractable from the semblance is mythic thinking. The eye cannot maintain the distinction between them, for the truth content "remains . . . hidden" in the work and dies out as concrete realities die out in the world. The distinction between them is mythic—or else it is perceptible only to the camera obscura of the "English *Lord*," who makes his appearance at the home of Eduard and Charlotte in the second part of *Elective Affinities*—to the viewpoint, namely, of the "*Lord* of Hosts (of angels)"— beyond the human eye.[9] This ineffable difference between the material and the truth content might be grasped as a continuously supplied resistance to understanding. But such "resistance" is itself also mythic and cannot undo the requirement of understanding. The relation between the semblance (in its specific character and in its historical mode of appearance) and the truth it veils remains a shifting and elusive one, and yet it is a matter of finding— thus de Man in *Blindness and Insight*—"just the right balance of opacity and transparency." Writers and readers faced with such difficulties might understandably prefer to return to Benjamin's work of destruction, and they would be only half-wrong to do so.

The proviso in truth-telling for Benjamin—that such telling is first of all and last of all a telling of the semblance—is central (although it is only one center): not to follow this proviso is to be captivated by the myth that of all myths alluded to in Benjamin's essay most invites shattering. Indeed, this telling brings about the shattering. (De Man's essay on Benjamin's essay "The Task of the Translator," on which I will comment at the close, will go only to the negative and avoid the salvational, except as the latter is itself an affair of the destruction of the semblance.) This myth that calls for shattering is that of a *daily* experience, pure and simple, of a *daily* ethics, a *daily* understanding that could stand in any substantial relation to truth whatsoever, and whose distinguished figure is marriage. (This, again, is not a point that de Man would have found obscure or in any way wrong.) But—this is also true!—recall Benjamin's turn: he populates the resulting void with allusions to that truth in flight, under such names as true love, the secret, beauty, God, and hope. Benjamin's God-terms are obscure—with the obscurity I call the good obscure—but it is not as if any post-Benjaminian discourse, however assertively rigorous, has actually done without such metaphysical siblings to these essence-terms, God-terms. Consider, in passing, such brothers and sisters as "rhetoric," *différance*, social construction, paranoia—it does not matter here that they are hypostases of the negative—*versus*—true love, the secret, beauty, God, hope.

It will come as no surprise, then, that Benjamin's essay provokes resistance on the grounds of its semblance-like distinctions between truth and its material sign—distinctions stretched on the diction of German Idealism (for not all the essay's categories are transparent, let alone on the topic of obscurity; rather, they are "metaphysical"). It also comes as no surprise that Benjamin's essay provokes resistance on the grounds of its distinctive density or obscurity of argument, its personal and flaunted obscurity, its esotericism (although, of course, this is also true: the essay itself is determined to be in no way banal). No, what makes such resistance finally interesting is the fact that even though Benjamin's essay is obscure in the places where it is exalted or undecidable, it is also all too familiar, all too intelligible and transparent in an everyday fallen way. This, at any rate, is an irresistible assumption when the *Sachgehalt* of the essay, its real-material content, involves us as closely as it does—namely, in the so-called divinity of marriage that is also only the daemon, the specious divinity, of marriage—in the divinity, or is it the daemon, of marriage bent on its own ruin. The same familiar uncertainty besets us with respect to the renunciation of happiness: Who is urging it on us? Is it a god or only the wicked daemon, the mythic divinity of renunciation, that does not want to reveal itself as what it is—someone else's selfishness?

These are matters close to us, so close, indeed, that one could wonder whether there is anything one writes, anything of what one is always talking about, that should not be construed as a reason for and against marriage—or, in other words, as a reason for and against selfishness (one's own and someone else's)—and hence, finally, as a reason for one's not being entitled to find Benjamin obscure.

So why do we nonetheless resist Benjamin's gift of so intimate a subject matter? The answer is there in the last paragraph. Marriage, according to this essay—and not only adultery!—is selfishness, and hence an aversion to truth; but adultery, according to this essay—and not only marriage!—is selfishness, and hence an aversion to truth. In many ways Benjamin's *Elective Affinities* suggests that the adultery between Eduard and Ottilie is prefigured and hence ordained by natural signs, by a welter of omens and coincidences—is, in a word, fated; yet the novel nonetheless strives, says Benjamin, to show that there is no truth in this passion: there is truth only in Ottilie's death. But if there is truth in Ottilie's death, it is not because she has lucidly intended it and might therefore be said to have expiated her sin by means of it. Furthermore, if there is no truth in her adulterous passion, it is not because adultery assaults and shatters the truth of marriage. In the space of a single paragraph Benjamin sweeps away as banal whole libraries of domestic criticism (on *Elective Affinities*, and much more), by writing:

> The subject of *Elective Affinities* is not marriage. Nowhere in this work are its ethical powers to be found. From the outset they are in the process of disappearing, like the beach under water at floodtide. Marriage here is not an ethical problem, nor a social problem either. It is not a form of bourgeois conduct. In its dissolution everything human turns into appearance, and the mythic remains solely as essence. (131)

The choice between marriage and adultery is delusory, because they are both in one essential dimension corrupt:

> For what the author shrouds in silence a hundred times can be seen quite simply enough from the course of things as a whole: that, according to ethical laws, passion loses all its rights and happiness when it seeks a pact with the bourgeois, affluent, secure life. This is the chasm across which the author intends, in vain, to have his figures stride with somnambulistic sureness upon the narrow path of pure human civility. That noble curbing and controlling is unable to replace the clarity that the author certainly knew just

how to remove from himself, as well as from them. . . . In the mute constraint that encloses these human beings in the circle of human custom, indeed of bourgeois custom, hoping there to salvage for them the life of passion, lies the dark transgression that demands its dark expiation. (343)

Yes—the passion that veils itself in the civility of custom might deserve death —but what about love, one might well ask. So I cite from the essay: "Yet in truth, marriage is never justified in law (that is, as an institution) but is justified solely as an expression of continuance in love, which by nature seeks this expression sooner in death than in life" (301). Marriage appears in the best of cases to be a banal simulacrum of death.

This entanglement, this transgression, is the sin of selfishness, which in *Elective Affinities* appears in exemplary form in marriage: there is no more compelling example of the selfish *passion for meaning* that wants continuance. In marriage this passion (for meaning) promises itself eternal fulfillment, a promise especially appealing where meaning is tinged with a certain natural-seeming, authentic-seeming obscurity, meaning as if coming from the depths of the world. Marriage offers the daily opportunity to feel obscurity (or depth) meaningfully, to feel in the banal a certain authenticating obscurity (or depth); indeed, what one marries par excellence is marriage, the marriage par excellence of the banal and the obscure.

I said earlier that I knew no other modern work so impatient of the claim of a banal, an everyday experience of essence, an untroubled, a domestic sense of the obscure; for the meaning of obscurity is precisely the veiled, the undisclosable character of whatever, like beauty, could redeem. And hence, "the essentially beautiful" stand opposite to life ("For everything living [the higher the quality of its life the more this is so] is lifted up beyond the domain of the essentially beautiful" [350]). Benjamin has a word for the view (as in Solger) that "beauty is truth become visible" (350), "that the truth of the beautiful can be unveiled"—that word is "philosophical barbarism" (351), which now appears to be the academic equivalent of marriage.

At the end, Benjamin's injunction could turn one to Nietzsche, not as the foe of Benjamin but rather his source. In *The Gay Science*, Nietzsche is Benjamin's predecessor in the intensity of his doubt of visible essence, philosopher of barbarism, perhaps, but precisely here no philosophical barbarian. Nietzsche writes:

There is a certain high point in life; once we have reached that, we are, for all our freedom, once more in the greatest danger of spiritual unfreedom, and no matter how much we have faced up to the beautiful chaos of existence and denied it all providential reason and goodness, we still have to pass our hardest test. For it is only now that the idea of a personal providence confronts us with the most penetrating force, and the best advocate, the evidence of our eyes, speaks for it—now that we can see how palpably always everything that happens to us turns out for the best. Every day and every hour, life seems to have no other wish than to prove this proposition again and again. Whatever it is, bad weather or good, the loss of a friend, sickness, slander, the failure of some letter to arrive, the spraining of an ankle, a glance into a shop, a counter-argument, the opening of a book, a dream, a fraud—either immediately or very soon after it proves to be something that 'must not be missing'; it has a profound significance and use precisely for us. . . .

I think that . . . we should . . . rest content with the supposition that our own practical and theoretical skill in interpreting and arranging events has now reached its high point. Nor should we conceive too high an opinion of this dexterity of our wisdom when at times we are excessively surprised by the wonderful harmony created by the playing of our instrument—a harmony that sounds too good for us to dare to give the credit to ourselves. Indeed, now and then someone plays with us—good old chance; now and then chance guides our hand, and the wisest providence could not think up a more beautiful music than that which our foolish hand produces then.[10]

This is Benjaminian *avant-la-lettre* in the strictness with which it resists the truth-claims of providence, with which it will not exonerate the character's blindness to his own invisibly rapid movements of interpretive dexterity. Harmony on this star is an affair, not of the sacred, but of interpretation and chance.

Epilogue

I promised a final reference to de Man's commentary on "The Task of the Translator." De Man refuses the messianic side for the side of destruction; at the same time, he is impatient for the *truth* of death.

De Man associates the thing "word" with *letters* in a process he calls "dis-articulation"—we could say the divorce of word and sentence. But "Word" (*Wort*) in German in fact signals eloquence, a thing not unrelated to beauty. For better or for worse—I think, worse—"eloquence" is not a word in de Man's lexicon, even when he writes on rhetoric.

I think the reality for Benjamin is that, in the final analysis, fine writing, eloquence is salvational; but de Man preferred not to say or see that.

EIGHT

Portrait of Melancholy (Benjamin, Warburg, Panofsky)

BEATRICE HANSSEN

Although Walter Benjamin's face was always turned toward the future, he never could quite relinquish the image of the past. Amid phrases and aphorisms that captured the hurriedness of modernity's present, that assessed the shock impact of modernity's turn to technology, one finds in his work encrypted kernels of insight that threaten to withdraw forever, to recede, to become irrecoverably lost, unless one is attentive to the flash of meaning they emit. These are images of incomparable beauty, laden with melancholic valor, for they memorialize tradition and past experiences. Amid pronouncements that precisely register the numbing, anaesthetic effects of film and its dehumanizing disassembly of the real—from amid such pronouncements emerge nostalgic glimpses of the past that speak of hands, and eyes, and mind, all coordinated organically, all synchronized, as Benjamin's reflections on the artisanal storyteller would put it.[1] One such image, barely visible as it punctuates a discussion of technology, concerns the photographic portrait. Drawing the last contours of the human portrait and transforming it into a site of melancholic loss, Benjamin writes in his technology essay:

> It is no accident that the portrait was the focal point of early photography. The cult of remembrance of loved ones, absent or dead, offers a last refuge for the cult value of the picture. For the last time the aura emanates from the early photographs in the fleeting expression of a human face. This is what constitutes their melancholy, incomparable beauty.[2]

Tellingly, the portraits of Walter Benjamin that have come down to us —from the hands of such renowned photographers as Gisèle Freund and Germaine Krull or lesser-known ones, such as Charlotte Joël (see Fig. 1)

Figure 1. Walter Benjamin. Copyright Theodor W. Adorno Archiv, Frankfurt am Main.

—invariably attest to just such a "melancholic, incomparable beauty." For they present the stills—hardly snapshots—of one of Weimar's last German-Jewish intellectuals, whose loss, when contemplated with hindsight, they incontestably mourn. More than simple *memento mori*, these portraits uncannily double the object they seek to represent. Mourning the loss of one of the twentieth century's most influential intellectuals and critics, these pictures depict a brooding, gloomy Benjamin, born under the sign of Saturn, whose languid pose and language of gestures—that is, downward gaze, chin leaning on a clenched fist—seem to quote from an ancient pictorial archive of mourning and melancholia.[3] Bidding the beholder to adopt the pose of an age-old face reader, they invite one to glean Benjamin's temperament, no less than his fate, from the lines that define his mimetic image. Against better insight, and in full knowledge of the fated dialectic that accompanied such natural arts, their beholder is lured into drawing on the enigmatic techniques of physiognomy, the hermeneutical practice of reading facial features as natural signs, popularized by Charles Le Brun and Johann Caspar Lavater—an art Benjamin much respected, as he did astrology, graphology, and chiromancy.[4] To be classified, then, somewhere between *mise-en-abîme*, or a picture-within-a-picture, and dialectical image, these sober portraits fixate gestures of melancholy, appropriately attesting to a century, now waning, now at a close, that was marked by trauma, historic catastrophe, and loss.

The reflections that follow use Benjamin's portrait as a "picture for meditation"—to appropriate a phrase of Gershom Scholem's—that is, as an image that allows one to ponder the relations between modernity and melancholy as well as Benjamin's pivotal position in a century that was ruled by visual culture, by pictorial and archival concerns. Yet, they will not pursue the perhaps more common, familiar path that aligns Benjamin's most publicly known persona with the essays on technology and film—essays said to foreshadow recent postmodern definitions of the twentieth century as an age of the virtual simulacrum. Recognizing the importance of his pathbreaking work on technology, these reflections nonetheless propose to take a somewhat lesser-traveled road, one that follows Benjamin into the hidden recesses of his scholarship where his thought threatens to become arcane, at times even hermetic.[5] It is a path that leads back to Benjamin's more obscure treatises, such as *The Origin of the German Mourning Play*, and to his elective affinities with the discipline of art history.[6] Indeed, as is well known, Benjamin's "habilitation" thesis was rejected in 1925 by the faculty of "general aesthetics" at the University of Frankfurt at the instigation of Hans Cornelius —Adorno's dissertation adviser—and his assistant, later Frankfurt school luminary, Max Horkheimer. Yet, against all odds, Benjamin managed to publish the study independently in 1928. More than just a philological tract, the *Trauerspiel* (mourning play) book was a broadly conceived philosophico-theological *tractatus*, which furnished Benjamin's first sustained analysis of modernity, filtered through a study of the baroque, in terms, precisely, of the predominant moods of mourning and melancholia. This move to melancholia, furthermore, provided Benjamin with the first outline of a dialectical conception of cultural history and with the first insights into the operations of what he later would call the "dialectical image." Pursuing this path into more unfamiliar, seemingly remote terrain therefore also means returning to Benjamin's lesser-discussed theoretical and philosophical affinities: those that link his emerging picture theory to the iconology of art historians Erwin Panofsky and Fritz Saxl and, crucially, to the new cultural-scientific history of the image (*kulturwissenschaftliche Bildgeschichte*) devised by Aby Warburg, the German-Jewish cultural historian, whose picture-library, salvaged from the Nazis, was relocated from Hamburg to what is now known as London's Warburg Institute.[7] In taking these seemingly circuitous paths, the reflections that follow seek to retrieve what risks getting lost in the perhaps all-too-nostalgic cult of remembrance that has accrued around the auratic figure of Benjamin. They aim to restore an oft-neglected cultural-historical frame as well as posthumously to rehabilitate and legitimize his emerging scholarship in the field of cultural history. Aiming to broaden the reception of Benjamin as a philosopher of melancholia, they also gesture toward a historical genealogy of the dialectical image, whose origins revert to philosophical picture theories.

Much like Aby Warburg, whose final, monumental but unfinished art project consisted in what he called the *Mnemosyne-Atlas*—a mnemic atlas of gestures, poses, and "pathos formulae," from antiquity to the Flemish Middle Ages to the Florentine Renaissance, and from early modernity to the present—so Benjamin ultimately became the archaeologist and archivist of images. From his early years in Berlin to his exile years in Paris, Benjamin constructed a private memory bank, whose holdings ranged from medieval allegories and baroque emblem books, Horapollo's hieroglyphs, arcane tracts on cabalistic demonology, to the deceptively innocent images of children's picture books, the pornographic drawings collected by Eduard Fuchs, and—not to forget—the revolutionary dialectical film images and salvos shot off by Eisenstein or

Pudovkin. Cultural history, in Warburg's but also Benjamin's book, henceforth was to be thought of as a memory bank of mnemic images (*Erinnerungsbilder*) in which the new and the old, the past and the present, enmeshed. In the writings of this self-described insatiable collector of texts, the idolatry of the image coexisted with the iconoclastic history of the people of the book. Both entwined in the dialectical image, whose presence, as Benjamin cryptically observed in the unfinished *Arcades Project*, was all the more perceptible in language.[8] For, in allegory and emblem—mnemic techniques of cultural storing and storage—these two antithetical, antinomical traditions dialectically clashed, exhibiting a montage of icon and text, image and caption, figure and legend. No longer purely a rhetorical device, but rather an emblematic image with caption, allegory, as laid out in Benjamin's *Trauerspiel* book, anticipated the dialectical image to be coined in the *Arcades Project* and the theses on the philosophy of history. Radically different from their archaic counterparts, found in the writings of Klages or Jung, such historico-dialectical images, he believed, presented "dialectics at a standstill," or "that in which the Then and the Now come together into a constellation like a flash of lightning"—a flash of historic insight that, he added, only could "enter into legibility at a specific time."[9] Transforming the iconic understanding of ideology already captured in Marx's memorable analogy of the camera obscura, Benjamin lodged these dialectical images in a collectively produced unconscious and rethought ideology critique as the retrieval of the unfulfilled potential of the past.[10] In the final analysis, his concept of history was eminently iconographical or, more precisely, iconological (to allude to Panofsky's distinction), meaning that he went beyond a narrowly defined thematic history of allegorical types to secure a history of cultural symptoms.[11] Borrowing from Warburg, Panofsky, and even Nietzsche, Benjamin proved especially dependent on Freud's model of the unconscious, recasting the historical-materialist analysis of utopia into Freudian wish and dream images, out of whose phantasmagoric lure the historical subject needed to awake. If cultural history was like an archive of images to be rendered legible by the historian, then she in turn was to remain vigilant, ever ready to seize the image of the past before it threatened to become extinguished or irretrievably lost. Pushed to the limit, as he sought to escape the flood of Nazism that was about to engulf the European continent, Benjamin finally conceived of history as a flux of memory images, whose dazzlingly rapid flow the near-drowning historical subject saw flit by.

From the scrolls, or the picture book, that make up Benjamin's cultural history, there is one image in particular that detaches itself, to borrow Nietzsche's metaphor from the second *Untimely Meditation*. Fluttering from Benjamin's theses on history came an image from the hands of Paul Klee, arguably one of the most accomplished hieroglyphists of the modern. Called *Angelus Novus*, or new angel (see Fig. 2), the image in question was a sober watercolor from the year 1920. Klee drew the image at a time when he already had contact with Rainer Maria Rilke, author of the *Duino Elegies*, a poetic cycle constructed around the encounter between angels and humans. Gershom Scholem recounts the vicissitudes of the picture, noting how, shortly after its purchase in Munich in 1921, it became "a picture for meditation," or "a memento of a spiritual vocation," which accompanied Benjamin through most of his travels and years of exile.[12] Before his final flight from Paris in 1940, it found a place among the manuscripts that Georges Bataille would store for him in the Bibliothèque Nationale. The frontal depiction of an angel—his wings spread, his mouth slightly open, sacred scrolls in place of locks—*Angelus Novus*, as Scholem suggested, delivered eminently a Jewish message, insofar as in Hebrew the word angel (*malakh*) was identical with the word messenger. Used originally for meditative purposes, the image eventually became the site of a host of meanings: Was it an angel or birdlike figure with claws? Did its mouth and eyes mimic the existential horror or desolateness of Eduard Munch's *The Scream*—an artist, incidentally, not unfamiliar himself with the state of melancholia—or did it, quite to the contrary, betoken celestial, hymnic jubilation? Migrating through Benjamin's life and work, the image at times stood for the "personal-mystical," that is, a guardian angel, representing a person's secret self; or it betokened a hymnic Talmudic angel, who, after having sung his hymn before God, ceased to exist, dissolving into naught; or, again—under the influence of excessive hashish consumption in 1933 on the island of Ibiza—it metamorphosed into an inhuman, demonic, even satanic angel with claws.[13] Honoring the spirit of the

Figure 2. Paul Klee, *Angelus Novus*. Copyright The Israel Museum, Jerusalem.

benevolent angel, Benjamin early on called the project for a periodical he hoped to publish in the 1920s *Angelus Novus*, emphasizing how the journal was to capture actuality's ephemeral fabric before it would forever dissolve. Yet, not until the final stages of his life and work did Klee's angel, whose clipped wings signaled the melancholy course of history, truly emerge as a dialectical image. Assuming its last guise in the ninth thesis of "The Concept of History" (1940), which Benjamin wrote in response to the Hitler-Stalin pact, this celestial figure now emerged as the saturnine angel of history. Now, the hallowed, theological course humanity's messianic guardian angel aspired to follow was radically impeded by a secularized history, propelled by the exigencies of technology and militarism. For, caught in the storm of progress, his face turned to the past, the angel relentlessly was driven into the future while the wreckage and debris of culture mercilessly piled up, turning history as we know it into a permanent state of exception. Bogged down by and mired in permanent catastrophe, the melancholic angel now appeared inactive, static, frozen in movement. Fixed between the storm of progress and the wind coming from paradise, the angel remained suspended in mid-air, unable to fulfill its apocalyptic or guiding task, unable to leap from the claustrophobic immanence of catastrophic history into the transcendence of redemption and salvation.[14]

At the heart of the theses on history, the Klee picture often has been read as the most vivid illustration of Benjamin's dialectical image, to whose apocalyptic message one should not remain deaf, lest one hope to halt history's downward course. Yet, behind the Klee picture hides another image, the image of another winged figure, albeit perhaps not necessarily that of an angel. It is a lesser-known image in Benjamin scholarship, one hardly ever commented upon—a picture, moreover, that could well be regarded to be the Renaissance counterpart or mirror-image to Klee's modernist watercolor, namely, Dürer's engraving *Melencolia I* from the year 1514 (see Fig. 3).[15]

Not surprisingly, Klee's *Angelus Novus* never found a place in Benjamin's major work of the 1920s, the *Trauerspiel* study. Nor did Benjamin ever bring to fruition the publication of the periodical *Angelus Novus*. Pressed by time and preparatory work for his "habilitation" thesis, he let go of the journal project, reporting the angel's "annunciation" to Scholem on October 14, 1922.[16] In its place, it seems, quite stealthily, moved Dürer's engraving. Benjamin chanced upon the picture relatively late into his habilitation, through Panofsky and Saxl's 1923 monograph on the print, whose impact on him was such that he urged Scholem to acquire it immediately for the newly opened library at the University of Jerusalem. That Erwin Panofsky later, upon Hofmannsthal's plea to help Benjamin, was less enthusiastic about the *Trauerspiel* book of which he had seen an excerpt, constitutes another chapter in Benjamin's fated biography and one of the many missed encounters with like-minded spirits.

Figure 3. Albrecht Dürer, *Melencolia I.* (1514).

Interestingly, unlike the later *Arcades Project* for which Benjamin would collect a (now lost) extensive picture scrapbook, or *Bilderbuch*, composed of photo prints he had made in the Cabinet des Estampes of the Bibliothèque Nationale, the *Trauerspiel* book itself remained remarkably imageless, devoid of illustrations, Benjamin making use instead, it seemed, of the ancient rhetorical technique of *ekphrasis*.[17] Given his emphasis on the cabalistic tradition of word and name in the study's epistemo-critical prologue, it is perhaps not altogether surprising that his nascent iconology has generally been neglected to the advantage of his somewhat more recognizable language philosophy. Yet, it was in the *Trauerspielbuch*'s central chapter, dedicated to mourning and melancholia, at whose hidden core lay the Dürer print, that Benjamin avowed his pronounced indebtedness to the budding new school in art history from whose archives would emerge Panofsky's iconology and Warburg's novel cultural-historical method, anchored in a dual analysis of word and image.[18] By seizing upon the Dürer engraving, Benjamin once again showcased what might well be called a multilayered "image-within-an-image." In the art history of the time, *Melencolia I* had become the quintessential scholarly enigma, or *rebus*, on whose hermeneutical deciphering a clear understanding of Renaissance humanism seemed to rest. Much like the Klee image, which traveled through Benjamin's oeuvre only to assemble a history of meanings along the way, so *Melencolia I* had already acquired an exemplary position in the work of contemporary art historians. Commonly regarded to be the greatest artist of the northern Renaissance, Dürer for these scholars became the foremost representative of this period's victory over the dark, mythic forces of the Middle Ages while his work at the same time already averted the kind of "deplorable excesses" that would come to distinguish "Baroque rhetoric."[19] Steeped in the work of these historians, Benjamin would cull the tools of dialectics from Saxl and Panofsky's exegesis of the engraving whereas his emerging conception of the dialectical image, for its part, owed its greatest debt to Aby Warburg's theory of the prophylactic image. It seems appropriate to turn first to Panofsky, later to Warburg.

For Panofsky and Saxl, Dürer's Renaissance engraving represented the end point in the vicissitudes of what they, going back to the neo-Kantian Ernst Cassirer, called the historical configurations of a mythical conceptual structure, or thought complex, named melancholy.[20] Focusing on one of the tradition's seminal junctures, the Hippocratic text *Of the Nature of Man*, they showed how this tract merged natural philosophy with an already existing humoralism, or the medical doctrine of the four humors: the choleric, phlegmatic, the sanguine, and melancholic, the latter being the medical state that pointed to an excess of black bile. In so doing, the Hippocratic treatise transformed the original medical understanding of melancholia as a *pathology*, caused by the imbalance of fluids, into a *physiognomy* of four temperaments or character types. Based on the legibility of bodily, natural signs, this physiognomical doctrine in late antiquity was projected onto a cosmological model, then codified eventually in the ninth century by the medical school of Salerno. The astrologer Abu Mashar further traced the nefarious influence of the planet Saturn on melancholy and—fusing the myths of Saturn and Cronus—established the Saturnine as the conflictual state of polarities, dualities, or extremes, the melancholic type being thrown between states of exultation and extreme despondency. If the European Middle Ages, so the art historians continued, combined this astrological legacy with the theological doctrine of *acedia*, or sloth (one of the seven deadly sins), then the Renaissance ushered in a classically defined anthropology and with it a novel, humanistic version of melancholia, whose high point they discerned in Dürer's engraving. To be sure, as Panofsky and Saxl readily admitted, Dürer's artwork still paid visual tribute to astrological and mythical systems inherited from medieval planetary zodiacs and the iconological folk tradition of the *Planetenkinder* (Children of the planets), which linked the predisposition for particular professions to the influence of certain ruling planets. Thus, Melancholy's purse, for example, exemplified the medieval emblem of saturnine miserliness while the dog emblematized the adverse workings of the spleen. The engraving, however, pointed even further back, to antique times, as signaled by the magical square of Jupiter, a time-honored object of alchemical exegesis, which was believed to be a charm against the demonic, planetary influence of Saturn. But, in the final analysis, so the authors established, the new humanistic credo of the Renaissance triumphed. Bidding farewell to an outmoded conception of melancholy, the etching heralded the figure of genius, or of a "winged melancholia" (*melancholia generosa*), a state attained through the art of geometry as emblematized by the tools of applied geometry scattered around the languid figure, among them the hammer, molding plane, sphere, sextant, ladder, grindstone, saw, compass, and polyhedron. In this way, Saxl and Panofsky emphasized, Dürer in fact rekindled a long-lost, positive conception of melancholia already lodged in Aristotle's *Problemata* and revived by the Italian Renaissance humanist Ficino, who associated it with Plato's divine frenzy, or *mania*. Even though melancholy still remained a state of polarities or extremes in which the afflicted oscillated between abject despondency and divine elatedness, *Melencolia I* fundamentally inaugurated an altogether new, even modern, sensibility. Announcing the coming of modernity, Dürer's engraving—located somewhere between representation and ideography—no longer was a medieval, talismanic *Temperamentsbild* (ideogram of a temperament), but rather a modern personification of a subjective disposition or mood (*Stimmung*), whereby the term *mood* itself already announced the existential individualism that would come to typify the modern era.

Seizing on Panofsky and Saxl's diagnosis of melancholy as a state dominated by polarities, or *extremitas*, whose dualities derived from the "inner structure of the mythological idea of Cronus [*Kronos*] as such," Benjamin further transformed this melancholic ambivalence, turning it into nothing less than the operations of the dialectic.[21] The seeming incongruities, even paradoxes, between the vignettes that make up the central mourning chapter of his habilitation thesis dissolve once one recognizes them as the transitional moments of a dialectical logic. Transposed from the pages of art history to the *Trauerspiel* book, Dürer's engraving appeared encased, secured between multiple frames, as melancholy was defined now phenomenologically and psychologically, now historically, now politically or theologically, and, not unimportantly, epistemologically. For melancholy, as Benjamin suggested, truly opened up a new methodology and theory of knowledge, requiring the cultural historian's immersion in natural and cultural objects.[22] Certainly, Benjamin invoked the humanistic revival of Aristotelian melancholia no less than the persistence of a Christian, Tomistic legacy of *acedia* in the Counter Reformation, but his main interest lay in reconstructing a physiognomy of the modern as melancholic—a physiognomy of epochal dimensions. Brought on by the flight of the gods, the epoch's metaphysical desolateness left a self-alienated, torpid human subject behind, crouched amid an array of petrified relics, allegorical fragments, and enigmatic cultural objects. Leaning on Dilthey's influential study of the Renaissance, Benjamin pointed to the resurgence of Stoicism's *apatheia* in the period's anthropology, of which Dürer's etching indeed was a vivid example.[23] Donning what seemed to be the pose of an existentialist philosopher or psychoanalyst, Benjamin observed that the "deadening of the [affects], and the ebbing away of the waves of life . . . can increase the distance between the self and the surrounding world [*Umwelt*] to the point of alienation from the body."[24] Throughout the ensuing analysis, he deployed the terms mourning and melancholia more or less indiscriminately, failing to adopt Freud's 1917 typology, which argued that in the normal, terminable process of mourning the outside world proved empty and void to the subject while in the lethargic condition of melancholy such impoverishment befell the ego. Remaining oblivious to these distinctions, Benjamin instead focused on how, in the pathological state of extreme depersonalization characterizing melancholia, even the most innocuous, simple objects (*Ding*) could be transfigured into ciphers of enigmatic wisdom. Looking ahead to the baroque's obsession with libraries, Dürer's prescient Renaissance etching, he implied, symbolized both the irretrievable loss of natural objects and the emergence of a predominantly hermeneutical mode of relating to the world. "It accords with this [new trend]," he wrote, "that in the proximity of Albrecht Dürer's figure, *Melencolia*, the utensils of active life are lying around unused on the floor, as objects [*Gegenstand*] of contemplation [*grübeln*]."[25] What else did this mean than that natural objects and the tools of active life, having lost their life-infusing link to the *Umwelt*, were now no longer "ready-at-hand," to evoke the Heideggerian term from *Being and Time*. Or, to put it in the perhaps more familiar—if somewhat anachronistic—language of Adorno and Horkheimer's *Dialectic of Enlightenment*, what remained was a disenchanted world of cultural, fetishistic artifacts, produced by the technological exploits of instrumental reason and captured in the instruments of applied geometry.

But what if one projects the portrait of Benjamin onto Dürer's engraving? It is not hard, then, to discern in *Melencolia I* a personification of the collector—the physiognomist of objects—sitting amid a sprawl of collectibles.[26] Furthermore, it is precisely at this juncture that the state of melancholia as mere alienated self-loss also turns inside out to reveal itself to be a mode of knowledge, disclosing the extent to which the outside object at once proved constitutive of the self—a thought Benjamin condensed years later in his Baudelaire study, when he spoke of the Proustian madeleine as the repository of involuntary memory. Under Benjamin's gaze, melancholy revealed itself to be an existentialist *mode*, not simply, then, an overwhelming indeterminate *mood* (*Stimmung*) but, fundamentally, a technique of disclosure and knowledge that replaced the old rationalistic epistemological model. Already the study's prologue had, in quasi-Husserlian terms, called for a return to "things themselves," *zu den Sachen selbst*, and—in a scholastic allusion— had defined the method of philosophy (playing on the Greek *methodos*, or path, in German *Weg*) as a detour, or *Umweg*, through which contemplation was to reach the thing. Now, Benjamin established in the central part of the *Trauerspiel* book, its privileged way of doing so was precisely melancholia. In fact, an earlier announcement for the journal *Angelus Novus* had defined the task of the new critique as "knowledge through immersion" [*durch Versenkung erkennen*], an immersion that would release both the material and truth contents (*Sach-* and *Wahrheitsgehalt*) of the object under investigation, yet always in such a way that any subjective intentionality eventually would make way for the imposition of truth, betokening the death of intention altogether.[27] The shift in Benjamin's work as a whole—from the pre-Marxist phase to the later materialistic method of cultural analysis—transpires, then, through the changed understanding of material objects. From the *Trauerspielbuch* to the later work, Benjamin moved from a concern *mit den Sachen selbst* to the material objects that are the staple of the collector, or to phrase it differently, from an intention toward the thing's essence, from the eidetic reduction of the empirical thing to the *Sache* (material and truth contents), or *Wesensschau*, to a more pronounced concern with the concrete collectible, material object (although the two concerns really coexisted from the start). In so doing, Benjamin never relinquished his mystical desire for the elusive natural thing, which—as the avid reader of Kant he remained throughout his life—had much in common with the *Ding an sich*, or the *Thing*.[28] Even in his late work a nostalgia for the natural object reappeared, displaced, often, as the "auratic," or as the lure of the natural in its original animistic, fetishistic manifestation, whose pull he seemed hard-pressed to forget. It is no coincidence, therefore, that the famed technology essay, in quasi-Kantian fashion, describes the aura of cultural objects, lost through the onslaught of technology's unrelenting force, as the withdrawal of the natural object from the grip of calculating knowledge and technological reproduction. Drawing the vivid mental picture of an idyllic summer afternoon, Benjamin describes an aesthetic subject, reposing in tranquil nature, who, in tracing the lines of a mountain range on the horizon or in beholding the branch of a tree, experiences their aura, "the unique phenomenon of a distance, however close it may be."[29] Wrapped in recollections of the natural, whose mimetic force to create similarities he unremittingly sought to fathom, Benjamin always was prone to the exegesis of natural signs, which may explain why, even in his Marxist phase, he seemed reluctant to give up his interest in astrology and graphology, destined, like Dürer's *Melencolia I*, to battle out the conflict between the forces of an age-old animism—a primitivism, emanating from time immemorial—and the counterforces of an enlightened modernity.[30]

It is this duality between the arcane and the modern, the mystical and self-enlightenment—now projected back onto Dürer's print—that may serve as a way of entry into a brief treatment of the last intellectual affinity that binds Benjamin's evocation of the etching to contemporary art history, specifically, to Warburg's theory of the prophylactic memory image.

More so than Panofsky or Saxl would do after him, Warburg's 1920 treatise, *Pagan-Antique Prophecy in Word and Image During Luther's Time*, had interpreted *Melencolia I* as nothing less than a pictorial representation or mnemic image of the fierce battle between the dark, so-called pagan, demonic, planetary powers and the forces of enlightenment, that is, ultimately, as the struggle between magic, logic, and science, emblematized again by the remarkable array of instruments or mantic tools collected around the languid figure. Maintaining that Dürer had displaced this struggle from the cosmological plane to the interiority of a humanistic subject, he went even further when he claimed that the victory over demonic antiquity came about through "the polar function of an emphatic pictorial memory bank," which, while conjuring up the demonic, at once overpowered it *in* and *through* the image.[31] In functioning as an icon that warded off these mythical demonic powers, *Melencolia I* itself took on the protective force of the magical Jupiter square, which, in fact, it effectively doubled.

But in sharp distinction to what one could call Panofsky's high cultural interests, Warburg's theory of the prophylactic function of pictorial memory itself was rooted in anthropological and ethnographic studies that he had conducted in 1896 among the Hopi Indians during a research trip through the United States. Not until more than twenty years later would he be able to give shape to his thoughts—in the form of a lecture called "Images from the Region of the Pueblo Indians of North America"—while hospitalized in Dr. Ludwig Binswanger's sanatorium in Switzerland, suffering from paranoia and a mental breakdown—the irony being that Binswanger himself would later acquire fame for his phenomenological analysis of melancholia. Much has been made of the therapeutic effect Warburg's lecture on the snake ritual was meant to have in that its author set out to prove to the Swiss clinic that he had regained his sanity by delivering a well-argued and structured lecture. Centering on counterphobic psychological mechanisms, Warburg believed that so-called primitive peoples and children generated memory images to ward off the fear of the radically unknown, a defense mechanism that was to be understood as a response to original, primeval fear, or as the "phobic reflex of cause projection."[32] Seeking to demonstrate the "elementary indestructibility of the memory of the serpent cult," his lecture moved from the snake ritual among the Hopi and Dionysian snake rites, to the healing brazen serpent idol associated with Moses in the Old Testament, to the sculpture *Laocoön*. Tracing the ritual's trajectory across history, he aimed to chart the transformation of mythical patterns of causation, their spiritual elevation and eventual displacement by the distancing effects of science, whose harmful consequences were exemplified by American modernism, with its fated dream of controlling the natural realm technologically. Without a doubt, the insights Warburg gathered among the Hopi would shape his emerging cultural-historical work, bound to cross the rigid margins that circumscribed academic art history. For, his later *Mnemosyne-Atlas* was to be an "inventory of basic human reactions," as Gombrich reports, a series of tableaux that comprised visual material documenting the genealogy of emotional as well as intellectual human gestures across the centuries. As such, the memory atlas hardly could be considered a formalist, iconographic art-historical endeavor or even ranked the parallel of a Dadaist montage. Rather, as a broadly conceived global atlas of gestures, it sought to freeze-frame the essence of the universal human disposition, presenting the optic symbol as the equivalent of the engram, or memory-trace, in the nervous system.[33] As it traced the transfiguration of icons such as the ecstatic maenad, the atlas mapped the thematic—not just formal—return, displacement, and recodification of *pathos formulae*, resulting in a highly complex visual lexicon of codified physiognomical gestures that expressed the pathos-laden bodily configurations and dispositions of human nature. More than simply attesting to the influence of Semon's theory of the memory-trace (the engram) or approximating Jung's conception of a collective unconscious, filled with archetypes, Warburg's grand endeavor to construct an archaic memory-bank paid tribute to the philosophical legacy of the image cult of the nineteenth century. After all, was it not, in truth, Nietzsche, who in the *Birth of Tragedy* had held the Apollonian defense mechanism of the image against the Dionysian iconoclastic caesura of music? And, was it not Nietzsche, further, who had described Hamlet as a melancholic for having peered too deeply into the Dionysian abyss? Yet, if Warburg appropriated Nietzsche for his art-historical purposes, he did so with one crucial distinction. Unlike the philosopher, he invariably favored the ascendance of a sobering rationality, establishing how artists like Rembrandt had conquered the eruption of the Dionysian through Apollonian poise and (Kantian) distance.

That Benjamin's own mnemic theory of cultural history, laid out in the later *Arcades Project*, sometimes seemed to come uncannily close to Warburg's and Nietzsche's is evident from the now famous correspondence he conducted with Adorno in the 1930s. Pressed by his Frankfurt School friend and critic, Benjamin, until the very last, painstakingly sought to discriminate the dialectical image from archaic, mythical, or eternal ones, of the sort propagated by Jung and Klages. But not to much avail. Singling out the phrase "chaque époque rêve la suivante" in Benjamin's unfinished Baudelaire book, Adorno chided his friend for turning the dialectical image into the content of an immanent collective unconscious, instead of seeing this historico-political unconscious as materialistically or dialectically produced by the fetishized commodity. Always more attuned to the caesura-like force of music than Benjamin, Adorno proved unable to go along with the exegetical routes his friend pursued through the arcades of modernity, shying away from what he considered to be idolatrous ocularcentrism. But if one peers beyond the entrenched, old-standing dispute between Adorno and Benjamin, then the distinctions that separate Benjamin's unfinished *Arcades Project* from similar, contemporaneous cultural-historical ventures, such as the *Mnemosyne-Atlas*, become visible. It is fair to say that, despite notable exceptions, Warburg's quasi-ethnographic atlas set out to document the frozen petrified images of expressive human gestures, which may well explain the pathos that his project exudes. The restless sensation that may beset its present-day beholder seems generated by the atlas's overwhelming, affective concern with the human figure. In contrast, Benjamin's *Arcades* study testifies to the disappearance of the human, capturing its alienation and uneasy survival in the face of too much man-made technology and instrumental reason. In leafing through the reconstructed remainders of the two unfinished projects one notices the palpable differences. As one's gaze moves from the *Mnemosyne-Atlas* to the *Passagen-Werk*, or from the frozen human figure to its virtual eclipse, it is as if one experiences, *in nuce*, the altered existential conditions of modernity, whose fading life-fabric during the first few decades of the twentieth century Benjamin so well described. Nowhere better than in his 1931 essay on photography did he draw modernity's fast-changing anatomy, when he devised that in place of excessive specular melancholia was to come a new political education of the gaze that could revolutionize the ocular sphere. Characterizing the medium as the revolutionary magnification of the "optical unconscious," the revelation of the physiognomical aspects that inhabit the minuscule, he favored the new urban photography of the Parisian Atget—strangely devoid of human life—and, seminally, the new social atlas, or physiognomy, of humankind, assembled by the socialist, later persecuted, German photographer, August Sander.[34] Starting out with a materialist account of early photography, the antiquated patina of the daguerreotype, Benjamin first evoked the melancholic, introverted gaze at the focus of early studio photographs. Bearing witness to a past age, these early, almost painterly portraits fixated the human face, covered by a shroud of silence in which the sitter's gaze was at rest. As if enveloped by an aura or nimbus from behind which their gaze met the beholder, these figures seemed comfortably at peace in their surrounding environment.[35] If later technological exploits during the *Jugendstil* period furtively aimed to recreate this lost aura by artificial means, then their false pretensions were eventually exposed by Atget's vast urban topographies. His photographs depicted Paris's streets as empty crime scenes—murder scenes from which the human subject had been eliminated; not lonely streets (for that would amount to pathetic fallacy) but empty ones, devoid of affect, of *Stimmung*, hence *stimmungslos*. Atget's vistas of urban Paris were the anarchistic products of a destructive photographer—not unlike Benjamin's destructive character—who cleared out the place, making room for the politically educated gaze, exchanging bourgeois intimacies and the Biedermeier *intérieur* for the illumination of previously unseen detail. As such, his urban topographies laid the ground for surrealistic photography's *Bild-Raum*, which further cleared the passage for the progressive alienation of humans from their *Umwelt*. The new political, spectatorial gaze to which all of Atget's images addressed themselves no longer was at home in representative portrait photography, just as little as the new Soviet cinema any longer depicted the human face auratically, making way instead for the nameless expression of revolutionary workers. But it was above all August Sander, renegade photographer and sociopolitical outcast, who would compile the new didactic manual or social atlas of the human figure, *Antlitz der Zeit* (Face of the time) — an "exercise atlas" [*Übungsatlas*], as Benjamin called it, that was to give shape to the revolutionary political gaze. Replacing the quaint medium of the picture book (*Bilderbuch*) or family album full of portraits with a new sociopolitical physiognomy, Sander transformed Lavater's naturalistic, deeply conservative art of physiognomy — an obvious precursor of the worst to come in the fascist pseudoscience of phrenology — into a new "scientific" method.[36] Benjamin summed up the atlas's inordinate political significance when, writing on the eve of National Socialism's ascendance to power, he observed that Sander's images acquired new actuality in light of the power displacements in Germany, a period during which the sharpening of the physiognomical had become a vital necessity. Under the circumstances, Warburg's mnemic atlas, illustrating humankind's expressive gestures, would be strangely out of place, just as much as left-wing melancholy, whose harmful effects Benjamin discerned in the aesthetic productions of Kästner and the New Objectivity. For, whether one aligned oneself with the right or the left, now one would have to be prepared to be interrogated by the lens, as to "where one comes from."[37] Still, despite such revolutionary intent, the movement Benjamin traced through the photography essay was highly ambiguous. Although he seemed poised to accept the far-reaching encroachment of modernity's new technologies upon the present, one is left with the curious anomaly that early photography for him — nothing more so than portrait photography — always remained inextricably invested not just with a "halo" or cultic "aura" but with the pathos of melancholia. Only thus can one understand the unusual fascination with which he lingered over a childhood photograph of Kafka's, in which he discerned the melancholic glance of sadness, noting how the young boy threatened to be pushed out of the picture's frame by the ornamental decor and oversized hat, were it not for his immeasurably sad eyes.[38]

Against better insight, something of the same ambiguous affect captures the beholder who contemplates Benjamin's portrait—a portrait to which we must now return, as we conclude the movement of mirrorings and framings between these multiple images. In it, we encounter an image, perhaps even pictorial trace, that could well be added to Aby Warburg's unfinished archive of gestures, the *Mnemosyne-Atlas*, which also included tableaux on mourning. Benjamin's portrait might well have been inserted in this picture gallery, not just because he seemed inclined to pose in languid manner, mimicking the anatomy of melancholy. Casting now a downward gaze, now a melancholic glance at the distanced spectator, Benjamin seems frozen, not unlike Klee's *Angelus Novus* or Dürer's fallen angel, or even his poetic double, Baudelaire, furiously parrying the shocks of modernity coming from outside. For, doesn't Benjamin, in his well-known Baudelaire study, refer to Freud's consciousness as the agency that fends off shocks and external stimuli, the unconscious itself becoming the repository of memory-traces, not fully contained, perhaps not fully experienced? When viewed against the Baudelaire study, Benjamin's portrait distantly seems to attest to *pathos formulae*, as Warburg tended to call them: age-old mantic gestures, devised to overcome fear—and, by extension—to ward off the return of the mythical and primeval in contemporary history. Perhaps, then, in a postmodern age marked by the deadening or waning of affect, Benjamin's portrait, laden with pathos, flashes as an image that, however briefly, might appear to serve as a potential antidote.[39] No longer simply a quaint image of history's picture book or photo album, Benjamin's portrait, looking deceptively familiar, detaches itself and for a brief moment—now—seems to enter into legibility.

PART 3

Rethinking History

NINE

History as the Delayed Disintegration of Phenomena

FRITZ BREITHAUPT

To the question what can and what cannot have a history, Benjamin gives a clear answer: there can only be a history of phenomena.[1] The logic of Benjamin's link of history and phenomena can be summarized as follows: history is that which enables a phenomenon to last. Thus, the possibility of having a history and a future is not secondary or coincidental to the structure of the phenomenon, but rather an essential part of it. It must be part of the structure of the phenomenon that it can be remembered, can be repeated, can have an afterlife. Thus, already in its first and maybe only appearance, the phenomenon must be more than a phenomenon. Something in the phenomenon must prevent it from completely exhausting itself, burning out, or using itself up so that something remains open for the future. According to Benjamin, this remaining open is a holding back: the phenomenon withholds something inside itself which is not revealed. *Within* the phenomenon there is something nonphenomenal that does not appear, and *within* the event there is something that does not take place. History—and that will be the subject of this examination—comes into play by delaying the appearance of this nucleus within the phenomenon.

We are at the starting point of a discussion with many questions and many paths that might very well be wrong tracks within Benjamin's writings. Why did Benjamin in the 1930s turn to negotiations about history when politics seemed to be the question of the day? Could Benjamin entertain a hope in history such as the Marxist or Messianic one? Another of the many questions: What can Benjamin's now-itself-aged notion of history, if he has one, do for us today? In order to comprehend Benjamin's thought on history and phenomenology, I will choose the figure of inclusion, the nonphenomenal nucleus, as the red thread of the discussion. This might not be the fastest way—and I have to apologize for the detours that this approach makes necessary—but it has the advantage of being close to Benjamin's own formulations. Benjamin locates the event of history in the making-phenomenal of the nonphenomenal nucleus of the phenomena. There can only be a history because the nucleus withholds its appearance until it finally reveals itself in the moment of recognizability (*Erkennbarkeit*). Several of Benjamin's projects are essentially informed by this notion of concealment; for example, the project of the *Passagen-Werk* as a whole aims for the emergence of what is (still) being held back from and by the nineteenth century.

History is not external to phenomena but, as Benjamin says, a "movement in their inside" [*Bewegung in ihrem Innern*].[2] This movement within each phenomenon is first of all an active withholding of the nucleus. Only by withholding itself does the nucleus exist. Since it is withholding itself, it does not appear *yet*; thereby it points to an unknown future in which it could appear. That is why Benjamin calls this nonphenomenal nucleus within the phenomenon its "historic index," or the secret index of the past, "by which it is referred to redemption," which points from within to a future of the phenomenon: namely, to the future in which this inside is turned out.[3] Benjamin also characterizes this relationship between the phenomenon and its future as a "being-drawn-to," as an "expectation," or a "heliotropism" that causes the past to turn toward the coming of the future.[4]

Benjamin gives a specific turn to the historic index: this pointing to the future is not an indefinite opening toward the future, but rather a concrete expectation of a specific recognizability in one specific—although not predetermined—moment in the future *that can be missed*. Because of this moment, every phenomenon is dated. It is dated not so much from the moment of its first appearance, but from the coming appearance in the "moment of recognizability" (the *Jetzt der Erkennbarkeit* or the *Augenblick der Erkennbarkeit*).[5] Until this point in time, something remains within the phenomenon that resists its complete appearance, its exhaustion, and its dissolution in appearing; only in the "moment of recognizability" does the nonphenomenal nucleus of the phenomenon emerge and become (if this is possible) phenomenal, thereby permitting the complete (and thus the only true) recognition of the phenomenon.[6] This is the completion of the phenomenon. It is a completion not in the sense of putting pieces together, but in the sense that a process comes to its end: it shows everything, causes everything to appear, is nothing but appearance, and therefore dissolves and consumes itself completely. It burns, as Benjamin says, and thereby experiences its redemption.[7]

On this basis, we have to ask what exactly this nonphenomenal nucleus within the phenomenon is. I quote one of Benjamin's fragments: "The coming awakening stands like the Trojan horse of the Greeks in the Troy of the dream."[8] The act of waking up, as one should recall, is for Benjamin identical with the moment of recognizability ("The Now of recognizability is the moment of awakening") so that it is far to conclude that Benjamin aims at the structure of recognition when he speaks about waking up.[9] The Troy of the dreams is visible and phenomenal, but inside the Trojan horse (which itself is within Troy) are the hidden, thus "nonphenomenal," Greeks who are waiting to emerge. The hour in which the Greeks climb out of the horse and appear, constituting the future moment of waking up and of recognizability, is the very hour in which the destruction of Troy is undertaken: Troy is burned down. The price that must be paid for the emergence of the nonphenomenal nucleus inside the phenomenon is the destruction of the phenomenon (dream) itself. Thus, the possibility that a phenomenon has a future (and a history) is identical with the possibility of its destruction.

Again we have to ask: What is the recognition that can take place in the "moment of recognizability" and awakening? Why does this awakening collide with the dream as a recognition? And why is this recognition at the same time a destruction or dephenomenalization?

Upon awakening, the dream is recognized for what it is: *a dream*. To recognize one's dream as simply a dream means to shake it off and to wake up; a dream seems to be real only as long as one does not know that it is a dream. Once recognized for what it is, the dream loses its authority over the realm of the real. Therefore, the recognition of the dream as a dream is possible only in the simultaneous end or destruction of the dream. This recognition of the dream as a dream (and likewise the phenomenon as a phenomenon) does not come from the outside. Rather, it comes from within the dream, as in the case of the Trojan horse. The dream is indeed a dream, and it is this state of being-a-dream that is recognized. In other words, that which can be recognized in the "moment of recognizability" is exactly that which makes the dream a dream and the phenomenon a phenomenon: namely, its dream-ness or phenomenality, which resides *within* the phenomenon while remaining nonphenomenal in itself. The phenomenon exists only because of its phenomenality *and* is destroyed by its phenomenality, thus constituting and destroying itself.[10] Phenomena have a history precisely because they are not "entities," but rather human constructs, be they dreams, illusions, cities, institutions, or a tradition whose existence is pending on perception and make-believe.

Benjamin presents a similar movement of *Desillusion* in the famous passage of the sock. A young Benjamin puts his hand in a sock and grabs the end of the sock, the seam, in order to pull out the *Mitgebrachte* as the "content" of the sock. However, when he turns the sock inside out, there is nothing: nothing more than the sock, nothing but a cover without an inside or content. "It taught me that form and content, cover and covered are one and the same" [*Es lehrte mich, daß Form und Inhalt, Hülle und Verhülltes dasselbe sind*].[11] The turning inside out exposes that which resisted appearing, the nonphenomenal nucleus. But it does not show the true content of the nucleus; rather, it shows the phenomenal cover from the inside, *as a cover*. What was previously understood to be real and substantial turns out to be a mere cover, deception, and fiction.[12] History is a history of fiction: or more precisely, history is a delay of the ending of fictions.

We have to follow Benjamin one step further before we can try again to tie the notions of phenomenon and history together. The recognition that might take place in this "moment of recognizability" is split. It is at the same time a recognition of the dream *and* of the "dream-ness" of the dream. The mask (the sock) is displayed from both sides: the mask as reality and as a *staging* of reality.[13] For this split cognition, Benjamin coined the term "dialectic image." The dialectic image is an image in which the vision of the image conflicts with the exhibition of the image-ness of the image. It is a *dialectic* image since its two sides, the phenomenal appearance and the possibility of the condition of this appearance, only exist by means of each other and by projecting each other as its precondition. For Benjamin, every phenomenon is a dialectic image since it only appears through its (hidden) phenomenality. The obvious dilemma, then, is that a recognition of the phenomenon is not possible; either the phenomenon is taken for real or the phenomenon is recognized as such and thus ceases to exist, leaving the recognition empty-handed.

It was in Goethe, Hölderlin, and Brecht that Benjamin found his first witnesses for this dialectic image; Benjamin quotes Hölderlin's strong words:

For the tragic transport is actually empty, and the least restrained.—Thereby, in the rhythmic sequence of the representations wherein the transport presents itself, there becomes necessary what in poetic meter is called caesura, the pure word, the counterrhythmic rupture—namely, in order to meet the onrushing change of representations at its highest point, in such a manner that not the change of representation but the representation itself very soon appears.[14]

Hölderlin's "onrushing change of representations" necessitates the "representation itself," meaning the representation *as a representation*, since it alone resists and interrupts the rapid flow. Benjamin rephrases this idea, writing that the caesura is that by which "every expression simultaneously comes to a standstill, in order to give space to the expressionless power inside all artistic media" [*jeder Ausdruck sich legt, um einer innerhalb aller Kunstmittel ausdruckslosen Gewalt Raum zu geben*].[15] This expressionless power *within* the expression of the artwork consists in the recognition of the expression *as an expression*. This is why Hölderlin can speak of the caesura as the "pure word," meaning the word that is recognized as a word, which cannot demand authority over the communication and the expression, but rather stands exposed as nothing but a word.[16] This ex-position does not contain a positive message, but it does "give space" [*Raum . . . geben*], a space not like Kant's sense of a space a priori (although it shares its essential emptiness and thereby openness with Kant's space a priori), but instead a space that is suddenly provided only because it is emptied out.

Now we are finally able to risk an answer to the question of what a phenomenon is for Benjamin. A phenomenon has two sides: the presentation of something *and* the claim that this presentation is to be taken for real. The claim to be real that is given to all phenomena is the phenomenality, a phenomenality that is empty since there is no reality to which it corresponds, but that alone posits the phenomenon as reality. It is not the norm of reality, but rather the force of its normation. Thus, the phenomenon is simultaneously something that appears and something that hides within its appearance the normation of its appearance. In short, every phenomenon is a dialectical image.

What is unmasked in the recognition of the dream as a dream, and likewise of the phenomenon as a phenomenon, is the ability of the phenomenon to qualify as something real that in truth exists only as a phenomenon, a dream, or a fiction. Only by "hiding" and suppressing the corrosive phenomenality "within" can the phenomenon claim to be in touch with and part of the real, a claim that constitutes the phenomenon since it only exists in the form of a claim. Thus, the nonphenomenal nucleus (the phenomenality) alone makes the phenomenon possible and posits it; but in the phenomenon, this phenomenality or force of positing compromises the phenomenon. The phenomenon can claim itself—its existence—only by simultaneously suppressing the claim; it can be a claim only by hiding this act of self-claiming and self-positing.

Perceivers and beholders facing phenomena are subject to what Brecht decided to call the "alienation effect": they observe the presentation and the presentation of the presentation at once. The phenomenon is fundamentally split (*zweideutig*). Once the mirror is lifted, and once the recognition in the "moment of recognizability" occurs, both sides are recognized at once. But between the two, no cooperation and integration is possible, only an over-integration, which is simultaneously the disintegration of the phenomenon. The recognition of the phenomenon in its phenomenality affects its self-postulated and therefore false claim of reality, thereby causing the destruction of not only the claim but also the phenomenon as such; the phenomenality destroys the phenomenon and the positing force deposits the posited, leaving nothing behind but a mere phantom and perhaps an empty space, a space that Werner Hamacher has called the "afformative political event."[17] While the remaining phantom or ghost cannot engender a recognition since it has lost its *Rätselcharakter* and can only continue to exist in the history books of certain pedagogical institutions, this space of the "afformative" is the stage for Benjamin's politics. Benjamin uses this conception of the dialectic image to characterize historical situations. The dialectic image presents the past along with the "past-ness" of the past, thereby ending the authority of the past over the present. The past is dated toward the future moment of its recognizability, in which it will be destroyed. This is what Benjamin calls the "Now-Time" [*Jetztzeit*]; Now-Time exists only as the place of the elimination of the past. Benjamin says: "Erst der erlösten Menschheit fällt ihre Vergangenheit zu." This is usually translated as: "Only the redeemed mankind appropriates its past." However, the German *zufallen* means both "to appropriate" and "to slam shut" like a door. Thus, we also have to read and translate: "Only for the redeemed mankind, does the door to its past slam shut." The redeemed mankind "appropriates" (*fällt zu*) its past precisely in the "slamming shut" (*zufallen*) of the past. It is only by *ending* the past's claim over the present time, that we "appropriate" the—ended—past. This is the way mankind is redeemed: it is redeemed of its past.

This conception of the phenomenon accounts for why Benjamin's phenomenology (theory of images) is at the same time a cultural theory, as it is in general a strength of Benjamin's thought that it does not need to separate the spheres of aesthetics, culture, and politics.[18] Indeed, Benjamin's conception of the phenomenon directly translates itself into politics where cultural institutions, political parties, and economic interests manifest themselves as "phenomena." I quote Benjamin's well-known lines:

> The story is told of an automaton constructed in such a way that it could play a winning game of chess, answering each move of an opponent with a countermove. A puppet in Turkish attire and with a hookah in its mouth sat before a chessboard placed on a large table. A system of mirrors created the illusion ("Illusion") that this table was transparent from all sides. Actually, a little hunchback who was an expert chess player sat inside and guided the puppet's hand by means of strings. One can imagine a philosophical counterpart to this device. The puppet called "historical materialism" is to win all the time [*gewinnen soll immer*]. It can easily be a match for anyone if it enlists the services of theology, which today, as we know, is wizened and has to keep out of sight.[19]

The *Witz* of Benjamin's conception is that the effect of the automaton is suspended in the very moment in which the dwarf inside is recognized as a dwarf, so that the illusionary machine is recognized as an illusionary machine. It is not the victory of a puppet or a school that is Benjamin's goal, but rather the suspension of puppets and parties. On the one hand, the dwarf allows for a smooth functioning of the game as long as he remains hidden; on the other hand, the dwarf interrupts the game as soon as he is presented, such as he is in Benjamin's text.[20] Benjamin has made his own position destructible since this puppet can be unmasked when the inside nucleus of the machine comes to the surface. Just as Benjamin's position is destructible, so is fascism, the enemy that Benjamin is addressing in this text. In the image of the fair's attraction, the *historischer Materialismus* does not significantly differ from the fascism Benjamin is fighting. One has to recover from the dangerous fascination with machinery that cannot be understood, and to which one thereby falls prey; the task is to find the ugly dwarf within fascism, especially since fascism does not reveal its nucleus as does *Historical Materialism*.

It is precisely through a suspension of the false claim to qualify for something it is not that a phenomenon can have a history. History is the correction and elimination of the claim to authority of a phenomenon, fiction, ideology, or institution. Thus, history does not directly happen to people, but to those reality-promising constructs and institutions that are based on the validity of their fiction — and on the fiction of their validity. This is why history is a political force. For Benjamin, there is not simply a "history of politics," since politics is structured as history, a history that wipes out and burns off its players, leaving nothing behind but heaps of rubble.

From this conception of history results Benjamin's vehement rejection of Historicism. In his *Theses on the Philosophy of History* (Über den Begriff der Geschichte), from which I have taken the passage of the chess-playing automaton, Benjamin rejects the historicist method of "identification" [*Einfühlung*], which abandons historical distance in order to breathe life into the spirit of a period ("nachzuerleben").[21] Someone who identifies with a historical period views the past as real and forgets to recognize the past *as a past*.[22] Therefore, Benjamin calls historicist historiography a history of the victors, since it affirms the authority of what seems to be a reality, without presenting the law of its illusion, the ugly dwarf within. According to this understanding, Historicism celebrates, unknowingly, the continuity of the victory of illusions and the continuation of mere fictions. For Benjamin, however, history is not a continuation of the past, but rather its finishing.

It comes as no surprise that Benjamin shows an active interest in comedy.[23] The occurrence of history, as it has been described, has the structure of comedy. Comedy rips off the mask of false authorities and dismantles their claims of being more than they are. As Hegel says, comedy consists of the play with the mask. In a related way, Marx has emphasized the importance of masks in the coming of the new era:

> The tradition of all the dead generations weighs like a nightmare on the
> brain of the living. And just when they seem engaged in revolutionizing
> themselves and things, in creating something that has never yet existed,

precisely in such periods of revolutionary crisis they anxiously conjure up the spirits of the past to their service and borrow from names, battle cries, and costumes in order to present the new scene of world history in this time-honored disguise and this borrowed language.[24]

But while Marx attempts to distinguish between two kind of masks—the positive tragedy that opens up the future, and the minor form of comedy that only parodies and remains stuck to the past—for Benjamin, it is comedy that allows for a break with the past.[25] This comedy rests upon repeatability, a structure Benjamin also sees made possible in modernity by technical means. In its repetition, the event is detached from its original context and shows by this very possibility that, even in its first appearance, it does not have a true content, but instead consists of nothing but a mere mask or cover that hides the essential emptiness below.

There is not much that remains in Benjamin's world, and there seems little to be gained from the destruction of the phenomena and fictions, not even the intellectual satisfaction of cognition. Even in the moment of recognizability, it is only recognized that there is nothing to be recognized. It is a recognition of nothing, and thus a nonrecognition or nonexperience. However, in "The Destructive Character" (Der destruktive Charakter), Benjamin comments on the value of destruction. It makes space, he says, which only exists because it was thought to be occupied by some phenomenon or fiction. When this fiction is emptied out, the space remains. In this space, the future is not blocked. Someone or something could arrive. Benjamin says: "There will be someone who might need this place without occupying it."[26] The empty space is the podium for possible speakers.[27] For Benjamin, this empty space is the only sphere for politics, *a politics of advent*. Benjamin does not make an image of this person who might come and need this space. Every image or phenomenon would only occupy the space and thereby block the future. Sometimes, Benjamin calls this coming and space-needing person the Messiah. This Messiah can only arrive in strict imagelessness. He or She does not even need to come because the empty space is the condition of possibility of his or her arrival, and that is all that is needed.

The question might arise whether we today still need to read Benjamin. This question is justified. In fact, there is at least one recent school of thought that claims to be beyond mere "positions" and their blindness, and thereby beyond history. For such a school, Benjamin must appear as outdated. It is a school of thought that is not hesitant to talk about history: New Historicism. This school has called on scholars to take a position in relation to it, and this invitation seems to be more than an academic ritual, a simple argument for or against an idea; rather the essence of New Historicism seems to consist in the debate around it. Thus, even one of its major proponents summarizes that "The New Historicism" is less "a definable project"; "rather . . . the term 'New Historicism' is currently being invoked in order to bring such issues into play and to stake out—or to hunt down—specific positions within the discursive spaces mapped by these issues."[28] (These "issues" being various questions about the status of literature as a "discourse"). New Historicism's "attack" of "traditional" positions is certainly honorable insofar as it continuously reevaluates the foundations of our thought. In this hunting game, academics escape an ideology that emanates from any one position, are not fooled by hidden dwarfs within these positions, and dismantle any position instead. So they claim. We are led to conclude that it is in fact even necessary for the term *New Historicism* to remain without a position so that someone— a literary scholar as it appears—can import his or her "issues" and can fill the empty term with an undetermined position in order to defend or attack it. This is consistent with the scholarship that has appeared in the name of New Historicism or some other names, in which many critics with quite different agendas use the term for their work in a more or less sympathetic way; thus, it also is not surprising that it seems more clear in the texts of its opponents than of its proponents what New Historicism is.[29]

Perhaps academic discussions have often circulated around undefined terms, but the blatantness with which New Historicists admit to and even insist on the undefinedness of their discussion—while at the same time continuing their work—should still make us pause and take a closer look. Is this the consequent next step beyond Benjamin, for whom recognition coincides with the destruction of the recognized? New Historicists and their like only bring up "issues" or "positions" to show how they can be "hunted down" or be part of a game. Thereby they do not fall prey to false beliefs or hidden dwarfs because they do not invest too much in any particular position they already know to be merely part of a game. The security of this game allows for a rather militant vocabulary. One could be astonished at the unshakable ease with which H. Aram Veeser and others use the vocabulary of war when they speak of attacks and "counterattacks": where some "lent covering fire," others "struck down" certain doctrines, where positions are "hunt[ed] down," books are "hostile," and one school of thought "threatens" the other, and so on.[30] However, the simple reason for this aggressive vocabulary is that all these fights, we are assured, are strictly academic fights, made possible within such an academic concept as New Historicism. While the "specific positions" and "issues" themselves appear to be only elements of the game, the real matter seems to be the perpetuation of an academia that needs to provide its members, the so-called intellectual community, with the safe superposition or institution from which they can take and destroy these "specific positions." Even when New Historicism invites us "to cross the boundaries" of the disciplines and "to take a position," we stay within the fortified city of academia. New Historicism, then, turns out to produce stability in the semblance of change and continuation in the guise of overcoming. Within its automaton we would not find an ugly dwarf but an academic with a notebook computer and dirty feet, sitting comfortably in his old armchair.

New Historicism, and that which has come out of this school of thought in recent years, is not beyond history, not beyond Benjamin, not beyond "positions." Even their relativistic nonpositions require stable institutions, the institution of an academy that can be taken for granted and thereby goes unquestioned. Benjamin, far from shying away from the metaphor of war, also writes about "taking a position": "The coming awakening stands like the Trojan horse of the Greeks in the Troy of the dream."[31] The "Troy of the dream" is indeed a position in the original military sense of the word, but this position is not attacked from the outside, not from some other position, but rather from within. *Inside* the dream, the Trojan horse, the academy, stands as the future moment of awakening. Thus, the positions Benjamin presents are internally equipped (literally "enhorsed") with destructibility. They are positions that can be taken—taken away, invaded, and destroyed by their own doing.

What distinguishes practitioners of New Historicism from the major thinkers of the last decades—Adorno, Derrida, Foucault, Lacan, and de Man, to name only those whose names are frequently evoked by New Historicists themselves—is that these thinkers have deeply doubted and exposed the academic positions they have occupied. Certainly, New Historicism raises its voice against disciplinarity and in favor of an (unclear whether such a thing can exist) interdisciplinarity, against false objectivity and in favor of "professional confessions," and against tradition and in favor of newness or "subversiveness"—all within the safe space of academia, whose rules are followed even and especially in its antitraditionalistic rhetoric. What is at stake is the practice of academia. Different from New Historicism, Benjamin's goal is not the constitution of new schools or trends within the safe frame of the institution of academia—*das kleine Spiel der Positionen und Positiönchen*— but rather the act of making the institutionalized intellectual unnecessary, and the awakening from this illusion as well. Thus, Benjamin distinguishes sharply between the "delivering of an apparatus of production [such as the university, I might add] and its change" [*Belieferung eines Produktionsapparates und seiner Veränderung*].[32]

New Historicism receives its name from "history," but New Historicism deals with history only insofar as it can tame and mold it into a mere topic of intellectual thought. This explains Montrose's description of Stephen Greenblatt's (as well as his own) project as "substituting for the diachronic text of an autonomous literary history the synchronic text of cultural system."[33] History, to say the least, contains no risk for these intellectuals but merely provides them with "material." For Benjamin, history is not a mere topic; rather, history is the name for an experience that resists being a "topic." While the perception of any change requires a stable point of reference with which one can evaluate the changing (as Kant has it, "Alle Zeitbestimmung setzt etwas Beharrliches voraus"), *history* occurs for Benjamin in the breaking down of those structures and forms that serve as the stable ground of one's own position (Kant's *Beharrliche*). This history is a history precisely of the possibility to observe what is happening. Thus, the breakdown of one's position neither permits one simply to observe what is going on nor to maintain a frozen position toward it; one is simply left with an empty space, not a position. Therefore, to take a position means first of all to take (away) your own position: to ex-pose it.

I might add one final thought. Although I indeed see the need to read Benjamin and to challenge those who proclaim the end of history, one question remains unaddressed. It is a question about the status of money and economics today. Political institutions and other fictions are perhaps destroyed in their recognition, but economic interests remain. This does not mean that money is not itself a fiction. Quite the opposite: money might well be the fiction of fiction, the signifier that claims to make everything compatible, the fetish of capitalism. Money remains even after the destructive character has emptied out the world. The question that I will not be able to answer here, and perhaps not even articulate in an answerable form, is what can prevent money from taking over the emptied place. Again, it is a question by, for, and to Benjamin.

TEN

Virtual Paris

Benjamin's 'Arcades Project'

KEVIN MCLAUGHLIN

All great texts contain their virtual translation [*virtuelle Übersetzung*].
—WALTER BENJAMIN, *"The Task of the Translator"*

The new translations of Walter Benjamin's writings, which are on a much larger scale than the earlier English collections of his essays, may be as sure a sign as any of the more than merely passing interest his work still holds today nearly sixty years after his untimely death.[1] The latest return to Benjamin in the English-speaking world can be explained in part by the much talked about turn to history and culture across the humanities, especially in North America. In Benjamin, North American scholars and critics have found a thinker with a philosophically informed approach to culture who at the same time pays close attention to politics, history, and the emergence of newer forms of mass media. In the North American context, as indeed in others, Benjamin has thus reemerged as a potential opportunity to rethink traditional conceptions of art and culture as they come into contact with an array of developments loosely termed *modernity*. Cynical dismissal of a figure with the originality and scope of Benjamin as a mere effect of passing fashion, an ephemeral response to the desire to "have it all," as one observer has put it, appears especially misguided in this case.[2] By the same token, however, accepting the challenges Benjamin presents to ways of thinking, and especially of not thinking, with which we have become comfortable—ways of thinking, for example, about the historical character of culture, of knowledge, and of experience—will not get any easier with the appearance of a broader range of his writings in translation.

In particular, the appearance in English recently of a broader sample of early aesthetic writings together with a translation of the late *Arcades Project* will, one hopes, stimulate a reconsideration of one of the uncritical assumptions that has contributed to the popularity of Benjamin among academic literary scholars in America, namely, the assumption that a turn to culture and history necessarily implies a turn away from the philosophical problems of aesthetics. An instructive example of this can be found in current discussions of aesthetic value. Much contemporary work in this area has been concerned to approach it as a sociological and historical question, and this has invariably led to Benjamin. John Guillory's influential book *Cultural Capital* is a case in point. Guillory cites as a call for sociological analysis Benjamin's remark in "Theses on the Philosophy of History" that "there is no document of culture which is not at the same time a document of barbarism."[3] Thus Benjamin becomes enlisted in Guillory's project "to translate the (false) philosophical problem of 'aesthetic value' into the sociological problem of 'cultural capital.'"[4] Benjamin would undoubtedly have sympathized with the attempt "to conceptualize the social effects" of literary works under capitalism, but for him this was anything but a matter of translating the question out of philosophy. On the contrary, from Benjamin's perspective aesthetic value derives from the capacity of the work to conserve a dimension of philosophy—to allow philosophy to take on a certain dimensionality. The value of the literary work for Benjamin may indeed be said to manifest itself in translation. But the starting and stopping of translation—the "plunging character" [*das Stürzen*] Benjamin so admires in Hölderlin's Sophocles translations—is valuable, not because it results in aesthetic or *cultural capital*, but because it makes possible the appearance of a philosophical dimension in art. At several key points in his writing, including at the end of the translation essay just mentioned, Benjamin describes this dimension as "virtual." The following analysis of this term in Benjamin's earlier aesthetic writings suggests how it is conserved in the later cultural and historical critique of the *Arcades Project*.

My aim is to counter the assimilation of Benjamin's cultural and historical criticism to the antiphilosophical approaches that regularly embrace his work, specifically, the assimilation exemplified by current work like Guillory's on the question of aesthetic value. The identification of aesthetic value with use-value, which Guillory (following Bourdieu) attributes to Kant, is no doubt a false philosophical problem. But the sociological translation envisioned by Guillory and others neglects the genuine philosophical problem broached by Kant and reinterpreted by Benjamin in his critical writings. The conservation Kant explores in his aesthetics is not that of "use-value" or "incommensurability," as is often claimed, but rather of a "power of judgment" [*Urteilskraft*] — of a potential to judge singularly, in a manner that is universal and at the same time not reducible to the application of concepts or forms. This critical moment is pursued by Benjamin in his aesthetic and cultural criticism. For him it is bound to the emergence of the image in a singular moment of reading. As he notes in the *Arcades Project*, "The image that is read [*das gelesene Bild*] — which is to say, the image in the now of its recognizability — bears [*trägt*] to the highest degree the imprint of the perilous critical moment on which all reading is founded."[5] The encounter with the image is critical in the etymological sense that it bears a decision or a judgment. "Virtual" is the word Benjamin uses in his early aesthetic writings to describe the philosophical ideal conserved by such aesthetic judgments. In this sense, as it becomes virtually philosophical in the late *Arcades Project*, Paris turns into a study of the kind of aesthetic conservation that had been the subject of some of Benjamin's earlier writings on the philosophy of art.

'Gehalt' Theories

A good place to start a reconsideration of the question of aesthetic value in Benjamin is with the question of "content" [*Gehalt*] in art. As with so many of the major terms in Benjamin's writing (the term "dialectic," for example), content is not quite what it seems.[6] Despite its recurrence as a topic of critical reflection throughout his work, the question of content has yet to attract special attention among Benjamin's readers. The reason for this lack of attention could well lie in the way Benjamin may seem merely to repeat a category that is central to traditional Hegelian thought. But as with dialectic, the category of content in Benjamin's work is far from a simple repetition of Hegel. Although we might have expected the question of content to appear and to play a leading role in his aesthetic writings, especially in view of its prominence in Hegel's aesthetic theory, there is nevertheless something surprising about the way Benjamin uses the term, something of a departure from the more traditional Hegelian concept of content in art. The repetition of Hegel in Benjamin's aesthetics cannot be assimilated to that mode of "dialectical repetition" [*Aufhebung*] that is its point of departure. This deviation is no small matter: it concerns principles that our way of viewing art shares with our way of understanding the world. With respect to such principles Benjamin uses the word "virtual" [*virtuell*] at key points in his aesthetic writings, inflecting the traditional, in particular Hegelian, concept of content in art and pulling this aesthetic matter toward debates in contemporary science over *principles of conservation*. The word virtual links fundamental aesthetic questions concerning the content and value of art—the element that makes possible what he calls the "afterlife" of works of art—to long-standing natural-scientific inquiry into the principles governing the conservation of matter in the physical world. Developments in nineteenth-century science, in particular the theory of the conservation of energy with its roots in Kant's *Naturphilosophie*, were of considerable importance to the philosophical culture of Benjamin's generation of German intellectuals.[7] It is part of the background against which Benjamin uses the word virtual as well as a source of his tendency to draw on the metaphors of energy and force field throughout his aesthetic writings. The natural-scientific connotation of the word virtual draws attention to Benjamin's aesthetic writings as attempting to elaborate a theory of conservation—in other words, a theory of aesthetic value.

This can be brought out more clearly in relation to the word *Gehalt* that is used to describe the "content" of art. Until the end of the eighteenth century, *Gehalt* described the amount of precious metal (gold or silver) contained in a coin (dictionaries at the time give the Latin *valor* as an equivalent).[8] Hegel, following Schiller somewhat it seems and adapting this metaphor to aesthetic theory, employs the term *Gehalt* to describe the essential substance or kernel of truth in the work of art. As such, *Gehalt* defines what is essential in art for philosophy according to Hegel. In an illuminating essay on this topic, Lukács speaks of what he labels Hegel's *Gehaltsästhetik*, declaring that this focus on the substance of truth, the *Gehalt* of the work of art, is itself the "hidden and fruitful kernel" [*verborgener und fruchtbarer Kern*] of Hegel's aesthetics. It is from such a kernel, Lukács concludes, that a genuinely historical aesthetic theory will grow.[9] The *Gehalt* of the work of art in Hegel, Lukács explains, does not "originate" out of the "individual activity of the aesthetic subject, the activity of the artist, or the recipient," but rather from the "independently existing objective social and historical reality."[10] For Lukács, the individual artist cannot fully grasp this substantial content, or *Gehalt*, of his work: he is rather in the grip of this *Gehalt* when it becomes the subject of his work. The one who *is* in a position to grasp the *Gehalt* of the work, according to this view, is the philosopher of art. The Hegelian philosopher occupies the necessary vantage point from which to observe and identify the substance of truth that exists impurely in the work of art.[11] This is also the standpoint from which the essential content of works of philosophy appear to this particular philosophical position, whether it be that of Hegel on the writings of his precursors or that of Lukács on the "essential kernel" of Hegel's philosophy.

The divergence of Benjamin from such a perspective is suggested by the word virtual that appears in the phrase at the end of the essay on translation: "All great texts contain [*enthalten*] their virtual translation [*virtuelle Übersetzung*]."[12] For the translator, the *Gehalt* of an original is not like a substance; it is not a purified intellectual essence to be extracted and infused into a foreign language. The translator does not, as Hegel and Lukács claim the philosopher does, subject the work to a process of cupellation, assaying and refining an essential substantial content that would form the *Gehalt* of the original.[13] This is what Benjamin is getting at in his translation essay when he says that, in relation to its content, a translation is always "inadequate, violent, and strange" [*unangemessen, gewaltig und fremd*].[14] It is, as he says, a "provisional" way of coming to terms with the strangeness of languages that manifests itself in translation. Here, in passing, Benjamin offers another somewhat covert hint to the alternative understanding of content in translation that he is after. The word "provisional" translates, provisionally, the German *vorläufig*—"alle Übersetzung nur eine irgendwie vorläufige Art ist, sich mit der Fremdheit der Sprachen auseinanderzusetzen."[15] *Vorläufig* (from *vorlaufen*: literally "to walk before") could also be translated as "passing," or perhaps "passing by." The translator is in a way a passerby, like the speaker of Baudelaire's poem by that title, "A une passante" (To a passerby), a poem that figures prominently in the extensive commentary on Baudelaire in Benjamin's *Arcades Project*. Like Baudelaire's poet, the translator can no more grasp the essential content of the original than the poet can seize and hold fast to the "fugitive beauté" of the *passante* in Baudelaire's poem.[16]

What comes to pass from the perspective of the translator is a matter, not of substance, but of potential—of "translatability" [*Übersetzbarkeit*], the "virtual translation" [*virtuelle Übersetzung*] contained by great writings. Baudelaire's poem is about a similar potential or virtuality in the encounter, or non-encounter, with the *passante* in the deafening Paris street. Thus Benjamin's characterization of translation as *vorläufig* suggests how his aesthetics are repeatedly grounded in his cultural and historical writing, and vice versa. This interconnection is rooted in a philosophy of aesthetic conservation involving virtuality.

Benjamin's writing is punctuated throughout with terms stressing potential: in addition to "translatability" [*Übersetzbarkeit*] and "recognizability" [*Erkennbarkeit*] there is, to name just some examples, "criticizability" [*Kritisierbarkeit*], "reproducibility" [*Reproduzierbarkeit*], and "legibility" [*Lesbarkeit*].[17] These are all parts of a vocabulary of virtuality that surfaces in his writings of the late 1910s and 1920s. This vocabulary emerges from Benjamin's approach to aesthetic content as a matter of divisibility (*Teilbarkeit*). An early example of this can be found in a fragment (probably from the late 1910s), published posthumously under the title, "On Aesthetics" [Zur Ästhetik].[18] Benjamin's specific concern here is with the question of content in relation to repetition:

> When grasped with the greatest exactitude the form and the content [*Gehalt*] of every work of art is always something that is unique and unprecedented. With regard to its concept, the material [*Stoff*] does not exist, in that it is to be thought of as at once inside and outside of the work of art. Every material [*Stoff*] of a work of art is something repeated in relation to the fundamental material [*Stoff*] that is its model, insofar as its existence in the work of art is thought of as being split [*gesondert*]. Whether the "material" ["*Stoff*"] of true works of art exists at all is indeed another question altogether. . . .
>
> The subject matter [*Inhalt*] of a work of art is either unique and unprecedented or it is essentially repetition. Thus the lyric poem is of the type that is unique and unprecedented content [*Gehalt*]: it is an original appearance in the medium of language. By contrast, the lyric is in the greatest opposition to the novel, which is a reflection [*Reflexion*] in the medium of language and which is with regard to its content [*Gehalt*] unconditionally and essentially repetition; and indeed repetition of an occurrence whose sphere is to

be determined as general as well as in every case particular. In general, this sphere is in any case not that of reality.[19]

It is striking here that content, or what is also referred to as "material" [*Stoff*], never actually presents itself in the work of art, according to Benjamin: it is rather split, severed (the German word here, *gesondert*, is related to the English "sundered"). The content is thus inside and outside of the work of art, which is to say that it is not simply identifiable with the work itself. In other words, the work is a medium of a divisible content.[20] Benjamin's stress on divisibility here is in keeping with the understanding of matter generally in the tradition of *Naturphilosophie* stretching back through Kant to Leibniz, the latter of whom is likely a key source for the term "virtual" in Benjamin— a tradition away from which Hegel and his followers turned with the aim of establishing the priority of truly philosophical *speculative* science over what they viewed as the inferior physical sciences that relied on mathematics.[21] In this sense Benjamin's early remarks on the divisibility of content in aesthetic media prepares the ground for what he will call "virtual" in several key passages from his writings of the 1920s. These early reflections on aesthetic conservation mark a departure from a more conventional view of art as involving a process analogous to the preservation of a substance through time.[22] The decision to employ the word virtual to describe the potential content of "great writings" in the translation essay involves aesthetic matters in the broader context of a critique of a classical, here Hegelian, concept of content in aesthetics—content as conserved substance. This is where Benjamin's aesthetic theory is linked to the broader natural-philosophical context going back to Kant and Leibniz.[23] Signs of Benjamin's interest in this broader scientific context can be found throughout his work: from early notes on Bertrand Russell (in connection with his essay on language) to the borrowings from Henri Bergson in his Proust commentaries, the long passage from Arthur Stanley Eddington's 1929 *The Nature of the Physical World* cited at the beginning of "Some Reflections of Kafka" and the theory of the dialectical image as a force field in his posthumous *Arcades Project*.[24] But let us look now more closely at virtuality in Benjamin's aesthetic writings of the 1920s before going on to suggest how it manifests itself in the later cultural and historical critique carried out in the Paris project.[25]

Virtual Sites

The language of virtuality—of force, power, energy, and so on—can be found throughout Benjamin's major aesthetic writings of the 1920s, from "The Task of the Translator" to the study of the German *Trauerspiel* (mourning play) and the essay on Proust. In his study of German *Trauerspiel*, for instance, the word virtual describes the dimension through which *ideas* are explored—literally, "paced off" [*abgeschritten*]—historically.[26] But the word virtual plays an important role in another key passage from this period that has special affinities to the approach to history and culture taken by Benjamin in his writings of the 1930s. It occurs in the essay on Goethe's *Elective Affinities* as Benjamin offers an image of the virtuality at work in the interaction between critique (*Kritik*) and aesthetic content (*Gehalt*):

> Yet an image . . . is perhaps allowed. Let us suppose that one makes the acquaintance of a person who is handsome [*schön*] and attractive but impenetrable, because he carries a secret within him. It would be reprehensible to want to pry [*verwerflich, in ihn dringen zu wollen*]. Still it would surely be permissible to inquire [*forschen*] whether he has any siblings and whether their nature could not perhaps explain somewhat the enigmatic character of the stranger. In just this way critique seeks to discover [*forscht*] siblings of the work of art. All genuine works have their siblings in the realm of philosophy. It is, after all, precisely these figures in which the ideal of philosophy's problem appears.[27]

Benjamin goes on to explicate this image as a philosophical issue; at this point the word virtual makes an appearance. He begins following up on his image of the impenetrable stranger by stating that there is no question we can ask that would have as its answer the system or ideal of philosophy. Like the stranger's secret, such philosophical unity is beyond question—it is both a given and insusceptible to direct questioning. This is where works of art and criticism come in:

> Even if, however, the system [of philosophy] is in no sense attainable through inquiry, there are nevertheless constructions [*Gebilde*] which, without being questions, have the deepest affinity [*Affinität*] with the ideal of the problem. These are works of art. The work of art does not compete with

philosophy itself—it merely enters into the most precise relation to philosophy through its affinity [*Verwandtschaft*] with the ideal of the problem. And to be sure, according to a lawfulness grounded in the essence of the ideal as such, the ideal can represent itself [*sich darstellen*] solely in multiplicity. The ideal of the problem, however, does not appear in a multiplicity of problems. Rather, it lies buried [*vergraben*] in a multiplicity of works, and its excavation [*Förderung*] is the business of critique. The latter allows the ideal of the problem to appear in the work of art in one of its manifestations. For critique ultimately shows in the work of art the virtual formulatibility [*virtuelle Formulierbarkeit*] of the work's truth content [*Wahrheitsgehalt*] as the highest philosophical problem. . . . If, therefore, one may say that everything beautiful [*Schöne*] is connected in some way to the true, and that the virtual site [*virtueller Ort*] of the true in philosophy is determinable, then this is to say that in every true work of art an appearance of the ideal of the problem can be discovered.[28]

First of all, the focus in this passage is on criticism in relation to works of art as *constructions* in the sense of the collective form of the German word for "image" (*Gebilde*), for it is the capacity of the image to become a site of conservation that persists in Benjamin's writing from the earlier aesthetic writings through the essay on Proust ("The Image of Proust") to the *Arcades Project*. As images, Benjamin proposes in the Goethe essay, works of art conserve a philosophical ideal. They are not questions; yet, they are like the nonexistent question that would designate philosophy's problem. More specifically, they have an "affinity" [*Verwandtschaft*] with the ideal of the problem of philosophy, in the sense of the "elective affinities" [*Wahlverwandtschaften*] of Goethe's novel. This affinity of artworks to the ideal is grounded in a law according to which the philosophical ideal can only be represented (*darstellt*) in multiplicity. Not in a multiplicity of problems, however, but in a multiplicity of works—juxtapositions of images—does it appear "buried" [*vergraben*]. As Benjamin puts it here, the business of criticism is *Förderung*: "excavation" in the sense of mining—taking something out of the earth—but in this case, more accurately, also "bringing to light" or, closer to the etymology it shares with the English word, "furthering." What comes to light here and what is furthered and conserved is identified with nothing substantial; conserved in fact is the possibility that what philosophy seeks—vainly in its questioning—can still potentially appear.

The proposition that this occurs at a place or a site that is virtual (*ein virtueller Ort*) appears itself to require more explanation.[29] Hence the image of the secretive stranger. The image of the work of art would represent for the reader a place of possibility, in fact would represent place as possibility—a "virtual site" in the sense of a material place that becomes a medium of philosophical potential, a place that becomes what Benjamin calls a "human language," a language that "must communicate *something* (something other than itself)."[30] By way of such virtual sites the ideal of philosophy can become mixed up in place and vice versa: place can become mixed up in the ideal of philosophy. As medium, place can give philosophy an opportunity to *represent* its *ideal* to criticism. Criticism, then, is given to bringing out and conserving a virtual dimension of philosophy's ideal in an experience of place that would be akin to the encounter with the secretive stranger in Benjamin's parable, as well as to the encounter with the "stance of the narrator" [*Haltung des Erzählers*] in Benjamin's critique of the *Elective Affinities*—the veiled figure that passes before us in the images of the novella's "open secret."[31] Such encounters are fundamental to the image of Paris as a site of conservation in the *Arcades Project*. Indeed, Paris is a sort of mnemonic site in this late work, a distinctively modern version of the ancient rhetorical topos of the city in the "arts of memory."[32] The modernity of Benjamin's Paris derives from the proposition that it is a place, not where the past is recalled by the present, but where "what has been comes together in a flash with the now to form a constellation."[33] Out of this sudden "coming together" [*zusammentreten*] of what has been with the "now" springs what Benjamin calls the "dialectical image." As we read at one point in the *Arcades Project*, "The place [*Ort*] where one encounters them [dialectical images] is language."[34] Paris is such a place in this project: "Through its street names," Benjamin notes for example, "the city is a linguistic cosmos."[35]

But what, we might ask, does Paris as language communicate? To which the response, as formulated by Benjamin in his early essay on language, would be: "It communicates itself" [*teilt sich selbst mit*].[36] That is to say, Paris is a place that communicates itself as a medium—not as a means to an end, but as a medium of names. The names, moreover, are the parts of a fallen language, a language of mediacy and thus of judgment. As Benjamin says, "In exchange for the immediacy of the [divine] name that was damaged by [the Fall], a new immediacy arises: the magic of judgment [*Urteil*]."[37] The fallen language of man is a medium of judgment; at the moment of judgment the mediacy of fallen language becomes immediate. In other words, if the Fall is a judgment (*Urteil*) consigning all communication (*Mitteilung*) to impurity and mediateness, then the mediateness of communication may also be understood impurely to conserve such a primal judgment. Benjamin does not say it, but it might be said that *Mitteilung* becomes the virtual site or place of *Urteil*. Perhaps this is the "magic of judgment"—that it is mixed up in communication and can be experienced immediately in what Benjamin calls the "chatter" [*Geschwätz*] of language as medium.[38] As a place, Paris in the *Arcades Project* is the virtual site of judgment in this sense.

Excursus: Walking

Paris communicates itself, then, through divisible sites or places that conserve judgment. In this sense the Paris of the *Arcades Project* would communicate and conserve the relation Benjamin seeks to make readable in his manipulation of the German root word *Teil* (part) in the essay on language— the relation of divisibility (*Teilbarkeit*) and communicability (*Mitteilbarkeit*) to judgment (*Urteil*).[39] Such conservation is the aim of the artful montage of citations and reflections placed before the reader in the section of the project devoted to Paris streets ("Convolute P"). Judging from early notes and drafts as well as from the two exposés to the project, the motif of the street was a repeated point of departure for Benjamin in the study.[40] The streets of Paris themselves—their names—now take the place of the *passante* in Baudelaire's poem. They are like the crowd in Benjamin's explications of Baudelaire: a "veil through which the familiar city beckons to the flaneur as phantasmagoria."[41] Paris streets are, in other words, a moving force:

> They spoke of Paris as *la ville qui remue*—the city that never stops moving.
> But no less important than the life of this city's layout is here the unconquerable power [*Kraft*] in the names of streets, squares, and theaters, a power which persists in the face of all topographic displacement. Those little theaters which, in the days of Louis-Philippe, still lined the Boulevard du Temple—how often has one of them been torn down, only to resurface, newly built, in some other *quartier*. (To speak of "city districts" ["*Stadt-*

teilen"] is odious to me.) How many street names, even today, preserve the name of a landed proprietor who, centuries earlier, had his demesne on their ground. The name "Château d'eau," referring to a long-vanished fountain, still haunts various arrondissements today. Even the better-known eating establishments are, in their way, assured of their small municipal immortality—to say nothing of the great literary immortality attaching to the Rocher de Cancall, the Véfour, the Trois Frères Provençaux. For hardly has a name made its way in the field of gastronomy, hardly has a Vatel or a Riche achieved its fame, than all of Paris, including the suburbs, is teeming with Petits Vatels and Petits Riches. Such is the movement of the streets, the movement of names, which often enough run at cross-purposes to one another.[42]

Such is the chatter of the city's street names. A communicating medium, Paris is a matter of divisibility—not of *Teile* but of *Teilbarkeit*, of "quarters." Rounded off, its arrondissements are "haunted" [*spukt*] by the infinite remainder of the place name, which persists in the case of "Château d'eau," for example, long after its source has vanished. The phantasmagoria of Paris street names bears the experience of mediacy Benjamin describes in his essay on language. Not the theaters of the Boulevard du Temple, but the theatricality of a medium with a capacity to enact "topographic displacement" is conserved here.[43] If this theatricality is linked to film by Benjamin in his essay on Brecht's "epic theater," then in the *Arcades Project* he speculates about the cinematic possibility of the Paris street map: "Couldn't an exciting film be made from the map of Paris? From the unfolding of its various aspects in temporal succession? From the compression of a centuries-long movement of streets, boulevards, arcades, and squares into the space [*Zeitraum*] of a half an hour? And does the flaneur do anything different?"[44] Cinema exposes the movement of the street names to the infinite divisibility of the film image. In the manner of time-lapse photography, with close-ups, slow motion, and so on, the film medium introduces us in this context to a cartographic unconscious that is an effect of the intense, indeed excessive, mediacy of Paris street names. As suggested at the end of the passage just cited, this divisibility of place in the Paris of the *Arcades Project* is actualized by the divagation of the flaneur. This brings us to one of the key analogies in Benjamin's approach to street names in his Paris study, namely the analogy between walking and reading. Reading the street "in the now of its recognizability" is involved in

walking. At one point in his analysis of the film image in the essay on technical reproducibility, Benjamin takes walking as an example of a site that film
can render divisible: "Even if one has a general knowledge of the way people
walk, one knows nothing of a person's posture [*Haltung*] during the frac-
tional second of a stride [*Sekundenbruchteil des Ausschreitens*]. . . . Here the
camera intervenes."[45] The bearing of the flaneur—like the bearing of the
reader of the streets in the *Arcades Project*—makes possible an experience of
Paris as communicative medium, as the virtual site of judgment. To show
how this manifests itself, a brief excursus is needed on the analogy between
reading and walking, one we have already encountered in the description of
translation as *vorläufig* and in the characterization of the historical life of
ideas as *ein Abschreiten*.

Benjamin is concerned with a kind of walking that is specific to the street
—the kind described in Poe's "The Man of the Crowd," one of the key
sources for this topic in the *Arcades Project*. "I was at a loss to comprehend
the waywardness of his actions," Poe's narrator says of the secretive stranger
he has been following, "the old man . . . stalked backward and forward without apparent object."[46] This is the mode of walking connected to the street
in the Paris project. The street here is not a means to an end, but rather
what Benjamin calls a "communicating" medium—a medium of the name—
as is explained in the following passage on the distinction between the names
"street" [*Strasse*] and "way" [*Weg*]:

> "Street," to be understood, must be profiled against the older term "way."
> With respect to their mythological natures, the two words are entirely dis-
> tinct. The way brings with it the terrors of wandering [*Irrgangs*], some
> reverberation of which must have struck the leaders of nomadic tribes. In
> the incalculable turnings and resolutions of the way, there is even today, for
> the solitary wanderer, a detectable trace of the power of ancient directives
> over wandering hordes. But the person who travels a street, it would seem,
> has no need of any waywise guiding hand. It is not in wandering that man
> takes to the street, but rather in submitting to the monotonous, fascinating,
> constantly unrolling band of asphalt. The synthesis of these twin terrors,
> however—monotonous wandering—is represented in the labyrinth.[47]

One cannot stray on a street because here straying is fundamental in the
sense that *street* and *Straße*, both from the Latin *strata via*, is the way that is

strewn or paved.[48] The street's lack of what Poe's narrator calls "wayward-ness" makes it the site of a way of walking that is also implied in Benjamin's critique of certain conceptualizations of history as end-oriented and progressive in his "Theses on the Philosophy of History." This implication passes by way of the connections in German between "advancing" [*fort-schreiten*], or "taking steps" [*Schritte*], and "progress" [*Fortschritt*]. Kant can speak, for example, of the relationship between the vision of history "advancing to its ultimate end" [*fortschreiten zum Endzweck*], on the one hand, and the image of the singular step taken by the angel of the apocalypse, on the other. The apocalyptic angel, Kant argues, is an image that expresses the desire to "take a single step [*Schritt*] out of the sensuous world."[49] For Benjamin, each step of the flaneur along the streets of Paris is something like this singular apocalyptic step. From this perspective, the famous "angel of history," described by Benjamin as backing into the future with his eyes on the ruins of the past, may also be imagined as a flaneur. But the flaneur's steps are *something* like—that is, not exactly like—the millenarian step character-ized by Kant. It would be more accurate to say that the flaneur's gait may be understood as involved in the possibility that at each pace it might repeat or point to such a primal, apocalyptic step. Each point of contact with the in-tense mediacy of the street would become a virtual site in the sense described by Benjamin in his parable of the secretive stranger. These steps would point to the one taken, not out of, but into the "sensuous world" of mediacy. Such streetwise steps, such *pas sages*, would gesture in fact toward one impossible to describe accurately as moving into or out of a medium because it is at the very point of the primal division—*das Urteil*—that is the origin of mediacy, the point at which, as Benjamin suggests, mediacy becomes immediate and vice versa.[50] In this way Paris streets become the virtual site of *Urteil* in the *Arcades Project*.

Virtual Paris: La Place du Maroc

The virtuality of Paris in Benjamin's *Arcades Project* thus issues a challenge to the utilitarian functionalism of much contemporary interest in the topic. If the Paris streets of the project have little in common with the virtuality of the "information superhighway," the walking of these streets is also a radical departure from the instrumentalized steps envisioned by current projects to, for example, develop a shoe computer for which the body's own force field becomes an energy source—a "Personal Area Network (PAN)," as the author of a recent report from the Massachusetts Institute of Technology Media Lab puts it. This utilization of the walking body as a "PAN," a process that would allow "physical gestures to take on logical meaning," is what the promoter of this invention calls "thinking."[51] "Planning" is the word used by Benjamin in a note from the *Arcades Project*.[52] "Virtual Paris" does not refer to a program to provide access to the "capital of the nineteenth century" through a virtual medium; rather, it describes an experience of Paris itself as a virtual medium. As such, Paris in the *Arcades Project* is the name of a place where names are mixed up in judgment in the sense of *Urteil* (primal division) and where divisibility makes it possible to read the judgment virtually conserved by place names. This is the presentation Benjamin repeatedly calls "dialectical" in the Paris project. It is one that is itself described in terms of divisibility in several of the reflections on method in "Convolute N" such as the following, highly suggestive note on "dialectical presentation" [*dialektische Darstellung*]:

> Every dialectically presented historical circumstance polarizes itself and becomes a force field in which the confrontation between its fore-history and after-history is played out. It becomes such a field insofar as the present instant interpenetrates it. And thus the historical evidence polarizes into fore- and after-history always anew, never in the same way. And it does so at a distance from its own existence, in the present instant itself—like a line which, divided [*geteilt*] according to the Apollonian section [*Schnitt*], experiences its partition [*Teilung*] from outside of itself.[53]

Especially noteworthy in this passage is that the dialectical image presents itself in a splitting image from the history of natural philosophy, that of the "Apollonian section" [*Schnitt*].[54] One might say that the "now" of Benjamin's presentation of the dialectical image (or of our reading of it) cuts into what the Apollonian image has been up to this point, except that the interpenetration of the images is such that the Apollonian image could just as accurately be said to cut into Benjamin's dialectical presentation. In this sense, the Apollonian image and Benjamin's image each, together, experience their partition from outside of themselves. Such partitioning is the point of the montage of the *Arcades Project*. As the variations on the root *Teil* at the end of this excerpt indicate, conserved at the decisive moment (of *Teilung*) would be the primal decision or *Urteil* that is, as it were, at the beginning of a history of division—an epic history.

By virtue of their divisibility the place and street names of Paris have the capacity to present images of this history—the history of which they are a part. In other words, the places and streets of Benjamin's project are themselves media in that they communicate themselves as names. As such they resist the many proposals, including that of Haussmann in the nineteenth century, to rationalize the streets and addresses of Paris—projects that aimed, for example, to make of Paris a symbolic capital of France, such as the 1801 plan Benjamin cites to rename the streets with the city and place names of France so as to "present an arrangement that would allow the traveler to acquire geographical knowledge of France in Paris and, reciprocally, of Paris in France."[55] Benjamin refers to many of these proposals—to rename, for example, the streets so as to "transform Paris into a map of the world" or to make it a truly revolutionary city with street names like "Justice," "Humanité," "Bonheur," or "Probité."[56] Such plans for making Paris into the capital of France, or of the world, or of the revolution were responses to the feelings of disorder expressed by many nineteenth-century Parisians and Paris visitors. One of Benjamin's favorites is Jean-Baptiste Pujoulx who wrote at the beginning of the nineteenth century. Pujoulx's exasperation over the Babel of the Paris street names describes quite well one experience of partition that interests Benjamin in the *Arcades Project*:

> I know of nothing more ridiculous and more inconsistent than the names of streets, squares, blind alleys, and culs-de-sac in Paris. Let us choose at random some of these names in one of the more beautiful neighborhoods, and we cannot but note this incoherence and caprice. I arrive by way of the Rue Croix-des-Petits Champs; I cross the Place des Victoires; I turn into the Rue Vuide-Gousset, which leads me to the Passage des Petits-Pères, from which it is a short distance to the Palais-Egalité. What a salmagundi! The first name calls to mind a cult object and a rustic landscape; the second offers military triumphs; the third, an ambush; the fourth, the memory of a nickname given to a monastic order; and the last, a word which ignorance, intrigues, and ambition have taken turns in abusing."[57]

It is precisely this disorienting, and for Pujoulx profoundly troubling, aspect of Paris streets that interests Benjamin in the *Arcades Project*. The city becomes in this way a montage of street names—of intersections. As the streets cut into one another they make possible what Benjamin at one point calls "the magic of the 'corner.' "[58] The arcades are such intersections; they mark a point where interior crosses with exterior space, "the interpenetration of street and residence."[59]

But the experience of intersection decried by Pujoulx can also occur as one is standing in place, as is illustrated by a piece of "personal" testimony of the sort encountered here and there throughout the *Arcades Project*. This time it is "Benjamin" himself who provides the example with an account of a *flânerie* that comes to a standstill:

> Excursus on the Place du Maroc. Not only city and interior but city and open air [*Freie*] can become entwined, and *this* intertwining can occur much more concretely. There is the Place du Maroc in Belleville: that desolate heap of stones with its rows of tenements became for me, when I happened on it one Sunday afternoon, not only a Moroccan desert but also, and at the same time, a monument of colonial imperialism; topographic vision was entwined with allegorical meaning in this square, yet not for an instant did it lose its place [*Ort*] in the heart of Belleville. And in such cases, in fact, street names are like intoxicating substances that make our perceptions more stratified and richer in spaces. One could call the energy [*Kraft*] by which they transport us into such a state their *vertu évocatrice*, their evocative power—but that is saying too little; for what is decisive [*entscheidend*] here is not the association but the interpenetration of images.[60]

If, as Benjamin asserts elsewhere in the text, the "dialectical image" is "a caesura in the movement of thought," then the *place* in this passage becomes a caesura in the movement of street names—a place where the "tension" [*Spannung*] that emerges with the split between the "topographic vision" of the desert and the "allegorical meaning" of monument comes to a "standstill" [*Stillstand*].[61] This is what Benjamin calls the "interpenetration of images." Suddenly, the divisibility of this place emerges from the name, from the fallen language that came to inscribe this place. As such a language—as a medium that "must communicate *something* (something other than itself)"—the place name here does not exactly name the place. It refers to a place in Africa, a place being carved out of Africa in order to become part of the empire of which Paris was the capital, just at the time in fact that the Place du Maroc was baptized as part of what became, under Haussmann and at the height of the empire (in 1860), the nineteenth arrondissement of Paris.[62] Emerging here, then, is that "genuine historical image" that "flashes up fleetingly" before the historical materialist in the passage Guillory cites from Benjamin's "Theses on the Philosophy of History." The Place du Maroc is a "document of culture" that is "at the same time a document of barbarism." Moreover, in this case a monument explicitly devoted to culture in the sense that it commemorates the arrival of culture in a place where there was none—the birth of culture in the desert and among the peoples of North Africa who bore the name of barbarian for the Romans. In the Place du Maroc we are at the very intersection of culture and barbarism, at the very point where culture cuts into barbarism and vice versa. Here culture has carved a name in the earth and called it a place (*ein Ort*), or a city in the sense of the German *Stadt*, which derives from the root for "place"; or perhaps, as is being suggested in "Convolute P" of the *Arcades Project*, a street in the sense of the French *rue* from the Latin *ruga* meaning "wrinkle," "groove," or "furrow."[63] To this day in fact streets are "pierced" in French: *perçer une rue*, one says. "The street," Benjamin notes in Marseille, "is like a cut made by a knife" [*die Straße . . . ist wie ein Schnitt, den ein Messer gezogen hat*].[64] In this way street may be understood to bear the trace of the primal decision or partition—*das Urteil*—whereby place and city become nameable in human terms, that is to say, in the mediate terms of human language.

Paris has become for us the name of such a place and of such a judgment. The judgment of Paris (*das Parisurteil*) marks in a sense the original fall to culture, specifically to the European culture of Ernst Robert Curtius and Georges Dumézil—and, one might imagine, their contemporary Benjamin.[65] "Remember Paris," Hubert Damisch has observed recently,

> the fortune of the legend of Paris in European literature demonstrates
> the dependence of Western culture on that ancient Mediterranean, and
> of the role played by the Middle Ages, Latin and then French, in transmit-
> ting a heritage constantly laid claim to even as it was being transformed.
> Everything in the *histoire* or "novel" of Troy comes to us secondhand, from
> its basic narrative material to the interpretative glosses on it dating from

the Hellenistic period. . . . A history of Greece as well as, through Virgil, of Rome, and (if we credit the "Trojan" genealogies) that of the entire Occident. A history within which Paris—to deliberately stretch a point—occupies a position comparable to that assigned in the Bible to Adam in the context of the history of humanity.[66]

The German Hellenist and contemporary of Benjamin, Karl Reinhardt, puts it succinctly: "Without the judgment of Paris, there would be no *Iliad*" [*Ohne Parisurteil keine Ilias*].[67] That is to say, the Homeric epic and the epic history of Western culture through which it is transmitted virtually conserve the judgment of Paris. And yet in Benjamin's Paris, as in the Place du Maroc, this "allegorical meaning" would also be entwined with "topographic vision"—the vision of the ancient Celts, the Parisii, whom the Romans found living on what is now the Île de la Cité and whose name was taken for the place.

Culture and Barbarism

At this point, at the intersection of these interpenetrating images of Paris, Benjamin's famous remark about culture and barbarism cited by Guillory becomes less familiar and more challenging. The question is how to read the "culture" and "barbarism," the interpenetrating images of which are, as Benjamin says, "decisive" [*entscheidend*]. The epic tradition of European culture—the culture of Curtius and Dumézil—provides us with occasional reflections on what might be called its own "barbarism." Long before Baudelaire's "Andromache, je pense à vous!" there was, for example, the hyperbolic and horrifying violence with which the honorable Hector is killed before the city of his birth in the *Iliad* or the sadness with which Virgil portrays Aeneas's slaughter of the "priestly Umbro" who is "mourned" by the waters and woods of his native countryside.[68] Such reflections on "what it takes" to establish an empire are themselves part of this epic culture. In his "Theses on the Philosophy of History" Benjamin may seem to be in line with this culture when he cites Flaubert's comment, made in the same year that the Place du Maroc became a part of Paris, about yet another barbaric, in this case specifically North African, site: "Few will be able to guess how sad one had to be in order to resuscitate Carthage."[69] But the sadness, or better the sorrow (*Traurig-*

keit), of Benjamin's historical materialist here does not, as he stresses, lead to "empathy" [*Einfühlung*]. It is tempting to read the statement about culture and barbarism as a call for identification with the victims. But the sorrow that concerns Benjamin excludes, not just empathy for the victor, but empathy as such. In this way Benjamin departs from the traditional epic identification by virtue of which the victor can imagine the loss of the victim as a tragic loss of a part of himself—his "innocence," his "freedom," or the collective "innocence" or "freedom" of his people that is the price of progress.[70] This is the perspective of the "historicism" in the "Theses on the Philosophy of History." But Benjamin also breaks here with a tradition of empathy for the victim, a tradition that has readily embraced his remark about culture and barbarism. This is the perspective of much recent interest in Benjamin's historical and cultural criticism.

Guillory, who wants to rescue judgment from the neglect it suffers from the defenders and the attackers of culture, explicitly rejects both of these alternatives. He begins by pointing out correctly that following the so often cited sentence Benjamin turns to focus on the process of cultural "transmission" [*Überlieferung*]: "And just as [the document of culture] is itself not free of barbarism," Benjamin goes on, "neither is the process of transmission by which it descends from one to another."[71] It is here that Guillory wants to intervene and to translate what he considers the false philosophical problem of culture into the genuine sociological problem of "cultural capital." The process of transmission is the basis on which Guillory makes his proposal for a "culture of universal access" and for "aesthetic judgment" as he understands it. "The point," Guillory concludes,

> is not to make judgment disappear but to reform the conditions of its practice. If there is no way out of the game of culture, then . . . there may be another kind of game, with less dire consequences for the losers, an *aesthetic* game. Socializing the means of production and consumption would be the condition of an aestheticism unbound, not its overcoming.[72]

In other words, by reforming the conditions in which aesthetic judgment is practiced and by making such practice universally accessible, barbarism would be removed from culture in the process of its transmission. But barbarism cannot be processed out of the culture Benjamin has in mind. The sentence Guillory quotes from Benjamin does not say that the process of transmission—the social conditions in which judgment is practiced—can be reformed so as to make culture more accessible and therefore less barbaric. It says that the process of transmission is, like the document of culture itself, "not free of barbarism." Guillory treats barbarism as if it were something external to culture, a condition to be "mapped" and reformed in the "social field" in which judgment is practiced.[73] But judgment is not practiced *in* conditions of cultural transmission; it *is* the very condition of cultural transmission—judgment communicates itself in the transmission of a culture interpenetrated by barbarism.[74]

In a sense the word *barbarism* as such demonstrates this interpenetration. According to the *Oxford English Dictionary*, barbarism derives from the Greek word meaning "foreign mode of speech":

> The Greek word had probably a primary reference to speech, and is compared with Latin *balbus* stammering. The sense-development in ancient times was (with the Greeks) "foreign, non-Hellenic," later "outlandish, rude, brutal"; (with the Romans) "not Latin or Greek," then "pertaining to those outside the Roman empire"; hence "uncivilized, uncultured," and later "non-Christian," whence "Saracen, heathen"; and generally "savage, rude, savagely cruel, inhuman."

Barbarism is to be compared to the word *Berber*. The latter, which was used in the ancient Arab world to describe the peoples of North Africa and of the areas south of Egypt, derives from an Arabic word that also means "to talk noisedly or confusedly." It is not clear whether the Greek word and the Arabic word are related or whether one or the other is descended from a foreign root—not clear, in other words, in which language, if in either, barbarism is not a barbarism. Philological history helps explain why Benjamin decides in his essay on translation to speak of the foreignness, not of language, but of languages (*die Fremdheit der Sprachen*)—of the foreignness of languages to one another. It also helps explain why documents of culture are documents of barbarism: barbarism names the foreignness borne by culture. Cultural transmission without barbarism would indeed be what Guillory calls "the condition of an aestheticism unbound," but it would also be a condition from which judgment had been lifted. It is not a culture from which barbarism has been removed, but a culture interpenetrated by barbarism that conserves judgment. The spoils of culture can be celebrated or decried or redistributed so as to become universally accessible. But the interpenetration of culture and barbarism, which is the virtual site of judgment, can only emerge when documents of culture, as Benjamin says, "have to reckon with a distanced observer" [*mit einem distanzierten Betrachter zu rechnen haben*].[75] With this moment of judgment the bearing of the historical materialist comes to the fore. This is what happens in the excursus on the Place du Maroc. The juxtaposition of documents laid before the reader in Benjamin's Paris project calls for such a bearing. At a time when universal access is increasingly seen as a way to overcome the barbarism of culture, the virtual Paris of the *Arcades Project* confronts us with the inaccessibility of a philosophical ideal—the ideal of a culture free from barbarism.

ELEVEN

Aesthetics? Philosophy of History? Theology!

NORBERT BOLZ

It is the appeal of Walter Benjamin's writings that, while they are constructed in an unusually sophisticated manner, it is hardly possible to say on what *theory* they are based. The basic question concerning Benjamin's "approach" misses the mark. This is why such incredibly contradictory opinions about his oeuvre exist. In other words, his lends itself like no other oeuvre to the projection of one's own considerations. There are, however, clear hints that Benjamin was not really concerned with the construction of a theory. On the contrary, we could say that he was concerned with a deconstruction (*Abbau*) of theory.

In the context of Brecht, Benjamin once spoke of a positive impoverishment of thinking. What could this mean? After all, an impoverishment is positive only if the prevailing wealth is false. We are thus suffering from an excess of opinions, positions, and concepts. In contrast, Benjamin wishes to fulfill Goethe's dream of constructing truth out of facts—this is probably the most binding directive for reading the labyrinth of the *Passagen-Werk*. The anti-Hegelian program par excellence is: "What is concrete erases thinking. Construction through a complete elimination of theory" (5:1033).[1]

The construction of facts erases thinking, apparently the way that blotting paper erases ink—it soaks it up. We are thus dealing in Benjamin's work with an overabundance of erased thoughts that must be read in the aggregate condition of "having been eliminated." This is true, too, of theological thoughts and opinions; we recall that Benjamin himself applied the image of ink and blotting paper to his relationship to theology. Therefore, Benjamin's thinking erases theology in order then to be itself erased by a construction of facts.

Let us attempt a self-application of this concept of a positive impoverishment of thinking. What follows is the suggestion to reduce the false wealth within the discussions of Benjamin. My basic thesis framing these thoughts is simple: Benjamin's aesthetics break down into a theory of media and a philosophical history of the aesthetic. I believe that Benjamin points the way toward the future especially as a *theorist* of media and design. One need only recall his critique of empire style, the *Neue Sachlichkeit*-like figure of the destructive character, and his aesthetic speculations on the connection of form and industry. But this—media and design theory—is not our topic here.

Benjamin's philosophical history of the aesthetic is grounded in an inverse theology that may be considered as the "basic science" [*Grundwissenschaft*] of the *Passagen-Werk* because capitalism has an "essentially religious structure" (6:100). Here, we must look more closely.

Aesthetics?

Benjamin belongs to the front of anti-Hegelians. For them, system, mediation, and dialectical sublation are all figures of thought of a "forced reconciliation" with the status quo. But the most savvy Hegelians do not attempt the impossible: to outdo Hegel. On the contrary, in light of the overwhelming structural wealth of Hegel's system, the strategy of impoverishing thinking becomes interesting. The philosophical system is undercut with ironic modesty—this is the significance of the essay as form. Instead of the system, just an "attempt"; instead of philosophy, just literary scholarship; instead of world mystery, just conjectures—I call this *essayistic occasionalism*. It is a shrewd technique of the incognito. "After all," Benjamin writes, "it is possible to say things in a critical analysis of others' views that otherwise one would not know yet how to present synthetically" (*B* 259). One presents highly problematic figures of thought "in the guise of critique" (3:383). The essayist is not concerned with the production of knowledge but—one is tempted to say on the contrary—with "the settlement [*Ansiedlung*] of knowledge" (*B* 323). Two examples of this, recommended to readers' independent verification: Adorno was never more compelling than in his interpretations of Eichendorff's lyric poetry, and Lukács's reflections were never more powerful than in his small essay on Novalis. These are masterworks of essayistic occasionalism.

Yet this technique of the incognito resolves not only a problem of presentation but also, in light of the false wealth of thoughts, an ethical problem. Here, interpretation appears as the only form in which one can still show oneself responsible for knowledge. Moreover, it provides a protected space in which one can loosen the safeguard mechanisms of thinking. When dealing with poetry one may make logical errors without punishment. The ironic modesty of form enables Benjamin's extremism of method. What his dialectic puts in the place of Hegelian mediation and sublation could be described as a configuration of extremes.

However, this essayistic occasionalism, this shrewd settlement of thought in poetry comes at a price. It leads, first of all, to an overtaxation of the aesthetic. The aesthetic now appears—at the end of philosophy and in an age of highly differentiated, blinders-wearing individual scholarly disciplines—as the last medium of integral cognition. It therefore also leads, secondly, to an explosion of the aesthetic. Aesthetic categories are dissolved into political and historico-theological concepts: "Perfected critique breaks the space of aesthetics" (6:179). Here are some pertinent symptoms:

Prose forms lift life out of its raw condition—this is why to perceive actually means to read.

Benjamin understands reading not as an act of empathy but one of incorporation. He refers us to the double meaning of the word *Gericht*, meaning both meal and court, to eat and to judge. The critic is also a destructive character.

Literary praxis explodes the literary framework; just think of newspapers and advertising. What is decisive for modernity is that writing leaves the book. To perceive now means to read the imagistic writing of fashion, advertising, and architecture.

All this motivates, thirdly, a new concept of the aesthetic. It should be left up to Benjamin's reader if he discerns here three evolutionary stages or three permanent options of the aesthetic. Of course it is possible to read Benjamin's explosion of the aesthetic equally emphatically in the direction of philosophy of history and of aesthetics—I myself have done so often enough. But this explosion of the aesthetic can also be interpreted as the preparation of a transformed concept of the aesthetic as a theory of perception in the age of apparati. Let us consider this more closely.

Time and again Benjamin emphasizes the position of the human being "in front of the apparatus." It possesses such a transformative power that we can speak of a new way for the human to become human. Benjamin is thus far from denouncing machines as inhuman—on the contrary. Only when they are eye-to-eye with the new media technologies do humans become human. What the golden age of Marxism liked to evoke as self-alienation is recognized as a productive power—as a chance for emancipation from the "old Adam."

Apparati are capable of liberating because humans themselves operate in an apparatuslike fashion and can thus be *remodeled*—this, after all, was Brecht's great motif. Benjamin's by now famous formula of a "refunctionalization of the human apparatus of apperception" (1:1049) thus also contains the suggestion that human perception is an apparatus. This has two decisive consequences: (1) the temporal-paradigmatic forms are in the machines; and (2) one must *innervate* the apparati in order to see the world. This all makes good sense if, as Benjamin's essay on reproducibility suggests, we refer the concepts of machine and apparatus concretely to media and communications technology. In Benjamin's work, media theory would assume its place next to theology as the second basic science.

Thus, my main thesis is: Benjamin's thinking can be described as an ellipsis moving around the focal points of theology and media theory.

It is in this context, too, that his infamous anthropological materialism should be situated. Benjamin replaces matter with a so-called collective body. I cannot clarify this concept here and only wish to suggest that it seems to be a question of resonant phenomena such as *mystical participation*. For our context, something else is important: Benjamin has an antiphysical concept of nature—he speaks of a "prying open of the teleology of nature" (5:777)—and, complementary to that, an organic concept of technology.

Thus, a mysticism of the moving collective body whose organ is technology results. The new media and technologies perform a kind of collective surgery on the social body. At stake here are symbioses between humans and machines. This very mysticism is for Benjamin the key to the most burning actual relevance. In order to perceive the reality of the masses and the masslike, natural optics must be transcended: apparati penetrate perception.

Philosophy of History?

So much for my reduction of the aesthetic problem. On the basis of what I have said, I will now even more rigorously reduce the philosophy of history to its *function* in Benjamin's work. You will see that everything pushes toward theology.

What is history? Certainly not evolution, neither the "flow of events" nor its description. For there to be history, a petrification is required, a crystallization, constellation, and interruption of its course. "History breaks down into images, not into stories," Benjamin writes (5:596). And this new aggregate condition of what occurs is the work of "politico-theological categories" (5:1023). We may only know history if we interrupt its unfolding—this is a question of presence of mind and thus of politics. But this means that historical cognition is a political problem for Benjamin.

The great question for the historian here is: How does one interrupt the flow of history without having everything dissolve into something amorphous? How can interruption give form? The answer is: through citation and montage. History is construction, not contemplation. It constructs a "new past" that has never existed (5:1000). Likewise, current relevance or actuality is a quality of the event, a quality that one can never find already in place but that one must construct. To actualize means to render history a scandal for the present. The most decided antithesis to this is the historicist position. The historicist is "caught in images," which for Benjamin means mythical self-consciousness. Thus, the sense of historical construction is the transformation of history into scandal. The Paulinian "scandalon" is apparently the prefiguration of the truly actual, the measuring stick of the philosophy of history.

Theology!

Benjamin decomposes and reconfigures both aesthetic concepts and those of the philosophy of history through politico-theological concepts. But this does not lead to an application of the concepts of the sacred to something profane—Benjamin is no theocrat. This difference is so important that he dedicated his most esoteric and suggestive model of thinking to it. After all, the "Theologico-Political Fragment" exposes a purely spiritual concept of theocracy. But in this framework a politics that *promotes* theocracy can only be *nihilistic*. This is why Benjamin emphasizes that God's kingdom is "not the goal, but the end" of history (2:203).

And what is the source of the consciousness of discontinuity that is so decisive for historical cognition? That is the central problem of his political theology: "to link revolutionary destruction with the idea of redemption" (1:1241). To set the problem once again into sharp relief: How does one avoid political theocracy without having to make do without political theology? Benjamin answers with a valorization of destruction. Destruction creates the synergetic effects between the profane and the messianic.

On multiple occasions, Benjamin enacted this significant figure of thought of a valorization of what is destructive. Already his book on the baroque shows the dialectical function of shattering, mutilation, and the fragment. In the Baudelaire essay he shows the "destructive force of allegorical intention" (1:661). And then there is above all, of course, the "Destructive Character" with his efforts to make room, to clean, to brush history against the grain. He delivers constructive power from the poverty of experience. Benjamin's explicit theology, too, is concerned precisely with "unleashing the destructive powers which lie in the idea of redemption" (1:1246). After all, the human being is redeemed primarily in his self-image. Because emancipation for Benjamin is thinkable only as a negation of humanistic human-likeness, he considers "destruction the climate of real humanity" (1:1243).

Descriptive Theology

Why is religion indispensable? Let us take a step back from Benjamin's work in order to address this question more generally. Religion lives off the tension between "actual" life (meaning) and social life (functioning). At least for the eternally waiting Jews and for Christians since the delay of Christ's return at Judgment Day, the function of religion is clear: to manage disappointments. Benjamin's great disappointment was the decline of the medium *experience*. He reacted to it with two gestures of thought. First, in Brecht's traces, with the desperately offensive theory of the poverty of experience. Secondly, with an intricate rescue mission for the ugly dwarf called theology.

The significance of theology for Benjamin lies in how it replaces the "concrete totality of experience" (2:170). But this can no longer be managed by theology; it has every reason to be ashamed and to hide. Theology therefore assumes a secular incognito. But what does this mean? Since Adorno, we are used to saying that whoever wants to save religion must secularize it. This is an error, however, to which Benjamin interestingly *did not* succumb. Religion is self-substitutive, which is why secularization is a form of self-misunderstanding. Only religion can replace religion. Other equivalents either ignore the world beyond (historical materialism, or HistoMat) or this world (ecstasy of drugs). This is why everything turns around the concept of *inverse theology*.

Theologumena are protected by inversion. This protection occurs, from Lukács to Adorno, in the form of an exodus from metaphysics to commentary. One could consider this an autology of the ban on images—it does not permit theologumena as such. Even the theological prohibition of theological concepts would contain too much theology. One sees now how important the question of the secular incognito becomes. As is well known, Benjamin found a nicely usable dummy to whom we today, however, no longer have access: historical materialism. Protected by the incognito of HistoMat, theology could become the "basic science" of his work. We could say that historical materialism was the formula of pathos for his messianism.

An even shrewder form of inverse theology is the transformation of a theologumenon into a method; one could call this the proceduralization of a belief's content. In this vein, Benjamin developed the method of "historical apokatastasis" (5:573), or "the bringing back of all." There is nothing in the world that is so bad that the distinction of good and bad could not be applied to it one more time—until "everything is good." At stake is the reentry of a differentiation (positive/negative) into what is differentiated (negative). This is a decisive step in the direction of formalism. The formalism of historical apokatastasis—that is, the procedural differentiation of positive and negative—is indeed the successful secular incognito of theology. because within it operates the religious differentiation between salvation and condemnation.

In short, religion, as the guarantor of totality, hides in the operation of differentiation. This is why humans may be content with what Benjamin barely grants them, "a *weak* messianic power." The unraveling of this paradox of the paradoxical formulation that locates a power in a weakness—strictly on a formal level—consists in the fact that totality is guaranteed by differentiation.

That Benjamin holds on to the religious guarantee of totality legitimates Jacques Derrida's evocation of the "formality of a structural messianism without religion." Yet, with this, Benjamin indeed still belongs to the *Specters of Marx*. One cannot follow this line. Today, we must make do with the guarantee that we will continue to be able to *differentiate*. For this, a religion without messianism is enough—for instance, a Christianity without happy ending. This has nothing to do with religious needs; the reader of this essay is surely above them, anyway. Certainly, humans can make do without religion, but society cannot. Religion is a symptom of the fact that one cannot reduce society to humans. This is why theology survives as a descriptive or, as Benjamin says, as a "basic science."

Translated by Gerhard Richter

PART 4

Figures of Finitude

TWELVE

Tragedy and Prophecy in Benjamin's 'Origin of the German Mourning Play'

PETER FENVES

Homer and the tragedians are the Moses and prophets for the Greeks.

—WILAMOWITZ

Benjamin Bound

The end of tragedy unfolds from its beginning, and so, too, the end of tragic theory.[1] For example, in the case of Benjamin: "This work," he writes to Scholem, "is for me a conclusion, in no way a beginning." With these words Benjamin leaves undecided the theory of tragedy he had proposed in "this work," *Ursprung des deutschen Trauerspiels* (Origin of the German mourning play). He will not dispute Gottfried Salomon-Delatour's contention that the conception of the tragic hero that Franz Rosenzweig advances in *Der Stern der Erlösung* (Star of redemption) and that Benjamin reworks is deeply indebted to Hegel—and for good reason: he has only skimmed over the relevant Hegelian texts.[2] (He also admits that he has not read Rosenzweig very thoroughly either.[3]) Benjamin's theory of tragedy, like tragedy according to this theory, ends in a *non liquet*: the decision—about the tragic hero, about the treatise in which his theory of tragic heroism is advanced—is final, to be sure, but not the case itself.[4]

Yet Benjamin's theory of tragedy bears an even closer resemblance to tragedy as it is defined by this theory, for the failure of tragic heroes, their defiant silence, corresponds to Benjamin's own failure. Benjamin's language is in this way "meta-ethical," as this term is understood by Rosenzweig: although incomprehensible to those who first condemned it, especially the academic judges at the University of Frankfurt, it nevertheless, like an "echo" —this is Benjamin's word—communicates to coming generations.[5] A new community first "learns to speak"—once again Benjamin's words—from the depths of this defiant refusal to engage in the language of the then-constituted Greek or academic community: "The farther the tragic word remains behind the situation . . . the more the hero escapes the old statutes to which, when they finally overtake him, he throws the dumb shadow of his being, his self, as a sacrifice, while his soul is saved into [*hinübergerettet*] the word of a distant community."[6] Whereas Benjamin cannot speak to the University of Frankfurt in 1926, his language, especially the preface to the *Trauerspiel* book, which is often described in terms usually reserved for Aeschylus—obscure, incomprehensible, forbidding, and for this reason magnificent—becomes, according to the logic of reversal for which tragedy has always been famous, the language of this very same university in, say, 1962. His soul is "saved over into" the word of this distant academic community. *Der Benjamin*, the last born, becomes Benjamin the first born, and once again, this corresponds to Benjamin's own words: "In respect of its victim, the hero, the tragic sacrifice differs from any other kind, being at once a first and last" (1:285). But the relation between Benjamin and the tragic hero whom he describes is more intimate still, for the infantilism of the hero and the Aeschylean sternness of Benjamin's language share a common root: tragic heroes, according to Benjamin, know that they are better than the gods, even those of Olympus, and for this reason they are struck dumb (1:288–89). So, too, Benjamin. Better than those who condemn him to academic oblivion, better than the gods of German academia, unwittingly sacrificed in preparation for a new academic community that will learn to speak his as yet incomprehensible language— a language for which he himself is equally unprepared: "I have lost every measuring-rod for this work"—Benjamin is struck dumb, condemned to this, a magnificently defiant silence.[7]

There is perhaps no more popular image of Benjamin. In countless portraits, he emerges as a heroic victim from whom new communities—and especially new academic communities—learn to speak. And at the heart of this tragedy is the failure of his theory of tragedy to secure an academic appointment. A recent version of "Walter hero" presents this image in particularly concise terms: "In the tragedy that Benjamin's life is generally taken to have been, the incomprehension of the Frankfurt jury charged with evaluating his doctoral thesis [it was, in fact, a *Habilitationsschrift*] ranks second only to the rise of Nazism as a node of embitterment."[8] The collapse of Benjamin's academic career, the rise of Nazism—thus Jeffrey Mehlman, who in a book called *Benjamin for Children* apparently need not distinguish between a dissertation and a *Habilitationsschrift*, for what, after all, do children care about these matters? Yet, even if we disregard Melman's way of characterizing "the tragedy that Benjamin's life is generally taken to have been," there is something wrong with this whole way of proceeding: Benjamin cannot be a tragic hero, and his life cannot be a tragedy, if the indispensable element of the theory of tragedy developed in the *Origin of the German Mourning Play* is in any way valid. To speak of the "tragedy" of Benjamin's life in the context of his *Habilitationsschrift* is to ignore Benjamin's first and in a sense final word about tragedy: it is a onetime, epoch-making dramatic form, never to be repeated, least of all revived in whatever describes itself in terms of *the tragic*. Tragedy is not only not *tragic*, but further it runs counter to sadness, sorrow, mourning—and "embitterment." The term *tragedy* belongs to fifth-century Athens, not twentieth-century Germany. One reason for Benjamin's rigorous delimitation of the historico-geographic horizon of tragedy is apparent from the very first paragraph where it is discussed. "Cultural arrogance" (1:280) gives rise to talk of "the tragic," and this arrogance consists for the most part in a pernicious sentiment according to which our "culture" is equal to the Greeks, which generally means, better than yours. At perhaps no other time was talk of the "return of tragedy" or "the return of the tragic age" more pervasive than in the Germany in the early part of the twentieth century. Benjamin's response to this talk is the only sober one: no, Attic tragedy was unique; there are no tragedies outside the theater of Dionysus.

But, as Benjamin also emphasizes, tragedy nevertheless claims an unsurpassable "topicality" [*Aktualität*]. These two traits—uniqueness, topicality—define the difficulty, or better yet, the density of tragedy as a *geschichtsphilosophische* (historico-philosophical) category. Tragedy does not return; but it—or something that claims it as its heritage—comes back again and again. Something in tragedy or something of tragedy comes back without tragedy itself ever returning, and this *something* distinguishes tragedy from itself, that is, distinguishes tragedy from what comes to be known under the rubric of *tragic* or, to cite the English translation of the title of Benjamin's book, "tragic drama."[9] As his attention is drawn toward a dramatic form whose stages wander from place to place—toward the *Trauerspiel*, in short—Benjamin tracks down this self-divisive *something* and calls it "prophecy."[10] Tragedy is not only distinguished from *Trauerspiel* by virtue of its prophetic character but also is distinguished from *itself*, for tragedy is, according to an enigmatic phrase of Benjamin, only the "preliminary stage of prophecy" [*die Vorstufe der Prophetie*] (1:297). Because it never goes beyond this "stage," however, it is forever distinguished from that which defines it: the prophetic as such. Tragedy opens onto a prophetic "step" or "stage" but is not itself prophecy. Beyond the distinction between tragedy and *Trauerspiel* lies the "internal" distinction between tragedy and prophecy, and this latter distinction not only demands a rigorous distinction between tragedy and *Trauerspiel* but also guarantees that tragedy—which is distinguished from prophecy by virtue of its preliminariness—will return as something other than itself: as *Trauerspiel*. Of prophecy *itself*, Benjamin has almost nothing to say in the *Origin of the German Mourning Play*. In this near silence—and perhaps only here—Benjamin's book touches on the tragic.

Nietzsche's Prometheus

Tragedy does not return. On this point Benjamin distinguishes himself from a crowd of his contemporary writers for whom the "decline of the West" implies the return of "the tragic age." Benjamin opens his discussion of tragedy in the second section of the *Trauerspiel* book with a polemic against those, like Johannes Volkelt, who make "the tragic" into a universal psychological experience of causal determinacy.[11] But this polemic is only a preparation for an altercation with a much more challenging antagonist: the young Nietzsche. *Die Geburt der Tragödie* (Birth of tragedy), according to Benjamin, "lays the foundation" (1:280) for the more recent lines of inquiry into the nature of tragedy pursued by Lukács and Rosenzweig; but it soon becomes apparent that Nietzsche lays a foundation by painting a dark background from which one can perceive the lucidity of a Lukács, a Rosenzweig, and, strangely enough, a Wilamowitz. What Benjamin describes as Nietzsche's original insights into the distinctive character of tragedy—"the connection of tragedy to legend [*Sage*]"—belongs in fact to his great opponent in the world of classical philology, and it is by connecting tragedy to legend that Wilamowitz hopes to undo the damaging effect of Nietzsche's "philology of the future" once and for all.[12] This is only the beginning of the complications of quotation and attestation in which Benjamin's theory of tragedy is enmeshed, and all these complications circle around in the name *Nietzsche*. Just as the allegorist exalts and at the same time devalues "the profane world" (1:351), Benjamin exalts and repudiates Nietzsche—exalts his repudiation of all moralizing interpretations of tragedy and devalues his replacement of moralism with an aestheticism in whose train a new and now Germanic tragic-artwork is supposed to appear. Nietzsche does not, of course, subject tragedy to the protocols of empirical psychology in the manner of a Volkelt, but he does something equally errant, according to Benjamin: he dissolves everything specific to the "state of affairs" [*Sachverhalt*] of Attic tragedy into the "abyss of aestheticism" (1:281). This dissolution of tragedy into the "eternal" play of appearance and disappearance—regardless of whether this play is affirmed or denied—doubtless disentangles tragedy from its entrapment in moralizing frameworks; but it also leaves the specificity of Attic tragedy undetermined. Tragedy can thereafter become something general, something "tragic," a matter for "Dionysiac man." And like Dionysus himself, Dionysiac man can wander beyond the theater of Dionysus and migrate to other and, in particular, more northern climates.

The Birth of Tragedy may not have given rise to the rebirth of tragedy, but it did give rise to incessant calls for its Germanic rebirth. These calls are sanctioned throughout the book, most conspicuously in the sections devoted to Wagnerian opera but also in its decisive, early sections. Tragedy, according to Nietzsche, not only can return; it already has done so—and with a clarity unknown to the Greeks. Thus Nietzsche writes in the ninth section of *The Birth of Tragedy*: "What the thinker Aeschylus has to say to us here [in *Prometheus Bound*], what, however, as a poet he only lets us intimate [*ahnen*] through this parable-like image [*gleichnisartiges Bild*], this is something that the young Goethe knew how to unveil to us in the bold words of his Prometheus."[13] This sentence summarizes one of the less trenchant tendencies of Nietzsche's early theory of tragedy; according to the young Nietzsche, a young German (Goethe) is incomparably more mature than an elderly Greek (Aeschylus, whose *Prometheus Bound* is often presented as a work of old age). Goethe lets "us," the Germans, know what Aeschylus surely thought but was unable to reveal to the Greeks—or even to himself. From this inability to bring thought into poetry arises the "parablelike image" of a still muffled, still uncreative Prometheus. When the Greeks came to know what they said, it was under the tutelage of the twin inventors of rationality and realism, Socrates and Euripides, whose confidence in the saving power of knowledge sentences tragedy to death. The stony silence of the first tragedian, and indeed the only tragedian who, like Wagner, was reputed to be a musician, can now be understood for what it is: Aeschylus was waiting for Goethe to reveal what he wanted to say.

No wonder a later Nietzsche will smell something unpleasantly "Hegelisch" in his first book.[14] The touchstone of a certain Hegelianism is this very thesis: Germania knows what Hellas merely intimated. And the proof of this statement lies close at hand: the *theory* of tragedy—the only theory of tragedy that has the courage to break with the late-born Aristotle—has blossomed on German soil. One might say that the Germans own a piece of Prometheus's rock. According to the ninth section of *The Birth of Tragedy*, the legend of the fire bearer is nothing less than a "primordial property of the entire Aryan congregation of peoples and a document of their gift for the meditative-tragic [*Tiefsinnig-Tragischen*]; indeed, it may not even be improbable that the same significance inhabits this myth for the Aryan that the myth of the Fall has for the Semitic."[15] The theory of tragedy has its roots in a talent for *Tiefsinn*, and this talent not only makes possible a revival of tragedy or a *tragic age* but may already be a revitalizing sign. That Benjamin concludes the *Origin of the German Mourning Play* by bringing the talent for *Tiefsinn* into connection not with the tragic but, on the contrary, with the fall of Satan—and thus with the "Semitic" myth of the fall—indicates at the very least a pointed repudiation of Nietzsche's conception of tragedy, but it also indicates in a subtle manner what has been at stake in the figure of Prometheus from the beginning: the relation between Greekness, Germanness, and Jewishness.

Nietzsche, of course, also repudiates his own call for a rebirth of tragedy under the auspices of German music, but others—and especially those who only took Nietzsche's fate as a "sign" and had little inclination to read his writings—went even further in this direction. One of these new "prophets" of tragedy plays a small but not insignificant role in the *Origin of the German Mourning Play*. When Benjamin first takes Nietzsche to task for his aestheticization of tragedy, he takes over a critique of *The Birth of Tragedy* launched by Leopold Ziegler, a student of Eduard von Hartmann and author of the 1902 book entitled *Zur Metaphysik des Tragischen* (Toward the metaphysics of the tragic). Just as Benjamin asserts that only "historico-philosophical or religious-philosophical concepts" [*geschichts- oder religionsphilosophischen Begriffen*] (1:283), not aesthetic ones, grant access to tragedy, Ziegler had maintained some twenty years earlier that "the tragic is closely connected with the *religious problem*," and this problem is world-historical.[16] More precisely, the problem is one of *cosmic* time:

> Just as there are religions that snuff out a self-radiating tragic, so there are religions that are nothing but the tragification [*Tragifizierung*] of the existence-process. In this sense it is no accident that *German* philosophy brings to completion theoretically the principal solution of the tragic problem, while the original mythology of the German race may be called the religion of the tragic.[17]

German theory of tragedy can solve the "tragic problem" because the Germans know that existence itself is problematic. "For they," Ziegler writes of the Germans, "already knew in the existence of the gods a mysterious, tragic primordial guilt [*geheimnisvolle tragische Urschuld*], and they believed that man is called upon to bring to completion the expiation of this guilt through the tragic end of the twilight of the gods."[18] And the Germans likewise know the solution to the problem of existence: "The mission of man" consists in the "redemption of God [*Erlösung Gottes*]." "By negating his will, man renounces the actuality of the divine will; by liberating himself from the burdensome curse of being an existence [*Dasein*] at the cost of God's being [*Sein*], he also frees God from this curse, this being-enclosed-in-itself."[19] From the knowledge that Nietzsche attributes to the young Goethe and that Ziegler, who was then a champion of Houston Stewart Chamberlain, attributes to the Germans as a "race," there arises the theory of tragedy, which, in turn, gives rise to a new tragic age. The tragic returns, according to Ziegler, as the catastrophic redemption of the cosmos in "a unique tragedy of totality" [*einer einzigen Tragödie der Allheit*].[20] Once redeemed, the tragedy of totality begins anew—without end. On the basis of an inner knowledge of the endlessness and purposelessness of the cosmos, Jewish-Christian religiosity can be overcome, and the Germans, as a result, can finally carry out the mission of man: redeem the gods of their own tragic individuality without falsifying existence as a whole by positing a creator God beyond the world.

Distinguishing Tragedy from 'Trauerspiel,' Jewish Silence from German Speech

Ziegler is not alone in proposing a German propensity toward *the tragic*. The ghost of tragedy haunts post-Nietzschean Germany, a ghost that makes itself known in farcical repetitions of the great Nietzschean announcement: *incipit tragoedie*. But the ghostliness of tragedy, its status as a *revenant*, means, for Benjamin, that tragedy has not returned: *Trauerspiel* has. Benjamin thus places his work in this context, the return of the baroque mourning play to Germany. Benjamin is quite explicit about this: instead of viewing Franz Werfel's *Troerinnen* (Trojan women) as evidence of the return of Euripides, for example, he presents it in the penultimate section of the preface as a return of seventeenth-century *Trauerspiel* (1:235). Thus does the mourning play return, and the theory of the mourning play shows these plays to be nothing but the ostentatious display of "returnees." The gods return, antiquity returns, spirits return; indeed *everything* returns in the play of mourning, for this is the law of mourning: everything must come back again and again. The law of mourning expresses itself in Nietzsche's doctrine of the eternal return of the same, which, in the hands of a Ziegler, constitutes nothing less than the knowledge that *tragifies* existence. For Benjamin, by contrast, it is only in the mood of mourning that everything returns. The schema of return defines thinghood for the mourner in the first and last place—and defines it as ghostly, haunted by apparitions from apparent beginning to apparent end. Things return to the mourner in this way because mourning consists in the experience of holding onto the play of disappearing appearances; under this melancholic but by no means unpleasant condition it is impossible for anything, least of all the dead, to depart *for good*: all appearances—and there are, for the mourner, nothing but appearances—are absorbed into an endless play of devaluation and disappearance.

Everything, therefore, returns in the play of mourning—*except tragedy*. Or, when tragedy returns, as it must, it does so as a "slave" to the mourning play, not on its own (1:278). And this is, to use Ziegler's imprecise terminology, the "religious problem" of tragedy: it does not return because it has nothing to do with mourning. If tragedy has nothing to do with mourning, then with what? To use another imprecise term: messianism. Mourning and messianism have absolutely nothing do with each other: *absolutely nothing*, because messianism—or to us a more precise term, *messianicity*—absolves itself of everything mournful.[21] Instead of appearances returning as they once were, everything is fulfilled as it never was. Just as history, according to Benjamin, disappears in the setting of the mourning play, and this setting freezes the "impure" history of "natural history" [*Naturgeschichte*], the destructive gesture of divine justice disappears from the scene of mourning only to be replaced by the endless play of unstable orders, each of which justifies itself on the basis of a *state of exception* whose violence—however brutal—never destroys the setting as such and is therefore never exceptional enough, which is to say, never exceptionally exceptional but only exceptional according to the rule.

Benjamin is drawn toward the German mourning play for precisely this reason: in it, more than in its English or Spanish versions, messianic time is absorbed into "natural history" without remainder—especially without the remainder to which Hamlet attests in his final words, "the rest is silence" (1:335). As Benjamin emphasizes from the title of the book onward, it is in the specifically *German* baroque mourning play that eschatology altogether vanishes and, in turn, the world appears altogether "empty." In view of this emptiness Benjamin presents the Idea of the *Trauerspiel*, for eschatology is the name for the gathering together of last things, and the presentation of an Idea, according to the methodological protocols of the "Epistemo-Critical Preface," depends on the analysis of phenomena into their elements, which, as extremes, are no longer susceptible to the scientific labor of conceptualization for the precise reason that they mark out the limits of the concepts—and therefore the transcendental consciousness—under which they are subsumed. In the case of the baroque *Trauerspiel*, the list of last things is a litany of woes: extremities of the state, states of exception; extremities of passion, martyrdom and tyranny; extremities of self-estimation, injured honor and self-glorification; extremities of loyalty and disloyalty, intriguer as both; extremities of kinship relations, incest; extremities of geographic space, the borderlands of Christendom; and finally the edge of the cosmos, Saturn, the most distant and slowest planet. But no extreme of time: in Greek, no *eschaton*. Instead of eschatological time, there is only time as limit. Thus does the *Trauerspiel* revolve around certain liminal moments and especially around the hour of midnight, the "very witching time of night" (*Hamlet*, quoted 1:314), the time in which not only the day but also counterparts to daylight—dreams, ghosts, specters—return. Midnight is not only *not* eschatological, not an extremity, still less a last time; it is not even properly historical but is, instead, only "natural historical," for, as Benjamin writes, "the spirit world is without history [*geschichtslos*]" (1:314). The *Trauerspiel* is defined by this, the absence of nonnatural—but not, for this reason *spiritual*—history, which is to say, its absolute nonrelation to, or absolution from, messianic time. And so the theory of tragedy not only becomes the place in which the historical can be articulated without reference to nature or natural history, it also bears responsibility for presenting, in whatever form, the one element whose absence grants access to the Idea of the *Trauerspiel*: the element for which there is absolutely no analysis because there are absolutely no concepts under which it can be grasped, the extremity par excellence, the eschaton *kat exochen*, or messianic time.

In view of this criterion, then, Benjamin makes a rigorous distinction between tragedy and *Trauerspiel*: tragedy is related—in an as yet unspecified manner—to messianic time, whereas the *Trauerspiel*, especially its German version, belongs to the temporality of eternal return and thus to natural history. Benjamin's earliest attempt to distinguish tragedy from *Trauerspiel* is clear on at least this point: "This Idea of fulfilled time," he writes in "Trauerspiel and Tragedy" some eight years earlier,

> is called in the Bible as its dominant historical Idea: messianic time. In any case, however, the Idea of fulfilled historical time is not to be thought at the same time as the idea of an individual time. This determination, which of course entirely transforms the meaning of fulfillment, is what distinguishes tragic time from messianic time. Tragic time is related to the latter as individually to divinely fulfilled time. (2:134)

Tragedy is defined by the same terms as messianicity—"fulfilled time"—and only because it is so defined can Benjamin undertake the critical work of distinguishing the time, temperament, and language of tragedy from those of the *Trauerspiel*. Tragedy has something to do with messianic time, not so the *Trauerspiel*. Benjamin understands this something as "fulfillment," but in the *Origin of the German Mourning Play* he imposes on himself a stern rule: he will not conduct what he calls a "frontal assault" on his subject matter.[22] Instead of speaking of "fulfillment," he only speaks of its negation: the novelty of an entirely "empty world" (1:317), contours and cataracts of which the great Lutheran dramatists of the seventeenth century set out to fathom. And instead of speaking of tragic time in relation to messianic time, Benjamin introduces a new term: a third term, as it were, which implies in its own way *both* the individuality of "individually fulfilled time" and the totality of "divinely fulfilled time," namely "the prophetic." Once tragedy is brought into relation with prophecy—which is at the very least a term for a certain experience of language and history—it silently refers to the messianic, and it is in this silence that Benjamin will find the decisive trait of everything "tragic."

After Benjamin had decided to draw on his early efforts to distinguish tragedy from *Trauerspiel* for his *Habilitationsschrift*, he asks Florens Christian Rang to help him clarify the relation between tragedy and prophecy: "I recall that we are very much in accord on this matter [the theory of tragedy], but unfortunately with regard to the details (like the relation of tragedy to prophecy and so forth) not with sufficient clarity."[23] Benjamin makes this request to Rang, who knew little Greek and less Hebrew, at the end of a long letter devoted to an apparently different topic: the relation of *Deutschtum* to *Judentum*. All of these polar terms—tragedy and prophecy, Germanness and Jewishness, tragedy and *Trauerspiel*—form a shifting kaleidoscope through which at least two images of "moral speechlessness" (1:289) are uneasily brought to light: the silence of the tragic hero, on the one hand, and contemporary Jewish silence, on the other. "In the most terrible moments of a people," Benjamin writes in the same letter to Rang, "only those are called upon to speak who belong to this people—even more to the point, those who belong to it in the most eminent sense, who not only can say *mea res agitur* but also *meam propriam ago*. The Jew certainly should not speak."[24] At issue in this injunction to silence is the question of guilt for the war and reparations for its victims to which Rang responds in his pamphlet, *Deutsche Bauhütte*.[25] Although only Rang would understand—and even Rang, the "authentic reader" of *The Origin of the German Mourning Play*, would perhaps only have understood up to a point—Benjamin has worked himself into a position where he no longer needs to pose the question of the silent hero as one of German foreknowledge but can pose it in terms of a certain Jewish messianism.[26] The silence of the hero echoes the silence of those who "should not speak" during the "most terrible moments of a people": those who have nothing to say and could not be heard in any case because they "do not belong," and they do not belong and in any case have nothing to say—tautologically or perhaps tautosigetically—because they cannot or in any case should not speak.

The silence of the tragic hero in the crisis of the Greek world corresponds to the silence of the Jews in the crisis of contemporary Germany—and, to add one more element to this constellation, which unfortunately cannot be drawn out here, the silence of the youth at the time of its congregation.[27] All of these silences at moments of crisis are paradoxically related to the category of prophecy: paradoxically, of course, because the prophet, as the word itself indicates, is precisely the one who speaks, indeed, the one who speaks before everyone else—in both senses of *before*. If it seems not only paradoxical but downright implausible that Jewish—or youthful—silence should be prophetic insofar as genuine prophets, unlike false ones, bear the burden of denouncing the sins of their own people, then it is equally implausible that tragic heroes, as Benjamin presents them, should be associated with prophetism, even if only as a preliminary stage. For prophets—at least those of the Hebrew Bible, according to innumerable authorities, including the imposing one of Hermann Cohen—speak out against nothing so much as the institution of sacrifice, which, for Benjamin, constitutes the very framework of tragic existence: "He throws the dumb shadow of his being, his self, as a sacrifice, while his soul is saved into the word of a distant community" (1:287–88).[28] The sacrifice of the tragic hero does not, however, belong to a continuous sacrificial tradition. On the contrary, "The tragic sacrifice differs from any other kind, being at once a first and last" (1:285). The end of sacrifice altogether would perhaps be announced if only the "dumb shadow" of the tragic hero could speak: no longer dumb, the shadow would instead be something like the angel with which, according to a Jewish tradition that Benjamin invokes in private, every soul is born and which, when revealed, marks the commencement of the messianic era.[29] The individually fulfilled time of tragedy would thus become the divinely fulfilled time in which what never was—call it the realm of shadows—is first and finally saved. The silence of

Greek heroes and that of contemporary German Jews is by no means equivalent, but in their respective enactments of a certain silence can prepare a stage for prophecy—or its renewal. For silence makes possible an entirely different practice of speech than those in which words are enmeshed in the juridical categories through which guilt, including guilt for the start of the war, is not so much judiciously determined as unjustly created. Evidence of the relation of the tragic to the Judaic, finally, would be the blossoming of tragic theory after Nietzsche in the works of a Lukács, a Rosenzweig, and of course, a Benjamin. *Trauerspiel*, by contrast, will be aligned with Germanness—or, more properly, with its return to Germany—and the link of Germany to the *Trauerspiel* will be forged finally by the latter's total exclusion of the tragic, which is to say, of the prophetic and so silently—of the Judaic. As for evidence of Benjamin's attraction to such a conception of his own project, one observation perhaps suffices: Benjamin finds occasion in his exposition of Greek tragedy to cite a biblical text and propose an interpretation—or midrash—of his own making: "'You shall not make for you any engraved image'—this serves not only as a defense against idolatry. With incomparable emphasis the prohibition on the presentation of the body guards against the illusion that the sphere in which the moral essence of the human being is perceptible can be made into an image [*abzubilden*]" (1:284; Exodus 20:4).[30] Nowhere in the entire *Origin of the German Mourning Play*, by contrast, does Benjamin cite a single passage from an ancient Greek playwright—not even when he seeks to distinguish Greek tragedy from German *Trauerspiel*.

Silence, Echo

The interaction between Benjamin and Rang, which both of them understood as something like a dialogue between *Judentum* and *Deutschtum*, cannot be so easily reconstructed, however, for Benjamin never articulates his understanding of the relation between tragic silence, prophecy, and his admonition that German-Jews remain silent. What Benjamin emphasizes in *The Origin of the German Mourning Play* is something else: the singularity of tragedy, its uniqueness from the perspective of *Geschichtsphilosophie*. In earlier drafts of his theory of tragedy, especially in "Fate and Character," Benjamin not only fails to emphasize the singularity of tragedy but even makes tragedy into a drama of *fate*, which, along with guilt or debt (*Schuld*), plots the ensnaring circle in which everything appears to return. Little of this survives into the *Trauerspiel* book, even though Benjamin finds occasion to quote "Fate and Character": tragedy, as Benjamin makes clear in the opening paragraph of his discussion (1:279), is no longer defined in terms of fate, guilt, and expiation, because any definition of this sort, any definition that would rely on the traditional notions of *moira* and *ananke*, to say nothing of *tragic guilt* or *tragic fault*, would immediately implicate tragedy in the temporality of eternal return and thus undo the rigorous distinction between tragedy and *Trauerspiel*.[31] Benjamin may be following a venerable philological tradition when he declares that Attic tragedy should not be compared with other supposed "tragedies" composed in other "tragic ages," but his declaration of tragedy's never-to-be-repeated status resembles nothing so much as the rabbinical doctrine that the time of prophecy is over—until, paradoxically, the messianic era comes and prophets, one or many, can then prophetize the coming of the messianic era.[32]

Benjamin enlists the theory of tragedy in two tasks: to disassociate Attic tragedy from all forms of *fate drama*, regardless of how these dramas conceive of their provenance, and to associate tragedy with prophecy. To accomplish the first of these tasks, Benjamin reworks Wilamowitz's philological studies and, more problematically, Rang's speculations concerning the conversion of the *thymele* from sacrificial altar into theatrical stage. Each of the elements of Benjamin's analysis of tragedy takes its point of departure from certain "pragmatisms" of Athenian public life, and especially its juridical forms and forums: the Aristotelian unities, in particular, are presented in terms of the space and time of the Attic courts and are therefore anything but rules for the production of plays outside of Athens. By presenting the "metaphysics of the tragic," to use Ziegler's title, in terms of the pragmatics of Athenian jurisprudence, Benjamin comes close to formulating in a precise, concise manner the methodological—or contramethodological—principle that gives direction to many of his later inquiries, including his massive study of the "primordial history" of the nineteenth century known as the *Passagen-Werk*: "As everywhere else, so here the most fruitful layer of metaphysical interpretation lies at the level of the pragmatic itself" (1:296). The presentation of the pragmatic, in other words, *is* metaphysics, and metaphysics, in turn, must be an interpretative—rather than deductive or intuitive—enterprise. Beyond

interpreting the Aristotelian unities in terms of Athenian juridical procedures, however, Benjamin does not follow through on his own suggestion.
Despite its great merits in developing an adequate account of Attic tragedy—
and the work of Vernant and Vidal-Naquet has gone in precisely the direction of Benjamin's analysis—this emphasis on the affinity between legal
forums and tragic spectacle comes to serve two specific functions within the
economy of the work as a whole.[33] On the one hand, it allows Benjamin to
avoid both the "abyss of aestheticism" toward which *The Birth of Tragedy* was
said to be drawn and the converse of this aestheticism, that is, the moralizing
interpretations of tragic figures and fates against which Nietzsche rebelled;
one the other, it makes Attic tragedy into the paradoxical representative of
singularity as such. These two perspectives meet at a single point: universalized singularity is what no mythic, legal, or conceptual order can ever grasp.
It takes up residence in the paradoxes of tragedy, and its home—if it can be
said to have one—would be among the Ideas, each of which, according to the
"Epistemo-Critical Preface," is singular, all of which together resonate the
indivisible and nonphenomenal Being of truth. The silence of the tragic hero
is the muted, infantile voice of singularity within the context of the *Origin of
the German Mourning Play*, for what this hero does without saying—and such
doing without saying is another name for heroic passivity—is to condemn
the legal order whose justification resides in myth: to condemn not simply
the demonic order of retribution against which law (*das Recht*) struggles but
also the Athenian form of distributive justice and, in turn, the order of *Recht*
as such.

In the space of the tragic contest Athens thus opens up an arena in which
the justice of its own legal order *would have been* condemned but *could not*
for lack of words—or because the only words for judgment and the space
of its jurisdiction were themselves defined by the prevailing legal order. The
opening up of the arena of contestation is, for this reason, incomplete. The
contest, in turn, can only be considered a *non liquet* (1:296). For Rang, whose
highly tendentious exposition of the tragic agon gives direction to the initial
moments of Benjamin's analysis, tragedy is nothing less than a cosmic process in which the astrological circle is partially opened up and turned into
the semicircle of the stage. The struggle, *das Ringen*, concerns, for Rang,
the ring, *der Ring*.[34] And so, too, for Benjamin, up to a point: whereas Rang
understands the Athenian stage according to the same schema through which

he sought to understand the Roman carnival—as a semicircle or semicircus in which astrological cycles are gradually perforated—Benjamin makes the opening up of the circle into the defining character of the specifically Athenian legal order.[35] Nowhere is *The Origin of the German Mourning Play* both closer to and farther from *The Birth of Tragedy* than in its account of this opening:

> For the Athenian legal order the most important and characteristic feature is the Dionysian puncture [*der dionysische Durchschlag*]—that the drunken, ecstatic word was allowed to break through [*durchbrechen*] the regular circling of the agon; that a higher justice develop from the persuasive power of living speech than from the trial of conflicting tribes by weapons or pre-scribed verbal forms. The logos breaks through the ordeal into freedom. This is at its deepest the affinity between the trial and tragedy in Athens. (1:295)

Dionysus carries out a juridical—and *not* an aesthetic—function: to free the word from fixed, Apollonian formulae. Because of its affinity with the Athenian order of right, tragedy can then be defined as "agonal prophecy" (1:286). The agon is for, as it were, free speech.[36] The prophecy, by contrast—and one can only understand this term by contrast—consists in a liberation of language from this *higher justice* for the *highest* justice, which, by virtue of its height, would destroy the perspectives of retribution and distribution alike. Without words for justice of this order, tragedy can only remain an incomplete opening of the circle, a thwarted breakthrough in which, as Benjamin writes, "The old legal order of the Olympians is disempowered" (1:285)—without, however, being destroyed.

By virtue of the "meta-ethical" character of the tragic hero—where the "meta-ethical" names the defiant experience of becoming a self—tragedy functions as a paradoxical representative of self-enclosed singularity. Unlike death in the *Trauerspiel*, which is "communal fate," death in tragedy (and indeed the death of tragedy) is singular, *Einzelgeschick* (1:314). The life of tragic heroes, according to Benjamin, is nothing but the framework of their death: so fitting is this framework that they have no life outside of it, which is to say, no oscillation of feeling and therefore no life at all. Without naming his source Benjamin then quotes—and quotes incorrectly—an aphorism from Nietzsche's *Jenseits des Gut und Böse*: "'Not the strength but rather the duration of high feeling makes the high human being'" (1:294).[37] To which Benjamin adds, as if it goes without saying that the "higher human being" for Nietzsche is the tragic one: "This monotonous duration of heroic feeling is only guaranteed in the pregiven framework of his life" (1:294). With this idea of the "'force of the framework'"—again a term Benjamin cites without giving the source of his citation—he can remove tragedy from its association with fate.[38] And he can do something more: suggest the direction from which tragedy comes to an end—not in an incomplete *non liquet* but in a complete liquidation: "Necessity, which appears to be built into the framework, is neither casual nor magic. It is the speechless [*sprachlose*] necessity of defiance, in which the self brings its utterances to light. Like snow before the south wind, it would melt at the slightest breath of the word. But only of an unknown word. Heroic defiance, closed in itself, contains this unknown" (1:294). The breath of the word—what is this but *ruah hakodesh*, the holy breath with which and sometimes of which the prophets speak? Ezekiel, for example: "And he said to me, Prophesy to the breath [*hinave' el-haruah*], prophesy, son of man, and say to the breath, Thus says the Lord God: Come from the four winds, O breath, and breathe upon these slain, that they may live" (Ezekiel 37:9).

Such speech is, of course, entirely out of place in Greek tragedy—not least because the "crisis of death" [*Todeskrisis*] (1:286) it stages devolves into a sacrifice of its heroes instead of resolving itself as the resurrection of the unjustly slain. Tragedy is nevertheless "epochal" (1:314) in a literal sense: it suspends the continuity of the mythic tradition in the same way that the phenomenological *epoche* suspends *natural attitudes*. Instead of the continuity of myth and mythic continuity, there is a break, and according to Benjamin, the break *with* tragedy—which runs counter to the thwarted breakthrough *of* tragedy— begins with Socrates. Platonic dialogue saves the Idea of justice at the cost of its historicity, which is to say, in terms of Benjamin's work, its originalness, or *Ursprungshaftigkeit*. Universal singularity takes refuge in a world beyond, and justice becomes an Idea in the Platonic sense. From the perspective of this Idea *everything* historical is debased and condemned. By converting justice into an eternal Idea, Plato does not transcend, complete, or even negate tragedy; on the contrary—and in contrast to Nietzsche—Benjamin claims that Platonic dialogue constitutes a *return* to an historical stage against which tragedy had silently, and therefore indecisively, protested. According to one of Benjamin's more audacious proposals, Platonic dialogue constitutes a restoration, a *Wiederherstellung*, of the *mysterium*; but it is precisely this—the *mysterium* and the mystery cults—that both tragedy and comedy had been in the process of "secularizing" [*Verweltlichung*], that is, making worldly.[39] Thus the strange and wholly undecidable sentence in which Benjamin speaks about the decision for *and* against tragedy:

> Den Kampf aber, den dessen Rationalismus der tragischen Kunst angesagt hatte, entscheidet Platons Werk mit einer Überlegenheit, die zuletzt den Herausforderer entscheidenender traf als die Geforderte, gegen die Tragödie [But Plato's work decides the struggle that its rationalism announces against tragic art with a superiority that in the end strikes the one who challenges more decisively than the one challenged—against tragedy].[40]

Plato's work—and philosophy in turn—is the decisive victor, but the very decisiveness of its victory makes this work more decisively stamped by the struggle with tragedy than tragedy itself, which in a sense *escapes* the struggle because the decision against it—"against tragedy," against its propheticism perhaps—is in the nature of tragedy itself. It is not, for Benjamin, the "rationalistic spirit" of Plato's dialogues that grants them "superiority" over tragedy but their dramatic, or "purely dramatic" [*reindramatisch*], form: dialogue does tragedy one better by doing away with everything impurely dramatic, everything nondramatic, everything in tragedy that disrupts the performance. Which is to say it does away with the inaction—or better yet, counteraction—of those heroes who contain the unknown word that would liquidate them. By contrast, nothing ever disturbs Socrates' dialogues, least of all the prospect of his death. Benjamin, who perhaps stands under the influence of the penultimate stanza of Hölderlin's "Der Rhein," does not refer to Socrates's statement in the *Apology* concerning his desire to engage in dialogue in the afterworld but to the conclusion of the *Symposium* in which Socrates, having outlasted the tragedian and the comedian, returns to speak in the agora: "The purely dramatic restores the *mysterium*, which in the forms of Greek drama had gradually been made worldly [*verweltlicht*]; its language is that of the new drama and also that of the *Trauerspiel*" (1:297).

Instead of offering a place for a defiant and therefore disruptive silence, dialogue gives voice to a restored *mysterium* in whose aura an unjust death sentence can be accepted, if not as a sacrifice, then at least as the ways of this, the debased because irrational world. Whereas the tragic agon, which realizes itself in a peculiar form of radical inaction, belongs to *this* world—to death, to prophecy, and implicitly to the messianic—the latter belongs to another world. Access to this world can be found in an academy, the very space that could not accommodate Benjamin's work. The silence of the tragic hero offers itself as the language from which a new community learns to speak. The purely dramatic language of dialogue, by contrast, has no place for *another* language—or something other than language, for all silence is taken up into self-conscious irony and therefore speaks after all. Not only has Socrates, the "hero" of this new dramatic form, already learned to speak a new language, but also he has already taught it to his "flock of youths, his young speakers" (1:297). This, in short, is Benjamin's response to Nietzsche's famous account of the death of tragedy at the hands of Socratic rationalism: the death of tragedy is, to be sure, the work of Socrates and Plato, yet tragedy does not die because of its "rational spirit" but because of its "rational mysticism" (to use a phrase of Lukács that Benjamin cites). The "worlding" in which tragedy and comedy alike are in the process of performing dies when the *mysterium* is restored. Mystery versus silence: this is the heart of the conflict. The *mysterium* guards its secrets and teaches the youth how to speak—and especially how *not* to speak, which is to say, how to be ironic. Instead of keeping or revealing the silence, a "popular community," Benjamin emphasizes from the beginning of his account of Attic tragedy, speaks *out of it*. But what does it mean to speak out of a silence? This question corresponds to a long-postponed one: *Who* learns to speak from tragic silence? Which *Volksgemeinschaft*?[41]

All the difficulties of Benjamin's theory of tragedy—and of his attempt to wrest tragedy away from those who proclaim its return—revolve around the question, the details of which, as he admits to Rang, are still unclear to him: How does tragedy relate to prophecy? This question comes down to a determination of those to whom tragic silence speaks after all. The *content* of this both agonistic and agonizing speech is incontestable: it speaks of a redemption (*Erlösung*) from the fateful cycle of retribution—an incomplete, postponed redemption, to be sure, and as such a redemption far removed from the one about which prophets, properly speaking, would perhaps be able to speak. As the "preliminary stage of prophecy," however, tragedy is scarcely in a position to say anything about the latter. All Benjamin, for his part, can say is that the preprophetic corresponds to the pretemporal: "Tragic is the word and is the silence of the pretime [*die Vorzeit*] in which the prophetic voice tries itself out [*sich versucht*], suffering and death where they redeem this voice" (1:297). If the time of the tragic is *die Vorzeit*, then the time of which its language speaks would have to be *die Zeit*: *the* time, which is to say *our time*, and *time itself*, and that means, to use an expression Benjamin avoids throughout his *Habilitationsschrift*, although it is implied in its first words—"Sketched 1916"—*erfüllte Zeit* [fulfilled time] (2:134). *Fulfilled time* gives tragedy an irreducible duplicity: it is at once altogether *topical* (as topical as a newspaper called "die Zeit") and completely foreign to *the times*, that is, to unfulfilled historical time, including the time of *Trauerspiel*, dramatic and nondramatic alike. In its topicality it always remains the condemnation of these times as unfulfilled precisely because the voice of the tragic remains preprophetic. Tragedy is for—and against *because* it is for—*the times*.

The place where "suffering and death redeem the prophetic voice" is likewise doubled: it is the place of tragic performance, Athens, to be sure, and yet again not *this* place: "In view of the suffering hero the community learns awesome thanks for the word with which his death endowed it—a word that, with every turn the poet wins from the legend, lights up another place as a renewed gift" (1:287–88). The "distant community" is, on the one hand, the community itself, and the temporal structure of the tragic performance is like that of Virgil's *Aeneid*: a "prophecy" of the very regime under which this "prophecy" is spoken. The time and place of "redemption" [*Erlösung*] is the time and place of the tragic performance. But, on the other hand, the community to which the word and the silence of the tragedy speaks is *distant*: in another place. Every new turn (*Wendung*) the poet extracts from the legend lights up the word "at another place" [*an anderer Stelle*]: what escapes the community, its laws, its gods, and its language. Benjamin's single reference to Hölderlin in the *Trauerspiel* book makes the law of this "lighting up" clear: tragedy turns from a judgment against the hero to a trial against the Olympians "at which the former gives testimony and, against the will of the gods, announces 'the honor of the halfgod'" (1:288)—an honor that would be his *own* honor, the honor of the hero, if the "halfgod" were indeed the hero and not, to use another term of Hölderlin, "an Other," other than a human being and other than a god, other than itself insofar as it, the halfgod, is precisely *halved*.[42] Neither human nor divine, destructive of this all-important distinction to the point of unimaginable monstrosity.[43] Or, in terms of the messianic poetics and politics of "Patmos," destructive of this distinction to the point of an irredeemable dispersal of everything it defines:

> . . . wenn die Ehre
> Des Halbgotts und der Seinen
> Verweht und selber sein Angesicht
> Der Höchste wendet
> Darob, daß nirgends ein
> Unsterbliches mehr am Himmel zu sehn ist oder
> Auf grüner Erde, was ist dies?[44]

> *[. . . when the honor*
> *Of the halfgod and of his (disciples)*
> *Blows away and his own face*
> *The highest turns*
> *Away, so that nowhere is an*
> *Immortal to be seen any longer in the sky or*
> *On the green earth, what is this?]*

Whatever "this" may be—and "Patmos" is concerned with little else— the announcement of the "honor of the halfgod" cannot be triumphal: it, like the honor itself, is blown away by a devastating wind. This wind does not have the power to melt away the frozen frameworks within which tragic heroes live out their deaths. The word that is then "saved over into the distant community" can only be a distancing, devastating, and divisive word— less *a* word than a sign of distance, division, and devastation. Benjamin no longer needs to pose the question Nietzsche touched on when he spoke of "the deep Aeschylean trait toward justice"—a phrase of Nietzsche that Benjamin cites but unjustly attributes to Max Wundt—the question, that is, of the tragedians only intimating what later generations know.[45] What is said in tragic silence does not belong to the order of knowledge, and even when the poet "wins" something of the tragic word for the "popular community," the people cannot claim this "word" as its own, for ownership of this "word" makes "the" people into—what else?—dumb shadows. And yet, according to the direction of Benjamin's argument, only by owning such a word can there be anything like *a* people in the first place.

Far from being a mystery around which a community gathers, tragic silence distances and divides the "popular community" [*die Volksgemeinschaft*], from itself. The singularity of the tragic, in other words, singularizes—without, it seems, any trace of universality. It does so because the silence from which the "distant community" learns to speak is not a source but is already an *echo*—an echo without source, hence a reverberation of emptiness.[46] The self of the hero—but this is, for Benjamin, drawing on Rosenzweig, the self as such—comes to light and comes to speech only by virtue of something unheard-of. Tragedy is the spectacle of the appearance of the self *e contrario*; but the origin of tragedy does not lie in the "sin" of individuation, according to a line of thought common to Schopenhauer, the young Nietzsche, and especially Ziegler. For the unheard-of is not the totality from which the individual departs to its peril; it is, rather, the very echo that the self repeats as the insignificant—because always inarticulate—sign of its selfhood. Tragic heroes say nothing because they have nothing to say, and they have nothing to say because they are dead from the start: "His life unfolds from his death, which is not its end but its form. . . . This has been expressed in many different ways. Perhaps nowhere better than in a casual reference to tragic death as 'merely . . . the outward sign that the soul has died'" (1:293). Benjamin takes—or rescues—this last quotation from Ziegler's *Zur Metaphysik des Tragischen*, and draws the following conclusion: "Yes, the tragic hero is, if one wishes, soulless. Out of the enormous emptiness [*ungeheuere Leere*] his interior resounds [*widertönt*] with the distant, new commands of the gods [*Göttergeheiße*], and from this echo coming generations learn their language" (1:293).[47] Coming generations do not simply learn to speak from an echo, but from an echo as "uncanny" or "enormous emptiness," an echo, therefore, that makes every word equally—or doubly—enormous, uncanny, and hollow. And the mark of this uncanniness can be found in Benjamin's own description: the commands that resound from the "soulless" hero are *multiple*, commands *of the gods*, not, as the English translator writes, "divine commands."[48] Whatever *Göttergeheiße* means (*heißt*), the gods who speak—whatever they may be called (*heißen*)—are many. If, as Benjamin writes when the question of tragic silence first arises, the tragic hero is offered "to the unknown God [*unbekannten Gott*], as the first fruits of a new harvest of humanity" (1:286), then this one god has multiplied into many by the time it—or they—speak(s): such is the uncanniness of the language the community learns to speak. One unknown god, the commands of a multitude—less a double bind than the mythic expression of the *Volksgemeinschaft* to whom tragic silence "speaks": sacrifice of one to one, reverberation of many in their multiplicity. No one, strictly speaking, is receptive to the tragic word, still less its silence. Where there is tragedy, when there is tragedy, there is always none, or too many: the dead soul of the living hero, the many gods who reverberate in the "enormous emptiness" of the "self."

But this is the singularity of tragedy: it may never have come even once. Tragic silence, true to its word, cannot be heard—not even by members of the *Volksgemeinschaft* who are supposed to learn to speak from its emptiness. And yet, only those who do learn to speak in this manner have a right to say anything about it: the rest—and the name for this rest in Benjamin's letter to Rang is "the Jews"—should remain silent. Benjamin, who, perhaps as a memorial to Rang, cites without quotation marks the last words of the dying Hamlet at the conclusion to the section of the *Origin of the German Mourning Play* entitled "*Trauerspiel* and Tragedy," keeps to the promise of these words— "the rest is silence" (1:335)—by not giving the rest any form or figure, still less a recognizable name. That there is a remnant, a *Rest*, however, may be the one prophetic saying that tragedy or its theory prepares: about everything else—what prophecy might be, what the term *Prophetie* might mean, and how it relates to tragedy after all—he remains silent.

THIRTEEN

Ornament, Constellation, Flurries

BETTINE MENKE

The graphic line is determined through its opposition to the surface. . . . To the graphic line is assigned, namely, its ground [*Untergrund*]. The graphic line provides its ground with an identity. The identity which the ground of a drawing has is completely other than that of the white surface of the paper on which it is located and which would probably be denied this identity if one were to perceive it as a surging [*Gewoge*] of white wavelengths of color [*Farbwellen*] (possibly indistinguishable with the naked eye).

—BENJAMIN, *"Über die Malerei oder Zeichen und Mal"*

Because of the *Divan* I was constantly renewing my investigations of oriental characteristics and spent much time in these pursuits; because however handwriting is of such great significance in the Orient, one will hardly find it strange that I devoted myself eagerly to calligraphy without any special linguistic training and attempted both in jest and in seriousness to imitate the oriental manuscripts which lay before me as well as possible and even with some traditional ornamental flourishes. The effect of these intellectual-technical endeavors will not escape the attentive reader upon closer examination of the poetry.

—GOETHE, in a letter concerning his *Western-Eastern Divan*

Discussions of writing always seem to involve models of what it is not as well; writing is modeled oppositionally—either in the familiar opposition between spirit and letter, or in its polarity to the image as representation or reflection. This polarity has been reformulated in terms of arabesque and ornament.[1]

The term *ornament* offers the classic oppositional concept to the mimetic image. An attempt to derive a concept of writing from a text on similarity must therefore seem quite remarkable. But it is in no way merely a question here of a rehabilitation of a relation of similarity between linguistic sign and referent. Rather, it is a question of the setting or "the configuration in the surface." The models of writing listed in the title above—ornament, constellation, flurries—bring writing into relation to the surface in which lines, signs, and sketches have their place. In these models, writing is brought into transitional or marginal zones, to points of transition between these models and to the limits of readability in the flurry (*Gestöber*) of letters.

My point of departure is Benjamin's "Lehre vom Ähnlichen," since this text elaborates a theory of reading and writing based on the concept of *"nonsensory* similarity."[2] The "strange ambiguity of the word reading in relation to both its profane and its magical meaning" (2:208–9), which is often cited in Benjamin criticism, is derived from a precise figure, namely the constellation as a model for writing and the concomitant practices of anagrammatical dispersion.[3]

The "Lehre[n] vom Ähnlichen" sketch out a historical transformation of both the "objects" and the "mimetic faculty, . . . which responds to them" (2:205). If this transformation occurred in a uniform direction, however, it was not due "merely to the growing decrepitude of this mimetic faculty." While the "metamorphosis" diagnosed by Benjamin can be understood initially in terms of loss: "obvious form [*Gestaltung*], obvious object-character existed once where we are no longer capable today of even suspecting it. For example, in the constellation of stars" (2:206), what has been lost is at the same time itself characterized as a certain readability, as linguistic, as the structurality of the written. Language and writing are accordingly not secondary to a prior magical-unmediated relation; they become rather themselves the primary model of "nonsensory similarity": "Fundamentally, one must assume that processes in the heavens were imitable by earlier peoples, and moreover both as groups and as individuals: that this imitation contained the concrete instruction to handle [*handhaben*] a certain similarity" (2:206). On the one hand, the term "handle" accentuates an essential constructivity at work in Benjamin's concept of the "mimetic," which is not stabilized by (pre)given "similarities," but rather defined as a "faculty" of the perception of these similarities through the "processes" of their production (2:204). As the "perception" of the "instruction for handling a certain similarity," reading "the processes in the sky" is literally determined as a "grasping [*Ergreifen*] of similarity, which is executed in an act of *becoming* similar" (2:956).[4]

On the other hand, "imitation" may of course "be an enchanting act; at the same time, however, the imitator disenchants nature, insofar as he brings it closer to language" (2:956). Imitation itself is thus not divorced from language, and reading achieves what imitation has always done.

According to Benjamin's categorical and fragmentary decree, "perception is reading" and what is "readable" is "what appears in the surface," namely, "the configuration of the surface" (cf. 5:32). The "handling" of the "processes in the sky" is its reading as constellation. It is not this perception that is lost—the developmental process conceptualized by Benjamin does not describe a substantial loss; rather, it lays claim to another place and another "archive," "the most perfect archive of nonsensory similarity," which is to say: "language and writing."[5]

In his notes to the "Lehre[n] vom Ähnlichen," Benjamin experimented with situating the "mimetic faculty" in various ways. On the one hand, the "human body" was described as having been the "first material on which the mimetic faculty was tried out." On the other hand, he experimented with the idea "that the *gaze* was the first motor of the mimetic faculty? That the first effort at mimicry [*Anähnlichung*] is carried out by the gaze? Is it possible to close the circle finally with the supposition that stellar constellations participated in the origin of ornaments? That the ornament fixes *Sternenblicke*" (2:858). This not only refers to views of the stars but also to the gazes of the stars themselves. Benjamin does not answer these questions here. They can serve, however, as clues for how to read the "stellar constellations" in the "Lehre[n] vom Ähnlichen." For Benjamin, the ornament serves as the place where the two media of the mimetic, the "body" and the "gaze," intersect. The ornament is not only figure and fixation of the "gazes of the stars" in their constellation; rather, it is "close to dance" as well—proximity being a metonymic relation. Further, "It provides a lesson on the production of similarity" (2:957). The proximity of ornament and dance is that of the prescription and inscription of the dance in the ornament.[6] The dancing body inscribes itself in space in its movements and gestures and leaves behind a trace in or as "ornament." According to Benjamin, this in its turn is the original model, the schema or figure "for the mimetic faculty" (2:958) that traces over it. A phrase of Mallarmé that speaks of dance in terms of its "gestural writing" [*l'écriture de ses gestes*], the writing of its gestures, confirms that these entries in space endure as written traces.[7] The "gesture which produces writing," according to Roland Barthes, manifests itself as the *Schriftzug*, the trait or the draw of writing, "by letting itself be drawn along" as well.[8] This model of the material traces of writing, of the inscription of gestures, serves Benjamin as the foundation of perception and representation and the concept of *mimesis*, intervening on their behalf: "Man corresponds to every form, to every outline, which he perceives, in the faculty of creating it. The dancing body, the sketching hand recreates [*bildet nach*] and takes possession of him" (4:613). Another note states what is meant by the verb *to correspond* and *to recreate*:

> One should thus ask oneself whether the earliest mimesis of objects in the presentation of dance and painting isn't to a large degree founded on the mimesis of activities [*Verrichtungen*], in which primitive man came in contact with these objects. Stone Age man was perhaps able to sketch an elephant so incomparably because the hand which led the stylus remembered the bow [*Bogen*] with which it killed the animal. (6:127)

Accordingly, the "mimesis of objects," which is traditionally conceptualized in terms of a binary logic of representation, *is* a "mimesis of activities" [*Verrichtungen*], the latter being a (remembering) relation of relations, of gestures, and not a re-presentation of something pregiven in these activities.[9] Following Benjamin, perception is defined as *reproduction* or presentation, and presentation is defined in its turn as a gestural inscription, a *Schrift-Zug* or trait of writing, which reproduces nothing, re-presents nothing but itself.

When Benjamin's "mimesis" is modeled on the pattern of the ornament, then the traditional counterterm to all presentation or representation of something, the *a-mimetic* ornament, functions as a "lesson [*Lehrvorgang*] on how to produce similarity."[10] Benjamin cites thereby Worringer's well-known, antimimetically inflected opposition between "abstraction and empathy," or ornament and imitation, and undermines its oppositionality.[11] The drawn line, which reflects nothing (but itself), the *ornament*, alone determines the surface of the presentation. It does not constitute the representational space within which something (beyond it) is illusorily presented. The gesture is a movement, a reference, not to something that it does not reach, but rather a demarcation in the space it occupies. It is written as a trace in the surface. The gesture relates metonymically to the line that it draws and translates. The line in which the gesture is fixed does not depict; it is not subject to the law of a metaphorical similarity to *something*, rather it sketches out and retraces the gesture. It translates the gesture it produces, and enters into a *metonymical* relation *to* the surface that it determines and *in* the surface, from trace to trace. Accordingly, Leroi-Gourhan speaks of a nonlinear "co-ordination of the gestures translated into material, graphic symbols" in their belated—written—"simultaneity" in the surface. The *ornament* is the figured simultaneity of having been inscribed in the surface, which is organized by this inscription.[12]

It is the gesture, the hand inscribing its trace, to which the gaze is related, not the seeing of the representational image of "something," but rather the *reading* of "configuration" (in) the "surface" (6:32). This points toward an implied affinity between reading and writing, the gaze and stellar-constellations, which are supposed to have participated in the emergence of ornaments. Benjamin's ornament is the interface between presentation as inscription of gestures (on the one hand) and of the gaze (on the other); thus they are intimately related to the thesis of Leroi-Gourhan who situates writing in the medium of interaction between hand and eye—"in the pairs: reading-face and sketching-hand"—and above all to Derrida's accentuating continuation of this reading.[13] Where Derrida speaks of writing, Benjamin conceives of the "ornament" on the model of the "constellation," which demands to be read differently, in a nonlinear fashion. By the same token, the ornament as written, which is here played off against representation (in its stead), determines writing itself as nonlinear organization.

Constellation and ornament provide a reading lesson. Just as the model of mimesis is developed *and* becomes untenable in the ornament conceived as writing, this model of the ornament by the same token gives rise to a non-signifying writing. Writing as the gestic trait, the metonymy of the ductus between hand and feather, "which produces writing by allowing itself to be drawn along," as Roland Barthes says, without (another) signified, would be a mere exercise in writing or a scribble, whose reading instructions would still have to be given. It would be, in other words, either writing as a supplement to or a remainder, beyond all information, of written characters (*Schriftzeichen*) that have lost their semantic and semiotic functions—of a postcalligraphic ornamentality such as, for instance, the arabesque, which still complies with the rules of ornamental typeface (*Schrift-Bild*).[14] Or it would be the scribble of gestures, which cover the paper, "a confusion, almost a smear, a mess," as is found in Cy Twombly's metathematic images of writing—"writing of which only the slant, the cursivity remains . . . : it falls, it rains in a fine spray, it bends like grass, it cancels out from idleness."[15] The dispersion, which "scatters" its elements over "vast spaces," "intervals" "thinly sown [and] full of holes," displays "on a screen (or on paper)" what makes writing possible.[16] Without intervals, there would be no drawings and no signs. These are defined by Benjamin in his early reflections on "Zeichen und Mal" through the organization of the surface in the distinctive and identifying relation of line and ground (2:603). The scriptural gesture can however always approach the "dirtying" [*Verschmutzung*], which sullies this determination, the opposition of line and surface, the condition of possibility of the sign, drawings and writing, black on white.[17] As Barthes suggests, "No surface . . . is virgin: everything is always already raw, rough, uneven, scanned by some incident: there is the grain of the paper, then the stains, the gridwork, the looping, the diagrams, the words."[18] The scribble of writing—full of holes and dispersed—gives up the distinction (of figure and ground, of the drawn line of the surface) constitutive of all written characters to the dirtying, which it is and from which it cannot distinguish itself as the latter's ground.

With the model of writing as constellation, Benjamin investigates the organization of writing: black-on-white. That this is not only a question of metaphoricity can be seen in the intensive coalescence of metaphoric/literal reading and metaphoric/literal constellations in Benjamin's texts: the constellation in the heavens and the text as pre-scriptive for reading stand in for each other in a displacement of metaphoricity and literality.[19] Just as the stellar constellation always already implies reading (to perceive of something *as* a constellation is called reading), the constellation is the *schema* of the reading of literal texts and the model of literal writing. The constellation of stellar points of light in the darkness of night: "The alphabet of stars," as Mallarmé writes with reference to an old tradition of scripture in the sky, is repeated in the negative on the white of the paper on which the text is arranged.[20] While the ornament's bond to the gesture accentuates it as manu-scripture, the displacement from ornament to constellation marks writing rather as an operation combining movable letters, thus as a typewriter. As the schema of reading, the *constellation* makes visible the surface marked with writing. It constitutes itself, namely, in the interplay between what is *constellat*ed and its background, between figure, constellation, and ground. Reading establishes as its *figure* the "constellation," which (according to the principle of the anagram) is bound up with the division and dispersion of elements in the surface (cf. 1:212–13), whose typo-graphic organization is readable as the figure written in the constellation (*Stern-Schrift-Bild*). And conversely, writing "does not fall away like slag while reading," but rather "enters into what is read as the latter's figure" (1:388), as Benjamin puts it in the *Trauerspiel* book, defining thereby the aspect of the "typeface" [*Schriftbild*] of what is written, the typographical organization of its persistence.

Hamann's comment that "the oldest writing was painting and drawing" leads to the thesis that writing "was even then already occupied with the *economy of space, its limitation and determination through figures.*"[21] This "economy" that constitutes the ornament as a mode of the written determines script as the "figure" of "limitation and determination" of the surface. Benjamin's discussion in "Zeichen und Mal" of the "sign" as "graphic line" and the surface on which it is found deserves to be cited and read in this context:

> The graphic line designates the surface and determines the latter by subordinating itself to it as its ground. Conversely, there is also a graphic line only on this ground, so that here for instance a drawing which would completely cover its ground would stop being one. The ground attains thereby a position which is indispensable for the meaning of the drawing, so that within the graphic two lines can determine their relation to each other only relative to their ground. (2:603)

The readability of signs is determined through their "position," through the positions in which they arrange themselves upon a ground.[22] In the model of the constellation of the stars and of the written characters, the figurality of reading as an (ornamental) arrangement on the surface is related to the ground and is determined through this relation, through what it is not, what is not there, what is not readable.

To accentuate the "economy of space" that constitutes writing and reading somewhat differently, the discussion of readability would have to return to the correspondence between the "gaze" and the "ornament" in "stellar constellations" and investigate the complexity of the formulation cited above, "that the first effort at mimicry [*Anähnlichung*] is carried out by the gaze," "that stellar constellations participated in the origin of ornaments" or "that the ornament fixes stargazes [*Sternenblicke*]" (2:858). This formulates a correspondence between the readable and reading, which is also called returning the gaze: "Are there earthly beings as well as things which gaze back from the stars?" that actually open their gaze for the first time in the sky?[23]

The conjunction, according to Benjamin, is "subject to" the "moment" [*Augen-Blick*] (2:207), that of its readability, the *Augen-Blick*, which adjusts and decides on the constellation.[24] In Benjamin's *Passagen-Werk*, the transitoriness of what is to be read is called the "now of readability" [*Jetzt der Lesbarkeit*] and the "principal" or "critical, dangerous moment which is the foundation of all reading." As a particular readability, the constellation of "stargazes" is a question of time: of the moment (*Augenblick*) and of fixation. The decision on readability, which fixes and thereby excludes (this is its "economy," "limitation and determination"), constructs what is read as a readable figure. Benjamin's concept of "magical reading" as a "reading out of stars, intestines, coincidences" (2:209) draws out its other aspect: "reading out of" is the name of the destructive constructivity of reading.[25] This means that reading, through processes of distinction, division, and dismemberment, decides on the *elements* and the background from which the elements are distinguished and arranges them in the surface which is constituted precisely through reading, in the decision on element and interval.[26] For the constellation, this implies a suspensive interruption in the binding of reading to the *Augenblick*, to the moment and the gaze, which in the act of reading is *captured as* constellation. The break, the caesura, which delimits and fixes what is *momentary*, is readability's condition of possibility.[27] It functions as the distinction of the unreadably undifferentiated and the endless differentiation and as the decision on the constellation, whose readability is its figure. It functions, in other words, as the suspension of time that constitutes the constellation and its figure or image, a suspension that lifts up the latter from its background.

This is how the "ornament" "*captures stargazes*," in Benjamin's terms.

"The images according to which stars are drawn together" remain stiff and staring (*starr und starrend*) in Benjamin's prose piece "Himmel":

> In a dream I came out of a house and saw the night sky. A wild brilliance radiated from it. For, starry [*ausgestirnt*] as it was, the images according to which stars are drawn together were there in sensory presence. A lion, a virgin, scales and many others *stared down* on the earth as dense clusters of stars. There was no moon in sight. (4:125)

In the homonymic play of the "staring down" [*herunterstarren*] of the images, "stargazes" are made readable as rigidified stares, crystallizations into constellations of stellar characters, into the "read image" [*das gelesene Bild*], which is the name of the interruptive standstill in the *Passagen-Werk* (5:N 3, 1). In its precipitation as con-figuration, reading—in the decision on readability—suspends (other) readabilities. Each readability is determined through the unreadabilities that not only accompany them but also determine them in their exclusion, their "suspension."[28] When it is a question of the internal relation of readability and unreadability, readings differentiate themselves from each other in the manner in which they realize what must be suspended in each decision on readability. In this way, reading could *read* precisely: the *un-readabilities* accompanying and conditioning each readability, each suspension and each interruption.

The model of the ornament stands for this as well: what becomes readable in the *ornament* is the prescription and inscription of *polysemic* readings.

> There is no ornament which cannot be seen from at least two different sides: namely, as surface form or as linear configuration. For the most part however the singular forms, which can be unified in various groups, allow a plurality of configurations. This experience alone points toward one of the most core peculiarities of hash [*crock*]: namely to its irrepressible readiness to derive a plurality of sides, contents and relations from one and the same state of affairs [*Sachverhalt*] for instance a décor or a landscape.[29]

The ornamental structuring or the "figure" cannot be definitively stabilized: the gaze sets up a constellation, reads a certain configuration from out of the texture of lineaments and its interlacings, and each time realizes a new relation of figure and ground. The "polysemy of the ornament" [*Mehrsinnigkeit des Ornaments*] that Benjamin mentions is derived from a specific fabrication of *readability* in specific *groupings* and *unions*; these are decisions on figure and ground. Each bears the possibility of a displacement into another image.

The necessity of decision and the tipping of the decidability of figure and ground are both confirmed by the pictures of Adolf Wölfli found in his "Negerhall" (1911) (see Fig. 4).[30] In order to see or read anything at all, a decision must be made between the written notation of language, textual and computational systems, catalogs, lists, numbers, interest rates, notes calculations, music, ornaments, maps, and pictures, where decidability is never guaranteed. They play out each respective background as a space of writing and use each respectively blank surface of figuration within a competing system of figuration.[31] The plural, mutually exclusive *views*, "namely, either as surface form or as linear configuration," reformulate the specific "polysemy" *as* ornament or *as* writing in their mutual dependence as it is staged in all typographical images: figure-poems (see Fig. 5), concettist calligrams (see Fig. 6), Jewish micrographs (see Fig. 7), and arabesques.[32] Arabesque, on the border between ornament and sign, would then name a *gestalt-switch*, an incessant oscillation of undecidable determinations, in which according to Benjamin all ornaments participate.[33] The difference between figure and ground or background, whose erasure would make ornaments, images, and arabesques impossible, is blurred in the undecidability of a *polysemy*, which is due precisely to the fact that decisions must be made constantly and that decisions always already have been made.

The potential displacement of every figure realizes—in absence, as excluded—the readability of the "plurality of sides, contents and relations," which in reading (or in a state of euphoria that for Benjamin is modeled on reading) can be derived from "one and the same fact [*Sachverhalt*]."[34] Each momentarily established "fact" is only given in a puzzling dis-location—and is thus *dis-placed* in the ornamental setting in which no figure and no image can be stabilized. It is displaced in the Benjaminian "state of similarity," not that of the "similarity of one with another, with which we are familiar" but rather that in which "what happens never emerges as identical, but rather as similar, inscrutably similar to itself" (2:314).

The ornament is a picture puzzle (*Vexierbild*) and as such is determined in a twofold sense: not only by its diversity of interpretability but also by its "characteristic experience of identity," which delimits and stabilizes this

Figure 4. Adolf Wölfli, *Negerhall* (1911). Courtesy the Adolf Wölfli Stiftung, Bern, Switzerland.

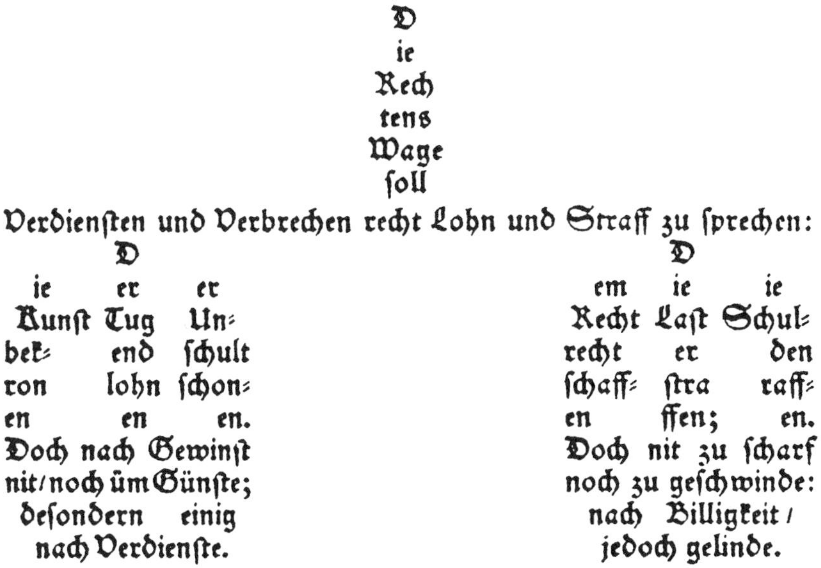

D
ie
Rech
tens
Wage
soll
Verdienſten und Verbrechen recht Lohn und Straff zu ſprechen:

D				D	
ie	er	er		em	ie	ie
Kunſt	Tug	Un=		Recht	Laſt	Schul=
beł=	end	ſchult		recht	er	den
ron	lohn	ſchon=		ſchaff=	ſtra	raff=
en	en	en.		en	ffen;	en.

Doch nach Gewinſt   Doch nit zu ſcharf
nit/noch ûm Günſte;   noch zu geſchwinde:
  beſondern   einig   nach Billigkeit /
  nach Verdienſte.   jedoch gelinde.

Figure 5. German figure-poem.

diversity. This *double* determination constitutes the functioning of the picture puzzle: it oscillates in its "inscrutable similarity to itself" precisely because it switches *between* different stabilizations and in mutually exclusive stabilizations, which is to say *images* (see Fig. 8).[35] Its perception *as* a picture puzzle can only occur in such a gestalt-switch between the realization of polysemy, on the one hand, in which identities are destabilized and dissolve in oscillation, and each respective — figural — stabilization, on the other, which excludes all other stabilizations as *polysemies*. The respective stabilization of an image in a picture puzzle on the background of respectively excluded possibilities must in its turn fall into dissolution, for its respectively *other* image to be stabilized and become visible. The "particular identity" *experienced* in the ornament is that of a readability, realized as a specific (momentary) interruption of the vexations and displacements. The ornament is unstable in the manner of a picture puzzle, insofar as the possibility of the respective image switching into one of the unrealized, excluded unreadabilities announces itself in each of its (respective) visibilities. Benjamin characterizes this permanent oscillation of readabilities in terms of a "quiet turmoil

Figure 6. Concettist calligram.

of the ornament" (4:123), exemplified by the Alcazar in Seville, an image of the lion court of Alhambra (see Fig. 9).[36] The edge of its disappearance, its nonvisibility is inscribed within the picture puzzle. It is then always there as a picture *puzzle* (*Vexier*bild) where it cannot exist as a self-identical image.

As a *picture puzzle*, the *ornament* is a model of readability, in the same sense that Benjamin writes of the constellation as a model of reading texts.[37] Benjamin programmatically defines the literal reading of alphabetic script as a *physiognomic* reading of sentences: "Even a sentence becomes . . . a face, not to mention individual words." Physiognomic reading, which (traditionally) inscribed readability, that is, translatable figures in a legend accompanying an illustration, and thus was the model and generator of semantic decidability, implies an organization in and of the surface.[38] Words and sentences, which as a rule are considered to be organized in linear terms although they may have always functioned as typefaces, are wrenched thereby out of their linear sequence. What is then decisive is that "this face [of the sentence] looks like that of the opposed sentence. . . . In this manner, every truth clearly refers to its opposite. . . . Truth becomes a living being, it lives only in the rhythm in which *Satz und Gegensatz*, sentence and opposition, are displaced in order to think themselves" (5:M 1a, 1).[39] Constellative reading performs this *rhythm*— the rhythm with which all readability is determined as "face," as readable constellation by the "opposed sentence," by its relation to "its opposite" into which it is displaced.[40] Elsewhere and in a somewhat different terminology,

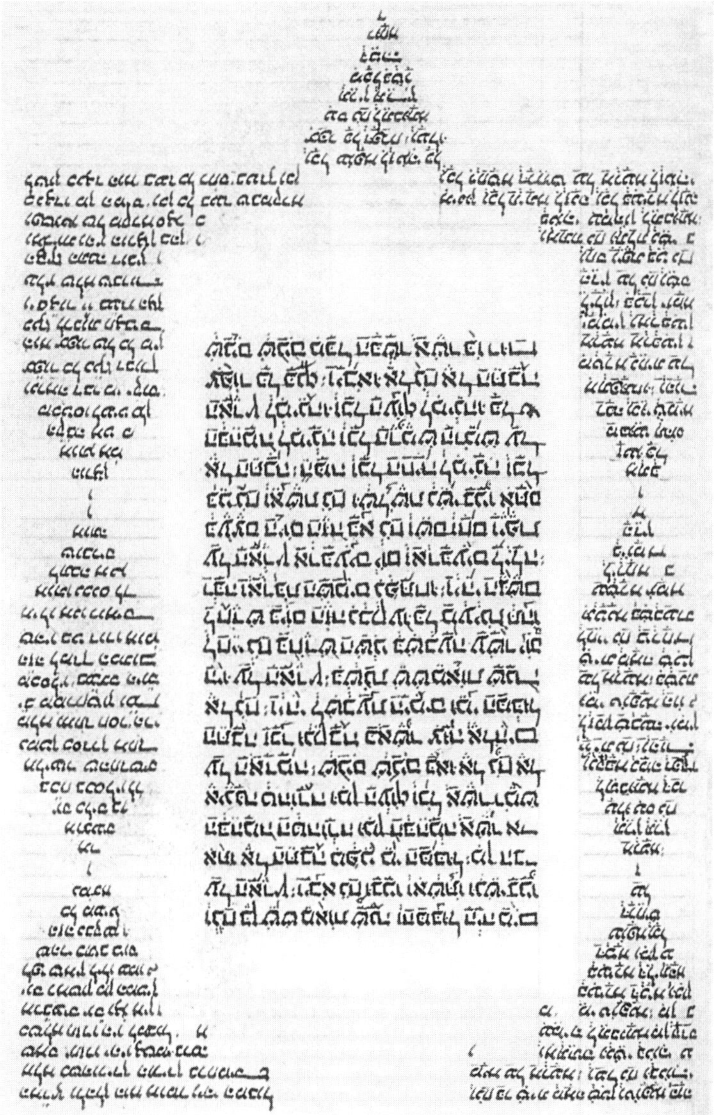

Figure 7. Jewish micrograph (1496).

Figure 8. Nineteenth-century German *Vexierbilder* (picture puzzles).

Benjamin writes that the "truth of a state of affairs [*Sachverhalt*]" not only functions as a constellation but also is "a function of the constellation of the veracity of all remaining state of affairs [*Sachverhalte*]" (6:46). This constellation of the "truth of a fact" does not only become readable in the "opposed sentence" [*Gegen-Satz*], but moreover in the nongiven constellation of all other sentences. The *truth* read in this way is not localizable; it "lives," Benjamin suggests, it takes place in the puzzling reciprocal mediality of "Satz und Gegensatz," *between* the one, the meaning stabilized in the *sentence*, and its other, that which is no longer an identifiable opposite or sentence. In the "realm" of linguistic constellations *between* "Satz und Gegensatz" and their respective stabilizations occurs that which is the object and structure of a different reading whose schema is the constellation: in a rhythm of displacements, in a presence, which is rather an absence, whose model is the picture puzzle (*Vexierbild*), the unreadable constellation of suspended sentences.

The relegation of the constellation to the intervals provides another set of reading instructions. To read "lineless," nonlinear writing, which entails reading (all) writing *as* constellation "with a modified principle of spatial organization," means, as Derrida puts it, "finally reading what wrote itself between the lines in the volumes."[41] If writing has *always* been determined through intervals as in the constellations that emerge in the night sky and organize themselves in the negative on the whiteness of paper, then this implies finally that what is to be read is what cannot be read, but that as such

Figure 9. The lion court of Alhambra.

is readability's condition of possibility: the suspended, absent and as such determinate intervals, grounds and backgrounds. Reading is devoted to dispersion to the extent that it perceives (which is to say, reads) the nonfinal functioning of the text and realizes it *as constellation*, as ordered arrangement in the space in which the elements are dispersed. In their suspended, blank, and unread interrelations, however, these dispersed elements are read *differently*.[42] Reading dislocates words out of the supposed self-identity of their meaning into the unresolvable puzzle of *self-similarity*.

Rather than givens, what is at stake are the relations and structures, bracings, "Verspannungen," (2:208, 212) and intervals that determine that which appears as given: the tension and the distance between writing and image, typeface (*Schriftbild*) and signified, between drawing and scribbling—and the self-distance, which enters into every text and every word; it disturbs and scatters the word into letters.[43]

I want to account for this by turning to another Benjaminian model of the materiality of script as "flurries" [*Gestöber*], which occur as the pulsing of the rhythm in which language constructs and withdraws meaning, insofar as every *something*, every figure remains bound to the (absently) determinant relations, as the *margin* of the constellation, as the—cloudy—border-zone of itself inscribed within the constellation. In the pulsing of the constellation organized by unreadable intervals, in the rhythm with which a figure, on the one hand, constructs itself as surface-figure or constellation and, on the other hand, returns to the surface, the ground, before which it lifts itself, the constellation is unreadably distorted into flurries. This *flurry of letters* comes from the Benjaminian repertoire of metaphorical models. It surrounds childhood reading like a storm of soundless *snow flurries*, out of which both the reader and the read emerge only to be driven about and to lose themselves within it. A "loosely woven world [*undichte Welt*][44] in which everything is displaced with each step," is given in the pages of books combining pictures and letters for *that* reading in which words appear in a masquerade ball whose director is precisely not "meaning": they "*whirl around* [as] *resounding snow-flakes*" (4:609).[45] The "looseness and flakiness [*Lockere und Flockige*], which cloud up in the core of things like snow flurries in a small glass ball" are found in the word "Mummerehlen," dislocated into misunderstanding. The phrase "clouds itself" becomes disfigured in its interior—"Mummerehlen," paronymically displaced between *Mummen* (mummery), *Mummelsee* (Mummel Lake), and the *Murmeln* (murmur) of words. These words direct anyone searching for their referent into that cloud of "flakiness" and "looseness," where words lose their contours and images cannot be resolved. Rather than being transgressed by the act of seizing the signified in an illusory referentiality, the "deceptive screen of the surface" (4:609) becomes loosened and destabilized in the "clouds" [*im Gewölke*] that detach words from their referents. Signs, signifiers, and signifieds lose themselves in the flurry of letters, words, and hieroglyph swirling disruptively through the pages. The clouds comprise a zone of the dis-solution or "loosening" of the identical, of self-contained images, into the "flakiness" [*Flockige*], which is opened out by language in the misunderstanding and dislocation of words—into the other similarity (with itself) that does not close onto itself, a space of noises, of unlocalized movements, oscillations, of mixing and flowing together.[46]

In the dispersion of writing in the "flurry [*Gestöber*] of changeable, colorful and quarrelling l e t t e r s" (4:103) and in the *new* typographical "*invasion of letters*" (5:F, 22) diagnosed by Benjamin, writing is realized as what it has always been: the materiality of black-on-white before and after the readability of meaning, a *pulsing surface*, in which the restriction of writing's commitment to the signified is dissolved. In the textual surface of flurrying dispersion, writing is abandoned to its law of black-on-white just as the latter in its pulsations loses itself again in the oscillations of visibilities/readabilities.[47] The "flurry" of "l e t t e r s" designates the organization in the surface as an endless oscillation of black-on-white, and hence its undemarcated boundary, a border-*zone* for all readability and textuality always already inscribed in writing.

The materiality of writing, black-on-white, realizes itself and loses itself in *flurries*—as it does in the dirtying *smear* in which gestural inscriptions and intervals approximate each other and collaborate. In their undecidability between sign and interval, they pass over into oscillations, into a *surging* (*Gewoge*) in which the scribble and the white surface of the blank page, a "*surging* (of indistinguishable) wavelengths" (2:603), become inseparable.

Translated by Anthony Reynolds

FOURTEEN

Eros and Language

Benjamin's Kraus Essay

SIGRID WEIGEL

Situating the Kraus Essay

In the vast wealth of readings and interpretations of Benjamin's work, the essay on Karl Kraus plays an oddly marginal role. The few studies that devote any attention at all to this at times cryptic and generally perhaps least accessible text by Benjamin always limit their discussion to specific aspects or motifs from it. The most prominent of these is undoubtedly the passage containing a short, condensed theory of quotation.[1] However, the connection between Eros and language, which is central to the essay, is one of the leitmotifs of Benjamin's thought that have hitherto remained largely overshadowed, above all by his heroines of modernity, the whores of Baudelaire's poetry.[2] Yet reflections on the relation between Eros and language form an often clear, at times concealed trace in Benjamin's theory and from his earliest writings appear repeatedly as a central preoccupation of his thinking. Within this trace, the Kraus essay of 1931 represents the attempt to set out a conclusive *systematic* argument concerning the connection between sexuality and intellectual production. The text juts out like a hermetic block into the midst of the more fluid mode of writing of Benjamin's late works, which are increasingly characterized by thought-images and miniatures, juxtaposed quotations, detail-readings, or single scenarios from the history of culture or the subject.

The figure of Karl Kraus and his traversal of the positions of *Allmensch* (cosmic man), demon, and *Un-Mensch* (monster or, more literally, nonhuman being) not only represents an analysis of the different textual practices of

Kraus the writer; at the same time, it is a masked reflection on and a rewriting of Benjamin's own earlier statements on this topic. The essay only really becomes decipherable in its larger context when read in relation to concepts from his early work such as the "Eros of the creative" (*Eros der Schaffenden*) and the figures of genius and whore, and when understood as a reformulation of the idea of *pure language* or the relationship between guilt and language. To this latter relationship Benjamin now introduces the dimension he had omitted from his consideration of the "Fall of Language-mind" (*Sündenfall des Sprachgeistes*) in his early philosophy of language: namely, the dimension of sexuality. The attempt to give a systematic theory of the relationship of language, Eros, creativity, and justice within modernity and to represent this relationship condensed within a single figure demanded a complexity that subverted the systematic intention within the mode of writing. For this reason I have chosen here to approach the topic via the detour of a very different text on the same topic, that is, via an aphorism.

"Überzeugen ist unfruchtbar"—To convince is unfruitful—is the briefest entry in *One-Way Street* (1928, 4:87), Benjamin's first nonacademic book publication. By the association with the word *unfruchtbar*, "unfruitful" or "infertile," Benjamin here indicates the meaning of *zeugen*, that is, "to conceive," "to beget," or "to procreate," as being part of *überzeugen*, to convince, because in German *über-zeugen*, to convince, is literally to overprocreate, overbeget.[3] The sentence appears under the phrase "FOR MEN," printed in small capitals aligned to the right-hand margin, which, as one of a series of words and phrases in this position and format, serves to divide the text without being clearly identifiable as title, heading, slogan, dedication, address, or motto. From the configuration of the two entries—"FOR MEN" and "To convince is unfertile"—there thus results an ambiguous wordplay that can be read as a monad for the meaning and representation of Eros in Benjamin's theory. This note from *One-Way Street* marks the precise point at which his theoretical reflections on language and on sexuality intersect. It should not be taken either as a *bon mot* or as a metaphorical figure intended simply to play on the ambiguity of sexual allusions. Rather, at issue is a linguistic practice, an attitude toward public statement that Benjamin rates as "unfruitful," uncreative because it uses language as a means to an end: this praxis is unfruitful for the precise reason that it is oriented toward a result. In a traditional metaphorical usage in which mental or intellectual production is represented in terms of corporeal procreation—using vocabulary from the fields of conception, generation, pregnancy, and birth—the act of convincing, *überzeugen*, would correspond with a procreative sexuality directed toward fertility and with an interest in engendering offspring. In playing on the traditional comparison, Benjamin uncovers the falseness of the analogy inscribed in it and the opposite effect achieved by it: in its outcome an intellectual attitude that behaves analogously to a sexual attitude oriented toward fertility proves itself unfruitful. A thought-image par excellence: the act of convincing, of over-conceiving, that is, of carrying over into language the economy of procreation, in its effect inverts the intended aim.

What remains implicit, not expressly mentioned in this phrase—finding linguistic expression rather in the play of allusions I have described—is another, different practice that would have to be called *not un*fruitful. Since the problematical effect arising from the comparison would necessarily follow, this different practice cannot be called fruitful as such. Benjamin's representation is thus based on an ambiguous sexual allusion that profits from the ambiguity of the comparison between creation and procreation. In the manner that he writes, however, this is transformed into another kind of allusion: into an allusive reference to an intellectual attitude that cannot be grasped unambiguously and that evades conceptual or metaphorical designation, a linguistic practice that can only be described as the other of convincing.

Language and Sexuality: The Genesis of the Connection

Benjamin discusses this paradigm in a number of different places, notably in the early writings, under the title of "genius." This title designates the male position of nonprocreative conception, which directs all potency toward intellectual activity. The attempt at a positive programmatic definition of the relationship between conception and creation dominates the first phase of his work on the Eros complex. While his contributions on the youth movement (1911 onward) behave in the first instance apologetically in relation to the interplay of the repression and metaphorization of the sexual, in 1915, after his return to Berlin, he complains of the "lack of erotic culture" (2:71f.).[4] In his well-known speech "The Life of the Students," he proposes the notion of a "unity in the existence of the creative and the procreating man" (83).

This reads as an emphatic program for the "Eros of the creative," which is targeted against the academic profession and the family alike, both of which Benjamin criticizes as sites in which sexual and intellectual energy is neutralized. The alliance of student and prostitute in Benjamin's early writings can be explained in terms of their common counterposition to these institutions. The "Eros of the creative" appears here as a mental attitude akin to sexual desire, as a desire directed toward knowledge and understanding and linguistic-intellectual articulation, which can perhaps best be understood as an antipole to work and instrumental rationality.

In the short essay "Socrates" of 1916, Benjamin characterizes the genius in contradistinction to the "demon" that degrades Eros to the status of a means toward an end. In this essay the twenty-four-year-old recapitulates his ideas on the "Eros of the creative" by a distinction from the notion of "pedagogical Eros," that is, from an understanding of the learning process as being propelled by an erotic element in the relation between teacher and pupils. Read as a text in which he is working through his own history in the youth movement and the bond between himself and Wyneken, Benjamin's anti-Socrates is a radical rejection of an order of knowledge that enlists Eros into its service. In the "graduated scale of eroticism" set out in the text, the genius designates a site produced by the dialectical transformation of the lowest point on the scale that is occupied by the demon; the genius is "sexless and yet of supraworldly sex." In a positive profile of the genius, Benjamin characterizes him as *Empfangender*, one who conceives/receives, and describes his "conception without pregnancy as the mental sign of the male genius" (131)—that is, as the male equivalent to the immaculate conception. But it is only the existence of the feminine and the knowledge of this existence that, according to Benjamin, guarantees the "sexlessness of what is mental."

In this way he situates the genius in a sphere beyond corporeal sexuality in which—in the knowledge of the existence of corporeal procreation and of the feminine—a "pure Eros" reigns. The "unity in the existence of the creative and the procreating man" thus means anything but a merging of the two spheres; what is meant is rather the unity of a purely mental Eros and a pure sexual love. The passage about the *methodos* of the question, about the contrast between, on the one hand, the Socratic question and, on the other, the "sacred question" that "waits for the answer and whose resonance is once again renewed in the answer" (130), makes it clear that the relation described in the intellectual sphere is modeled on a figure of desire: it is structured as a relation to the Other. The *methodos* of the "sacred question" organizes a constellation similar to the "desire to be desired." Thus Benjamin rescues from the Symposium a figure of desire that has been translated into the mental sphere while at the same time rejecting the degradation of desire to the status of a cognitive instrument.

Although the motif of procreation and creation is a peripheral concern in Benjamin's work of the 1920s, a number of his anthropological notes of the early 1920s nevertheless form a hidden trace that prepares the ground for the motif's reformulation. Benjamin's theoretical conceptualization of intellectual and imaginary processes within a matrix of (corporeal) excitations, together with his work on the topos of closeness and distance, bring about an obvious displacement in the figures of desire in his writings: toward the *Eros of distance* and toward the concept of a *Platonic love* that possesses the beloved in name—in awareness of the sexual dimension, and yet beyond it. The Eros of distance is not a figure understood as being without physical dimension; rather, it is conceptualized in analogy to longing or desire as a kind of "presence of mind incarnate" [*leibhaftige Geistesgegenwart*]. Perceptions, images, and words are here bound to processes of excitation in the individual subject.

In the genesis of this topic, the study on "Goethe's *Elective Affinities*" marks a caesura in relation to the notion of purity that implicitly structures the concept of a unity between "purely mental Eros" and a "pure sexual love" in the writings of the young author, thus highlighting the problem of the entanglement of his own earlier ideas in Christian mythology. In the discussion of the figure of Ottilie, the embodiment of innocence in Goethe's novel, Benjamin now explicitly links the idea of purity to the Christian ideal of virginity and rejects its function as the opposite of a mythical guilt arising from sexuality. Sexual being, he argues, cannot be taken as the basis of a "natural innocence," since this is only possible as a mental state. This marks a reappearance of his earlier postulate of a "unity in being" [*Einheit im Dasein*], but now reformulated in the notion of an individuality and concept of a "character" for whom sexual and mental life, and thus guilt and innocence, form a unity.

If in "Socrates" the positive counterimage to the grotesque portrait of the demon emerged as a male equivalent to the immaculate conception, then in "Goethe's Wahlverwandtschaften" this model is definitively rejected and with it an idea of purity that has sexual connotations—although Benjamin does here attempt to retain a concept of purity entirely free of sexual allusions. Ambiguity and lack of ambiguity are in this sense not discussed as criteria of meaning; rather, his critique refers to the mingling of the mental and the sexual. Thus ambiguity always refers to ambiguity in a sexual-linguistic sense, or in the sense of allusion to sexuality. In this, the work on Goethe's *Wahlverwandtschaften* (written in 1920–1922, published 1924–1925) can be seen as a parallel piece to the essay on "The Task of the Translator," written during the same period, in which the concept of a *pure language* forms a kind of leitmotif. Given that this pure language takes as its orientation the "immediacy" of Adamite language, it is the negative evaluation of mediacy, the rejection of every kind of mediation and instrumentality, that represents the vanishing point at which the concepts of language and Eros meet—even if they are here discussed in parallel in two different texts. In the midst of the omnipresence of a language organized as a system of signs, such as above all dominates in journalism and in a public sphere organized as the circulation of opinions, it is the position in the Now-Time, the *Jetzt-Zeit*, which in the 1920s forms the experiential horizon for Benjamin's reflections on language and guilt.

In the notes that make up *One-Way Street*, this situation becomes thematically central. The book has its place in the context of an attempt to differentiate mind and sexuality (*Geist* and *Sexus*), whereby the position of the genius is set apart from the instrumental use of language, apart from the public circulation of opinions, and the predominating type of contemporary journalism. The Kraus essay (1931), which brings this project to its conclusion, discusses the dual counterpositions to this situation under the contrary headings of *Allmensch* and demon, in order then to win from this constellation the site of the *Unmensch*, the nonhuman being. In this text the concept of the genius, which had disappeared from the writings of the 1920s, returns in modified form. The site in which the text culminates is achieved through a dialectical movement that, taking as its starting point the negation of a language of the public sphere, then passes through the demonic, the sphere of the ambiguity of mind and sexuality. In the course of this movement, the erotic is taken up into the concept of a Platonic love, a love that possesses the beloved in name—in awareness of the sexual, but beyond it.

The transferral of the erotic into the intellectual, which represents a clear trace in Benjamin's theoretical work, is thematized in his work of the 1930s as both a biographical and a historical experience; thus the passage of the intellectual through the sphere of the sexual is seen both in the perspective of the history of the individual subject and in broader historical perspective. The autobiographical threshold scene "Sexual Awakening" (4:251), located at the transition from the *Berlin Chronicle* to *Berlin Childhood Around 1900*, leads, as part of the shift from the recollections of the individual subject to those of the collective in the *Arcades Project* and the *Baudelaire* book, to an extensive and multilayered "science of thresholds" [*Schwellenkunde*], to a panorama of the ur-history of modernity. The prostitutes, who in the early writings were called *Dirnen* and regarded as accomplices of the genius because of their counterposition to procreation, make their return here as the whores. Described as "guardians of the threshold," they become the allegories of modernity because they represent the significance of Eros within cultural memory or recall the element of the sexual that is contained within language. The author of modernity is now both in competition and in league with them.

The Dialectical Conception of the Kraus Essay

The tripartite composition of the Kraus essay illumines the figure of Kraus from changing viewpoints, a construction which, as far as the mind-sexuality paradigm is concerned, brings about a significant shift in relation to the Socrates model. Where the demonic Socrates was characterized as "inhuman" (2:131), in the Kraus essay the concept and standard of what is human have been inverted. The sequence of chapter headings, *Allmensch, Dämon, Un-Mensch*, from which the profile of Karl Kraus emerges, is intended by Benjamin as a representation of a dialectical movement, in the course of which Kraus's "inter- or sub-human traits are conquered by a true non-humanity" (2:358; *OWS* 281, trans. mod.). This nonhuman being is not inhuman in the everyday sense of the word; rather, in calling him *unmenschlich*, Benjamin is characterizing his position as other to the established image of "humanity." Benjamin describes Kraus as the messenger not of an ideal, but of a real humanism, whose humanity "proves itself by destruction" (367; 289).

The "Eros of the creative," meanwhile, has been transformed in the Kraus essay—as it were under the conditions of a language impure because of its mediatory status—into a totally different concept. "He [the demon] fell in the beginning because he came into the world as a hybrid of mind and sexuality. His sword and shield—*concept* and *guilt*—have fallen from his hands to become emblems beneath the feet of the angel who slew him" (360; 283, trans. mod.; emphasis mine).[5] With "concept and guilt" those two aspects are named which are at issue in the primal scene of the biblical attainment of knowledge. In the context of his theory of language-magic Benjamin had examined this scene as a constellation of the "Fall of language-mind" in the first instance only with reference to the problem of language. Yet it is at the moment of this fall, that is, the moment when language loses its immediacy and becomes signs and names become concepts, that sexuality and gender difference also enter the world: the guilt, in short, which, in the essay on Goethe's *Wahlverwandtschaften*, Benjamin had described as natural guilt in the sexual life of the individual. Concept and guilt mark the distance that opens up from the origin and from paradisiac creation out of and within language in the very moment of biblical (re)cognition. Concept and guilt are then attributes of a combative Kraus figure and, at the same time, define his distance from immediacy and purity both in terms of sexuality and in language.

Now the ideas developed in the Kraus essay, in particular the paradigm of "mind and sexuality" and the "law of ambiguity" discussed in it, are relevant to the construction of a site oriented toward the "Eros of the creative," although at the same time being sure that "pure mind" is a chimera (354; 277). Both ideas revolve around a possible practice that can take account of the guilt of a mediatory language and the natural guilt of sexuality, but without falling prey to the ambiguity of the demonic.

> Kraus fails to see this, because pure mind and pure sexuality in their complete identity, that is, in the demonic, are to him so much the sphere of his existence that he is unable to see through them in terms of their construction. This is, however, compensated for by his dialectical activity which unfolds within this sphere, never going beyond it, yet which is continuously splitting itself, thus constantly disavowing this sphere, blasting it apart. (2:1093)

In this passage from the preliminary notes for the essay, Benjamin's attitude in the writing of the Kraus portrait becomes clear. He tries to make manifest the "strange interplay between reactionary theory and revolutionary practice" (2:342; *OWS* 265) so significant for Kraus and at the same time to represent in his text "in terms of [its] construction" that which Kraus (like the younger Benjamin himself) has failed to see through: namely, the structure that underlies this interplay. This attitude means that Benjamin's text remains suspended between critique and apologia. In certain respects, notably in view of the second section of the essay, Kraus is presented as the successor to the demon (Socrates). However, Benjamin now no longer constructs a counterposition in terms of a unity of pure mind and pure sexuality, certainly not in terms of a "unity in the existence of the creative and the procreative." Instead, he works on a dialectical method of passing through different positions, in the course of which movement Karl Kraus emerges as constituted of three parts and thus as a thoroughly unharmonious and unbeautiful figure.

The effect is not only that the transposition of corporeal procreation onto "intellectual creation" is rejected, but so too is the norm of creativity altogether. At the end of the essay the emphasis is on destruction, through the image of a kind of work that destructively intervenes in its material, so that creation as the criteria for intellectual work is negated: "For far too long the accent was placed on creativity" (366; 289). Thus the Kraus essay culminates in the intimation of a practice that replaces the idea of *intellectual creation* and all those related notions such as *work*, *original*, *authorship*, and so on, a practice that, under the name *allegorical method*, will become central for Benjamin's theory: this is a method whereby traditional representations are broken asunder, or single images broken out of the continuum in order to make possible a changed view of what has been in the past, or: "'Construction' presupposes 'destruction'" (5:587).

The figure of Kraus presented in the first section of the essay under the name of *Allmensch* could be taken as the embodiment of that new, other magic of judgment and abstraction in the "world after creation" that arises at the same moment as the character of language as sign out of the "threefold significance" of the Fall of language-mind: "The immediacy [*Unmittelbarkeit*] (this is the linguistic root) of the communicability [*Mitteilbarkeit*] of abstraction resides in judgment," as Benjamin wrote in his early essay "On Language as Such" (2:154; *OWS* 120, trans. mod.). It is in this sense that Kraus's mode of speaking is placed in the context of a public sphere, which is interested in judgments, as opposed to a public sphere that functions as the circulation of commodified opinions. This position in a world beyond creation also situates him beyond procreating and convincing, *Zeugung* and *Überzeugung*: "His testimony [*Zeugnis*] can be decisive only for those for whom it can never become a procreation [*Zeugung*]" (2:341; *OWS* 265, trans. mod.). The significance of Kraus's texts as testimony emerges only out of the destruction of the myths of creation and procreation in the conceptualization of the intellectual. In this context what is also at issue is the specific meaning that an attitude of *Recht-haben* attains, a word associated with the spheres of both justice and truth, to being right and having the right. "Many will be right one day. But it will be a right(ness) resulting from my [*Unrecht*] wrongness/injustice today," Benjamin quotes Kraus and concludes, "That is the language of true authority" (343; 266). In this sentence the emphasis is on language, for it is in his theory of language that Kraus displays his authority, in order thus to win from the empty phrases of the newspapers the "news" in the original sense of the word: as an event that takes place through and within language.

In the second section of the essay, which examines the "demon in Kraus," the connection between "being right" and language is taken further, specifically with regard to the difference between *Klage* and *Anklage*, between "lament" and "accusation." The argument here concerns the caesura to which Benjamin's critique of Kraus's practice refers. The caesura that divides the "world after creation" from the "world of creation" positions Kraus at the transition between lament and accusation. Although himself already in the position of one who judges, he nevertheless has the world of creation at his back, and he is still aware of what has been lost. "If he ever turns his back on creation, if he breaks off from lamentation, it is only as an accuser before the world's tribunal [*Weltgericht*, a word also with connotations of the Last Judgment]" (272, trans. mod.). The break in Kraus's linguistic practice that Benjamin illumines here denotes a literally and corporeally understood about-turn, from lament in the face of (God's) creation to accusation before the seat of judgment, with creation at his back.[6] While the lament directed at a divine authority has nothing to do with being right, as soon as the seat of judgment is addressed the lament becomes accusation, that is, becomes a discourse that has always been about being right or having the right.[7]

In Kraus's "theory of language," as described by Benjamin, there is, however, an instance within the practice of accusation that goes beyond this same discourse. What Benjamin calls Kraus's "linguistic rules of court" [*Sprach-*

prozeßordnung] could also be described as the accusation of accusation, as the complaint filed by language, specifically the language that recalls the sphere of creation or of lament, against the complaint of legal discourse. For Kraus, writes Benjamin, everything falls within the sphere of justice, but in the legal chamber that every thought can become, it is language that presides. It is this complex relation between language and justice that motivates Benjamin's reference to Kraus's "linguistic rules of court": "It is a misunderstanding of his theory of language if one does not see it as a contribution to the linguistic rules of court, if one understands the word of someone else in his mouth only as a *corpus delicti*, and his own only as a 'judging word'" (349; 272, trans. mod.). The linguistic rules of court are not part of the order of law, but on the contrary an accusation leveled against it. Benjamin explicitly stresses that the issue for Kraus is not the accusation of the law in its effect—which might mean where there are miscarriages of justice, cases of injustice, or the like—but rather "the law in its substance," which means in its claim to represent justice. This is why Kraus's charge is that of "the betrayal of justice by law. More exactly, of the word by the concept," for "over right-saying/jurisdiction stands right-spelling/orthography" (349; 273). In claiming to represent justice, the legal system has expropriated justice from its divine origin and wrested it from the one context in which it can continue to exist, namely in the connection of justice and language. As for Judaism in general, so too for Kraus "justice and language remain founded in each other." Kraus's worship of the image of divine justice as language, particularly in the German language, is thus seen by Benjamin as "the genuinely Jewish somersault by which he tries to break the spell of the demon" (349; 272).

The reverse side of this act of rescuing divine justice from the order of law within language is not unknown to Kraus. It is described in that section of the essay that presents Kraus under the name of "demon" and places him— with reference to the relation of mind and sexuality—in a sphere of ambiguity. Kraus, writes Benjamin, "nevertheless" invokes the law, however much he has seen through it, "precisely because his own demon is drawn so powerfully by the abyss it [that is, the law] represents," and moreover most clearly "where mind and sexuality meet—in the trial for sexual offences" (350; 273). This "nevertheless" in Benjamin's Kraus portrait shows that the accusation of the order of law before and through language is disturbed when sexuality invades this sphere and can no longer be overlooked. If the theory of language of Benjamin's Kraus moves along the same lines as Benjamin's own early language theory, then the invasion of the sexual here once again makes it clear that something had been omitted from it. The "demon in Kraus" brings this to light and motivates the author of the Kraus essay to rethink the relation between his theories of language and of Eros.

"Mind and sexuality," writes Benjamin, move in the sphere of ambiguity: the obsession of demonic sexuality, that is, the ego *and* obsessed mind, that is, the joke. The "law of ambiguity" that rules where mind and sexuality seem identical is portrayed by Benjamin in an image that represents an intersection of procreativity between sexuality and language, arriving at a final figuration with reversed terms: "Neither of them reaches its object, the ego its women no more than the joke its words. Disintegration has taken the place of procreation, stridency that of secrecy; yet now they shimmer in the most beguiling nuances: in the witticism lust, and in onanism the punch line come into their own" (350; 273, trans. mod.). This is no more a *bon mot* than was the note on the unfruitfulness of convincing; nor is it mere rhetoric. If, in this oxymoron, body and language cross over (witticism-lust and onanism-punch line), it is through the heterogeneity of body and language inscribed in this crossover that the rhetoric is simultaneously distorted, and the oxymoron becomes a *Denkbild*, a "thought-image." It drives the ambiguity that remains enclosed within the metaphorical equation of the sexual and the mental to the surface of visibility, representing this ambiguity as a law of meaning. It is clear from this thought-image how the essay is structured by a mode of writing different from a conceptually systematic representation, although the text in fact has a clear scheme as its basis. A sketch of this scheme, for which the law of ambiguity is the underlying basis, appears in Benjamin's notes for the essay:

> Language: Mind = Eros: Sexuality
>> Eroticism: the prism of lust, its development
>> Language: the blasting apart of the mind, its destruction
>> Dialectic is the relation of language to Eros,
>> ambiguous is that of the mind to sexuality. (2:1096)

The theoretical task following from this scheme is the transformation of the ambiguity of mind and sexuality into the dialectic of Eros and language. To examine the law of ambiguity means that the precondition for the metaphorical equation (of mind and sexuality) must necessarily be discussed. Thus Benjamin sees the correspondence of the "forms of existence—life under the aegis of mere mind or of mere sexuality" as the condition for the solidarity of the man of letters with the whore. It is the condition of possibility for Kraus's comparison of journalism with prostitution (352; 275), which also makes indirect reference to the closeness between student and prostitute in Benjamin's own early writings. In an exemplary commentary on an ambiguous passage from Kraus about the "late-comer, who brings the woman the joy [*Lust*] of the sequence and will triumph as the last in it," an ironic and sexually allusive revolt against the idea of the original, Benjamin pursues the image further, and in so doing his writing uncovers the death fantasies contained in the comparison of woman and language that end with "Jack the Ripper" (353; 276).

In the third section of the essay there appears under the name of *Unmensch*, and in the place of (1) the yardstick of pure language and (2) the (demonic) law of ambiguity, the dialectic of language and Eros. The former idea of purity is here substituted by a detour that, taking place within the sphere of language, will lead back to immediacy. Kraus's language here becomes the scene of a "sanctification of the name," whereby this poetic practice is, in order to avoid misunderstandings, clearly distinguished from the hymnic and conciliatory variant of a Stefan George. Comparable rather with the theory of a dialectic of the semiotic and the symbolic in the signification process (Julia Kristeva), Kraus's linguistic gesture operates with the "two poles of linguistic expression—the enfeebled [*depotenziert*] pole of humming and the armed pole of pathos," in order thus to become "the scenario of a sanctification of the name" and at the same time "with Jewish certainty" to set itself "against the theurgy of the 'word's body'" (359; 282).

The essay can be read as a commentary on Kraus's phrase "origin is the goal," quoted at various points in Benjamin's works.[8] Here it is explained in terms of a philosophy of language as a method of passing through or overcoming the interpersonal (of the *Allmensch*) and the subhuman (of the "demon") to arrive at the position of a nonhuman: "intellectuality as a deviation . . . leading back to immediacy" (360; 283).[9] The discovery of the *origin* is not an *original* discovery, but rather a "discovery that has a curious element of rediscovery. The theatre of this philosophical recognition scene in Kraus's work is poetry, and its language rhyme" (360; 283).

This philosophical recognition scene of, and within, poetry becomes for Benjamin the sphere in which the Eros of distance takes on linguistic form, in which Eros has become language or in which language, separated from mind, is now linked to Eros: "'The more closely you look at a word the more distantly it looks back.' This is a Platonic love of language. The closeness from which the word cannot escape, however, is solely rhyme. So the primal erotic relationship between closeness and distance is given voice in his language: as rhyme and name" (362; 285). The paradigm of "language and Eros" thus formulated—replacing the rejected paradigm of "mind and sexuality"—sets the frame for interpreting different literary and linguistic figures. The dedication, for example—discussed by Benjamin in relation to Kraus's "Die Verlassenen" (The forsaken, from the fifth volume of *Words in Verse*), in which Benjamin sees the "most intimate interpenetration of language and Eros"—now takes on a beautiful meaning as the declaration of Platonic love, "which does not do penance for its desire in what it loves, but possesses it in name and lavishes attention on it in name. This man, preoccupied with himself, knows no other self-renunciation than giving thanks. His love is not possession, but thankfulness. Thankfulness and dedication—for to thank is to place feelings under a name" (362; 285, trans. mod.). In other words, the Eros-become-language in the literary figure of the dedication no longer has half an eye on sexuality. And quotation, too, Kraus's "basic polemical procedure," is revealed in relation to the idea of name as a method that, by breaking words out of their given context, "calls [them] by name," thus recognizing them at origin: quotation, then, as detour and return to immediacy.

> In the quotation that both saves and chastises, language proves the matrix of justice. It summons the word by its name, wrenches it destructively from its context, but precisely thereby calls it back to its origin. Not without rhyme and reason [*nicht ungereimt*], it appears sonorously, sound in the structure of a new text. As rhyme it gathers the similar into its aura; as name it stands alone and expressionless. In quotation the two realms—of origin and destruction—present themselves before language. And conversely, only where they interpenetrate—in quotation—is language consummated. In it is mirrored the angelic tongue in which all words, startled from the idyllic context

of meaning, have become mottoes in the Book of Creation. (363; 286, trans. mod.)

Rhyme, name, dedication, quotation. Language filled with Eros no longer attempts to imitate (divine) creation as *intellectual creation.* At the most in the quotation there appears for a moment a mirroring of that language in which, maybe not the Book of Creation is written, but mottoes from it are preserved. Comparable to the conceptualization of Now-Time (*Jetzt-Zeit*) as a model of messianic time, the quotation here appears as a model of the language of the angels.

The Shifts in Benjamin's Theory of Language and Eros

If one compares the link between language and Eros as set out in the third section of the Kraus essay with Benjamin's early Eros theory, it becomes clear that he adheres to the postulate of *immediacy*, both of language and of sexuality. However, this immediacy is no longer contrasted with an epistemological means to an end as it was in the Socrates model. Rather, it is the vanishing point of a movement in the look backward that is won from a perspective "in the midst of mediacy," giving rise to recognition and incorporating moments of destruction.[10] At the same time, the translation of the sexual into the mental, such as is found in the concept of "intellectual creation" in its classical form, is rejected. It is, though, rejected after the traversal (both in the Kraus essay and within the genesis of Benjamin's writings) and the overcoming of everything that is metaphorical, of comparisons, equivalences, and so on, in order, via the detour of the figure of the "Eros of distance," to replace the ambiguity of mind and sexuality with an interpenetration of language and Eros.

In the course of this transition, a metamorphosis has taken place in Benjamin's ideas from the "Eros of the creative" to an Eros that has entered into language. At the same time the idea of creation in the intellectual sphere has been dismissed, so that within language there is no longer any aspiration for a mimesis of either corporeal procreation or divine creation. The structure of intellectual production modeled on the figure of *desire* has now taken on a genuinely linguistic form. The idea of Platonic love, which Benjamin already took as his orientation in the Socrates model, is no longer bound to notions of sexual purity or innocence; rather, it serves to link Eros and language in the form of love in the name.

In one of the thought-images from "Short Shadows" (1929), Benjamin had already formulated this notion of Platonic love, in part in language identical to passages from the third section of the Kraus essay. In this thought-image, Platonic love is defined in its "only genuine, only relevant sense":

> as the love which does not do penance for its desire in the name, but which loves the beloved in name, possesses her in name and lavishes attention on her in name. That it protects and preserves intact the name, the forename of the beloved woman, that alone is the true expression of the suspense, the inclination across distance that is called Platonic love. For this love, the existence of the beloved, and even the work of the lover, comes forth, as rays from the heart of the fire, from her name. Thus the *Divine Comedy* is nothing but the aura that surrounds the name Beatrice; the mightiest representation of the fact that all the forces and all the figures of the cosmos are produced from the name that has risen forth unscathed from love. (4:369f.)

The name that has risen forth from love, and out of which the work of the beloved emerges—this marks a return to the immediacy of language via the path of love or in the relation to the Other. That this idea of Platonic love in Benjamin is not linked to the dismissal of sexuality becomes clear in the thought-image that follows, "Once Is Not Once" [*Einmal ist keinmal*]. In a passage rich in allusion, the ambiguity of the title phrase is transposed from mere sexual innuendo into the elaboration of the two possible meanings that the singular fulfillment seen as "not once" can take on: either the possibility of the eradication of doubt or alternatively "sheer, naked fulfillment," which in recollection becomes worthless (369).

In another thought-image, "After Completion" [*Nach der Vollendung*], the conceptual image of creation in the field of art is once more presented and at the same time deconstructed by being turned into a dialectical image.[11] In this image the implications of the concept of *genius*, including related concepts such as *master, completion,* and *creation,* are made visible. Here the devaluation of the corporeal, of the maternal body, inscribed into the established notion of *intellectual creation*, is addressed:

> For creation in its completion gives birth anew to the creator. Not in terms
> of his femininity, in which the creation was conceived, but in relation to his
> male element. He blissfully surpasses nature: for he will now owe this exis-
> tence, which he first received from the dark depths of his mother's womb, to
> a brighter realm. His home is not where he was born; rather he comes into
> the world where his home is. He is the male first-born of the work that he
> once conceived. (438)

The formulation "the male first-born of his work" makes it clear that the
concept of intellectual creation is a variant of those "bachelor machines" in
which the corporeal origin from woman is denied. Benjamin will pursue this
motif further, in the image of the competition between modern authorship
and pregnancy, in his Baudelaire essay.

While the latter work sees the reappearance, together with the figure of
the whore, of another figure from the early writings, that of love between
women, it is striking that Benjamin did not, after the caricature of "Socrates,"
devote any systematic attention to male homosexuality. It is mentioned only
marginally in the Proust essay (2:319; *I* 205), or, for example, in a short note
written in Siena that might be assigned to the motif of the "Eros of distance":
"The rite teaches us: the Church did not develop on the basis of overcoming
male-female love but homosexual love. That the priest does not sleep with
the choirboy: that is the miracle of the Mass. (Siena Cathedral 28 July 1929)"
(6:204).

What is striking in the thought-images written in parallel to Karl Kraus
that address the same thematic area—Eros and language versus mind and
sexuality—is the lightness and fluidity of the presentation in this "incon-
spicuous form" in which, nevertheless, nothing of the difficulty and complexity of the connections is lost. The Kraus essay, by contrast, stands there
in the sequence of Benjamin's texts like a granite block. It is undoubtedly
the contradictory relationship of systematic intention and the work on a different mode of writing that characterizes the intermediary position of the
Kraus text in the history of Benjamin's writings; this also explains in part the
problems in its reception and the marginal position that this text has hitherto
occupied in the studies of Benjamin's work. If this essay is compared with
the texts that followed it, then it becomes clear that Benjamin from then
on turned away from the systematic intention in the sense of programmatic

works to embrace a new practice of writing: adopting a cultural-historical perspective and aided by his "Copernican revolution in remembrance" (5: 1058). In these later writings Eros, too, takes on a different position; at stake no longer is a programmatic and systematic theory of Eros, but rather the reading of the images of what has been and the consideration of histori-cally distinct phenomena in which Eros makes its appearance on the cultural scenery.

Translated by Georgina Paul

Reference Matter

Notes

INTRODUCTION

1. In the case of references to Benjamin, the first citation refers to the English translation, the second to the German original. In the case of a single citation, there is no standard English translation, and the translation from the German source indicated is my own. For the English citations, I use the following abbreviations: (D) "Doctrine of the Similar," trans. Knut Tarnowski, *New German Critique* 17 (1979): 65–69; (F) "Eduard Fuchs: Collector and Historian," trans. Edmund Jephcott and Kingsley Shorter, in *One-Way Street and Other Writings* (London: New Left Books, 1979), 349–86; (*I*) *Illuminations*, ed. Hannah Arendt, trans. Harry Zohn (New York: Schocken, 1968); (N) "N [Theoretics of Knowledge; Theory of Progress]," trans. Leigh Hafrey and Richard Sieburth, in *Benjamin: Philosophy, Aesthetics, History*, ed. Gary Smith (Chicago: University of Chicago Press, 1989), 43–83; (*R*) *Reflections*, ed. Peter Demetz, trans. Edmund Jephcott (New York: Harcourt Brace, 1978); (*SW*) *Selected Writings*, vol. 1: 1913–1926, ed. Marcus Bullock and Michael Jennings (Cambridge, Mass.: Harvard University Press, 1996). The German edition cited is *Gesammelte Schriften*, ed. Rolf Tiedemann and Hermann Schweppenhäuser, 7 vols. (Frankfurt am Main: Suhrkamp, 1972–1989).

2. Reinhard Markner and Thomas Weber, eds., *Literatur über Walter Benjamin. Kommentierte Bibliographie 1983–1992* (Hamburg: Argument, 1993).

3. See the comic book by Howard Caygill, Alex Coles, and Andrzei Klimowski, *Introducing Walter Benjamin* (New York: Totem, 1998); and the novel by Jay Parini, *Benjamin's Crossings* (New York: Henry Holt, 1997).

4. For a seminal meditation on spectrality as a cultural and political category, see Jacques Derrida, *Specters of Marx: The State of the Debt, the Work of Mourning, and the New International*, trans. Peggy Kamuf (New York: Routledge, 1994).

5. Gershom Scholem, *Walter Benjamin: The Story of a Friendship*, trans. Harry Zohn (Philadelphia: Jewish Publication Society of America, 1981), 61. As Scholem tells us, Benjamin distinguished between "two historical ages of the spectral and the demonic" [*Weltalter des Gespenstischen und des Dämonischen*], in order to suggest that

the "real content of myth was the enormous revolution that polemicized against the spectral [*das Gespenstische*] and brought its age to an end" (61).

6. See his *Schwellenkunde. Walter Benjamins Passage des Mythos* (Frankfurt am Main: Suhrkamp, 1986).

7. The tradition that conceives of Paris in terms of the ghostly, from Baudelaire to Hugo, Breton and beyond, is usefully delineated by Margaret Cohen, *Profane Illumination: Walter Benjamin and the Paris of Surrealist Revolution* (Berkeley and Los Angeles: University of California Press, 1993). Throughout the *Passagen-Werk*, Benjamin comments on and inscribes himself into this tradition of being haunted by the ghosts of Paris. In "Convolute P," entitled "The Streets of Paris," for instance, we read: "The name of the 'Château d'Eau,' a former fountain that is no longer there, still today haunts several city quarters" (5:643).

8. For a recent discussion, by a historian, of the possibility of writing and reading cultural history today, see Mark Poster, *Cultural History and Postmodernity: Disciplinary Readings and Challenges* (New York: Columbia University Press, 1997).

9. For an extended analysis of the dialectical image, see Michael Jennings, *Dialectical Images: Walter Benjamin's Theory of Literary Criticism* (Ithaca, N.Y.: Cornell University Press, 1987).

10. See Peter Bulthaupt, ed., *Materialien zu Benjamins Thesen "Über den Begriff der Geschichte." Beiträge und Interpretationen* (Frankfurt am Main: Suhrkamp, 1975); Jeanne-Marie Gagnebin, *Zur Geschichtsphilosophie Walter Benjamins* (Erlangen: Palm and Enke, 1978); John McCole, *Walter Benjamin and the Antinomies of Tradition* (Ithaca, N.Y.: Cornell University Press, 1993); Michael Steinberg, ed., *Walter Benjamin and the Demands of History* (Ithaca, N.Y.: Cornell University Press, 1996); and Eduardo Cadava, *Words of Light: Theses on the Photography of History* (Princeton, N.J.: Princeton University Press, 1997).

11. Derrida, *Specters of Marx*, 181.

12. Theodor W. Adorno, "Ernst Bloch's Spuren: On the Revised Edition of 1959," *Notes to Literature*, vol. 1, trans. Shierry Weber Nicholsen (New York: Columbia University Press, 1991), 210.

13. Bill Readings, *The University in Ruins* (Cambridge, Mass.: Harvard University Press, 1996); J. Hillis Miller, "Literary Study in the Transnational University," *Profession* (1996): 6–14.

14. Fredric Jameson, "The Theological Hesitation: Benjamin's Sociological Predecessor," *Critical Inquiry* 25, no. 2 (1999): 267. For insightful discussions of the theoretical and political stakes of mimesis today, see Tom Cohen, *Ideology and Inscription: "Cultural Studies" After Benjamin, De Man, and Bakhtin* (Cambridge: Cambridge University Press, 1998); and Martin Jay, "Mimesis and Mimetology: Adorno and Lacoue-Labarthe," in *The Semblance of Subjectivity: Essays in Adorno's Aesthetic Theory*, ed. Tom Huhn and Lambert Zuidervaart (Cambridge, Mass.: MIT Press, 1997), 29–53.

15. Paul de Man, "The Resistance to Theory," *The Resistance to Theory* (Minneapolis: University of Minnesota Press, 1986), 19.

CHAPTER I

1. "Das dialektische Bild malt den Traum nicht nach—das zu behaupten lag niemals in meiner Absicht. Wohl aber scheint es mir, die Instanzen, die Einbruchsstelle des Erwachens zu enthalten, ja aus diesen Stellen seine Figur wie ein Sternbild aus den leuchtenden Punkten erst herzustellen" (Benjamin to Gretel Adorno on 16 August 1935). Theodor W. Adorno and Walter Benjamin, *Briefwechsel 1928–1940* (Frankfurt am Main: Suhrkamp, 1994), 157. Benjamin quotations included in parentheses in the text are from *Gesammelte Schriften*, ed. Rolf Tiedemann and Hermann Schweppenhäuser, 7 vols. (Frankfurt am Main: Suhrkamp, 1972–1989). Translations are my own.

2. "Die Ebne des Zeichens liegt—vom Menschen aus gesehen horizontal, die des Males vertikal." Walter Benjamin, *Gesammelte Briefe*, vol. 1: 1910–1918 (Frankfurt am Main: Suhrkamp, 1995), 418.

3. "Selig sind die Zeiten, für die der Sternenhimmel die Landkarte der gangbaren und zu gehenden Wege ist" (Georg Lukács, *Die Theorie des Romans* [Berlin: Paul Cassirer, 1920], 9).

4. "[T]ranszendentale Obdachlosigkeit" (ibid., 23f.)

5. Quotations of Hölderlin are from the Frankfurt edition (*FA*): *Sämtliche Werke. Frankfurter Ausgabe*, ed. D. E. Sattler (Basel and Frankfurt am Main: Stroemfeld and Roter Stern, 1975–).

6. "In der äußersten Gränze des Leidens bestehet nemlich nichts mehr, als die Bedingungen der Zeit oder des Raums" (*FA* 16, 258).

7. "Das älteste Systemprogramm des deutschen Idealismus. Ein handschriftlicher Fund von Franz Rosenzweig" (Heidelberg: Sitzungsberichte der Heidelberger Akademie der Wissenschaften. Philosophisch-historische Klasse, 1917), 5. "Abhandlung," 5–7. For a full documentation and discussion of this text, see Christoph Jamme and Helmut Schneider, eds., *Mythologie der Vernunft* (Frankfurt am Main: Suhrkamp, 1984).

8. Jamme and Schneider, *Mythologie der Vernunft*, 11. Italics corresponds to underlining in the manuscript.

9. Ibid., 12, 13.

10. There is, as far as I can see, no evidence that Benjamin refers to the "Systemprogramm"; the thoughts developed in his text are firmly rooted in his own philosophical development. However, the objective historical constellation remains striking.

11. "Dieses das Handeln bestimmende Wissen gibt es. Es ist jedoch nicht als 'Motiv,' sondern kraft seiner sprachlichen Struktur bestimmend. Das sprachliche Moment in der Moralität hängt mit dem Wissen zusammen. . . . Mit dem Begriff des Tao dürfte dieses bestimmende Wissen sehr verwandt sein. Dagegen ist es dem Wissen der Sokratischen Tugendlehre strikt entgegen gesetzt. Denn dieses ist für das Handeln motivierend, nicht den Handelnden bestimmend" (6:48f.).

12. Among the many passages of Nietzsche, see the following passage from "Morgenröthe": "Sokrates und Plato, in diesem Stücke grosse Zweifler und bewunderungswürdige Neuerer, waren doch harmlos gläubig in Betreff jenes verhängnisvollsten Vorurtheils, jenes tiefsten Irrthums, dass 'der richtigen Erkenntnis die richtige Handlung folgen müsse',—sie waren in diesem Grundsatze immer noch die Erben des allgemeinen Wahnsinns und Dünkels: dass es ein Wissen um das Wesen einer Handlung gebe" (Friedrich Nietzsche, *Sämtliche Werke. Kritische Studienausgabe* [Berlin and Munich: De Gruyter and DTV, 1980], 3:108f., #116).

13. "Das Dasein der Sprache erstreckt sich aber nicht nur über alle Gebiete menschlicher Geistesäußerung, der in irgendeinem Sinne immer Sprache innewohnt, sondern es erstreckt sich auf schlechthin alles" (2:140).

14. Jacques Derrida, *Of Grammatology* (Baltimore, Md.: Johns Hopkins University Press, 1976), 158.

15. This is presented most explicitly in the preface to *The Origin of the German Baroque Mourning Play* (1:207–37).

16. Benjamin's "Lage der Wahrheit" recalls the "plain of truth" [*alêtheias pedion*] in Plato's *Phaidros* (148b).

17. Again we may recall Plato's concept of the "plain of truth," of truth as a plain (*pedion*).

18. Jürgen Habermas, *Der philosophische Diskurs der Moderne* (Frankfurt am Main: Suhrkamp, 1985).

19. "Säumen—das Säumen der Kinder, das Trödeln: sie ziehen die Fransen aus den Erlebnissen, strähnen sie. Darum trödeln die Kinder, 'Saumseligkeit'—so könnte man wohl den besten Teil diese Glücksgefühls nennen" (6:614f.). The term means "tardiness" or "sluggishness," but literally it also means "blissfulness at the seam."

20. "Ob sich nicht das Gefallen an der Bilderwelt aus einem düstern Trotz gegen das Wissen nährt? Ich sehe in die Landschaft hinaus: da liegt das Meer in seiner Bucht spiegelglatt; Wälder ziehen als unbewegliche stumme Masse an der Kuppe des Berges herauf; droben verfallene Schloßmauern wie sie schon vor Jahrhunderten standen; der Himmel strahlt wolkenlos, in 'ewiger Bläue,' wie man es nennt. So will der Träumer es, der sich in diese Landschaft vertieft" (6:427).

21. "Die Franzosen sagen allure, wir: Haltung. Beide Worte sind aus dem 'Gehen' genommen. Um aber das gleiche—in wie begrenztem Sinn es das gleiche ist, sagt aber diese Bemerkung, zu bezeichnen, spricht der Franzose vom Gange selber—allure—, der Deutsche von seiner Unterbrechung—Haltung" (6:425).

22. "Die Kurve eines Lebens unter diesem Gesichtspunkt zu zeichnen: in welchem Verhältnis steht die Zahl der Lebenden, die er kennt zu den Toten, die er gekannt hat? Definiert durch Überwiegen der letztern" (6:415).

23. "Wer dieses Gedicht gelesen hat, ist durch den Dichter hindurchgegangen wie durch ein Tor, auf dem in verwitterter Schrift ein B.B. zu lesen ist" (2:554). Benjamin's commentary has provoked symptomatic reactions by literary critics who naively believe in the simple opposition of "proper" and "metaphorical" speech without giving

much thought to the nature of language and the constitutive functions of tropes that Nietzsche already pointed out, as Paul de Man rightly recognizes: "The trope is not a derived, marginal, or aberrant form of language but the linguistic paradigm par excellence. The figurative structure is not one linguistic mode among others but it characterizes language as such" (Paul de Man, "Rhetoric of Tropes [Nietzsche]," in his *Allegories of Reading: Figural Language in Rousseau, Nietzsche, Rilke, and Proust* [New Haven, Conn.: Yale University Press, 1979], 105). In one of those symptomatic German "scientific" academic investigations of the 1970s, a particularly clever critic makes the amazing discovery that the gate in Benjamin's text is inconsistent as a metaphor because it can no longer be applied to Brecht when Benjamin writes that it might have stood there for centuries. See Harald Fricke, *Die Sprache der Literaturwissenschaft. Textanalytische und philosophische Untersuchungen* (Munich: Beck, 1977), 135.

CHAPTER 2

Work on this essay was made possible by a fellowship from the John Simon Guggenheim Memorial Foundation. For critical readings, research, and inspirations, I wish to thank Bill Brown, Victoria de Grazia, Michael Geyer, Philip Gossett, Andrew Hebard, Martin Jay, David Levin, Eric Santner, Lesley Stern, Yuri Tsivian, and the participants of the Angelus Novus conference, held at Yale University in September 1997. Unless otherwise noted, translations of texts not yet published in English are mine.

1. Walter Benjamin, "On Some Motifs in Baudelaire" (1939), in *Illuminations* (hereafter cited as *I*), ed. Hannah Arendt, trans. Harry Zohn (New York: Schocken, 1969), 184; *Gesammelte Schriften*, ed. Rolf Tiedemann and Hermann Schweppenhäuser (Frankfurt am Main: Suhrkamp, 1974), 1:642. References to the *Gesammelte Schriften* are given in the text by volume and page number. For a more sustained elaboration of the affinity between Benjamin and the problematics of Hong Kong cinema, see Ackbar Abbas, *Hong Kong: Culture and the Politics of Disappearance* (Minneapolis: University of Minnesota Press, 1997).

2. In a running gag, the protagonists are repeatedly shown at an automatic-teller machine through an alternation between the balances on the monitor and reaction shots from the viewpoint of the machine (which may or may not be that of an internal surveillance camera).

3. In his 1989 Hong Kong feature *The Killer*, Woo paid hilarious homage to Disney by having the perversely paired cop and killer refer to each other as "Mickey Mouse" and "Dumbo." In Chan's film, the romantic counterpart to Mickey Mouse is Hollywood icon William Holden, whose image and memory are invoked as the elusive American dream, as it were, of the character of Rosie, the male protagonist's dying aunt.

4. Walter Benjamin, *One-Way Street* (1928), trans. Edmund Jephcott, in *Selected Writings* (hereafter cited as *SW* in the text), vol. 1: 1913–1926, ed. Marcus Bullock

and Michael W. Jennings et al. (Cambridge, Mass., and London: Harvard University Press, 1996), 476 (trans. mod.); *Gesammelte Schriften*, 4:132.

5. Benjamin, *Selected Writings*, 1:476. For Benjamin's revisionist approach to kitsch, see his "Dream Kitsch: Gloss on Surrealism" (1927), in *Selected Writings*, vol. 2: 1927–1934, ed. Michael W. Jennings et al. (Cambridge, Mass., and London: Harvard University Press, 1999): 3–5; "Some Remarks on Folk Art" (c. 1929), in ibid., 278–80; and *Passagen-Werk*, K 3a, 1: "Kitsch [. . .] is nothing more than art with a 100 percent, absolute and instantaneous availability for use"; *The Arcades Project*, trans. Howard Eiland and Kevin McLaughlin (Cambridge, Mass., and London: Harvard University Press, 1999), 395 (trans. mod.). For a related, although distinct, reevaluation of kitsch, see Ernst Bloch, "Hieroglyphs of the Nineteenth Century," in *Heritage of Our Times*, trans. Neville Plaice and Stephen Plaice (Berkeley and Los Angeles: University of California Press, 1990), 346–51.

6. Hansen, "Of Mice and Ducks: Benjamin and Adorno on Disney," *South Atlantic Quarterly* 92, no. 1 (January 1993): 27–61.

7. Benjamin, Letter to Gretel Adorno, June 1934, *Gesammelte Schriften*, 2:1369; also see his letter to Gershom Scholem, of 29 May 1926, in which he characterizes his attitude in all things that really matter as "always radical, never consistent." *The Correspondence of Walter Benjamin*, trans. Manfred R. Jacobson and Evelyn M. Jacobson (Chicago: University of Chicago Press, 1994), 300 (trans. mod.); Benjamin, *Briefe*, ed. G. Scholem and T. W. Adorno (Frankfurt am Main: Suhrkamp, 1978), 1:425. On the antinomic structure of Benjamin's thinking, see, among others, Anson Rabinbach, "Between Enlightenment and Apocalypse: Benjamin, Bloch, and Modern German Jewish Messianism," *New German Critique* 34 (1985): 78–124; Irving Wohlfarth, "The Measure of the Possible, the Weight of the Real and the Heat of the Moment: Benjamin's Actuality Today," *New Formations* 20 (summer 1993): 16–17; Wohlfarth, "No-Man's Land': On Walter Benjamin's 'Destructive Character,'" in *Walter Benjamin's Philosophy: Destruction and Experience*, ed. Andrew Benjamin and Peter Osborne (London and New York: Routledge, 1994), 155–82; Gillian Rose, "Walter Benjamin—Out of the Sources of Modern Judaism," *New Formations* 20 (summer 1993): 59–81; John McCole, *Walter Benjamin and the Antinomies of Tradition* (Ithaca, N.Y.: Cornell University Press, 1993).

8. McCole, *Benjamin and the Antinomies* 3, 21–30; Wohlfarth, "Measure," 16.

9. Benjamin, "Experience and Poverty" (1933), in *Selected Writings*, 2:731–36.

10. The trope of a forgotten future appears frequently in Benjamin; see, for instance, "Berliner Kindheit um Neunzehnhundert," *Gesammelte Schriften*, 4:252; "A Berlin Chronicle," trans. E. Jephcott, in *Selected Writings*, 2:634–35; and "Little History of Photography," trans. Edmund Jephcott and Kingsley Shorter, in *Selected Writings*, 2:510; *Gesammelte Schriften*, 2:371. On Benjamin's concept of experience, see Marleen Stoessel, *Aura. Das Vergessene Menschliche. Zu Sprache und Erfahrung bei Walter Benjamin* (Munich: Carl Hanser, 1983); Martin Jay, "Experience Without a Subject: Walter Benjamin and the Novel" (1993), in his *Cultural Semantics: Keywords of*

Our Time (Amherst: University of Massachusetts Press, 1998); and, more recently, Howard Caygill, *Walter Benjamin: The Colour of Experience* (London and New York: Routledge, 1998), a study that usefully brings to bear Benjamin's early writings on perception and color on his theory of experience but neglects the ways Benjamin's concept of "aura," developed *in conjunction* with his shift of attention (rather than simply in opposition) to urban-industrial modernity, informs key aspects (temporality, reflexivity) of his effort to reconceptualize the possibility of experience in modernity.

11. McCole, *Benjamin and the Antinomies*, 9 and passim; Rose, "Benjamin," 76. For a discussion that complicates these oppositions, in particular with regard to Benjamin's analysis of fascism, see Alexander García Düttmann, "Tradition and Destruction: Walter Benjamin's Politics of Language," trans. Debbie Keates, in Benjamin and Osborne, *Benjamin's Philosophy*, 32–58.

12. Susan Buck-Morss, "Aesthetics and Anaesthetics: Walter Benjamin's Artwork Essay Reconsidered," *October* 62 (fall 1992): 3–41.

13. "Eduard Fuchs, Collector and Historian" (1937), trans. Knut Tarnowski, *New German Critique* 5 (spring 1975): 34; *Gesammelte Schriften*, 2:475. Also see Benjamin, "Theories of German Fascism" (1930), trans. Jerolf Wikoff, *New German Critique* 17 (spring 1979): 120–28, 126ff.; *Gesammelte Schriften*, 3:238–50, 247ff.

14. Benjamin, "Surrealism: The Last Snapshot of the European Intelligentsia" (1929), in *Selected Writings*, 2:217–18; *Gesammelte Schriften*, 2:307–10.

15. In his letter responding to the artwork essay, 18 March 1936, Adorno makes this point with particular reference to Benjamin's enthusiasm for Mickey Mouse and slapstick comedy, whose revolutionary implications, he argues, are belied by the (bourgeois-)sadistic laughter of the cinema audience; this laughter, as Adorno was to expound in his critique of jazz and the culture industry, promoted only the internalization of terror and masochistic conformism; "Letters to Walter Benjamin," trans. Harry Zohn, in *Aesthetics and Politics*, ed. Fredric Jameson (London: New Left Books, 1977), 123–24. Adorno invokes Anna Freud's concept of "identification with the aggressor" verbatim in "Benjamin's *One-Way Street*" (1955), rpt. in Theodor W. Adorno, *Notes to Literature*, vol. 2, trans. Shierry Weber Nicholsen (New York: Columbia University Press, 1991–1992), 326.

16. My references to the artwork essay here are largely to the second version, which was Benjamin's first typed and, for him, definitive version. This typescript was not published until 1989, in *Gesammelte Schriften*, 7:350–84; see notes by the editors, Rolf Tiedemann and Hermann Schweppenhäuser, 7:661–65. Adorno's letter of 18 March 1936, responds to—and contains references that only make sense in relation to—this version. The English version of the essay that appears in *Illuminations* not only suffers from an unreliable translation but also is based on the most compromised German version of the essay, as edited by Adorno and Friedrich Podszus and first published in 1955.

17. Benjamin, *Correspondence*, 322, trans. mod.; Benjamin, *Briefe*, 455.

18. See Tiedemann, "Einleitung des Herausgebers," *Gesammelte Schriften*, 5:39; and Tiedemann, "Anmerkungen des Herausgebers," *Gesammelte Schriften*, 5:1067–1205. See also Buck-Morss, *The Dialectics of Seeing: Walter Benjamin and the Arcades Project* (Cambridge, Mass., and London: MIT Press, 1989), 47–54.

19. Some of the implications of these texts for film theory are explored in my essay "Benjamin, Cinema, and Experience: 'The Blue Flower in the Land of Technology,'" *New German Critique* 40 (winter 1987): 179–224.

20. Siegfried Kracauer, *The Mass Ornament: Weimar Essays*, trans. and ed. Tom Levin (Cambridge, Mass., and London: Harvard University Press, 1995), 201 (trans. mod.).

21. See, for instance, the exchange of letters between Bloch and Kracauer in 1926, in Ernst Bloch, *Briefe 1903–1975*, vol. 1, ed. Karola Bloch et al. (Frankfurt am Main: Suhrkamp, 1985), 269–75.

22. Ernst Bloch, "Revue Form in Philosophy" (1928), in *Heritage of Our Times*, 334–37.

23. Jean Laplanche and J.-B. Pontalis, *The Language of Psychoanalysis*, trans. D. Nicholson-Smith (New York: W. W. Norton, 1973), 213. Also see editor's note to Freud's *The Interpretation of Dreams*: "'Innervation' is a highly ambiguous term [*keineswegs eindeutig*]. It is very frequently used in a structural sense, to mean the anatomical distribution of nerves in some organism or bodily region. Freud uses it . . . often (though not invariably) to mean the transmission of energy into a system of nerves, or . . . specifically into an *efferent* system—to indicate, that is to say, a process tending towards discharge" (*The Standard Edition of the Complete Psychological Works of Sigmund Freud*, trans. and ed. James Strachey [London: Hogarth Press, 1953–1974], 5:537; Freud, *Studienausgabe*, ed. Alexander Mitscherlich, Angela Richards, and Strachey [Frankfurt am Main: Fischer, 1982], 2:513).

24. *Oxford English Dictionary*, s.v. "innervation."

25. Sigmund Freud, "The Neuro-Psychoses of Defence (I)" (1894), *Standard Edition*, 1:49, 51, 55; see also Freud, "Further Remarks on the Neuropsychoses of Defence," *Standard Edition*, 3:175.

26. Freud, *Standard Edition*, 5:537 (emphasis mine).

27. Freud, 18:31, 30; and Freud, *Studienausgabe*, 3:241, 240.

28. Buck-Morss, "Aesthetics and Anaesthetics," 17 n. 54.

29. Freud, too, speaks of a "conversion in the opposite direction," but assumes that such a conversion, as pursued by Breuer, would be effected "by means of thought-activity and a discharge of the excitation by talking" (Freud, "Neuro-Psychoses of Defence," 3:49, 51).

30. See S. M. Eisenstein, "The Montage of Attractions" (1923), and "The Montage of Film Attractions" (1924), in his *Selected Works*, vol. 1, ed. and trans. Richard Taylor (London: BFI; Bloomington and Indianapolis: Indiana University Press, 1988), 33–38, 39–58; Ludwig Klages, *Ausdrucksbewegung und Gestaltungskraft* (Leipzig: Johann Ambrosius Barth, 1923). On Eisenstein and Klages, see Oxana Bulga-

kowa, "Sergej Eisenstein und die deutschen Psychologen: Sergej Eisenstein und sein 'psychologisches' Berlin—zwischen Psychoanalyse und Gestaltpsychologie," in *Herausforderung Eisenstein*, ed O. Bulgakowa (Berlin: Akademie der Künste der DDR, 1989), 80–91; on Benjamin and Klages, see McCole, *Benjamin and the Antinomies*, 178–80, 236–40, 242–52.

31. In James's famous assertion, it is "the more rational statement . . . that we feel sorry because we cry, angry because we strike, afraid because we tremble, and not that we cry, strike, or tremble, because we are sorry, angry, or fearful, as the case may be" (William James, *The Principles of Psychology* [Cambridge, Mass.: Harvard University Press, 1983], 1065f.). James's critique of Wundt's category of "Innervationsge-*fühl*" (1880) is directed not against the concept of *innervation* as such but against the idealist notion of innervation being coupled with, and depending on, a sentient, conscious "feeling" rather than the physiological fact of "discharge into the motor nerves" (1105). On Eisenstein's and Meyerhold's reception of James, see Alma Law and Mel Gordon, *Meyerhold, Eisenstein and Biomechanics: Actor Training in Revolutionary Russia* (Jefferson, N.C., and London: McFarland, 1996), 36f., 207 and passim.

32. Named after Dr. William Carpenter, a nineteenth-century British physiologist who first discovered that we tend unconsciously to mimic the movement of another person whom we are observing (*Principles of Mental Physiology, with Their Applications to the Training and Discipline of the Mind, and the Study of Morbid Conditions* [New York: Appleton & Co., 1878]); see Bulgakowa, "Eisenstein," 83. Also see James, on "ideo-motor action," *Principles*, 1130ff. I am much indebted to Yuri Tsivian for drawing my attention to, and sharing his wisdom on, the Carpenter Effect and its implications for theories of acting and identification.

33. In a fragment of 1929–1930, "Notizen zu einer Theorie des Spiels" (Notes toward a theory of gambling), Benjamin parenthetically equates the term "motoric innervation" with "inspiration," foregrounding the etymological connection between inspiration and breathing (*Gesammelte Schriften*, 6:189).

34. Both the appeal and the anachronism of the recourse to Yoga practices in Western modernity are registered by Freud in a sarcastic comment in *Civilization and Its Discontents* (1929–1930), *Standard Edition*, 21:72–73; Freud, *Studienausgabe*, 9:204–5.

35. Benjamin, "Kunstwerk," *Gesammelte Schriften*, 7:359f.; see also the French version, *Gesammelte Schriften*, 1:716–17.

36. Max Horkheimer and Theodor W. Adorno, "Odysseus or Myth and Enlightenment," in their *Dialectic of Enlightenment* (1944, 1947; rpt. New York, Seabury, 1969), new translation by Robert Hullot-Kentor, *New German Critique* 56 (summer 1992): 109–41; Ernst Jünger, "Über den Schmerz" (1934), in his *Sämtliche Werke, Zweite Abteilung: Essays*, vol. 7 (Stuttgart: Klett-Cotta, 1980), 143–91, esp. 158–59, 181–88.

37. Benjamin, *Gesammelte Schriften*, 7:359; see also the section "To the Planetarium," *One-Way Street*, in *Selected Writings*, 487. The emphasis on play and inter-

play, that is, on both ludic and ecological possibilities, in Benjamin's notion of second technology, is key to his critique of fascism. Against Nazi efforts "to fold second nature back into the first (blood and soil)," it is necessary "to accentuate the ludic form [*Spielform*] of second nature: to oppose the serenity [*Heiterkeit*] of communism to the beastly seriousness of fascism" (draft note for the first version of the artwork essay, *Gesammelte Schriften*, 1:1045).

38. The notion of technology as a "key to happiness" rather than a "fetish of doom," appears in Benjamin's "Theories of German Fascism" (1930), trans. Jerolf Wikoff, *Selected Writings*, 2:321, a text that represents an important, if problematic, relay between Benjamin's speculations on technology in *One-Way Street*, especially in "To the Planetarium," and the respective passages in the artwork essay; on the upsurge of the "German feeling for nature" in the context of World War I, see ibid., 318–19. On the concept of "second nature," a key source for which was Georg Lukács's *Theory of the Novel* (1916), see Steven Vogel, *Against Nature: The Concept of Nature in Critical Theory* (Albany: State University of New York Press, 1996), 17 and passim. The term goes back to Hegel's *Philosophy of Right*, paragraph 151.

39. Benjamin, "Outline of the Psychophysical Problem" (1922–1923), in *Selected Writings*, 1:396; *Gesammelte Schriften*, 6:81. Benjamin's reflections on the body involve the distinction, in German, between *Körper* and *Leib*, which, however, is not crucial in this context (see translator's note, *Selected Writings*, 1:401).

40. Jünger, "Schmerz," 181. On Jünger's aesthetics/politics of technology, see Andreas Huyssen, "Fortifying the Heart—Totally: Ernst Jünger's Armored Texts," *New German Critique* 59 (summer 1993): 3–23; for a different approach, see Helmut Lethen, *Verhaltenslehren der Kälte: Lebensversuche zwischen den Kriegen* (Frankfurt am Main: Suhrkamp, 1994), esp. 187–202.

41. This image, from the second version of the artwork essay, also appears in the section on Fourier in the *Passagen-Werk* (W 7, 4), *Arcades Project*, 631, dating from the "middle" period (June 1935 and December 1937) when Benjamin was working on the artwork essay (Buck-Morss, *Dialectics of Seeing*, 50–51). On Benjamin's interest in cognitive development, especially in comparison with the theories of Jean Piaget, see Buck-Morss, *Dialectics of Seeing*, 262–64. It is striking how Benjamin's montage image of child, moon, and ball resonates with the poetics of imagism, specifically T. E. Hulme's neoclassicist inversion of Benjamin's trope: "Above the quiet dock in midnight, / Tangled in the tall mast's corded height, / Hangs the moon. What seemed so far away / Is but a child's balloon, forgotten after play"; Hulme, *Speculations: Essays on Humanism and the Philosophy of Art*, ed. Herbert Read (London: Routledge and Kegan Paul, 1924), 266.

42. See, for instance, the last of Benjamin's "Theses on the Philosophy of History": "'In relation to the history of organic life on earth,' writes a modern biologist, 'the paltry fifty millennia of *homo sapiens* constitute something like two seconds at the close of a twenty-four-hour day. On this scale, the history of civilized mankind would fill one-fifth of the last second of the last hour.' The present, which, as a model

of Messianic time, comprises the history of the entire species in a gigantic abridgment, coincides exactly with *that* figure which the history of mankind cuts in the universe" (*I* 263, trans. mod.; *Gesammelte Schriften*, 1:703). On Benjamin's concept of "natural history," see Beatrice Hanssen, *Walter Benjamin's Other History: Of Stones, Animals, Human Beings, and Angels* (Berkeley and Los Angeles: University of California Press, 1998), a study that traces Benjamin's effort to reconceptualize history from a materialist, nonhumanist, nonhermeneutic perspective, although it occludes the significance of technology for such a history. For the latter, consider Benjamin's intense interest in the utopian visions of Charles Fourier (*Passagen-Werk*, "Konvolut W" and passim) and the science fiction of Paul Scheerbart, to whose novel *Lesabéndio* (1913) Benjamin returned repeatedly: "Paul Scheerbart: *Lesabéndio*," *Gesammelte Schriften*, 2:618–20, *Gesammelte Schriften*, 2:1423–25; "Experience and Poverty," 733–34. See also Burckhardt Lindner, "'Natur-Geschichte': Geschichtsphilosophie und Welterfahrung in Benjamins Schriften," *Text + Kritik* 31–32 (1971): 41–58; Susan Buck-Morss, *The Origin of Negative Dialectics* (New York: Free Press, 1977), 52–57; and Buck-Morss, *Dialectics of Seeing*, 58–77, 160–61.

43. "On account of our corporeality, in the end most immediately through our own body, we are placed into the world of perceptions, that is into the highest layers of language. [We are,] however, blind, and for the most part incapable of distinguishing between the natural body, between appearance and being according to the measure of the messianic shape. It is very significant that our own body is in so many ways inaccessible to us: we cannot see our face, our back, not even our whole head, that is, the most noble part of our body" ("Wahrnehmung und Leib," *Gesammelte Schriften*, 5:76).

44. Gertrud Koch, "Cosmos in Film: On the Concept of Space in Walter Benjamin's 'Work of Art' Essay," trans. Nancy Nenno, in Benjamin and Osborne, eds., *Walter Benjamin's Philosophy*, 205–15, 209–10. For a contemporary reflection similar to Benjamin's, see Freud's famous pronouncement that, thanks to modern technology, "man has, as it were, become a kind of prosthetic God," in *Civilization and Its Discontents*, *Standard Edition*, 21:91–92; Freud, *Studienausgabe*, 221–22.

45. *Passagen-Werk*, W 8a, 5; *Arcades Project*, 635. See also "Micky Mouse" (1931), trans. R. Livingstone, in *Selected Writings*, 2:545–46.

46. Sigrid Weigel, "Passagen und Spuren," in *Leib- und Bildraum. Lektüren nach Benjamin*, ed. Sigrid Weigel (Köln, Weimar, Wien: Böhlau, 1992), 52. Also see Sigrid Weigel, *Body- and Image-Space: Re-reading Walter Benjamin* (London and New York: Routledge, 1996); and Sigrid Weigel, *Entstellte Ähnlichkeit. Walter Benjamins theoretische Schreibweise* (Frankfurt am Main: Fischer, 1997).

47. Draft notes for the second version of the artwork essay, *Gesammelte Schriften*, 7:666–68. The concept of *Schein* is of course central to Benjamin's major early essay, "Goethe's *Elective Affinities*" (1919-1922; 1924–25), *Selected Writings*, 1:297–360; also see the unpublished fragments "On Semblance," *Selected Writings*, 1:223–25; and "Beauty and Semblance," *Selected Writings*, 1:283. On "semblance and play" in the

context of the artwork essay, see Burkhardt Lindner, "Benjamins Aurakonzeption. Anthropologie und Technik, Bild und Text," in *Walter Benjamin 1892–1940. Zum* 100. *Geburtstag*, ed. Uwe Steiner (Bern, Frankfurt am Main, New York, and Paris: Peter Lang, 1992), 217–48.

48. The meanings of the German *Spiel* (play, game), *spielen, Spieler* also include the game of chance, gambling, and the gambler, a topic that Benjamin explored as a particular figure of modern temporality (boredom, empty time, chance); see, for instance, "On Some Motifs in Baudelaire" (1939), *I* 177–80. Kracauer speaks of the turn to the photographic media as the *vabanque* or "go-for-broke game of history" in his important essay "Photography" (1927), *Mass Ornament*, 47–63, 61–62. The affinity of photography with chance and material contingency (versus narrative, dramatic "fate") is crucial to Kracauer's *Theory of Film* (1960), especially the early drafts written in Marseille, following Benjamin's suicide; see Hansen, "'With Skin and Hair': Kracauer's Theory of Film, Marseille 1940," *Critical Inquiry* 19, no. 3 (spring 1993): 437–69.

49. See, for instance, Paul Virilio, *Aesthetics of Disappearance* (1980), *War and Cinema* (1984), *The Vision Machine* (1988; rpt. Bloomington: Indiana University Press; London: BFI, 1994); Friedrich Kittler, *Grammophon, Film, Typewriter* (Berlin: Brinkmann and Bose, 1986); and Norbert Bolz, *Theorie der neuen Medien* (Munich: Raben Verlag, 1990). For the notion of a "historical a priori of mediality," see editors' introduction, *Armaturen der Sinne. Literarische und technische Medien 1870 bis 1920*, ed. Jochen Hörisch and Michael Wetzel (Munich: Fink, 1990), 13.

50. Buck-Morss, "Aesthetics and Anaesthetics," 5.

51. Benjamin, *Selected Writings*, 1:482–83. Scipio's exclamation puts this gesture into closer vicinity with a modern history of colonialism and imperialism than Benjamin might have intended. On a similarly repressed ambivalence toward that history, see John Kraniauskas, "Beware Mexican Ruins! 'One-Way Street' and the Colonial Unconscious," in Benjamin and Osborne, eds., *Walter Benjamin's Philosophy*, 139–54.

52. Ludwig Klages, *Vom kosmogonischen Eros*, in Klages, *Sämtliche Werke*, ed. E. Frauchiger et al., vol. 3, *Philosophische Schriften* (Bonn: Bouvier Verlag Herbert Grundmann, 1974), 353–497. Klages emerges as a significant influence on Benjamin himself, particularly his phenomenology of dreaming and waking (a key motif in the *Passagen-Werk*) and the temporal inflection of distance and nearness as key terms in the transformation of sensory-somatic perception (cf. Benjamin's concepts of "aura," "masses," and "kitsch"). In "Outline of the Psychophysical Problem," *Selected Writings*, 1:397–400, Benjamin lists Klages's essay on dream consciousness, "Vom Traumbewußtsein" (1919), in *Selected Writings*, 1:155–238, but not *Vom kosmogonischen Eros*, the more specific source on distance and nearness; see especially chapters 4 and 5 (410–41).

53. This argument appears in all versions of the artwork essay; see "Preface," *I* 217–18. Benjamin further elaborates his critique of capitalist-imperialist technology in "Theories of German Fascism" and, specifically in view of contemporary fascist

aesthetics, in "Pariser Brief I: André Gide und sein neuer Gegner" (1936), in *Gesammelte Schriften*, 3:482–95.

54. "Imperial Panorama: A Tour Through the German Inflation," in *Selected Writings*, 1:451. In a long note to the second version of the artwork essay, Benjamin takes up this pessimistic discourse with explicit reference to Gustave LeBon and mass psychology, as he contrasts the "compact mass" of the petite bourgeoisie, defined by "panic-prone" behavior such as militarism, anti-Semitism, and blind striving for survival, with the "proletarian mass." The latter in fact, Benjamin argues, ceases to be a mass in the LeBonian sense in the measure that it is infused with class consciousness and solidarity. Ultimately, the proletariat "works toward a society in which both the objective and the subjective conditions for the formation of masses no longer exist" (*Gesammelte Schriften*, 7:370f.). In a variant to this note, he likens the cinema audience to "random masses" such as the "population of a city" or the category of those who are "color-blind" (ibid., 668). For a discussion of Benjamin's concept of the mass(es) in relation to Kracauer's, see Hansen, "America, Paris, The Alps: Kracauer (and Benjamin) on Cinema and Modernity," in Leo Charney and Vanessa Schwartz, eds., *Cinema and the Invention of Modern Life* (Berkeley and Los Angeles: University of California Press, 1995), 362–402.

55. For a historical survey situating Benjamin and Adorno in relation to other revivals of the concept of *mimesis* (notably Erich Auerbach's), see Gunter Gebauer and Christoph Wulf, *Mimesis. Kultur—Kunst—Gesellschaft* (Reinbek bei Hamburg: Rowohlt, 1992); also see Martin Jay, "Mimesis and Mimetology: Adorno and Lacoue-Labarthe," in *Cultural Semantics*, 120–37; Michael Cahn, "Subversive Mimesis: T. W. Adorno and the Modern Impasse of Critique," in *Mimesis in Contemporary Theory*, ed. Mihai Spariosu (Philadelphia and Amsterdam: John Benjamins, 1984), 27–64; Josef Früchtl, *Mimesis: Konstellation eines Zentralbegriffs bei Adorno* (Würzburg: Königshausen + Neumann, 1986), on Benjamin, 17–29; Karla L. Schulz, *Mimesis on the Move: Theodor W. Adorno's Concept of Imitation* (Bern, Frankfurt am Main, New York, and Paris: Peter Lang, 1990). For an interesting reanimation of Benjamin's concern with the mimetic from an anthropological perspective, see Michael Taussig, *Mimesis and Alterity: A Particular History of the Senses* (New York and London: Routledge, 1993); and Michael Taussig, *The Nervous System* (New York and London: Routledge, 1992).

56. Benjamin, "On the Mimetic Faculty" (1933), *Selected Writings*, 2:720 (trans. mod.); *Gesammelte Schriften*, 2:210–13, 210. Also see the first, longer version, "Lehre vom Ähnlichen," in *Gesammelte Schriften*, 2:204–10; "Doctrine of the Similar," trans. Knut Tarnowksi, *New German Critique* 17 (spring 1979): 65–69. For the darker implications of the mimetic gift, see the same phrase in "Berliner Kindheit um Neunzehnhundert," *Gesammelte Schriften*, 4:261, where Benjamin recalls the impossibility of resemblance with oneself in the alienating nineteenth-century environment of the photographer's studio ("I am distorted by resemblance with all the things that here surround me"). Adorno prolongs this negative connotation of mimesis as an unreflected mimicry of/onto reified and alienated conditions, a compulsion to self-

reification and self-alienation, in his analysis of mass culture; see especially the sequel to the excursus on the culture industry in *Dialectic of Enlightenment*, "The Schema of Mass Culture," trans. Nicholas Walker, in Adorno, *The Culture Industry: Selected Essays on Mass Culture*, ed. J. M. Bernstein (London: Routledge, 1991), 53–84.

57. See the section on childhood in *One-Way Street*; "Enlargements," in *Selected Writings*, 1:463–66; and the autobiographical texts on turn-of-the-century Berlin childhood, "Berliner Kindheit um Neunzehnhundert" (1933–1934), *Gesammelte Schriften*, 4:235–304, the recently discovered later version of that text, *Gesammelte Schriften*, 7:385–433, and the earlier draft, "A Berlin Chronicle," *Selected Writings*, 2:595–637, *Gesammelte Schriften*, 6:465–519. The emphasis on the figural, rather than overt, quality of mimetic correspondences relates to the mnemonic status of childhood experience, the element of distortion (*Entstellung*) that characterizes both memory traces and the forgotten/remembered moment of similitude, and it is no coincidence that Benjamin develops the notion of a "distorted similitude" in his essay on Proust, "On the Image of Proust" (1929), in *Selected Writings*, 2:240. On the significance of Freud's concept of memory for Benjamin, and on the distinction between "distorted similitude" and "nonsensuous similitude," see Weigel, *Body- and Image-Space*, xvii, chaps. 8 and 9; Weigel, *Entstellte Ähnlichkeit*, 9–11, 27–51.

58. Benjamin, "Franz Kafka" (1934), in *Selected Writings*, 2:810; "Surrealism," in *Selected Writings*, 2:210. Benjamin's vision of modernity as *Ur*-history, combined with the notion of capitalism as a "dreamsleep" and the political project of "awakening" the collective from that dream while preserving its utopian energies, is central to his work on the Paris arcades, especially in its early stages; see, in particular, "Konvolut K [Dream City and Dream House, Dreams of the Future, Anthropological Nihilism, Jung]." Also see Buck-Morss, *Dialectics of Seeing*, chaps. 5 and 8.

59. Benjamin, *Passagen-Werk*, K 1a,3, *Arcades Project*; interpretive translation in Buck-Morss, *Dialectics of Seeing*, 274. On Benjamin's insistence on the historicity—and historiographic significance—of childhood, especially children's experience of technology, see ibid., 261–65, 273–79.

60. Benjamin, *Selected Writings*, 1:449 (trans. mod., emphasis mine); *Gesammelte Schriften*, 4:92. See also "Berliner Kindheit," *Gesammelte Schriften*, 4:244, 262–63.

61. Benjamin, "Negativer Expressionismus" (ca. 1921), in *Gesammelte Schriften*, 6:132.

62. Benjamin, *Gesammelte Schriften*, 7:377f.; *Gesammelte Schriften*, 1:1040, 1047; and draft notes for the Kafka essay, *Gesammelte Schriften*, 2:1256–57. Also see Benjamin, "Chaplin in Retrospect" (1929), in *Selected Writings*, 2:222–24; "Chaplin" (1928–1929), in *Gesammelte Schriften*, 6:137–38; and the fragment in which he compares Chaplin and Hitler (in 1934, six years before *The Great Dictator*), "Hitler's Diminished Masculinity," in *Selected Writings*, 2:792–93.

63. On the question of a particular modern(ist) sense of "things," I am much indebted to discussions with Bill Brown and his work-in-progress on *The Secret Life of Things*; see Bill Brown, "How to Do Things with Things (A Toy Story)," *Criti-*

cal Inquiry 24, no. 4 (summer 1998): 935–64; and Bill Brown, "The Secret Life of Things (Virginia Woolf and the Matter of Modernism)," *Modernism/Modernity* 6 (April 1999): 1–28.

64. The phrase in parentheses occurs in "Dream Kitsch," in *Selected Writings*, 2:4. The alignment of nearness with "things" (and, implicitly, of distance with the "image," *Bild*) can be found at great length in Klages's *Cosmogonic Eros* (416ff.), a text whose generally antimodernist, antitechnological pathos must have provided a contrasting foil for *One-Way Street*.

65. Commenting on "This Space for Rent," Taussig emphasizes the "two-layered character" of Benjamin's modernist mimetics, the interconnectedness of the copying functions of the technical media with their ability to effect psychosomatic contact, that is, a new, corporeal form of understanding or embodied knowing; see Taussig, *Mimesis and Alterity*, 24–31; and Taussig, *Nervous System*, 145.

66. See above, note 5.

67. ". . . wird die gesundete Sentimentalität amerikanisch frei, wie Menschen, welche nichts mehr rührt und anrührt, im Kino wieder das Weinen lernen" (*Gesammelte Schriften*, 4:132).

68. When Benjamin evokes the force of "money" in this context, the field of reference is more likely Simmel's *Philosophy of Money* (1900) than Marx's *Capital*.

69. This "speculative image," to use Howard Caygill's term, resonates with Benjamin's early reflections on the philosophy of color, which Caygill (*The Colour of Experience*, 9–13, 82–88, 150–52) has shown to be central to his concept of experience; see Benjamin, "Der Regenbogen. Gespräch über die Phantasie" (1915), *Gesammelte Schriften*, 7:19–26; "Aphorisms on Imagination and Color" (1914–1915), "A Child's View of Color" (1914–1915), and "Notes for a Study of the Beauty of Colored Illustrations in Children's Books" (1918–1921), in *Selected Writings*, 1:48–51, 264–66; *Gesammelte Schriften*, 6:109–12, 123–25, and other fragments in the section "Zur Ästhetik," in ibid., 109–29. Specifically, the image of the "fiery pool" reflecting, and dissolving, the actual neon sign recalls qualities of "chromatic phantasy" or imagination that Benjamin discerns in children, their fascination with rainbows, soap bubbles, and pictures produced by decals and magic lanterns—color's fluidity ("moistness"), its freedom from contours and substance (color in opposition to form), its intensive infinity of nuances, its availability for shifting patterns and transformations. These qualities may also have played a part in Benjamin's adult fascination with animated film, in particular the metamorphoses of objects and characters, the freewheeling interchange between the animate and inanimate world, in early Disney films (see "Experience and Poverty," in *Selected Writings*, 2:735).

70. For examples of Kracauer's play with the trope of commercial lighting, see "Boredom" (1924), in *Mass Ornament*, 331–34; "Lichtreklame" (1927), in Kracauer, *Schriften* 5.2, ed. Inka Mülder-Bach (Frankfurt am Main: Suhrkamp, 1990), 19–21; and "Ansichtspostkarte" (1930), ibid., 184–85. Benjamin recognized, and appreciated, Kracauer's mimetic sensibility for the afterlife of things in characterizing him as a

Lumpensammler, or "ragpicker" (Baudelaire's *chiffonnier*); see his review of Kracauer's *Die Angestellten*, "An Outsider Makes His Mark" (1930), in *Selected Writings*, 2:305–11, 310.

71. See Benjamin's fragment, "Die Reflexion in der Kunst und in der Farbe" (1914–1915), in *Gesammelte Schriften*, 6:117–18, in which he claims that color has an inherent reflexivity: "Das Aussehen der Farben und ihr gesehen Werden ist gleich / Das heißt: *die Farben sehen sich*" [The look of the colors is the equivalent of their being seen / This is to say: *the colors see themselves*] (118).

72. Jürgen Habermas, "Consciousness-Raising or Redemptive Criticism: The Contemporaneity of Walter Benjamin" (1972), trans. P. Brewster and C. H. Buchner, *New German Critique* 17 (spring 1979): 45–46. For a related attempt to think "things" in terms other than the philosophical subject/object relation, see Adorno, *Negative Dialectics*, trans. E. B. Ashton (1966; rpt. New York: Continuum, 1997), part II; also see Brown, "The Secret Life of Things"; and Hanssen, *Benjamin's Other History*.

73. See Benjamin, "Einiges zur Volkskunst," *Gesammelte Schriften*, 6:187; "Some Remarks on Folk Art," in *Selected Writings*, 2:279: "Die Kunst lehrt uns in die Dinge hineinsehen / Volkskunst und Kitsch erlauben uns, aus den Dingen heraus zu sehen" [Art teaches us to look into (the inside of) things / Popular art and kitsch allow us to look outward from the inside of things] (trans. mod.).

74. Benjamin discusses the *mémoire involontaire* in photographic, or rather, proto-filmic terms in a speech delivered on his fortieth birthday: "Aus einer kleinen Rede über Proust, an meinem vierzigsten Geburtstag gehalten," *Gesammelte Schriften*, 2.3:1064.

75. Caygill, *Colour of Experience*, 94.

76. "Reply to Oscar A. H. Schmitz" (1927), in *Selected Writings*, 2:18 (trans. mod.).

77. Hansen, "Of Mice and Ducks," 41ff.

78. Wohlfarth, "Measure," 14; see also the section, "Fire Alarm," in *One-Way Street*, in *Selected Writings*, 1:469–70.

79. See, among others, Patrice Petro, *Joyless Streets: Women and Melodramatic Representation in Weimar Germany* (Princeton, N.J.: Princeton University Press, 1989). Kracauer was one of the first to recognize and analyze the formation of this new mass public, particularly in and through the cinema and other institutions of leisure culture; see his pathbreaking study, *Die Angestellten. Aus dem neuesten Deutschland* (1929), *The Salaried Masses: Duty and Distraction in Weimar Germany*, trans. Quintin Hoare, intro. Inka Mülder-Bach (London and New York: Verso, 1998). as well as his important, if somewhat notorious, article series, "The Little Shopgirls Go to the Movies" (1927), *Mass Ornament*, 291–304.

80. Norbert Bolz, "Die Zukunft der Zeichen: Invasion des Digitalen in die Bilderwelt des Films," in *Im Spiegelkabinett der Illusionen: Film über sich selbst*, Arnoldshainer Filmgespräche, vol. 13, ed. Ernst Karpf, Doron Kiesel, and Karsten Visarius (Marburg: Schüren, 1996), 57. Bolz also includes Kracauer in this assessment.

CHAPTER 3

1. A useful general point to the theory of images in Benjamin may be found in Sigrid Weigel's remark: "Benjamin's use of the term ["similitude," *Ähnlichkeit*] is associated with his concept of the image, not as reproduction, but, in an older tradition, as likeness, resemblance. Latin similitudinem." See her *Body and Image-Space: Re-reading Walter Benjamin* (London and New York: Routledge, 1996), 176. Adding to Weigel, I might specify an ancient precursor to Benjamin's theory of images: *Lucretius. De Rerum Natura*, trans. W. H. D. Rouse, Loeb Classical Edition (Cambridge, Mass.: Harvard University Press, 1937), see, for example, Bk. 4, ll. 722–823. This anticipates Benjamin's *cinematic* (!) image theory.

2. Walter Benjamin, "Konvolut N," in *Das Passagen-Werk, Gesammelte Schriften*, ed. Rolf Tiedemann and Hermann Schweppenhäuser, 7 vols. (Frankfurt am Main: Suhrkamp, 1991), 5:570–611; the passage cited is from 5:591–92. All parenthetical references to N are from this collage of notes for the *Arcades Project* (the book to be written on "Paris, the Capital of the 19th century"); they are cited as *GS* along with volume and page number.

3. The stupendous shift from silent film to talkie, while greeted by most with the customary alacrity given to any new development in mass technology, was criticized even before the transition was achieved. (It should be remembered that the silent films, generally accompanied by music, were silent with respect to diegetic sound.) Sergei Eisenstein, for example, states (in 1928): "To use sound in this way [in the "talking film"] will destroy the culture of montage, for every ADHESION of sound to a visual montage piece increases its inertia as a montage piece . . ." (Sergei Eisenstein et al., "A Statement on Sound," in *Film Theory and Criticism*, 4th ed., ed. Gerald Mast, Marshall Cohen, and Leo Braudy (New York: Oxford University Press, 1992), 318. Eisenstein's notion of "dialectical montage" is close to Benjamin's "dialectical image" in important respects: "A shot. A single piece of celluloid. A tiny rectangular frame in which there is . . . a piece of an event" (Sergei Eisenstein, "The Cinematographic Principle and the Ideogram," in *Film Theory and Criticism*, 132). Other early critics in this vein include Rudolf Arnheim (1933), Béla Balázs (1945), and Theodor W. Adorno (1947). In *Composing for the Films* (1947), a joint composition with Hans Eisler, Adorno restates the case against talkies in terms that recall Benjamin's theory of tragedy: "There is even reason to believe that the more closely pictures and words are co-ordinated, the more emphatically their intrinsic contradiction and the actual muteness of those who seem to be speaking are felt by the spectators." Quoted in Robert Hullot-Kentor's foreword (xvii) to his translation of Theodor W. Adorno, *Kierkegaard: Construction of the Aesthetic*, trans. Robert Hullot-Kentor (Minneapolis: University of Minnesota Press, 1989).

4. Here the same line of reasoning used by Benjamin in "A Small History of Photography" (1931) may be applied to silent film. In that essay he discerns a graphic les-

son for materialist history in the early history of photography (some ninety years before the time of writing, in 1931), where "the physiognomic aspects of visual worlds" (*One-Way Street*, trans. Edmund Jephcott and Kingsley Shorter [London: New Left Books, 1973], 243; hereafter *OWS*), first becoming legible, reach into the present time to disclose something hitherto unperceived: "the human countenance," which "had a silence about it in which the gaze rested." In Benjamin's texts the face serves as a privileged site for a reading of cultic image archives: as "the camera," for example, which "transforms the human physiognomy into a huge field of action" ["The Work of Art in the Age of Mechanical Reproduction," in *Illuminations*, trans. Harry Zohn (New York; Schocken, 1976), 237; hereafter WA]; or as the "frozen face of natural history" and facies hippocratica of the *Trauerspiel* book. Whereas the snapshot image memorializes the temporal uniqueness of its subject in the still, the flashing image of the film would, in this critical frame, perform that uniqueness through the rapid "flashing" (cutting) of montage.

5. Walter Benjamin, "Paris, Capital of the Nineteenth Century," in *Reflections*, trans. Edmund Jephcott (New York: Schocken, 1978), 157.

6. "In quotation the two realms—of origin and destruction—justify themselves before language. . . . Where they interpenetrate—in quotation—is language consummated. In it is mirrored the angelic tongue" (Benjamin, "Karl Kraus," *Reflections*, 269).

7. As in the case of "epic theater," which "is by a definition a gestic theater. For the more frequently we interrupt someone in the act of acting, the more gestures result" (Benjamin, "What is Epic Theater?" *Illuminations*, 151).

8. Gerald Mast, *A Short History of the Movies*, 6th ed. (Needham Heights, Mass.: Allyn and Bacon, 1996), 88. This point, the brevity of the comedy scene (skit, joke, gag) is easily obscured when one identifies comedy with an entire narrative, which identification tends to fudge over in the episodic nature of its genre, especially where the discrete gags serve to advance the plot, as in 1930s "Screwball Comedies" and their modern comedy-romance spin-offs.

9. Benjamin, *Gesammelte Schriften*, 1:702–3. Hereafter, this edition is referred to by volume and page number. (The passages, in Zohn's translation, correspond to Theses XVI and XVII of the "Theses on the Philosophy of History," *Illuminations*, 262–63.

10. Associations from later films could be superimposed over "prisoner's uniform" and "aristocrat's pajamas"—for example, the "bicycle racer" from René Clair's *A Nous la Liberté* (1931), where a convict takes advantage of his prison uniform to blend in with a group of bicycle racers (themselves now being montaged to fugitives). For a critical reading of Hitchcock that turns on bar images and iconography, see Tom Cohen, *Ideology and Inscription: Cultural studies After Benjamin, De Man, and Bakhtin* (Cambridge: Cambridge University Press, 1998), 169–200, with my review in *Textual Practice* 15, no. 1 (spring 2001): 142–48.

11. Benjamin, *Reflections*, 190; 2:307. Jephcott's translation of this piece obscures

crucial articulations, which makes it hard to follow the rapid shifts of thought in Benjamin's coherent but demanding essay.

12. "By the 1920s," writes Noël Carroll, "the sight gag is the leading type of film comedy." While "sight gags are everywhere in the history of film (and television)," there may be "a deep thematic connection between the sight gag and silent film." See "Notes on the Sight Gag," in *Comedy/Cinema/Theory*, ed. Andrew Horton (Berkeley and Los Angeles: University of California Press, 1991), 39–40. In a tentative taxonomy of sight gags, Carroll differentiates six types that bear on the sight gag as a structured relation between one set of events (images, interpretations) and an alternative set; this relation may be interrogated along different variables, for example, whether the relation of the two sets is simultaneous or sequential; whether the two sets interfere with one another or are collateral; whether the characters themselves are aware of the alternatives.

13. Benjamin, "Paris," *Reflections*, 157.

14. "Thinking involves not only the flow of thoughts, but their arrest as well. Where thinking stops in a configuration pregnant with tensions, it gives that configuration a shock, by which it crystallizes a monad . . . the sign of a Messianic cessation of happening" (Benjamin, Thesis XVII, "Theses on the Philosophy of History," *Illuminations*, 262).

15. The passage continues: "In the context of allegory the image is only a signature, only the monogram of essence, not the essence itself in a mask" (Walter Benjamin, *The Origin of German Tragic Drama*, trans. John Osborne [London: Verso, 1977], 214). To label an "image" as "a form of writing" is both a critical imperative and a definitional statement. "Writing" (which may also be called an "image" and is itself full of images) still depends on an "optic" (a visual metaphor or pictorial organization, an apparatus related to spatiality). There can be optic without writing, but writing begins from the optical and seems tethered to it: "Das ursprüngliche Interesse an der Allegorie ist nicht sprachlich sondern optisch. 'Les images, ma grande, ma primitive passion (Baudelaire)" (Benjamin, "Zentralpark," 1:686). The present essay emphasizes this optical beginning or tether. If allegory involves the loss of visibility, *la perte d'auréole* (665), it keeps returning to the optical (as the pictorial image or sight metaphor) as the means to keep its own graphic eclipsing of sight "in sight." The clarion call, "Jedes Bild als Schrift" thus collapses the difference between image and writing while asserting that difference as a critical imperative. "Dialectical images" both speak to and fall into this deeply aporetic scenario. In a critical review of earlier scholarship, Anselm Haverkamp rightly insists on the multiplex levels (and aporia) of dialectical images. See "Notes on the Dialectical Image," *diacritics* (fall–winter 1992): 70–80.

16. Benjamin, "Rückblick auf Chaplin," *Gesammelte Schriften*, 3:159.

17. Benjamin, *Gesammelte Schriften*, 2:310; and Walter Benjamin, "Surrealism: the Last Snapshot of the European Intelligentsia," in his *One-Way Street* (London: Verso, 1992), 239.

18. Benjamin, "Zentralpark," 1:683. Translations from "Zentralpark" are by the author. See also 1:1243 and passim.

19. Ibid., 1:676.

20. Ibid., 1:679. The paragraph entry begins "Eine Invektive gegen Cupido aufzufinden."

21. "Die Rettung hält sich an den kleinen Sprung in der kontinuierlichen Katastrophe" (ibid., 1:683).

22. Walter Benjamin, *The Origin of German Tragic Drama*, trans. John Osborne (London: Verso, 1977), 157; 1:334.

23. In a rare appearance of the subject in Benjamin criticism, Peter Osborne refers to "the comic aspects of Jewish theology," as this emerges in the Benjaminian reading of Kafka and in epistolary conversations with theologian Gershom Scholem. See "Small-Scale Victories, Large-Scale Defeats," in *Walter Benjamin's Philosophy*, ed. Andrew Benjamin and Peter Osborne (London: Routledge, 1994), 79. In a further footnote comment, Osborne phrases the issue nicely: Benjamin "extends this point about the comic character of the historically redundant comedy to both Surrealism and the lyric . . . Such comedy is a product of the new form of historical time, and soon overtakes it in turn. As Adorno put it in the 1960's: even the label 'avant-garde' begins to conjure up 'comical associations'" (103–4, n. 77). Following up Osborne's hints, one could formulate the relation of Adorno and Benjamin along the diacritical lines of comedy that resonates in "negative dialectics" and that provides "insight into the constitutive character of the nonconceptual in the concept" (see Theodor W. Adorno, *Negative Dialectics*, trans. E. B. Ashton [New York: Continuum, 1997], 5). One example of this failure to engage the nonconceptual is "logic, a defense mechanism of the materialized consciousness" (56). Comedy carries out the project of negative dialectics, but makes its point before concepts set in to make it. There is a vast difference between a comic and a theorist of comedy.

24. A passing remark in Hegel's *Encyclopedia of Philosophical Knowledge* (in section 401, under "Anthropology," several way-stages before "Psychology" [where Spirit attains the level of "thought"]) brings in laughter as a graphic exposé of dialectical operation: laughter demonstrates dialectical mastery, where the one who has "mastery" [*Macht*] is the one who laughs. Indeed, Hegel calls this laughing mastery "pure dialectic." Laughter is structural as much as topical: if fascists laugh just as heartily as nonfascists, the reverse is also true. G. W. F. Hegel, *Enzyklopädie der philosophischen Wissenschaften*, vol. III (Frankfurt am Main: Suhrkamp, 1970), 114.

25. Sigmund Freud, *Joking and its Relation to the Unconscious*, vol. III, trans. L. Strachey (New York: W. W. Norton, 1960), 127, emphasis mine.

26. Benjamin, *Origin of German Tragic Drama*, 125–28.

27. Compare Thesis II of "The Theses on the Philosophy of History": "Our image of happiness is *thoroughly colored* by the time" (emphasis mine). Freedom, like comedy and tragedy, is necessarily off-color: "The vision of [comic and tragic] character is liberating in all its forms: it is linked to freedom" (*OWS* 131). "Happiness," too

much under the sway of "our image" of it, falls from its messianic anonym. (These materials find some resonance in Wallace Stevens or John Ashbery's poetry, where color and colorization are used as modernist and postmodernist tropes of reflection on the writing of poetry—broad strokes for its lingering histories and enabling fixations.) On "freedom," as something to be articulated through the generic relation of comedy and tragedy, compare George Steiner: "Tragedy and comedy move to an identical vanishing-point on the horizon of human perception" (George Steiner, "Tragedy Pure and Simple," in M. S. Silk, *Tragedy and the Tragic* [Oxford: Oxford University Press, 1996], 535). (But "horizon of human perception" is too historically undifferentiated.) The statement seems right that the many "magisterial treatments (i.e., of tragedy) from Aristotle to Dr. Johnson, from Johnson to Nietzsche and Walter Benjamin—contrast strikingly with the paucity of first-order theoretical examinations of comedy" (534); but it does not seem right to posit tragedy (as Steiner does) as the more accessible of the two: "Very likely comedy is the more difficult, and the more elusive, of the two genres." It seems better to argue that it is not so much texts themselves that are accessible or not, but critical traditions, which, handling texts, make them seem more accessible (or not).

28. Benjamin, Thesis III, *Illuminations*, 254.

29. Compare "blasted . . . out of the homogeneous course of history" (Benjamin, Thesis XIII of the "Theses on History"). In 1929, Sergei Eisenstein had also compared montage to "the series of explosions of an internal combustion engine . . . the impulses driving forward the total film" (Eisenstein, "The Cinematographic Principle" [1929], in *Film Theory and Criticism*, 4th ed., ed. Gerald Mast et al. (New York: Oxford University Press, 1992), 134.

30. "Joking confirms our ability to hold on to Symbolic operation in the same moment as it allows a 'play' of the energies which militate against that" (Susan Purdie, *Comedy: The Mastery of Discourse* [Toronto: Toronto University Press, 1993], 35). Norms are disrupted in comedy (because comedy is that disruption), yet the joke (the main emphasis of Purdie's book) only leads back in its effects to the "reinscription of boundaries" (116). One might join with these reflections by differentiating "comedy" from "humor" (acknowledging that this differentiation may often prove hard to draw in practice): if one may think of "humor" as secondhand comedy, if humor is comedy as a quotation of a more original comedic incident that has not yet become just a citation, then laughter attends "humor" as a compensatory miming of the original (comedy). Laughter (which need not accompany comedy) may authenticate comedy just as it may sometimes falsify it. Laughter may work to pass off humor as comedy, to make it seem as if there had been no quotation. As may be seen from these remarks, the relation of comedy to humor is analogous to the relation of an original (source) text to its translation. (This is theorized in Benjamin's "The Task of the Translator" essay, but many strands in his translation theory go back to different precursors.) As a way to demonstrate the recursive loops in this topic but also (hopefully) to make a point, I quote myself (from the paragraph that ends section II

in the body of the essay): "To miss seeing the quotation (which wouldn't be signaled by quotation marks) within the texts one reads is to invite catastrophe, the ongoing 'catastrophe' that is 'to have missed the opportunity; the critical moment—the status quo threatens to hold firm'" (*GS* 10, 2).

31. Benjamin, *Origin of German Tragic Drama*, 139.

32. Walter Benjamin, *Briefe*, ed. Gershom Scholem and Theodor Adorno (Frankfurt am Main: Suhrkamp, 1966), 1:132.

33. Benjamin, Thesis XVIII. (My thanks to Bruce Palmer of the UHCL history faculty for the stimulating discussions under which this essay began.)

CHAPTER 4

A more extended version of the argument presented in this chapter can be found in Lutz Koepnick, *Walter Benjamin and the Aesthetics of Power* (Lincoln and London: University of Nebraska Press, 1999). I am grateful to the University of Nebraska Press for allowing me to make use of previously published material.

1. Walter Benjamin, *Illuminations: Essays and Reflections*, ed. Hannah Arendt, trans. Harry Zohn (New York: Schocken, 1969), 236.

2. Anne Friedberg, "Cinema and the Postmodern Condition," in *Viewing Positions: Ways of Seeing Film*, ed. Linda Williams (New Brunswick, N.J.: Rutgers University Press, 1995), 60; see also Friedberg's more comprehensive study, *Window Shopping: Cinema and the Postmodern* (Berkeley, Los Angeles, and Oxford: University of California Press, 1993).

3. Benjamin, *Illuminations*, 223.

4. See the various essays gathered in Victor Burgin, *In/Different Spaces: Place and Memory in Visual Culture* (Berkeley, Los Angeles, and London: University of California Press, 1996).

5. Hans Jürgen Syberberg, *Vom Unglück und Glück der Kunst in Deutschland nach dem letzten Kriege* (Munich: Matthes und Seitz, 1990), 50.

6. For a more thorough version of this argument, see my "Rethinking the Spectacle: History, Visual Culture, and German Unification," in *Wendezeiten— Zeitenwende. Positionsbestimmungen zur deutschsprachigen Literatur 1945–1995*, eds. Robert Weninger and Brigitte Rossbacher (Tübingen: Stauffenburg Verlag, 1997), 151–70.

7. George L. Mosse, *The Nationalization of the Masses: Political Symbolism and Mass Movements in Germany from the Napoleonic Wars to the Third Reich* (Ithaca, N.Y.: Cornell University Press, 1975), 47–72.

8. See, for example, Thomas Meyer, "Repräsentativästhetik und politische Kultur," in *Kunst, Symbolik und Politik. Die Reichstagsverhüllung als Denkanstoß*, ed. Ansgar Klein et al. (Opladen: Leske und Budrich, 1995), 317–24.

9. Jim Collins, *Architectures of Excess: Cultural Life in the Information Age* (New York: Routledge, 1995), 25.

10. Andreas Huyssen, "Monumental Seduction," *New German Critique* 69 (fall 1996): 187

11. Benjamin, *Illuminations*, 188.

12. Heide Schlüpmann, "Kinosucht," *Frauen und Film* 33 (October 1982): 45–52.

13. Miriam Hansen, "Early Silent Cinema: Whose Public Sphere?" *New German Critique* 29 (spring–summer 1983): 180.

14. Max Horkheimer and Theodor W. Adorno, *Dialectic of Enlightenment*, trans. John Cumming (New York: Continuum, 1995), 135.

15. Theodor W. Adorno, "On Popular Music," in *On Record: Rock, Pop, and the Written Word*, eds. Simon Frith and Andrew Goodwin (London: Routledge, 1990), 308.

16. Theodor W. Adorno, "On the Fetish-Character in Music and the Regression of Listening," in *The Essential Frankfurt School Reader*, eds. Andrew Arato and Eike Gebhardt (New York: Urizen Books, 1978), 280.

17. Patrice Petro, *Joyless Streets: Women and Melodramatic Representation in Weimar Germany* (Princeton, N.J.: Princeton University Press, 1989).

18. Ibid., 67.

19. Miriam Hansen, "Benjamin, Cinema and Experience: 'The Blue Flower in the Land of Technology,'" *New German Critique* 40 (winter 1987): 202.

20. Benjamin, *Illuminations*, 238.

21. Walter Benjamin, *Gesammelte Schriften*, eds. Rolf Tiedemann and Hermann Schweppenhäuser, 7 vols. (Frankfurt am Main: Suhrkamp, 1974), 2:205.

22. Siegfried Kracauer, "Cult of Distraction," in *The Mass Ornament: Weimar Essays*, trans. Thomas Y. Levin (Cambridge, Mass.: Harvard University Press, 1995), 327.

23. Benjamin, *Illuminations*, 232.

24. See Tom Gunning, "The Cinema of Attraction(s)," *Wide Angle* 8, nos. 3–4 (1986): 63–70; see also Gunning's essay "An Aesthetic of Astonishment: Early Film and the (In)credulous Spectator," *Art & Text* 34 (1989): 31–45.

25. Hansen, "Benjamin, Cinema and Experience," 209.

26. David Harvey, *The Condition of Postmodernity: An Enquiry into the Origins of Cultural Change* (Oxford: Basil Blackwell, 1989), 124.

27. Peter U. Hohendahl, *Prismatic Thought: Theodor W. Adorno* (Lincoln: University of Nebraska Press, 1995), 145.

28. Friedberg, "Cinema and the Postmodern Condition," 74; see also Iain Chambers, "The Aural Walk," in *Migrancy, Culture, Identity* (London and New York: Routledge, 1994), 49–53.

29. Benjamin, *Illuminations*, 232.

30. See Gerhard Schulze, *Die Erlebnisgesellschaft. Kultursoziologie der Gegenwart* (Frankfurt am Main: Campus Verlag, 1992), 33–89.

31. See Sherry Turkle, *Life on the Screen: Identity in the Age of the Internet* (New York: Simon and Schuster, 1995).

32. Helmut Dubiel, *Ungewißheit und Politik* (Frankfurt am Main: Suhrkamp, 1994), 90.

33. Gerhard Schulze, "Das Medienspiel," in *Kulturinszenierungen*, eds. Stefan Müller-Doohm and Klaus Neumann-Braun (Frankfurt am Main: Suhrkamp, 1995), 370.

34. Jürgen Habermas, "What Theories Can Accomplish—and What They Can't," in his *The Past as Future*, trans. Max Pensky (Lincoln: University of Nebraska Press, 1994), 119.

35. Anthony Giddens, *The Consequences of Modernity* (Stanford, Calif.: Stanford University Press, 1990), 55–78.

36. Hal Foster, *The Return of the Real* (Cambridge, Mass.: MIT Press, 1996).

37. Andreas Huyssen, "Escape from Amnesia: The Museum as Mass Medium," in *Twilight Memories: Marking Time in a Culture of Amnesia* (New York: Routledge, 1995), 16.

38. Martin Jay, *Downcast Eyes: The Denigration of Vision in Twentieth-Century French Thought* (Berkeley and Los Angeles: University of California Press, 1994). Barbara Maria Stafford, *Good Looking: Essays on the Virtue of Images* (Cambridge, Mass.: MIT Press, 1996).

39. Jim Collins, *Uncommon Cultures: Popular Culture and Post-Modernism* (New York: Routledge, 1989), 1–27.

40. Michael P. Steinberg, "The Collector as Allegorist: Goods, Gods, and Objects of History," in *Walter Benjamin and the Demands of History*, ed. Michael P. Steinberg (Ithaca, N.Y.: Cornell University Press, 1996), 107.

41. As, for instance, in the 1996 show "Kunst und Macht im Europa der Diktatoren 1930 bis 1945," put together by the Hayward Gallery in London for successive exhibition in London, Berlin, and Barcelona.

CHAPTER 5

1. All citations in the following are from the so-called second version of the essay, found in *Gesammelte Schriften*, ed. Rolf Tiedemann and Hermann Schweppenhäuser, 7 vols. (Frankfurt am Main: Suhrkamp, 1972–1989), volume 1. All other works by Benjamin are cited from this edition, indicated by volume and page number. The page references to the English translation of the artwork essay (*Illuminations: Essays and Reflections*, ed. Hannah Arendt, trans. Harry Zohn [New York: Schocken Books, 1969], 217–51) have been included as a general reference; most of the translations have been altered.

2. See Susan Buck-Morss, "Benjamin's *Passagenwerk*: Redeeming Mass Culture for the Revolution," *New German Critique* 29 (1983): 211–40.

3. Jürgen Habermas, "Bewußtmachende oder rettende Kritik—Die Aktualität Walter Benjamins," in his *Kultur und Kritik. Verstreute Aufsätze* (Frankfurt am Main: Suhrkamp, 1977), 302–44.

4. Surprisingly, Benjamin did not include the program and manifesto among the literary genres considered in the surrealism essay. With their performative and interventional character, such texts deal with unmediated experience: "Whoever has recognized that the writings of this circle do not concern literature, but rather something else: manifestation, slogan, document, bluff, forgery, if you will, but above all not literature. Whoever has recognized this knows also that it is literal experience, and not theories, even less phantasms, that is at stake here" (2:297).

5. Theodor W. Adorno, "Einleitung zu Benjamins 'Schriften,'" in his *Noten zur Literatur* (Frankfurt am Main: Suhrkamp, 1981), 579. The critical thrust of his observations becomes more clear in the following: "The gesture of his language takes on something authoritarian" (579). The *"devastating* evidence of his experience" (ibid., emphasis mine) with which Adorno credits Benjamin is at once the starting point of his critique, which aims at the lack of mediation in Benjamin. Adorno reads the latent violence of the linguistic gesture as its symptom. That Benjamin, who had repeatedly claimed that the "firm, seemingly brutal grasping" (5:592) belongs to redemption, had commended of all things the "cannibalistic qualities" of his essay to Adorno gives pause for thought.

6. Burkhardt Lindner, "Technische Reproduzierbarkeit und Kulturindustrie: Benjamins 'Positives Barbarentum' im Kontext," in *Walter Benjamin im Kontext*, ed. Burkhardt Lindner (Königstein/Ts.: Athenäum, 1985), 189.

7. Benjamin succinctly recapitulated the theses in the "Paralipomena" as follows: "Technological reproduction leads to a literaricization [crossed out and replaced with] politicization" (1:1039). Literaricization is apparently not the equivalent of fascist aestheticization, but rather a synonym of politicization.

8. Uwe Steiner, *Die Geburt der Kritik aus dem Geiste der Kunst. Untersuchungen zum Begriff der Kritik in den frühen Schriften Walter Benjamins* (Würzburg: Königshausen und Neumann, 1989).

9. Adorno, *Noten zur Literatur*, 578.

10. The problem of representation in the mourning play study marks the difference between knowledge and truth: "The more clearly mathematics demonstrates that the total elimination of the problem of representation—which is claimed by every rigorous didactic system—is the sign of genuine cognition, the most conclusively does it reveal its renunciation of that area of truth to which languages refer" (1:207).

11. In the "Program of the Coming Philosophy," Benjamin criticizes the poverty of Kant's concept of experience. But he maintains, with Kant, that the "knowledge of which we have the most pure account will at once also be the most deep" (2:157).

12. The chemical metaphors that will later return in the preface to the study on the German mourning play appear for the first time in Benjamin's work on the concept of art criticism. Here, representation is understood "as the generation of one substance through a determinate process to which others are subjected" (1:109).

13. The objection that the "fundamental relations" are independent of temporal-

quantitative alterations, and that capitalism has thus remained the same in its structure from the beginning, is refuted by Benjamin's own text, for the "fundamental
relations" of the technology of reproduction do not in fact remain self-identical:
"Quantity has been transmuted into quality" (1:503; *Ill.* 239). This applies not only
to the masses that Benjamin refers to at this point, but rather also to the technology
of reproduction, the development of which would, as Benjamin represents it, be un-
thinkable without the masses.

14. Architecture constitutes an exception to the quasi-typological—quasi to the
extent that it is first created in the representation—structure of reference. Architecture seems to be an anthropological constant, immune to the historical functional
transformation to which all other arts are susceptible: "Architecture has always represented the prototype of a work of art the reception of which is consummated by a
collectivity in a state of distraction. . . . Buildings have been man's companions since
primeval times. . . . But the human need for shelter is lasting" (1:540; *Ill.* 239-40). The
reason behind the exceptional role played by architecture in aesthetics from Hegel to
Schopenhauer cannot be sought with reference to this classical tradition alone. Like
film, architecture belongs in Benjamin's thought to those "motifs" that manifest the
convergence of method and object in an obvious manner. One recalls the immanent
significance of architecture for a work that features an architectural innovation of
the nineteenth century in its title, the organizational principle of which itself has architectural traits: the arcades. In the artwork essay, architecture is excluded from the
process of construction, since it is the essence of construction.

15. Under these circumstances, Adorno's critical lament that the realities of the
culture industry appear less positive to him than to Benjamin, falls short of its mark;
Benjamin makes no claim to describe primarily contemporary realities. Adorno's
desire for "more dialectic" (1:1004) misses the point entirely. One could rather criticize Benjamin for an "excess" of dialectic, because he made his text not the organ
but rather the stage for the dialectic of the history of philosophy. That is why Benjamin responds to Adorno's desire to see more dialectic with such calm: "It generally
seems to me that our investigations [the essay on the work of art and Adorno's study
'Über Jazz,'—E. G.] are like two spotlights, directed from opposite angles at an object, to make the contours and dimensions of contemporary art comprehensible in
an entirely new and much more productive manner than has been the case to date"
(1:1022).

16. Benjamin develops his theory of shock above all in the Baudelaire studies and
in the surrealism essay.

17. This simultaneity is what Benjamin has elsewhere referred to as "topicality"
[*Aktualität*]. Grzimek writes in his analysis of the concept: "Accordingly . . . the struc-
ture of the concept of true topicality is defined in a temporality that is at once tran-
scendent." Martin Grzimek and Dietrich Harth, "Aura und Aktualität als ästhetische
Begriffe" in *Walter Benjamin—Zeitgenosse der Moderne*, eds. Gebhardt, Grzimek, and
Harth et al. (Königstein/Ts.: Athenäum, 1976), 127. According to this, topicality

would be the state of simultaneity of time and transcendence. Grzimek mistakenly claims that the concept of topicality is absent in the artwork essay, since "Benjamin attempts to analyze the development of art as the result of technology alone" (135). Firstly, the concept is not absent (see 1:477); secondly, the artwork essay cannot be the place where an explanation is provided, since its task consists above all in demonstrating its own topicality and positioning itself historically, while at the same time avoiding the assumption of a fixed standpoint or position. In the execution of its representation, the text produces its topicality. And this execution entails the program of topicalization.

18. See Rolf Tiedemann, *Dialektik im Stillstand. Versuch zum Spätwerk Walter Benjamins* (Frankfurt am Main: Suhrkamp, 1983).

19. This is the only passage in which Benjamin uses the future tense. This could mean that he has great hopes for this development but little faith. Perhaps the future tense also marks Benjamin's own uncertainty with regard to whether his investigation is science or art. As early as the study on the German mourning play Benjamin had already thematized the relationship between art and science with respect to the problematic of representation. The philosopher achieves "the elevated middle between the researcher and the artist." The researcher is "connected to the philosopher through his interest in the eradication of mere empirical data, the artist through the task of representation" (1:212).

20. See Werner Hamacher's discussion of the problem of pure mediality in "Afformative, Strike," *Cardozo Law Review* 13, no. 4 (1991): 1133–57. Also published in German as "Afformativ, Streik," in *Was heißt darstellen?*, ed. Christiaan Hart-Nibbrig (Franfurt am Main: Suhrkamp, 1994).

21. That is why it is inaccurate to claim that the instance of "transformation is privileged over that of mediation" (Tiedemann, *Dialektik im Stillstand*, 36). Even for Hegel, the dialectical transformation is possible only in a universe of mediations. This is all the more the case in Benjamin's radicalized rendering.

22. "The invention of the woodcut may be said to have struck at the root of the quality of authenticity even before its late flowering" (1:476; *Ill.* 243).

23. In the epistemological preface to the mourning play study, this procedure belongs to the postulates of philosophical style: "the art of breaking off as opposed to the chain of deduction" (1:212).

24. Habermas, "Bewußtmachende oder rettende Kritik," 316.

25. Hegel, *Introductory Lectures on Aesthetics*, trans. Bernard Bosanquet, ed., with an intro. and commentary, Michael Inwood (New York and London: Penguin Classics, 1993), 12.

26. Ibid., 12.

27. Ibid., 4.

28. Ibid., 13.

29. It is above all Adorno's *Aesthetic Theory* that struggles with this problem: "Therefore art requires philosophy, which interprets it in order to say what it is un-

able to say, while art is only able to say it by not saying it." (Theodor W. Adorno, *Gesammelte Schriften*, eds. Gretel Adorno and Rolf Tiedemann, vol. 7 [Frankfurt am Main: Suhrkamp, 1984], 113).

30. In its abbreviated form, the formulation recalls similar ones from Benjamin's dissertation, especially "the thinking of thinking." Benjamin's demonstration of the equivocal structure of this philosopheme undermines the canonical form of reflection. This marks the difference between Fichte's and Schlegel's respective concepts of reflection (1:30).

CHAPTER 6

This essay was originally commissioned to respond to the question or panel topic "Benjamin as Freudian," for the 1997 MLA meeting, held in Toronto.

1. Walter Benjamin, *Ursprung des deutschen Trauerspiels*, in *Gesammelte Schriften*, *Werkausgabe* edition, 4 vols. (Frankfurt am Main: Suhrkamp, 1980). References to this edition are indicated by volume and page number.

2. Walter Benjamin, "Bücher von Geisteskranken. Aus meiner Sammlung" (1928), in *Gesammelte Schriften*, 4:615–16.

3. Alexander Mette, "Benjamin, Walter: Ursprung des deutschen Trauerspiels. E. Rowohlt, Berlin 1928," *Imago* 17, no. 4 (1931): 536–38.

4. See Walter Benjamin, "Alexander Mette, Über Beziehungen zwischen Sprach-eigentümlichkeiten Schizophrener und dichterischer Produktion. Dessau, Dresden: Dion-Verlag 1928. 99 S.," 3:165.

5. Ibid., 3:165.

6. Ibid., 3:165–66.

7. Ibid., 3:334.

8. See Alexander Mette, "Benjamin, Walter," 537.

9. Ibid., 537–38.

10. Ibid., 538.

11. Ibid. Mette continued to serve as happy medium (via displacement and in the mode of survivorship) for Benjamin's internal management of materials. As Mette found out firsthand, the analytic model had a staying power that was passed right on down, through the Third Reich. A context that has been so obscured that Ernst Jünger, for example, could be awarded, after the fact, after the big repression, a lead-ing role in the agon of influence, needs to be restored right now: back then the so-called Frankfurt school was engaging really only one main competitor on death drive, the eclectic psychotherapeutic brand and band that had grown up between the wars in the afterglow of Freud's success stories, his science's mythic healing of war neurosis. The military-psychological or psychotechnical competition (in relation to which Jünger was the dilettante who took his opportunism) was way advanced, along the double lines Benjamin explored in the essays on mechanical reproducibility and on Baudelaire's motives, the two-track taping together of psychoanalysis and media

technology. There was no Marxism in the competition's mix, and not because it was the one -ism that would have blown it all away. The competition only used what worked, and that meant Freud and technology. For the content and decoration of certain psychological war moves Jung would be used up front and Marx would be deployed between the lines of analyses of the tensions going down in target societies. But in theory and in praxis even the Nazis couldn't find any internal use for Jung and Marx. Benjamin's interest in the Marxist discourse, which he deployed, by all accounts, metaphorically or allegorically and not dialectically, was all about its abandoned status, as seen from the fast lane of the competition on death drive. Benjamin was drawn to lost places deep inside the recent past (the past that always also represents primal time). He knew all about the evil-eye powers of defeated discourses. The fascist grasp of the intersecting places between technology and the unconscious was too advanced to be outdistanced on its own terms, at least in the short run. But the performative mix Benjamin attempted in the essay on film culture, which culminated in the slogan designed for reproducibility, the one about aestheticization of politics and politicization of art, kind of won in the longer run. This is not a judgment call made against psychoanalysis but against the reversal of psychoanalysis internal to the Nazi techno-bond. Politicization in the name of Marxism, a third-party discourse outside analysis, means put the reversal into reverse, and up the "anti" on the therapeutic, on the all-out healing while promoting analytic and intrapsychic interventions. The call was put through to the same gadget lovers, the distracted teen testers, the teen experts in their own replication or reassembly, who were already plugged into the Nazi takeover of live or life's transmissions on death drive. Mette therefore displaces, enacts over time, becomes the afterlife of Benjamin's strategy. His publications during and inside the Third Reich make coded reference to Freud, in other words to the "depth psychology" under construction and exploration at the institute in Berlin. Under the direction of Mathias Göring, the other Göring's cousin, Freudian, Jungian, and Adlerian therapies and theories were to be mixed into one at once eclecticized and totalized "German" psychotherapy. Just the same, the institutional mix-up tended to give the analytic model the upper hand (for example the clinic was run by members of the A-Group, the former "Freudians"). In his 1940 study, *The Psychological Roots of the Dionysian and the Apollonian* (Alexander Mette, *Die psychologischen Wurzeln des Dionysischen und Apollinischen. Ein neuer Versuch* [Berlin-Steglitz: Dion-Verlag, 1940]), Mette writes above or ahead of annotated reference to Göring's institute: "The depth psychological study of ill and healthy life has taught us to recognize the significance of that zone which appears least intelligible to reason and which lies in the outer limits of the unconscious. With that a gate has been opened wide for the biological perspective, which Nietzsche like no other initiated, and limits have been set to that old standard of reason, which claims that only that which originates in it is of value" (63). Mette fixes his focus on the comedic aspect of alle-gory, the clown as late arrival of Dionysus. Only the depth psychologist and, intuitively, the artist can understand that the regressive violence of all clowning around is also the allegorical sign of a tearing apart of the original mother and child dyad. The clown, Mette argues, is unconsciously in the transit phase of individuation and separation (59, 53). Somewhere in Mette's own transitional objective, among these concluding pages, reference is made to the Dionysian articulations of the baroque period.

After the war Mette chose to remain in the Communist zoning out of Germany. In a collectively authored history textbook, *The Physician in Socialist Society* (with Gerhard Misgeld and Kurt Winter, *Der Arzt in der sozialistischen Gesellschaft* [Berlin: Akademie Verlag, 1958]), Mette cosigns the reading of an American competitor in this specialized market of books as a late arrival of Freud's influence, which is further analogized with art for art's sake, and thus, to fill in the ellipsis in Benjamin's terms, with a certain retrenchment of aura, which, Mette and company continue, gets symptomatized in the overemphasis on diagnosis (or interpretation) and the neglect of therapeutic concerns (which in the theory takes the form of privileging "the Unconscious"). The predominance of psychoanalysis in pre-Communist Europe matched the growing brutality of the imperialist ideology at that same time (58, 60, 63). On his own, in another textbook, *I. P. Pavlov: His Life and Work* (Berlin: VEB Verlag Volk und Gesundheit, 1959), Mette sets his biographical subject ahead of Freud in terms of biological know-how, so far ahead that any attempted coupling of Pavlov and Freud must fail, given the entirely "speculative" nature of Freud's work (46–47). Mette finds a better "biological" connection postwar with Pavlov. Now Mette's resistance is addressed to what for Freud, as Derrida has argued in *The Post Card* (*The Post Card: From Socrates to Freud and Beyond*, trans. Alan Bass [Chicago and London: University of Chicago Press, 1987]), remains inseparable and nonsuperimposable: the biological and the biographical, science and speculation (or spookulation). In 1976, in another textbook-style publication, Mette published a biography of Wilhelm Griesinger (*Wilhelm Griesinger. Der Begründer der wissenschaftlichen Psychiatrie in Deutschland* [Leipzig: BSB B. G. Teubner Verlagsgesellschaft, 1976]), who is granted the subtitle: "The Founder of Scientific Psychiatry in Germany." Mette has to "and" it to Griesinger's precursor contributions to Pavlov's material-dialectical psychiatry. Among the missing links we find Paul Flechsig, the psychiatrist in charge of the Schreber case. The Griesinger-through-Flechsig transmission begins with a change in the material conditions of the mentally ill. Before Griesinger and the rest pushed through their reforms, treatment had depended on therapeutic-punitive machines, special chairs and beds to which patients were strapped and that turned around forty to sixty times per minute. Because these devices already represented progress over the total neglect that had attended patients in chains throughout the Christian era of holding the insane morally responsible for their afflictions, the resistance to the even newer model of smaller clinics out in the countryside with emphasis on occupational therapies was considerable. But what accompanied Griesinger's relocation of the mentally ill to the suburbs was the merely more secular inside view that the brains of the deranged must ultimately be held responsible. The punitive machinery was thus internalized, and years later reached new points of externalization, for example, in the practice of lobotomy. The illustrations of the period that Mette includes in the book to show just what Griesinger was up against resemble the harnesses Schreber's father designed to promote the moral and physical well-being of all children (a kind of preventive or preemptive approach) at the same time as he prescribed suburban garden plots for the whole urban family. He certainly tried out his hygiene machines and theories on his two sons. There was more than one way to be a Skinner in a box. There remains only one echo of a "Freudian" objection to all this. It comes via Virchow, who was given back then—but completely as colleague, with interest and respect—to disagree with Griesinger's view that mental illness was always a physical disorder in the brain (75).

12. Sigmund Freud, "Psychoanalytic Notes Upon an Autobiographical Account of a Case of Paranoia (Dementia Paranoides)" (1911), in *Collected Papers*, ed. Ernest Jones, trans. Alix and James Strachey (New York: Basic Books, 1959), 3:457.

13. Ibid., 3:458.

14. Benjamin, "Bücher von Geisteskranken: Aus meiner Sammlung," 616–17.

15. Ibid., 619.

16. Benjamin, "Das Kunstwerk im Zeitalter seiner technischen Reproduzierbarkeit" (both the 1935 and the 1936 versions), in *Gesammelte Schriften*, 1:462.

17. Benjamin, "Über einige Motive bei Baudelaire," in *Gesammelte Schriften*, 1:605–53.

CHAPTER 7

1. This gesture recurs in de Man's critical writing; here is one example: "[Kleist's] *Marionettentheater* has produced fine articles of considerable subtlety, erudition, and wit (next to others of distressing banality)" ("Aesthetic Formalization: Kleist's *Über das Marionettentheater*," in his *The Rhetoric of Romanticism* [New York: Columbia University Press, 1984], 271).

2. "Goethes Wahlverwandtschaften," *Gesammelte Schriften*, ed. Rolf Tiedemann and Hermann Schweppenhäuser, 7 vols. (Frankfurt am Main: Suhrkamp, 1972), 2:126–201 (first published in Hofmannsthal's *Neue Deutsche Beiträge* in 1924–1925). "Goethe's Elective Affinities," trans. Stanley Corngold, in *Selected Works*, ed. Michael Jennings and Marcus Bullock (Cambridge, Mass.: Harvard University Press, 1997), 1:297–360. Hereafter indicated by page number.

3. Michael Jennings, doctoral diss. "Walter Benjamin's Literary Criticism" (University of Virginia, 1981), 135.

4. Cf. Werner Fuld, *Walter Benjamin. Zwischen den Stühlen. Eine Biographie* (Munich: Hanser, 1979): "It is untrue that Ottilie becomes silent; rather, she speaks frankly about her relation to Eduard" (134).

5. I say "at once, and more than" because obscurity is at once the condition of the

semblance through which beauty in art necessarily appears; and yet, in *Elective Affinities*, it is the condition of the appearance of Ottilie and hence a kind of obscurity not normally found in works of art. This impasse will require Benjamin to introduce distinctions among *kinds* of semblance—but I do not wish to get ahead of myself at this point.

6. Paul de Man, *Blindness and Insight: Essays in the Rhetoric of Contemporary Criticism*, 2d ed. rev. (Minneapolis: University of Minnesota Press, 1983), 13.

7. Occultatio: namely, "a figure where, with the appearance of keeping silent about something, one does in fact name it" (*Friedrich Nietzsche on Rhetoric and Language*, ed. and trans. Sander L. Gilman, Carole Blair, and David J. Parent [New York and Oxford: Oxford University Press, 1989], 82).

8. Note that I do not say "material content" [*Sachgehalt*], the medium of veiling manifestation in which the veiling effect is misrecognized. Of this content, Benjamin writes, "Of course the material content itself, which yields only to philosophical perception—or, more precisely, to philosophical experience—remains inaccessible to both, but whereas the latter leads into the abyss, the former attains the very ground where true knowledge is formed" (299). The material content, unlike the material thing or the material sign, is the beginning of wisdom, a knowledge of essence that, in principle, can be had short of death.

9. This identification was made by Jochen Hörisch. Further, cf. Arthur Schopenhauer, *The World as Will and Representation*, trans. E. F. J. Payne (New York: Dover, 1969), 1:266–67. "If the whole world as representation is only the visibility of the will, then art is the elucidation of this visibility, the *camera obscura* which shows the objects more purely, and enables us to survey and comprehend them better. It is the play within the play, the stage on the stage in *Hamlet*."

10. *The Gay Science*, ed. and trans. Walter Kaufmann (New York: Random House, 1974), 223–24.

CHAPTER 8

1. Walter Benjamin, "The Storyteller: Reflections on the Works of Nikolai Leskov," in his *Illuminations* (New York: Schocken Books, 1969), 108.

2. Benjamin, "The Work of Art in the Age of Mechanical Reproduction," in *Illuminations*, 226.

3. On Benjamin's propensity for melancholia, see especially Susan Sontag, "Introduction," in Walter Benjamin, *"One-Way Street" and Other Writings*, trans. Edmund Jephcott and Kingsley Shorter (London: Verso, 1985), 7–28.

4. Of the many notable references to the art of physiognomy that are scattered through Benjamin's writings one might cite his discussion of the skull in *The Origin of the German Mourning Play*, the description of the collector as physiognomist of objects in "Unpacking My Library," as well as his "Hashish in Marseille," "Berlin Childhood," and the early notes on graphology, telepathy, and astrology, in Walter Ben-

jamin, *Gesammelte Schriften*, eds. Rolf Tiedemann and Hermann Schweppenhäuser, 7 vols. (Frankfurt am Main: Suhrkamp, 1985), 6:185–94.

5. On Benjamin's concept of technology, see especially Susan Buck-Morss, "Aesthetics and Anaesthetics: Walter Benjamin's Artwork Essay Reconsidered," *October* 62 (fall 1992): 3–41; Miriam Hansen, "Benjamin, Cinema and Experience: 'The Blue Flower in the Land of Technology," *New German Critique* 40 (winter 1987): 179–224; and Sigrid Weigel, *Body- and Image-Space: Re-Reading Walter Benjamin* (London: Routledge, 1996).

6. For a lengthier discussion of the *Trauerspielbuch*, as well as Benjamin's early work, see Hanssen, *Walter Benjamin's Other History: Of Stones, Animals, Human Beings, and Angels* (Berkeley, Los Angeles, and London: University of California Press, 1998); and Hanssen, "'Dichtermut' and 'Blödigkeit': Two Poems by Hölderlin Interpreted by Walter Benjamin," *MLN* 112 (1997): 786–816.

7. Aby Warburg coined the term *kulturwissenschaftliche Bildgeschichte* in his book, *Heidnisch- antike Weissagung in Wort und Bild zu Luthers Zeiten* (Pagan-antique prophecy in word and image during Luther's time) (Heidelberg: Sitzungsberichte der Heidelberger Akademie der Wissenschaften, 1920). On the difficulties of translating the German term into English—apparent in the fact that the KBW or *Kulturwissenschaftliche Bibliothek Warburg* was simply renamed the *Warburg Institute* in London, see Ernst Gombrich, *Aby Warburg: An Intellectual Biography* (Chicago: University of Chicago Press, 1986), 15–16.

8. Walter Benjamin, "Re The Theory of Knowledge, Theory of Progress," in *Benjamin: Philosophy, History, Aesthetics*, ed. Gary Smith (Chicago: University of Chicago Press, 1989), 49.

9. Ibid., 50.

10. Karl Marx and Friedrich Engels, *The German Ideology Part One, with Selections from Parts Two and Three, together with Marx's "Introduction to a Critique of Political Economy,"* ed. C. J. Arthur (New York: International Publishers, 1970), 47. On the figure of the camera obscura, see also W. J. T. Mitchell's "The Rhetoric of Iconoclasm: Marxism, Ideology, and Fetishism," in his *Iconology: Image, Text, Ideology* (Chicago: University of Chicago Press, 1986), 160–208.

11. See Erwin Panofsky, "Iconography and Iconology: An Introduction to the Study of Renaissance Art," in his *Meaning in the Visual Arts* (Chicago: University of Chicago Press, 1982), 41. To be sure, Panofsky's precise qualification of iconology as concerned with detecting the "intrinsic meaning or content" of allegories, images, stories, which "[constitute] the world of 'symbolic' values," beyond allegorical exegesis, can only with great difficulty be applied to Benjamin's cultural-historical method, which rested on a thoroughly reconfigured, dialectical notion of allegory. Not only the *Trauerspiel* study, but also later essays such as "On Some Motifs in Baudelaire," pitted the disjunctive force of allegory's negative dialectic against the holistic, organic force of aesthetic symbols.

12. Here and in what follows, I rely on Gershom Scholem's comprehensive "Wal-

ter Benjamin and His Angel," in *On Walter Benjamin: Critical Essays and Recollections*, ed. Gary Smith (Cambridge, Mass.: MIT Press, 1991), 51–89. See also Stephane Moses, *L'ange de l'histoire. Rosenzweig, Benjamin, Scholem* (Paris: Seuil, 1992).

13. See Scholem's discussion of the cryptogram "Agesileus Santander" in "Walter Benjamin and His Angel," 59ff.

14. See also Scholem, "Walter Benjamin and His Angel," 85.

15. For a compelling contemporary analysis of the engraving, see Hartmut Böhme, *Albrecht Dürer, Melencolia I im Labyrinth der Deutung* (Frankfurt am Main: Fischer, 1989).

16. See Gershom Scholem and Theodor W. Adorno, *The Correspondence of Walter Benjamin 1910–1940*, trans. Manfred R. Jacobson and Evelyn M. Jacobson (Chicago: University of Chicago Press, 1994), 203.

17. The editors of Benjamin's collected works, Hermann Schweppenhäuser and Rolf Tiedemann, report that Alfred Sohn-Rethel, while in Paris, had seen Benjamin's album with collages of such illustrations, meant as iconic documentation for the *Passagen-Werk*. See their comments in *Gesammelte Schriften*, 5:1324.

18. See Walter Benjamin, *The Origin of German Tragic Drama*, trans. John Osborne (London: Verso, 1985), 140ff.

19. See Gombrich, *Aby Warburg*, viii.

20. Erwin Panofsky and Fritz Saxl, *Dürers "Melencolia I." Eine quellen- und typengeschichtliche Untersuchung* (Leipzig, Berlin: Studien der Bibliothek Warburg, 1923), 4.

21. Benjamin, *Origin*, 150.

22. The present essay privileges Benjamin's conception of melancholia within the context of his emerging theory of knowledge. For a more extended discussion of Benjamin's philosophical analysis of the baroque and modernity, see Hanssen, *Walter Benjamin's Other History*, passim.

23. Wilhelm Dilthey, *Weltanschauung und Analyse des Menschen seit Renaissance und Reformation. Abhandlungen zur Geschichte der Philosophie und Religion*, in Dilthey, *Gesammelte Schriften*, ed. Georg Misch, vol. 2 (Leipzig: B. G. Teubner, 1929).

24. Benjamin, *Origin*, 140.

25. Ibid.

26. Benjamin, "Unpacking My Library: A Talk About Book Collecting," in *Illuminations*, 60.

27. Benjamin, "Ankündigung der Zeitschrift. Angelus Novus," in *Gesammelte Schriften*, 2:242.

28. There exists a remarkable connection, here, to Kristeva's psychoanalytic interpretation of melancholia, which understands this pathological state as the interminable mourning of the irrepresentible, inaccessible *Thing*, or preobject. See Julia Kristeva, *Black Sun: Depression and Melancholia*, trans. Leon S. Roudiez (New York: Columbia University Press, 1989), esp. 13 and 95–103.

29. Benjamin, "The Work of Art in the Age of Mechanical Reproduction," in *Illuminations*, 222.

30. See Benjamin, "On the Mimetic Faculty," in his *Reflections: Essays, Aphorisms, Autobiographical Writings*, trans. Edmund Jephcott (New York: Schocken, 1986), 333–36.

31. In German the phrase reads: "Eine Art polarer Funktion des einfühlenden Bildgedächtnisses." On Warburg's memory project, see also Fritz Saxl's 1930 essay, "Warburgs Mnemosyne-Atlas," in Aby M. Warburg, *Ausgewählte Schriften und Würdigungen*, ed. by Dieter Wuttke (Baden-Baden: Valentin Koerner, 1979), 313–15; Kurt W. Forster, "Aby Warburg: His Study of Ritual and Art on Two Continents," *October* 77 (summer 1996): 5–24.

32. Gombrich, *Aby Warburg*, 218. See also Aby Warburg, *Images from the Region of the Pueblo Indians of North America*, trans. Michael P. Steinberg (Ithaca, N.Y.: Cornell University Press, 1995), passim; as well as Michael Steinberg's introduction to the edition, and Joseph Koerner's review article, "Paleface and Redskin," *The New Republic* 216, no. 12 (24 March 1997): 30–38. For a discussion of the lecture in the context of cultural history and cultural studies, see Sigrid Weigel, "Aby Warburg's *Schlangenritual*: Reading Culture and Reading Written Texts," *New German Critique* 65 (spring–summer 1995): 135–53.

33. As Gombrich notes, Warburg's conception of cultural history as memory, as a vast collective "storehouse" of images, gestures, and symbols, as a "primeval vocabulary of passionate gesticulation," was influenced by Semon's notion of the trace, or "engram," and Jung's emerging conception of the "collective unconscious." While Warburg's original conception of the atlas was modeled on the ethnographic work of Bastian, according to Gombrich, it is evident that he did not strive to document ethnic diversity, but rather to offer the hologram of universal human nature.

34. Benjamin, "Kleine Geschichte der Photographie," in *Gesammelte Schriften*, 2.1:371. For an English translation, see Walter Benjamin, "A Small History of Photography," in his *"One-Way Street" and Other Writings*, 240–57. In what follows, I have provided my own translations whenever appropriate.

35. Benjamin, "Kleine Geschichte der Photographie," 372, 376.

36. Benjamin here quotes from Alfred Doeblin's introduction to Sander's photo atlas. See ibid., 380.

37. Ibid., 380–81. In order to complete this genealogy of the social physiognomy of photographs and the recurring figure of the "atlas," one must trace the development of this topos in postwar modern art. For, unexpectedly and with considerable delay, the term *atlas* returns in pictorial history, appropriated by the postwar German photographer-painter Gerhard Richter, who brought its program to surprising completion when he compiled an extensive photographic collection of found and constructed photographs—from intimate family portraits to newspaper clippings —all *Vor-bilder* for his photo-paintings, which he called *Atlas*. Including a section dedicated to the physiognomies of "German Intellectuals," Richter's *Atlas* was first exhibited in 1972 and, most recently, at the 1997 international Documenta in Kassel, Germany. In these successive photographic transformations of social physiog-

nomies—from Benjamin to Warburg to Sander to Richter—cultural history is re-interpreted, reconceptualized as an expansive atlas of memory-images, or mnemic icons, although the aesthetic and political articulation of these pictorial traces shifts markedly, moving gradually from humanistic presuppositions to a postmodern post-humanism.

38. Benjamin, "Kleine Geschichte der Photographie," 375.

39. That the postmodern predicament is characterized by the dwindling of affect is a point that has been stressed by Jean-François Lyotard, *The Postmodern Condition: A Report on Knowledge* (Minneapolis: University of Minnesota Press, 1984); Fredric Jameson, "Postmodernism, or, the Cultural Logic of Late Capitalism," *New Left Review* 146 (July–August 1984): 61–62; and Naomi Schor, "Depression in the Nineties," in her *Bad Objects: Essays Popular and Unpopular* (Durham, N.C., and London: Duke University Press, 1995), 159.

CHAPTER 9

I thank Jill S. Smith and David J. Hinz for their careful and insightful editing of this text.

1. In most of his later writings, Benjamin preferred the term "image" [*Bild*] over "phenomenon" [*Phänomen*]. However, a text from the *Passagen-Werk* indicates that Benjamin was concerned with distancing himself from the concept of phenomenology that was dominated with the name of Heidegger. Walter Benjamin, *Gesammelte Schriften* (Frankfurt am Main: Suhrkamp, 1972–1989), 5:577 [N 3, 1]. That Benjamin is still heading toward a new concept of phenomenology, a phenomenology for which history does not remain purely abstract, is indicated by the same text. For the context of my argument, it is therefore acceptable to speak of a phenomenology even when Benjamin himself favors the term image in his later writings. For a discussion of this fragment, see Christopher Fynsk, "The Claim of History," *diacritics* 22, nos. 3–4 (1992): 115–26.

2. Benjamin, *Gesammelte Schriften*, 5:578 [N 3, 1].

3. Ibid., 5:577 [N 3, 1]. Also, "Durch den sie auf die Erlösung verwiesen wird" (*Gesammelte Schriften*, 1:693).

4. Benjamin, *Gesammelte Schriften*, 5:1006. Also *Gesammelte Schriften*, 1:693–95. For these forms of tropes of turning, compare David S. Ferris, "Introduction: Aura, Resistance, and the Event of History," in *Walter Benjamin: Theoretical Questions*, ed. David S. Ferris (Stanford, Calif.: Stanford University Press, 1996), 1–27.

5. Compare the *Konvolut N* of the *Passagen-Werk*, *Gesammelte Schriften*, 5:570–609, as well as Benjamin, *Gesammelte Schriften*, 1:695.

6. In his *The Narrator* [*Der Erzähler*], Benjamin characterizes narration similarly as that which does not exhaust itself (*verausgaben*) and which remains like an egg to be hatched ("das Ei der Erfahrung") and thereby passes through time (Benjamin, *Gesammelte Schriften*, 2:445–46).

7. Benjamin, *Gesammelte Schriften*, 1:211. Compare about the connection of redemption and ending: Giorgio Agamben, "Walter Benjamin und das Dämonische. Glück und geschichtliche Erlösung im Denken Benjamins," in *Walter Benjamin, 1892–1940, zum 100. Geburtstag*, ed. Uwe Steiner (Bern: P. Lang, 1992), 189–216.

8. "Das kommende Erwachen steht wie das trojanische Pferd der Griechen im Troja des Traums" (Benjamin, *Gesammelte Schriften*, 5:495 [K 2, 4]).

9. "Das Jetzt der Erkennbarkeit ist der Augenblick des Erwachens" (ibid., 5:608 [N 18, 4]). Compare also *Konvolut K* of the *Passagen-Werk*: "Erinnerung und Erwachen sind auf das engste verwandt" and "Der Traum wartet heimlich auf das Erwachen" (ibid., 5:492, 491).

10. Andrew Benjamin and Peter Osborne articulate that for Benjamin "the idea of destruction (Destruktion) as a condition of the possibility of experience (Erfahrung)" would be central, and I would add that the destruction is at the same time the *result* of the recognition and experience (Andrew Benjamin and Peter Osborne, eds., *Walter Benjamin's Philosophy: Destruction and Experience* [London: Routledge, 1994], xi).

11. Benjamin, *Gesammelte Schriften*, 7:416–17; compare with Sigrid Weigel, *Entstellte Ähnlichkeit. Walter Benjamins theoretische Schreibweise* (Frankfurt am Main: S. Fischer, 1997), 52–57.

12. Thus argues Helga Geyer-Ryan, "The Pictorial is destroyed when its existential emptiness is pointed up" ("Effects of Abjection in the Texts of Walter Benjamin," *MLN* 107 [April 1992]: 506).

13. Rainer Nägele has discussed the implications of such a "presentation of the presentation" and the caesura it invokes in several of his intriguing readings of Benjamin. See *Theater, Theory, Speculation: Walter Benjamin and the Scenes of Modernity* (Baltimore, Md., and London: Johns Hopkins University Press, 1991).

14. "Der tragische Transport ist nemlich eigentlich leer, und der ungebundenste. —Dadurch wird in der rhythmischen Aufeinanderfolge der Vorstellungen, worin der Transport sich darstellt, das, was man im Sylbenmaase Cäsur heißt, das reine Wort, die gegenrhythmische Unterbrechung notwendig, um nemlich dem reißenden Wechsel der Vorstellungen, auf seinem Summum so zu begegnen, daß alsdann nicht mehr der Wechsel der Vorstellung, sondern die Vorstellung selber erscheint" (Benjamin, *Gesammelte Schriften*, 1:181–82). Also Walter Benjamin, *Selected Writings*, Marcus Bullock and Michael W. Jennings, eds. (Cambridge, Mass.: Belknap Press of Harvard University, 1996), 1:340–41. For an analysis of Hölderlin's caesura, compare Philippe Lacoue-Labarthe, *Typography: Mimesis, Philosophy, Politics*, ed. Christopher Fynsk (Cambridge, Mass.: Harvard University Press, 1989), 208–35.

15. Benjamin, *Gesammelte Schriften*, 1:182.

16. On Benjamin's "pure" language and "pure word," see Aris Fioretos, "Contraction (Benjamin, Reading, History)," *MLN* 110 (April 1995): 540–64; and Werner Hamacher, who summarizes Benjamin's project as a "politics of pure mediacy": "For Benjamin the means for such a politics may be termed 'pure' because they do not

serve as means to ends situated outside the sphere of mediacy" ("Afformative, Strike," *Cardozo Law Review* 13 [1991]: 1133).

17. Hamacher, "Afformative," 1133; compare also notes 12 and 16 of his text.

18. Norbert Bolz has emphasized this connection of cognition and culture in the thought of Benjamin in several readings; in our context compare, "Bedingungen der Möglichkeit historischer Erfahrung," in *Passagen. Walter Benjamins Urgeschichte des neunzehnten Jahrhunderts*, eds. Norbert Bolz and Bernd Witte (Munich: Fink, 1984), 137–62.

19. Benjamin, *Gesammelte Schriften*, 1:693; Walter Benjamin, *Illuminations*, ed. Hannah Arendt, trans. Harry Zohn (New York: Harcourt, Brace & World, 1968), 253.

20. This dwarf is called theology since the dwarf and theology both promise a redemption. But Benjamin's dwarf does not offer redemption in the sense of a fulfillment. Rather, the dwarf promises and enables a *redemption of* illusion and position. In this *redemption of* historical materialism takes place; it constitutes a position only in the moment that its position is taken away.

21. Benjamin, *Gesammelte Schriften*, 1:696.

22. This is also the reason why Benjamin says that the recognition of the phenomenality and fictionality that is made possible by the "now of recognizability" can be missed. Benjamin emphasizes the uniqueness of the chance of getting hold of this recognition; if one misses the date and the one chance of recognition, then the phenomenon is lost and forgotten or is conserved only in the false fame that historicism attributes to the past.

23. Thus, Benjamin kept in the first two versions of "The Artwork in the Age of its Technical Reproducibility" a formulation according to which "the collective laughter" brings about a "therapeutic explosion of the unconscious" ("therapeutische Sprengung des Unbewußten") and its "sadistic phantasies or masochistic imaginations" ("Wahnvorstellungen"). The context of this passage is again the awakening, Benjamin, *Gesammelte Schriften*, 1:462; and Benjamin, *Gesammelte Schriften*, 7:377.

24. "Die Tradition aller todten Geschlechter lastet wie ein Alp auf dem Gehirne der Lebenden. Und wenn sie eben damit beschäftigt scheinen, sich und die Dinge umzuwälzen, noch nicht Dagewesenes zu schaffen, gerade in solchen Epochen revolutionärer Krise beschwören sie ängstlich die Geister der Vergangenheit zu ihrem Dienste herauf, entlehnen ihnen Namen, Schlachtparole, Kostüme, um in dieser altehrwürdigen Verkleidung und mit dieser erborgten Sprache die neue Weltgeschichte aufzuführen" (Karl Marx, "Der achtzehnte Brumaire des Louis Bonaparte," in Karl Marx and Friedrich Engels, *Werke* [Berlin: Dietz, 1973], 8:115). (MEGA: I.11; 97); *The Eighteenth Brumaire of Louis Bonaparte* (Moscow: Foreign Languages Publishing House, 1948), 15.

25. Derrida has chosen this text as an occasion for a remarkable reading and criticism of Marx, showing the uncanniness of Marx's concept of "labour" as the force that both establishes and threatens all institutions. Still, it is surprising to note how

quickly Derrida at times articulates his accusation of Marx and the generalizations he allows himself to make. Where Marx says, "The tradition of all the dead generations weighs like a nightmare on the brain of the living," Derrida reformulates: "death" itself weighs on the living brain of the living ("la mort pèse sur le cerveau vivant des vivants") (Jacques Derrida, *Spectres de Marx* [Paris: Galilée, 1993], 177). When he replaces "the tradition" by "death," Derrida certainly supports his claim that Marx wants to forget the dead. But Derrida does not consider that there can be a tradition, detached from the dead, which preserves itself in false institutions and relations of power that deserve to be destroyed independent of the necessity of a remembrance. In a different passage, Derrida makes fun of the outspoken goal of all revolutionaries for Marx to break out of the eternal repetition of the "phrase," in order to "attain their own content" [*bei ihrem eigenen Inhalt anzukommen*]. Derrida views this "*proper* content and appropriated content" [*le contenu* propre, *le contenu approprié*] (187) as a complete suppression of all others and as a naive belief that such a new beginning is possible. That one can hear in Marx's word for content, "Inhalt," also the interrupting (also "Inhalt" from the German *Innehalten*), the caesura, which stops, and thereby opens the phrase, is not considered by Derrida, even though he demands "sharp ears" of Marx's readers, and even though Marx's text as a whole is dedicated to the historical caesura of revolution that resists instrumentalization.

26. Benjamin, *Gesammelte Schriften*, 4:397. Compare also "Erfahrung und Armut," as well as other passages in which Benjamin discusses the writings of Paul Scheerbart and his project of glass architecture (Benjamin, *Gesammelte Schriften*, 2:618–20). For a detailed reading of *Der destruktive Charakter*, see Irving Wohlfahrt, "No-man's-land: On Walter Benjamin's 'Destructive Character,'" in *Walter Benjamin's Philosophy*, eds. Andrew Benjamin and Peter Osborne (London: Routledge, 1994), 155–82.

27. For Benjamin's usage of notions of space, see the rich text by Samuel Weber, *Mass Mediauras: Form, Technics, Media* (Stanford, Calif.: Stanford University Press, 1996), 76–107.

28. Louis A. Montrose, "Professing the Renaissance: The Poetics and Politics of Culture," in *The New Historicism*, ed. H. Aram Veeser (London: Routledge, 1989), 19. Catherine Gallagher goes so far as to hold it against the opponents of New Historicism that they expect New Historicism to have a political position. After stating that the politics of New Historicism "are so difficult to specify," she goes on to highlight the "most valuable insights" of New Historicism "that no cultural or critical practice is simply a politics in disguise, that such practices are seldom *intrinsically* either liberatory or oppressive, that they seldom contain their politics as an essence. . . . The search for the new historicism's political essence can be seen as a rejection of these insights." These are the assertions of an academic who has found a secure nest within academia and against whom no argument can be raised. She can discredit anyone who might criticize this attitude in the name of some "insights," by holding that he or she does not control his discourse. Our question, then, is why we should even bother

at all with New Historicism since it only receives a position by someone relating to it. See Gallagher, "Marxism and The New Historicism," in *The New Historicism*, ed. H. Aram Veeser (London: Routledge, 1989), 37.

29. Joel Fineman, to mention only one of several critics, uses the debate surrounding New Historicism for several interesting discussions: see, for example, his "The History of the Anecdote: Fiction and Fiction," in *The New Historicism*, ed. H. Aram Veeser (London: Routledge, 1989), 49–76. See Hayden White, "New Historicism: A Comment," in *The New Historicism*, ed. H. Aram Veeser (London: Routledge, 1989), 293–302; and Stanley Fish, "Commentary: The Young and the Restless," in *The New Historicism*, ed. H. Aram Veeser (London: Routledge, 1989), 303–16.

30. H. Aram Veeser, ed., *The New Historicism* (London: Routledge, 1989), introduction, ix–xvi, ix; and Montrose, 15–37, 19.

31. Benjamin, *Gesammelte Schriften*, 5:495 [K 2, 4].

32. Ibid., 2:692.

33. Montrose, 17; for an examination, see Hayden White, "New Historicism: A Comment," *The New Historicism*, ed. H. Aram Veeser (London: Routledge, 1989), 293–302.

CHAPTER 10

1. The first two of three volumes of *Selected Writings* from Harvard University Press have already appeared: Walter Benjamin, *Selected Writings*, vol. 1: 1913–1926, eds. Marcus Bullock and Michael W. Jennings (Cambridge, Mass.: Harvard University Press, 1996) and *Selected Writings*, vol. 2: 1927–1934, eds. Michael W. Jennings and Howard Eiland (Cambridge, Mass.: Harvard University Press, 1999). In addition, an English translation of Benjamin's massive study of nineteenth-century Paris has just appeared: *The Arcades Project*, trans. Howard Eiland and Kevin McLaughlin (Cambridge, Mass.: Harvard University Press, 1999).

2. See Dominick LaCapra's response to Paul de Man's lecture on Benjamin's "The Task of the Translator" in de Man's essay, "Conclusions: Walter Benjamin's 'The Task of the Translator,'" in his *The Resistance to Theory* (Minneapolis: University of Minnesota Press, 1986), 102.

3. John Guillory, *Cultural Capital: The Problem of Literary Canon Formation* (Chicago: University of Chicago Press, 1993), 55–57. Walter Benjamin, "Über den Begriff der Geschichte," in *Illuminationen. Ausgewählte Schriften* (Frankfurt am Main: Suhrkamp, 1977), 254; "Theses on the Philosophy of History," in *Illuminations: Essays and Reflections*, trans. Harry Zohn (New York: Schocken, 1978), 256. I have translated the German *Kultur* as "culture"; Zohn translates it as "civilization."

4. Guillory, *Cultural Capital*, 327.

5. Benjamin, *Das Passagen-Werk* (Frankfurt am Main: Surhkamp, 1982), 578; *Arcades Project*, 463.

6. On *dialectic*, which in Benjamin's writing is, as several commentators have

noticed, far from simply identical with the conventional Hegelian understanding of this term as *reconciliation* or *synthesis*, see Samuel Weber, "Genealogy of Modernity: History, Myth and Allegory in Benjamin's *Origin of the German Mourning Play*," *MLN* 106, no. 3 (April 1991): 467–68; and my *Writing in Parts: Imitation and Exchange in Nineteenth-Century Literature* (Stanford, Calif.: Stanford University Press, 1995), 4 and 124–37. Paul de Man makes a similar observation about Benjamin's use of the term *messianic* in an exchange with Dominick LaCapra that appears after de Man's essay, "Conclusions: Walter Benjamin's 'The Task of the Translator,'" 103. It should be noted that throughout Benjamin's work, there is something of a repeated attempt to smuggle in his divergent views under the cover of official critical discourse. An example of this is offered by his doctoral dissertation, *The Concept of Criticism in German Romanticism* (published in 1920), about which Benjamin wrote in a letter: "Even though I would never have taken it on without external inducement, my work on the dissertation is not wasted time. What I have been learning from it—that is, insight into the relationship of a truth to history—will of course hardly be at all explicit in the dissertation, but I hope it will be discerned by astute readers" (Benjamin, *The Correspondence of Walter Benjamin*, trans. Manfred R. Jacobson and Evelyn M. Jacobson [Chicago: University of Chicago Press, 1994], 135–36).

7. Important examples here, especially for Benjamin, were Heinrich Rickert (Benjamin's teacher in Freiburg) and Hermann Cohen. See, for example, Rickert's *Kulturwissenschaft und Naturwissenschaft* (Tübingen: Mohr, 1921), originally published as a lecture in 1899; Hermann Cohen, *Platonsideenlehre und die Mathematik* (Marburg: Universität Marburg, 1878); and Hermann Cohen, *Das Prinzip der Infinitesimal-Methode und seine Geschichte* (Berlin: Dummler, 1883).

8. J. L. Frisch, for example, in his 1741 *Teutsch-lateinisches Wörterbuch*, gives *valor* as the Latin equivalent of *Gehalt*. The Grimms' dictionary registers the emergence, in the late eighteenth century, of the application of the term to aesthetics. Under the following general signification of *Gehalt*: "gehalt von münzen . . . was sie an reinen silber, gold, an wirlichen wert in sich helten, enthalten," the Grimms note the extension of this meaning of *Gehalt* to aesthetics with Schiller, and in particular with the 1781 preface to *The Robbers* and the phrase "ein gewisser Gehalt von Geisteskraft" [a certain amount of spiritual power] necessary, according to Schiller, for the adequate reception of the play (*Die Räuber, Schillers Werke*, vol. 3 [Weimar: Hermann Böhlhaus Nachfolger, 1953], 7); an English translation of the passage can be found in Schiller, *Works* (Boston: Household, 1884), 2:136. A useful historical survey of the word *Gehalt* can be found in the *Historisches Wörterbuch der Philosophie*, vol. 3, ed. Joachim Ritter (Basel: Schwabe and Co. Verlag, 1974), 139–45.

9. Lukács identifies what he calls the "priority of content (*Gehalt*)" in Hegel's understanding of the "dialectical interaction of form and content" [*dialektische Wechselwirkung [zwischen] Gehalt und Form*]. Georg Lukács, "Hegels Ästhetik," in Georg Wilhelm Friedrich Hegel, *Ästhetik*, vol. 2, ed. Friedrich Bassenge (Berlin: Verlag das Europäische Buch, 1985), 620.

10. Ibid., 599.

11. This is the point of view, for example, from which Hegel in the *Phenomenology* philosophically cites Diderot's *Rameau's Nephew*, repeating while subjecting to conceptual distillation the prephilosophical mime. See my "Losing One's Place: Displacement and Domesticity in Dickens's *Bleak House*," *MLN* 108, no. 4 (December 1993): 881–83.

12. Walter Benjamin, "Die Aufgabe des Übersetzers," *Gesammelte Schriften* 4, no. 1 (Frankfurt am Main: Surhkamp, 1972), 21; Walter Benjamin, "The Task of the Translator," trans. Harry Zohn, *Selected Writings*, 1:263. Zohn translates "virtuelle" as "potential."

13. On what might be called the substance-based ontology of Hegel's epistemology—that dialectical "sublation" [*Aufhebung*] extends the substance metaphor to the realm of "rationality," or *Geist*, and ultimately requires Hegel to deny the existence of the "irrational" in nature—see Emile Meyerson, *L'explication dans les sciences* (Paris: Payot, 1921). While Hegel rejects and mocks the scientific tendency to "explain change by denying it, by affirming the identity of things through time," as Meyerson notes (656), the empirical facts of nature are viewed by him as including a measure of "scoria" that must be subject to "purification" by experimental science so that what exists in them—what in them is identical with reason (*Geist*)—can be separated by philosophy from what does not exist—what is not identical with reason (399–400, 481). Thus what Meyerson calls Hegel's "play on words" (144, n. 2 and 399) in the term *aufheben* (to conserve and to abolish) in fact describes a process whereby the substance of *Geist* is separated from the scoria of what is not-*Geist* (Meyerson's general argument here is that Hegel "only allows within his 'science' for a unique irrational, the *Andersein*, while declaring it by the way *rational*, while our science [one that does not postulate the identity of reason and nature] recognizes a whole series of them" [400]).

14. Benjamin, "Aufgabe des Übersetzers," 15; "Task of the Translator," 258.

15. Benjamin, "Aufgabe des Übersetzers," 14; Benjamin, "Task of the Translator," 257.

16. See Benjamin's comments on Baudelaire's "A une passante" in Walter Benjamin, *Charles Baudelaire. Ein Lyriker im Zeitalter des Hochkapitalismus* (Frankfurt am Main: Suhrkamp, 1974), 119; Benjamin, "On Some Motifs in Baudelaire," in *Illuminations*, 168–69; and Benjamin, *Illuminations*, 168–69.

17. "Criticizability," "reproducibility," and "readability" are the subjects of, respectively, Walter Benjamin, *Der Begriff der Kunstkritik in der deutschen Romantik* (Frankfurt am Main: Suhrkamp, 1973), 73–74 (Benjamin, *Selected Writings*, 1:159–60); Benjamin, "Das Kunstwerk im Zeit seiner Reproduzierbarkeit," in *Das Kunstwerk im Zeitalter seiner technischen Reproduzierbarkeit. Drei Studien zur Kunstsoziologie* (Frankfurt am Main: Suhrkamp, 1977), 17–18 (Benjamin, *Illuminations*, 224); and Benjamin, *Passagen-Werk*, 1:577 (*Arcades Project*, 462). To this list could also be added "citability" (in the Brecht essay) and "communicability" (in the early essay on language).

18. Walter Benjamin, "Zur Aesthetik," in *Gesammelte Schriften* (Frankfurt am Main: Suhrkamp, 1985), 6:109–29.

19. Ibid., 125.

20. In his study of German Romantic aesthetic theory, Benjamin describes the German Romantics' interest in this potential of literary works as their possible appearance in a critical reading or reflection. In this sense works become, he says, "centers of reflection. See Walter Benajamin, *Der Begriff der Kunstkritik in der deutschen Romantik* (Frankfurt am Main: Suhrkamp, 1973), 67.

21. On the divisibility of matter, see Immanuel Kant, *Metaphysicae cum geometria iunctae usus in philosophia naturali, cuius specimen I. contient monadologiam physicam, Werke in Zehn Bänden* (Darmstadt: Wissenschaftliche Buchgesellschaft, 1983), 1:534–39. For an account of Kant's debts to Leibniz with regard to the theory of the infinite divisibility of matter, see Mary B. Hesse, *Forces and Fields: The Concept of Action at a Distance in the History of Physics* (New York: Philosophical Library, 1961), esp. 175. On Hegel's relationship to natural science, see Meyerson, *L'explication dans les sciences*, 457–68.

22. This is one way of reading Benjamin's statement in another of the early fragments that "the medium through which works of art operate on later times is always different from the one through which they operated on their time" (Benjamin, "Zur Ästhetik," 126). This is also what Benjamin seems to be pointing to when, in yet another early fragment, he speaks of "the latent operation of myth" [*das latente Wirken des Mythos*]—of the ancient Greek "mythological motifs" memorialized in Homeric poetry or of the Christian "mythological motifs" functioning latently in the beautiful form of German *Plays of Mourning* (Benjamin, "Zur Ästhetik," 128).

23. Leibniz seems behind such statements as the following from "The Task of the Translator":

> One might, for example, speak of an unforgettable life or moment even if all men had forgotten it. If the nature of such a life or moment required that it be forgotten, that predicate would imply not a falsehood but merely a claim unfulfilled by men, and probably also a reference to a realm in which it *is* fulfilled: God's remembrance. Analogously, the translatability of linguistic creations [*Gebilde*] ought to be considered even if men should prove unable to translate them. ("Die Aufgabe des Übersetzers," 10; "The Task of the Translator," 254)

Compare this to the following passage from Leibniz on virtuality: "Now it is evident that all the predication has some basis in the nature of things and that, when a proposition is not an entity, that is, when the predicate is not explicitly contained in the subject, it must be contained in it virtually [*virtuellement*]," *Discours de métaphysique, Die Philosophische Schriften von Gottfried Wilhelm Leibniz*, vol. 4, ed. Gerhardt (Berlin: n.p., 1875–1890), 433; *Discourse on Metaphysics, Philosophical Essays*, trans. Roger Arien and Daniel Garber (Indianapolis, Ind.: Hackett, 1989), 41. Other discussions of virtuality (*virtualité, virtualism, virtuel*) in Leibniz can be found, for example, in a letter in

French to Burnet (1707) (*Philosophische Schriften*, 3:315), in an untitled Latin fragment from 1679 on proof (*Philosophische Schriften*, 7:300) and in sections 40, 43, and 54 in the *Monadology*. A gloss on Leibniz by Emile Meyerson is illuminating here: "God alone knows these truths a priori and sees reason in them, which is always the inclusion of the predicate in the subject, while human reason is obliged to be satisfied with an imperfect knowledge which comes by way of experience. In this case the proposition is only virtually identical" (Emile Meyerson, *Du Cheminement de la pensée* (Paris: Félix Alcan, 1931), 1:267. On virtuality and infinite divisibility, see Léon Brunschvicg, *Les Étapes de la philosophie mathématique* (Paris: Félix Alcan, 1912), 201–4. For a perceptive critical assessment of Leibniz (contemporary with Benjamin's *Trauerspiel* study) in the context of the German baroque and in German academic philosophy in the nineteenth and early twentieth centuries, see Hermann Schmalenbach, *Leibniz* (Munich: Drei Masken Verlag, 1921), 10–18. On the baroque of special interest is Schmalenbach's comments on continuity as "task" [*Aufgabe*] in Leibniz (462–65); this is to be compared with Benjamin's characterization of the continuity or conservation effected by translation as a "task" [*Aufgabe*]. It should also be mentioned here that, although the editors of the *Selected Writings* have assigned little (perhaps insufficient) importance (see 1:502), Benjamin's professor and dissertation advisor, Richard Herbertz, published a study dealing with what we here might call the virtuality of unconscious ideas in Leibniz. Herbertz's discussion of Leibniz's theory of *petites perceptions* — perceptions divisible into infinitely small parts not registrable immediately to consciousness — would be worth comparing to Benjamin's own reflections on similar perceptions in his work on Baudelaire (see, for example, Richard Herbertz, *Die Lehre vom Unbewußten im System des Leibniz* [Halle: Max Niemeyer, 1905], 47–51).

24. The note to Russell, written in connection with the essay "On Language as Such and on the Language of Man," can be found in Benjamin, *Gesammelte Schriften*, 6:9–15; the influence of Bergson is probably most evident in "On Some Motifs in Baudelaire" (see, for example, Benjamin, *Illuminations*, 157–60); the quotation from Eddington appears in *Illuminations*, 141–42.

25. I have elaborated more extensively on this natural-philosophical aspect of Benjamin's aesthetics, in particular in relation to the preface to his study of the German *Trauerspiel*, in my "The Coming of Paper: Aesthetic Value from Ruskin to Benjamin," *MLN* 114, no. 4 (December 1999): 975–77.

26. "The representation of an idea can under no circumstances be considered successful unless the whole range of possible extremes it contains has been virtually explored [*virtuell … abgeschritten*]. The exploration [*Abschreiten*] remains virtual [*virtuell*]" (Benjamin, *Ursprung des deutschen Trauerspiels* [Frankfurt am Main: Suhrkamp, 1974], 29; *The Origin of German Tragic Drama*, trans. John Osborne [London: Verso, 1985], 47).

27. Benjamin, "Goethes Wahlverwandtschaften," in *Gesammelte Schriften* (Frankfurt am Main: Suhrkamp, 1974), 1:172–73; Benjamin, "Goethe's Elective Affinities," in *Selected Writings*, 1:334.

28. Ibid., 173; 334.

29. Although we cannot do so here it would be worth comparing the significance of the German *Ort* here to Heidegger's discussion of *Ort* and *Medium* in *Einführung in die Metaphysik*. With reference to Plato's *Timaeus* 50e, Heidegger says, for instance, "Das, worin etwas wird, meint jenes, was wir 'Raum' nennen. Die Griechen haben kein Wort für 'Raum.' Das is kein Zufall; denn sie erfahren das Räumliche nicht von der extensio her, sondern aus dem Ort [*topos*] als *chora*, was weder Ort noch Raum bedeutet, was aber durch das Dastehende eingenommen, besetzt wird" (Martin Heidegger, *Einführung in die Metaphysik* [Tübingen: Max Niemeyer, 1953], 50). For elaborations that would be highly suggestive for a comparison of Benjamin and Heidegger on this point, see Jacques Derrida, *Khôra* (Paris: Galilée, 1993), 15–38.

30. Benjamin, "Über Sprache Überhaupt und Über die Sprache des Menschens," in *Gesammelte Schriften* (Frankfurt am Main: Suhrkamp, 1974), 2.1:153; Benjamin, "On Language as Such and on the Language of Man," in *Selected Writings*, 1:71.

31. Benjamin, "Goethes Wahlverwandtschaften," 200, 146; Benjamin, "Goethe's Elective Affinities," 355, 313.

32. See Quintilian, *Institutio oratoria*, XI.ii.17–22; and Frances Yates, *The Art of Memory* (London: Routledge, 1966), 21–26.

33. Benjamin, *Passagen-Werk*, 1:576; *Arcades Project*, 462.

34. Ibid.

35. Ibid., 1:650; 522. See also 1:1007–8; 840.

36. Benjamin, "Über Sprache," 142; "On Language," 63.

37. Ibid., 153; 71.

38. Ibid., 154; 72. I am borrowing the translation of *Geschwätz* as "chatter" from Peter Fenves's highly illuminating study of this term, *"Chatter": Language and History in Kierkegaard* (Stanford, Calif.: Stanford University Press, 1993).

39. These manipulations are variations on themes from Kant's natural-philosophy and aesthetics, especially on the link between "divisibility" and "judgment." See, for example, *Versuch, den negativen Größen in die Weltweisheit einzuführen, Werke*, 2:779–81; and *Metaphysische Anfangsgründe der Naturwissenschaft, Werke*, 8:47–62.

40. See, for example, Benjamin, *Passagen-Werk*, 2:54–56, 69–72, 993, 1041, 1044; *Arcades Project*, 10–11, 21–23, 827, 871, 873.

41. Ibid., 1:54; 10.

42. Ibid., 1:643; 516.

43. See Benjamin's remarks on theatricality in "Was ist das epische Theater?" in *Gesammelte Schriften*, 2.2:534–36; Benjamin, "What is Epic Theater?" in *Illuminations*, 150–51; and Benjamin, "Franz Kafka. Zur zehnten Wiederkehr seines Todestages," in *Gesammelte Schriften*, 2.1:418–21; and Benjamin, "Franz Kafka: On the Tenth Anniversary of His Death," in *Illuminations*, 121–23.

44. "Like the pictures [*Bilder*] in a film, epic theater moves in spurts" (Benjamin, "Was ist das epische Theater?" 537; "What is Epic Theater?" 153). To compare with the comments on the actor in this essay would be similar remarks in Benjamin, "Das

Kunstwerk im Zeitalter seiner Reproduzierbarkeit," *Das Kunstwerk im Zeitalter seiner Reproduzierbarkeit. Drei Studien zu Kunstsoziologie* (Frankfurt am Main: Suhrkamp, 1977), 24–27; Benjamin, "The Work of Art in an Age of Mechanical Reproduction," in *Illuminations*, 229–30. And Benjamin, *Passagen-Werk*, 1:135; *Arcades Project*, 83.

45. Benjamin, "Das Kunstwerk im Zeitalter seiner Reproduzierbarkeit," 36; Benjamin, "The Work of Art in an Age of Mechanical Reproduction," 237.

46. Edgar Allan Poe, "The Man of the Crowd," *Tales of Mystery and Imagination* (London: J. M. Dent, 1993), 114–15.

47. Benjamin, *Passagen-Werk*, 1:647; *Arcades Project*, 519.

48. On the related German word *streuen* (the root of *Zerstreuung*, which is also central to Benjamin's analysis of film), and on its significance in Benjamin and in Heidegger, see Samuel Weber, *Mass Mediauras: Form, Technics, Media* (Stanford, Calif.: Stanford University Press, 1996), 92–93.

49. Kant, "Das Ende aller Dinge," in *Werke*, 9:183.

50. That the word *passage* may be divided into meaning "imprudence" and "wise step" is invited by the following comment by Benjamin: "Gamut [*Tonleiter*] in the word passage" (Benjamin, *Passagen-Werk*, 2:1007; *Arcades Project*, 801). Benjamin may be thinking of the punning of such titles as Breton's 1924 collection of essays, *Les Pas perdus*, or Robert de Montesquieu's memoirs, published in 1923 under the title of *Les Pas éffacés*.

51. Neil Gerschenfeld, *When Things Start to Think* (New York: Henry Holt, 1999), 50–52.

52. Benjamin, *Passagen-Werk*, 2:962; *Arcades Project*, 801.

53. Ibid., 1:587–88; 470. For another example of this stress on divisibility in Benjamin's reflections on his method of "culture-historical dialectic," see ibid., 1:573; 459.

54. The reference here may be to the discussion of tangents in the conic theory of Apollonius of Perga. See Apollonius of Perga, *Treatise on the Conic Sections*, ed. T. L. Heath (Cambridge: Cambridge University Press, 1896), 22–30. "A straight line drawn through the extremity of the diameter of any conic parallel to the ordinates of that diameter . . . will touch the conic, and no other straight line can fall between it and the conic." Yet "the straight line drawn in the manner described will fall without the conic" (22). The tangent would be the point at which the conic cuts "into" the line and the line "into" the conic; but the "cut into" in this case would "fall without." On Apollonius, see G. J. Toomer, "Apollonius of Perga," *Dictionary of Scientific Biography* (New York: Charles Scribner's Sons, 1970), 1:179–93. This reference to conic sections recalls Henri Bergson's use of these figures in the chapter of *Matter and Memory* devoted to "the survival of images." This discussion is preceded by some remarks on "virtual objects." See Henri Bergson, *Matter and Memory*, trans. W. Scott Palmer (New York: Zone Books, 1988), 129–30, 152–62. See also Gilles Deleuze, *Bergsonism* (New York: Zone Books, 1988), 56–61.

55. Benjamin, *Passagen-Werk*, 1:647; *Arcades Project*, 521–22.

56. Ibid., 1:644, 649; 517, 521.

57. Ibid., 1:649; 521.

58. Ibid., 2:1008; 840.

59. Ibid., 1:534; 423.

60. Ibid., 1:645–46; 518.

61. Ibid., 1:595; 475.

62. See Alfredo Fierro, *Vie et histoire du XIXe arrondissement* (Paris: Editions Hervas, 1987), 33–35, 140.

63. *Stadt* derives from the root for *Ort* and *Stätte*. See Friedrich Kluge, "Stadt," *Etymologisches Wörterbuch der deutschen Sprache*, 22d ed. (Berlin: Walter de Gruyter, 1989); "rue," according to Littré, is from the Latin *ruga*, meaning "ride, au sens du sillon."

64. Benjamin, "Haschisch in Marseille," in *Illuminationen. Ausgewählte Schriften*, 325.

65. See Ernst Robert Curtius, *European Literature in the Latin Middle Ages*, trans. Willard R. Trask (Princeton, N.J.: Princeton University Press, 1953); and Georges Dumézil, *Mythe et épopée, I, L'idéologie des trois fonctions dans les épopées indo-européens* (Paris: Gallimard, 1968).

66. Hubert Damisch, *The Judgment of Paris*, trans. John Goodman (Chicago: University of Chicago Press, 1996), 187–88.

67. Karl Reinhardt, *Das Parisurteil* (Frankfurt am Main: Vittorio Klostermann, 1938), 21.

68. Charles Baudelaire, "Le Cygne," in his *Les Fleurs du mal* (Paris: Garnier, 1961), 95; Virgil, *Aeneid*, trans. Robert Fitzgerald (New York: Vintage, 1990), VII.1034–47. On this scene, see Adam Parry's classic essay, "The Two Voices of Virgil's *Aeneid*," in *Virgil: A Collection of Critical Essays*, ed. Steele Commager (Englewood Cliffs, N.J.: Prentice Hall, 1966), 107–23. On Hector as a man of *aidos* (responsibility and honor), see J. M. Redfield, *Nature and Culture in the Iliad: The Tragedy of Hector* (Chicago: University of Chicago Press, 1975), 118.

69. Benjamin, "Über den Begriff," 254; Benjamin, "Theses on the Philosophy of History," 256. The quotation is from Gustave Flaubert, *Correspondence—1860* (Paris: L. Conard, 1926–54), 348. It is noteworthy that Flaubert's letter was to his friend Ernest Feydeau, the author of a book on Algiers, written in 1860, the year of the annexation of the Place du Maroc as part of Paris's new arrondissements. Feydeau's book focuses on the city of Algiers as being at the intersection between culture and barbarism, which interested Benjamin. See, for instance, the final chapter that proceeds from a discussion of urban renewal (specifically, the dangers of trying to make Algiers "une cité européene") to a denunciation of the colonialist sentiment Feydeau sums up with the phrase "malheur aux vaincus!" Ernest Feydeau, *Alger* (Paris: Michel Lévy Frères, 1862), 269–80.

70. This, simply put, is Redfield's interpretation of the *Iliad* as tragedy (see 109–10, for example).

71. Guillory, *Cultural Capital*, 55.

72. Ibid., 340.

73. "The advantage of a sociological analysis of [aesthetic] discourse is its capacity to map the social field, and so to map the necessary conditions for such a discourse" (ibid., 327–28).

74. "Barbarism lurks [*steckt*] in the very concept of culture," Benjamin notes at one point in the *Arcades Project*—"the concept of a fund of values which is considered independent not, indeed, of the production process in which these values originated, but of the one in which they survive" (*Passagen-Werk*, 1:584; *Arcades Project*, 467).

75. Benjamin, "Über den Begriff," 254; "Theses on the Philosophy of History," 256 (trans. mod.). The "distance" here may be understood in Kant's terms between "pity" [*Mitleid*] and "participation" [*Teilnehmung*] in his *Grounding for Metaphysics of Morals*. See Immanuel Kant, *Grundlegung zur Metaphysik der Sitten, Gesammelte Schriften* (Berlin: Walter de Gruyter, 1900), 6:455–56; *Doctrine of Virtue*, trans. Mary J. Gregor (Philadelphia: University of Pennsylvania Press, 1964), 125–26. On this distinction, see Peter Fenves, *A Peculiar Fate: Metaphysics and World-History in Kant* (Ithaca, N.Y.: Cornell University Press, 1991), 263–67.

CHAPTER 11

1. [Translator's note: References to Benjamin's text follow the standard German edition, Walter Benjamin, *Gesammelte Schriften*, ed. Rolf Tiedemann and Hermann Schweppenhäuser, 7 vols. (Frankfurt am Main: Suhrkamp, 1977–1989). They are given by volume and page number. References to his letter follow the German edition *Briefe*, ed. Theodor W. Adorno and Gershom Scholem (Frankfurt am Main: Suhrkamp, 1966); they are indicated in the text by the abbreviation *B*, followed by the page number. All translations are mine.—G. R.]

CHAPTER 12

1. Ulrich von Wilamowitz-Moellendorff, *Einleitung in die griechische Tragödie* (Berlin: Weidemann, 1907), 95. Wilamowitz was fond of comparing the tragedians to the prophets; see, for example, *Griechische Tragöedien*, trans. U. V. Wilamowitz-Moellendorff, 4th ed. (Berlin: Weidemann, 1904), 2:47. It is worth noting that Wilamowitz's analogy seems to have had little influence on either biblical or classical studies. In an otherwise fine collection of essays on the relation of Greek poetry to Hebrew prophecy, none of the Greek tragedians is even mentioned, much less discussed; see James Kugel, ed., *Poetry and Prophecy* (Ithaca, N.Y.: Cornell University Press, 1990).

2. Walter Benjamin, *Gesammelte Briefe*, ed. Christoph Gödde and Henri Lonitz (Frankfurt am Main: Suhrkamp, 1995–), 3:15. In a previous letter to Salomon-Dela-

tour Benjamin describes his theory of tragedy as "a crux" — one, however, that he will not be able to avoid entirely.

3. Ibid., 2:300.

4. See Benjamin's remark to Florens Christian Rang, who, as Benjamin admits, is almost the coauthor of the theory of tragedy that he proposes in the *Trauerspiel* book; see Benjamin, *Gesammelte Briefe*, 2:416.

5. See Franz Rosenzweig, *Der Stern der Erlösung* (1921; rpt. Frankfurt am Main: Suhrkamp, 1988), 67–90.

6. Walter Benjamin, *Gesammelte Schriften*, ed. R. Tiedemann and H. Schweppenhäuser, 7 vols. (Frankfurt am Main: Suhrkamp, 1977–1985), 1:287–88. All other references to these volumes are in the text; all translations are my own.

7. Benjamin, *Gesammelte Briefe*, 3:14.

8. Jeffrey Mehlman, *Walter Benjamin for Children* (Chicago: University of Chicago Press, 1993), 1–2.

9. See Benjamin, *The Origin of German Tragic Drama*, trans. John Osborne (New York: Verso, 1985).

10. Nowhere in the *Origin of the German Mourning Play* does Benjamin engage in any exposition of what he means by "Prophetie" (which should sometimes be translated as prophetism or prophetic tradition, rather than the ambiguous term prophecy), and his correspondence does not give the impression that he ever undertook a comprehensive study of the concept of the prophet (*nabi*) as it develops in the Hebrew Bible. Nor does it appear that he had anything but a passing acquaintance with the kind of reflections that led a theologian like Leo Baeck — to mention only one instance of this trend — to present Judaism's prophetic tradition as "tragic" by virtue of its defiant "optimism": "Moral and tragic pathos here becomes one. The Bible is a world of this fortifying and optimistic tragedy, and by experiencing its truth Judaism grasped the meaning of the prophets and their successors" (Leo Baeck, *Das Wesen des Judentums* [Berlin: Hüpeden & Merzyn, 1905]; *The Essence of Judaism*, trans. I. Howe, V. Grubenwieser and L. Pearl [New York: Schocken, 1948], esp. 86). Nor even does Benjamin stake out a position with respect to various proposals for a "renewal of prophetic Judaism," including the one proposed by the young Martin Buber: "The self-affirmation of the Jew has its tragic aspects as well as its grandeur. . . . And to live as a Jew means to absorb this tragic aspect as well as the grandeur of self-affirmation" (*Drei Reden über das Judentum* [Frankfurt am Main: Rütten & Loening, 1911]; *On Judaism*, ed. N. Glazer, trans. E. Jospe [New York: Schocken, 1967], 21). Even though his exposition of tragedy relies upon the formula "preliminary stage of prophecy," Benjamin shows little interest in such matters as the much-debated question concerning the significance of the prophetic tradition in Judaism, the contentious problem of the historical end to this tradition (which gave certain anti-Semitic polemicists the opportunity to accuse postprophetic Jewry of having lost its former "creativity"), or the idiosyncratic suggestions that the prophetic tradition can somehow be renewed; on these matters see also note 32 below.

One of those who understood his work in part as a preparation for a renewed reception of the gift of prophecy did, however, attract Benjamin's attention during the time he wrote the *Trauerspiel* book, even as his presence physically repulsed him: Oskar Goldberg, who could not be further removed from Leo Baeck in the wide spectrum of early twentieth-century Jewish thought (see, for example, Benjamin's comments in *Gesammelte Briefe*, 3:111). Although Goldberg favored the prescriptive rites of the Books of the Torah over the "moralizing tendency" of the prophetic books, he nevertheless expected to receive the *ruah hakodesh* (holy spirit or breath) once again, just as Buber—from an entirely different direction—conceived of his activity in terms of a "renewal of Judaism." For an extensive inquiry into Goldberg, see Manfred Voigts, *Oskar Goldberg* (Berlin: Agora, 1992); see also the brief but spirited remarks of Jacob Taubes, "From Cult to Culture," *Partisan Review* 21 (1954): 387–400; for Benjamin's interest in the Goldberg circle, see the account of Gershom Scholem, *Walter Benjamin: The Story of a Friendship*, trans. H. Zohn (New York: Schocken, 1981), 95–98. Although it would have made sense to only a very few, if any, Benjamin's talk of a "preliminary stage of prophecy" may implicitly refer to the work of Goldberg, even as it seeks to determine the distinctive character of Attic tragedy.

11. See Johannes Volkelt, *Ästhetik des Tragischen*, 3d ed. (Munich: Beck, 1917).

12. Benjamin generally presents the work of Wilamowitz under the allegorical title of "philology" (perhaps because, as the case of Kurt Hildebrandt attests, Wilamowitz was still involved in university affairs; see Benjamin, *Gesammelte Schriften*, 2:441–42). According to Wilamowitz, Attic tragedy is defined by its relation to, and transformation of, Homeric legend. This fundamental trait of tragedy "distinguishes it from all other dramatic poetry that has hitherto emerged and, most likely, will ever do so" (Wilamowitz, *Einleitung*, 119). Benjamin makes use of this trait but makes no allowances for probability. Once "philology" has secured its results, they can be presented from the perspective of what he calls "Geschichtsphilosophie."

13. Friedrich Nietzsche, *Die Geburt der Tragödie*, in *Sämtliche Werke*, ed. Giorgio Colli and Mazzino Montinari (Berlin: Walter de Gruyter, 1967–1977), 1:67. Of the many peculiarities of this sentence, at least three should be mentioned: (1) the impossibility of deciding on the nature of a *gleichnisartiges Bild* as long as every *Bild* (image, picture) is understood to be *gleichnisartig* (in the nature of a likeness, parable-like); (2) the removal of quotation marks around the term *ahnen* (intimate). Only a few pages before Nietzsche had ridiculed another, specifically political use of this latter term: "With reference to the classical form of the chorus as we know it from Aeschylus and Sophocles, we would also consider it blasphemous to speak of an intimation of a 'constitutional representation of the people' [*Ahnung einer 'constitutionellen Volksvertretung'*], a blasphemy from which others have not shrunk. The ancient constitution of the state *in praxi* knew nothing about a constitutional representation of the people, and it is to hoped that they have not 'intimated' [*'geahnt'*] it in their tragedy" (*Sämtliche Werke*, 1:52–53). At stake in this "intimations" is the question:

Who is the "proper" heir to tragedy? Who learns to speak its own language from its infantilism? And (3) the passage from Goethe's *Prometheus* also figures prominently in Schopenhauer's *Welt als Wille und Vorstellung* (World as will and representation), but far from indicating anything about the intimate relation between Germans and Greeks, it designates a "standpoint" that can also be found in the *Bhagavad Gita*, Bruno, and Spinoza (Schopenhauer, *Die Welt als Wille und Vorstellung*, § 54; *Werke in fünf Bänden*, ed. Ludger Lütkehaus [Zürich: Haffmanns-Verlag, 1988], 1:373. The passage in which Schopenhauer discusses the "standpoint" designated by Goethe's *Prometheus* is of particular importance in any assessment of the relation of young Nietzsche to Schopenhauer, because this is the passage in which he first articulates the "standpoint" of the "affirmation of the will to life," precisely the point, according to Nietzsche, on which Greek tragedy stands or falls. And, of course, Goethe's *Prometheus* also figures prominently in the so-called *Pantheismusstreit* of the 1780s in which the relation of *Judentum*, represented by both Spinoza (the heretic) and Moses Mendelssohn (the defender of the faith), to *Deutschtum*, represented by Lessing (the heretic) and Jacobi (the defender of the faith), first enters philosophical discourse.

14. See Nietzsche, *Ecce Homo*, in *Sämtliche Werke*, 6:310.

15. Nietzsche continues, "And between these two myths there exists an affinity like that between brother and sister" (*Sämtliche Werke*, 1:68–69), that is, between active and passive, public heroism and private cunning.

16. Leopold Ziegler, *Zur Metaphysik des Tragischen. Eine philosophische Studie* (Leipzig: Dürr, n.d.), vii.

17. Ibid., vii.

18. Ibid., viii.

19. Ibid., 81–82.

20. Ibid., 102.

21. This term has been recently revived by Jacques Derrida as, for instance, in *Specters of Marx*, trans. Peggy Kamuf (New York: Routledge, 1994), 167–69. Benjamin was not unaware of this concept, although in the *Trauerspiel* book he presents it only in its Greek translation, perhaps as a homage to Florens *Christian* Rang, namely *Christlichkeit*; see Peter Fenves, "Marx, Mourning, Messianicity," in *Identity, Violence, and Self-Determination*, ed. Samuel Weber and Hent de Vries (Stanford: Stanford University Press, 1997), 253–70.

22. This is Benjamin's term for his earlier procedure. See his letter to Hugo von Hofmannsthal where he insists that he will no longer treat "Schicksal" (fate) in the same manner as he had done in his essay on Goethe's *Wahlverwandtschaften* and, one may assume, in "Schicksal und Charakter" (Benjamin, *Gesammelte Briefe*, 2:410).

23. Ibid., 2:371.

24. Ibid., 2:368.

25. See Florens Christian Rang, *Deutsche Bauhütte. Ein Wort an uns Deutsche über mögliche Gerechtigkeit gegen Belgien und Frankreich und zur Philosophie der Politik* (Leip-

zig: Eberhard Arnold, 1924). In addition to Benjamin's short letter (reprinted in Benjamin, *Gesammelte Schriften*, 4:791–92), Rang's book has addenda from Martin Buber, Ernst Michel, and Karl Hildebrandt among others.

26. Benjamin, *Gesammelte Briefe*, 3:16.

27. See especially Benjamin's essay, "Die Jugend schweigt" (*Gesammelte Briefe*, 2:66–7).

28. See Hermann Cohen, *Religion der Vernunft aus den Quellen des Judentums* (Leipzig: Fock, 1919); *Religion of Reason Out of the Sources of Judaism*, trans. Simon Kaplan, 2d ed. (Atlanta: Scholars Press, 1995), 165–77, chap. 10, "Das Individuum und das Ich." This chapter of Cohen's *Religion* corresponds to the section of Rosenzweig's *Star of Redemption* devoted to the "meta-ethical," and in both cases the "origin" of the self — or the individual — is understood in terms of Greek tragedy. This is hardly surprising. Even if neither Cohen nor Rosenzweig mention neither Schopenhauer nor Nietzsche, the basic scenario by which the latter philosophers recount the emergence of tragedy dovetails with the former two philosophers' account for the birth of the self: individuation. For Schopenhauer, it is a "sin"; for Cohen, an advance beyond paganism and pantheism to "religion"; for the young Nietzsche, an eternal game of disappearing appearances; and for Rosenzweig, a propaedeutic for any philosophy that seeks to come to terms with the ineluctable distinction among the three points of the star of redemption: world, human being, and God.

29. See the strange autobiographical text of Benjamin that famously Scholem analyzes in terms of its Kabbalistic intentions, "Agesileus Santander," in Gershom Scholem, *Walter Benjamin und sein Engel* (Frankfurt am Main: Suhrkamp, 1992), 40–43; see also the remarks of Giorgio Agamben, "Walter Benjamin and the Demonic: Happiness and Historical Redemption," in *Potentialities*, ed. and trans. Daniel Heller-Roazen (Stanford: Stanford University Press, 1999), 138–59.

30. For Benjamin's notes to this midrash, see *Gesammelte Schriften*, 1:923–94.

31. See, especially, *Gesammelte Schriften*, 1:288–89. Benjamin's discussion of tragedy in the *Trauerspiel* book is peculiar in at least one other respect: although "Schicksal und Charakter" was written before Benjamin could have had any familiarity with Rosenzweig's *Stern der Erlösung*, the two works are surprisingly similar in their description of tragedy as a decisive stage of *pagan man*. Although these two works are not interchangeable, Benjamin leaves the impression that the presentation of tragic "infantilism" in his own essay is largely the same as Rosenzweig's exposition of tragic silence. For an incisive investigation into the relation between Benjamin and Rosenzweig, see Stéphane Mosès, *L'Ange de l'histoire: Rosenzweig, Benjamin, Scholem* (Paris: Editions du Seuil, 1992).

32. A canonical account of the end of the prophecy can be found in the Talmudic treatise *Sanhedrin*:

> Our Rabbis taught: Since the death of the last prophets, Haggai, Zechariah and Malachai, the Holy Spirit [of prophetic inspiration] departed from Israel; yet

they were still able to avail themselves of the Bath-kol {daughter of the voice}. Once when the Rabbis were met in the upper chamber of Gurya's house at Jericho, a Bath-kol was heard from Heaven, saying: "There is one amongst you who is worthy that the Shechinah {the divine presence} should rest on him as it did on Moses, but his generation does not merit it." The Sages present set their eyes on Hillel the Elder. And when he died, they lamented and said: "Alas, the pious man, the humble man, the disciple of Ezra [is no more]." (*Sanhedrin*, 11a13–15; small brackets are included in the text of the English edition of the Talmud published by the Soncino Press; large brackets are my own; see also 1 Macc 4:46 and 14:41)

For a consistently insightful inquiry into the complicated question of the end of the prophetic tradition, see Benjamin Sommer, "Did Prophecy Cease? Evaluating a Reevaluation," *JBL* 115 (1996): 31–47. Sommer quotes a passage from *Tanhuma Beha'alotka* 6 concerning this matter: "When the temple was destroyed . . . five things were hidden away: the ark, the menorah, the fire, the holy spirit [*ruah hakodesh*], and the cherubim. And when the Holy One, blessed be He, rouses Himself in His mercy and rebuilds His temple, he will return them to their place" (36).

33. See, for example, the compilation of Jean-Pierre Vernant and Pierre Vidal-Naquet's writings published under the title, *Myth and Tragedy in Ancient Greece*, trans. Janet Lloyd (New York: Zone, 1990), esp. "Intimations of the Will in Greek Tragedy," 49–84.

34. Rang's notes on tragedy are reprinted in Benjamin, *Gesammelte Briefe*, 2:425–27.

35. See Florens Christian Rang, *Historische Psychologie des Karnevals*, 2d ed. (Berlin: Brinckmann & Bose), 1983.

36. Both Rang and Benjamin draw heavily from Jacob Burckhardt, *Griechische Kulturgeschichte*, ed. Jakob Oeri (Berlin & Stuttgart: Spemann, 1898–1902), which, in turn, draws inspiration from Nietzsche's early interest in Greek agonistics.

37. Nietzsche, by contrast, writes, "Not the strength but rather the duration of higher sensation [*hohen Empfindung*] makes the higher human being" (*Sämtliche Werke*, 5:86; *Beyond Good and Evil*, § 72).

38. Not only does the "force of the framework" [*Gewalt der Rahmen*] remove tragedy from fate; it also removes antiquity as a whole from the vicissitudes of fashion. Or at least, such is the supposition Benjamin briefly considers in the *Passagen-Werk*: "Were there fashions in antiquity? Or did the 'force of the framework' preclude them?" (5:115; B 2, 4).

39. Benjamin's proposal finds an echo in the writings of Jan Patočka, especially his *Essais hérétiques sur la philosophie de l'histoire*, trans. Erika Abrams (Lagrasse: Verdier, 1981; Czech ed. Prague, 1975).

40. Benjamin, *Gesammelte Schriften*, 1:297. In one of the most rewarding essays on the *Trauerspiel* book yet published, Samuel Weber has drawn attention to this strange

sentence and proposed a reading of it; see "Genealogy of Modernity: History, Myth, Allegory in Benjamin's *Origin of the German Mourning Play*," *MLN* 106 (1991): 465–500.

41. As Weber indicates in "Genealogy of Modernity," the term *Volksgemeinschaft* was one of the categories most dear to Nazi ideology. In *Passagen-Werk*, Benjamin outlines the relation between the appearance of classless masses and the invention of this ideological category:

> Considered apart from the various classes that join in its formation, the mass as such has no primary social significance. Its secondary significance depends on the set of relations through which it is constituted at any moment. A theater audience, an army, the population of a city comprise masses that in themselves belong to no particular class. The free market multiplies these masses, rapidly and on an immense scale, insofar as each piece of merchandise now gathers around it the mass of its buyers. The totalitarian states have taken this mass as their model. The *Volksgemeinschaft* aims to expel from single individuals everything that stands in the way of their wholesale fusion into a mass of consumers. (5:469; J 81 a, 1)

Hannah Arendt goes one step further in this direction. By indicating the temporal distortion through which the ideological category of *Volksgemeinschaft* functions, she evokes (without any intention of doing so) Benjaimn's theory of tragedy:

> To a certain extent, the *Volksgemeinschaft* was the Nazis' attempt to counter the Communist promise of a classless society. . . . The even greater advantage of the *Volksgemeinschaft* [over the idea of the classless society], however, was that its establishment did not have to wait for some future time and did not depend upon objective conditions: it could be realized immediately in the fictitious world of the movement. (Arendt, *The Origins of Totalitarianism* [New York: Meridian, 1958], 361)

But the word *Volksgemeinschaft* was also used in other contexts, one of which may have had a certain importance for Benjamin's deployment of the term in the *Origin of the German Mourning Play*. Whereas Benjamin explicitly contrasts his concept of origin from that of Hermann Cohen (1:226), he implicitly associates the *Volksgemeinschaft* that learns to speak from the word and silence of the tragic hero with the *Volksgemeinschaft* to which Cohen sometimes refers as he seeks to define the "national" character of the people whose historical mission consists in advancing the idea of monotheism: "I hope to have demonstrated that the religious substance of Jewish monotheism is compatible with a historically conceived Christianity and is sufficient for a *Volksgemeinschaft*" (Cohen, *Jüdische Schriften*, ed. B. Strauß [Berlin: Schwetschke, 1924], 78).

42. As he indicates in the notes, Benjamin is quoting from the first version of Hölderlin's "Patmos" (ll. 144–45), and this alone is enough to indicate the eschatological

character of Benjamin's theory of tragedy. Needless to say, "Patmos" concerns "der Christ," which is to say, translating literally from the Greek, "the messiah."

In another essay, "Abyssal Moods, Art-Destructive Character," I seek to show that the structure of the *Origin of the German Mourning Play* owes its origin to Hölderlin's poetological reflections. The dynamic tension between *Grundstimmung* (basic mood) and *Kunstcharakter* (art character), according to Hölderlin, sets a poem into motion, determines its subsequent *Wechsel der Töne* (alteration of tones), and thus defines the character of its final resolution. Each of the three modes of poetic composition Hölderlin analyzes—lyric, epic, and tragic—corresponds to one of the basic moods: naive, heroic, and ideal, respectively. What does not enter into the system of tonal alterations are, however, the two moods that are, as it were, more basic than the basic ones: joy (*Freude*) and mourning (*Trauer*). Together, they may perhaps be called *Abgrundstimmungen*, "abssyal" (rather than fundamental) moods. Benjamin has the audacity—or, as he writes, the "chutzpah" (*Gesammelte Briefe*, 3:14)—to do what Hölderlin refrained from doing: determine the "art character" that corresponds to the mood of mourning. Such is allegory, the character of which is art-destructive. Both the abyssal mood of mourning and the art-destructive character of allegory, moreover, are subject to the law of alteration: having gone through all the stations of mourning, melancholia (in the figure of Hamlet) overcomes itself in the spirit of *Christlichkeit* (which is to say, messianicity [1:335]), and having run through the "infinity of hopelessness," allegory, in turn, turns around in "*one* about-turn" [einen *Umschwung*] (1:406). The law under which they stand is, however, a law of rigorous infidelity, for, as Benjamin writes at the close of the penultimate section of the work, "The intention [of allegory] does not faithfully rest in the contemplation of bones but faithlessly [*treulos*] leaps over itself and into resurrection" (1:406). Once again, with this law of infidelity, Benjamin draws his resources from Hölderlin's late poetological writings, especially his "Remarks on Antigone," which Benjamin studied for the preliminary outline of his argument (1:917). For all these reasons, the reference to "Patmos" gains the utmost significance on reflection: the "honor of the halfgod," blown away, is the devastated emptiness in which allegory takes up residence and reigns—until the utter emptiness, too, is allegorized. The "until," however, cannot be understood according to any temporal schemata other than the paradoxical one of messianic time.

43. See the central stanza of "Der Rhein," in Friedrich Hölderlin, *Sämtliche Werke*, Große Stuttgarter Ausgabe, ed. Friedrich Beißner (Stuttgart: Kolhammer, 1943-1985), 2:145.

44. Ibid., 2:169; "Patmos," first version, ll. 144-50. Benjamin cites the edition initiated by Norbert von Hellingrath.

45. "Der tiefe aischyleische Zug nach Gerechtigkeit" (1:288)—this phrase, which Benjamin attributes to Max Wundt, appears in § 9 of the *Birth of Tragedy* (*Sämtliche Werke*, 1:71) at precisely the same point where Nietzsche presents Goethe's *Prome-*

theus as the fulfillment of Aeschylus's *Prometheus Bound*. It is worth comparing Nietzsche's remarks on "the deep Aeschylean trait [or pull] toward justice" with Hermann Cohen's very positive assessment of the Aeschylean solution to tragic fate in his *Religion of Reason*: "Thus with Aeschylus too [as in both philosophical consciousness and among the Jewish prophets] ethics leads to religion" (*Religion der Vernunft*, chap. 10, § 8; *Religion of Reason*, 169).

46. On the thematics of the echo in Benjamin, see Rainer Nägele, *Echoes of Translation* (Baltimore, Md.: Johns Hopkins University Press, 1997).

47. As a counterpoint to his approbation of Ziegler's *Zur Metaphysik des Tragischen* at this point in the text, Benjamin harshly condemns the same work later in the same section for its presumptuous condemnation of *Hamlet* (see 1:315). Benjamin may have borrowed the word *seellos* from Hölderlin, more specifically from the famous central lines of "Andenken": "Nicht ist es gut, / Seellos von sterblichen / Gedanken zu sein" (ll.30–32). On the peculiarity of this word as the crux of the poem, see Tim Bahti, *Ends of the Lyric* (Baltimore, Md.: Johns Hopkins University Press, 1996), 143–45.

48. Benjamin, *Origin*, 114.

CHAPTER 13

1. The present essay was originally written for the 1992 conference on the concept of sign as arabesque, "*Zeichen zwischen Klartext und Arabesque*," held in Konstanz, Germany, and appeared in German in the proceedings of the conference, published under the same title: *Zeichen zwischen Klartext und Arabesque*, eds. S. Kotzinger and G. Rippl (Amsterdam and Atlanta: Rodopi, 1994), 307–26.

2. This text exists in two unpublished versions: "Lehre vom Ähnlichen" and "Über das mimetische Vermögen," 2:204–10 and 210–13, respectively.

3. Unless otherwise noted, quotations of Benjamin are from the *Gesammelte Schriften*, ed. Rolf Tiedemann and Hermann Schweppenhäuser, 7 vols. (Frankfurt am Main: Suhrkamp, 1972–1989), and documented with the respective volume number and page number.

4. The relationship between reading (or the reader) and what is read can also be formulated in a textual metaphoric: "What the constellation [*Gestirnstand*] effected [*wirkte*] in a human existence thousands of years ago, was woven in on the basis of similarity" (Benjamin, *Gesammelte Schriften*, 2:210). "Wirkte" is brought into a homonymic suspension (through weaving), into the ambiguity of a weaving and texture metaphoric (*wirken*), on the one hand, and a causal metaphoric (*bewirken*), on the other. The reading of constellation and the life that is similar become entwined in and as texture(s). Similarities that are read affect the reader as (ornamental) inscriptions, interweavings, interlacings of what is read and the reader / life.

5. "Thus [is] language the highest application of the mimetic faculty" (Benjamin, *Gesammelte Schriften*, 2:209) and the "medium, into which the previous forces of mimetic productivity and comprehension have completely entered" (2:213). Compare,

for instance, "Mummerehlen" from the *Berliner Kindheit*, a first attempt at a "Lehre vom Ähnlichen":

> In good time I learned to wrap myself . . . in words [*in die Worte . . . mich zu mummen*]. The gift of recognizing similarity is nothing other than a weak resi-due of the ancient compulsion to conform [*ähnlich zu werden*] and to behave. Words exerted this compulsion over me. Not those which made me imitate patterns of civilized behavior but rather those which made me similar to apart-ments, furniture, clothes. With the sole exclusion of my own image and it is for this reason that I became so helpless when similarity with myself was demanded of me. (4:261)

6. Cf. Benjamin, *Gesammelte Schriften*, 2:211–12. Benjamin himself refers to Valéry's *L'Ame et la Dance* (1923), in which he read "contributions to the doctrine of the mimetic faculty" (2:957).

7. Mallarmé quoted in Jacques Derrida, "The Double Session," *Dissemination* (1972), trans. Barbara Johnson (Chicago: University of Chicago Press, 1981), 173–286, 195, cf. 240ff.

8. Roland Barthes, *Cy Twombly* (Berlin: Merve, 1983), 9.

9. Under the title "Le geste et la parole," André Leroi-Gourhan elaborates the concept of writing as "gesture." He suggests that, "at its origin," this fine art is "a symbolic transposition rather than a reproduction of reality. That is, between the graphic sign, in which one sees a bison, and the bison itself exists the same distance as between the word and the tool" (*Hand und Wort. Die Evolution von Technik, Sprache und Kunst* [Frankfurt am Main: Suhrkamp, 1974], 240). Leroi-Gourhan posits writ-ing as the original site of art and opposes thereby the idea that writing stems from pictography and hence from imitation (243).

10. On the opposition of ornament and imitation in Hegel, and in his reevaluation since Riegl by Pater and Worringer, cf. Hans Günter Schwarz, *Orient und Okzident* (Munich: Judicium-Verlag, 1990), 220, 232.

11. Benjamin cites and thereby radicalizes Worringer's book title *Abstraktion und Einfühlung* and his thesis on abstraction as (in Riegl's terms) primal "artistic will" prior to all depiction as follows: "The ornament is a model for the mimetic fac-ulty. This abstraction is the *haute école* of empathy" (Benjamin, *Gesammelte Schriften*, 2:958).

12. Just how little this simultaneity is that of a self-identical present will be ad-dressed in the following line of argumentation. Cf. Derrida's objection to the concept of *simultaneity* in *Of Grammatology* (1967), trans. Gayatri C. Spivak (Baltimore, Md.: Johns Hopkins University Press, 1974), 85–7.

13. Leroi-Gourhan, *Hand und Wort*, 266. "The history of writing is erected on the base of the history of the *grammē* as an adventure of relationships between the face and the hand" (Derrida, *Of Grammatology*, 84).

14. The arabesque as meaningless arabic letters, as desemanticized calligraphy in-

dicates transitional points where the letters as signs and/or ornaments both enter into competition with each other and serve each other as reciprocal models or patterns. On the concept of *Schriftbild*, see Benjamin, *The Origin of German Tragic Drama*, trans. J. Osborne (New York: Verso, 1977), 174–77. Cf. Bettine Menke, *Sprachfiguren. Name—Allegorie—Bild nach Walter Benjamin* (Munich: Fink, 1991), 186–94.

15. According to Barthes, Cy Twombly's "Work of Writing" has "something to do with calligraphy—. . . . A painting by Twombly is only writing's field of allusions (the rhetorical figure of allusion consists in saying something in order to allow something else to be heard out of it. Twombly refers to writing . . . and then goes somewhere else" (Barthes, *Twombly*, 8–9). "The gestures with which Twombly states (one is tempted to say 'spells') the materiality of the stroke: first, the scribble . . . ; second, the stain . . . ; third, the smear" (68–69). And ibid., 17, in text.

16. Ibid., 72–73.

17. Ibid., 69.

18. Ibid., 13–14. "For Twombly, the drawing disappears for the benefit of the region which it inhabits, mobilizes, works, cancels out—or thins out" (30).

19. In the "Epistemo-Critical Prologue" to the *Origin of German Tragic Drama*, the constellation, projected down from the sky, became the model of presentation, and designated the relation between the conceptually analyzed phenomenon and the "idea," which Benjamin characterized as a "handling" and establishing "interpretation." The ideas relate to phenomenon, namely, "as" the "constellation" to the individual stars. The "constellation" is the schema of a "handling" reading, of a reading of the "elements" scattered throughout and organized within the "constellation," elements whose readability is called "Stern-Bild," the image given in the constellation. In the "Doctrine of the Similar," conversely, the "reading" of the literal constellations in the sky, of "the conjunction of two stars," becomes the paradigmatic case of the perception of "nonsensory similarity." Conversely yet again, "language" is the "canon according to which the opacity associated with the concept of nonsensory similarity can be elucidated." If therefore, on the one hand, metaphorical reading of the literal constellation becomes the paradigm of reading, yet in its moment of "nonsensory similarity," on the other hand, it can only be determined by citing literal reading as the latter's model.

20. Compare the titles: "The book, the sky" in Blanchot's *The Song of the Sirens* (Frankfurt am Main, Berlin, Vienna: Ullstein, 1982), 86; and "The Sky as Book, the Book in the Sky" in Blumenberg's *Lesbarkeit der Welt* (Frankfurt am Main: Suhrkamp, 1986), 22. On the traditional relationship between letter and constellation, see Dornseiff, *Das Alphabet in Mystik und Magie* (Leipzig, Berlin: Teubner, 1925), 3, 15, 19, 38, 81f., 89–90.

21. J. G. Hamann, *Sämtliche Werke*, ed. J. Nadler, (Vienna: Herder, 1951), 3:286, emphasis added.

22. Musical notation fulfills this constellative determination of writing, which remains a factor in all alphabetic writing: its elements are nothing in themselves; they

are namely always the same; they indicate positions. The "lines of notation" do not merely constitute a linear sequence, but provide instructions on positionality as well. The (always at the same time constellative, that is, compositive) dissolution of linear reading in the anagram attempts to approach this.

23. "Are the stars, as the gaze from afar, the urphenomenon of the aura?" (Benjamin, *Gesammelte Schriften*, 2:958). Benjamin's well-known concept of the "investing gaze" [*belehnender Blick*] in the auratic appearance is thus preformed here: "To experience the aura of an appearance," means "*to invest it with the faculty of opening the gaze*" (1:646–47, emphasis added).

24. The "perception of similarity" is a type of "behavior," "derived" from "grasping similarity, which is completed in an act of conforming [*Ähnlichwerden*]" (Benjamin, *Gesammelte Schriften*, 2:956): "[The] similarity between two objects is constantly mediated by the similarity which man finds in himself with both or which he assumes to have with both" (2:956). "Like the perception of similarity by man, its production by man is in many and especially the most important cases [2:206, 'in every case'] bound up with a sudden illumination" (2:203). It is namely "just as fleeting and transitory as a constellation" (2:206, 956). "It is like the intervention of a third, of the astrologer, to the constellation of two stars, which are to be grasped in a single moment. In the opposite case, the astrologer remains unrewarded despite the accuracy of his instruments of observation" (2:207; cf. 2:209). A corresponding, although inverse model is to be found in Benjamin's collection of letters, *Deutsche Menschen*, in which a constellation (Orion), because of its link with a moment of conjunction, becomes a reference point of distant views and is supposed to bring views into constellation: those of Wilhelm Grimm and Jenny von Droste-Hülshoff (4:198–99).

25. The organization of the unreadable into writing as constellation has a temporal and spatial implication: "What is readable is [what appears] in the surface . . . surface which is configuration" (Benjamin, *Gesammelte Schriften*, 6:32). This implies that the varying distances of the stars within the constellation are not visible and just as irrelevant as the question of when the stars that are read in conjunction began to shine. This question is irrelevant and even distorted in the moment (*Augen-Blick*) of the *common* visibility of the stars.

26. The logic of figure and ground is clarified by J. F. Herbart for the "cognitive journey" through the map:

> Thus what is less significant must be conceived of as residing in between, as contained in the region, which has been previously determined by stranger points. The latter must be emphasized, must be separated from the rest, and understood only in connection with each other, be they ever so far apart. . . . This leads to triangulation. . . . The more felicitously the youthful imagination has recognized the representative of the earth's surface on the map, the more easily and readily can our triangles be raised to the *starry* heavens. Its shining points are obviously better suited than the cities of maps to be apprehended with the help

of those preliminary exercises. . . . On occasion one may give names to the constellations, although the child is himself at liberty to sketch out animals, cities,
foundations, and maps in the heavens. (*Pestalozzis Idee eines ABC der Anschauung
untersucht und wissenschaftlich ausgeführt*, in Johann Friedrich Herbart's *Päda-
gogische Schriften*, ed. O. Willmann and T. Fritzsch, 3 vols. [Osterwieck/Harz u.
Leipzig: Zickfeldt, 1919], 293 ff., 403–6)

27. Cf. Derrida: "The other originally collaborates with meaning. There is an
essential *lapse* between significations, which is not the simple and positive fraudulence
of a word, nor even the nocturnal memory of all language. . . . The caesura does not
simply finish and fix meaning: . . . But, primarily, the caesura makes meaning appear" (Jacques Derrida, "Edmund Jabès and the Question of the Book," *Writing and
Difference*, trans. Alan Bass [Chicago: University of Chicago Press, 1978], 64–78, 71).
On the function of the caesura and its connection to rigidification (*Erstarrung*), see
Benjamin, *Gesammelte Schriften*, 1:181, 4:425, 5:593.

28. "The interruption of semiotic reference generates meaning," generates readability in the "effect of a hesitation," as Samuel Weber puts it in another context
on Saussure's model of differentially determined signs: Interruption exists "only as a
kind of suspended reference to something else"; for "only in the suspended relation
to something else can the proper/interior differentiate itself. That which is excluded
thereby . . . becomes, as excluded, the enabling condition of that which excludes"
(Samuel Weber, "Postmoderne und Poststrukturalismus. Versuch, eine Umgebung
zu benennen," in *Ästhetik und Kommunikation* 63, no. 17 (1986): 105 f., 108, 110–11).

29. Walter Benjamin, *Über Haschisch* (Frankfurt am Main: Suhrkamp, 1972), 57.

30. Adolf Wölfli, "Negerhall" (1911). From "*Von der Wiege bis zum Grab. Oder,
Durch arbeiten und schwitzen, leiden, und Drangsal hettend zum Fluch,*" *Schriften 1900–
1912*, Adolf-Wölfli-Foundation, Kunstmuseum Bern, ed. Dieter Schwarz and Elka
Spoerri (Frankfurt am Main: Fischer Verlag, 1985), 2:167.

31. The pictures of Adolf Wölfli constitute a specifiable canon of forms of such
gestalt-switches, particularly the repertoire of the *birdies* and related, allusive *variables*.

32. Figure-poems (such as the figure-poem by Sigmund Birken, in "Pipenbur-
gische Rath-Stelle," 1650, shown in Figure 13.2) establish, on the one hand, a (secondary) reproductive relation (or rather, an emblematic relation) between the written characters as a surface construction and what is said; on the other hand, the
object presented and represented through the letters (but as black areas rather than
as letters) itself "speaks" of itself. The material body of the letter is used in its differential surface-extension with a concettist exposition of the relation between signifier and signified—and for the most part only the mere fact of this spatial extension
is used and not the literal forms of the letter's material body, such as for instance
in arabic calligraphy which figurally distorts the letter (see, for example, in Figure
13.3 the name of god in braided *Kufi*). Cf. B. Reinert, "*Der Concetto-Stil in den isla-*

mischen Literaturen," in *Neues Handbuch der Literaturwissenschaft,* vol. 5: Orientalisches Mittelalter (Wiesbaden: Akademische Verlags-Gesellschaft Athenaion, 1990), 365–408. Irregularities in baroque figure-poems, such as changes of the direction of linear sequences of letters for instance, necessitate ingenious techniques of synthesizing reading, which *momentarily* produces the literalizing linearity (a line that will also draw ornamental flourishes), allowing signifieds to be read, as for instance in Jewish micrography (see figure 13.4, micrography [1496], Bibliothèque nationale Paris, Mss. or., hébreu 50, fol. 9v). The *instance of the letter* is doubled: as a point of blackness with which the surface is filled out and as the next letter to be discovered, which is intended to secure meaning in the sequence.

33. Cf. the reading of arabesques which Oesterle characterizes as "the artificial tension between an 'ornamental mode and a figural mode,'" the shifting, often hardly noticeable transition from one dimension into the other, the complicated reciprocal play of formative factors which respectively support and undermine illusion," the "play between illusion and disillusion, between surface and spatial depth" (Günter Oesterle, *"Arabeske, Schrift, Poesie in E. T. A. Hoffmanns Kunstmärchen 'Der goldene Topf,'"* in *Athenäum. Jahrbuch für Romantik* 1, [München, 1991], 69–107, here 90–91 and 92–93).

34. On euphoria and arabesque, cf. Oesterle, *Arabeske, Schrift und Poesie,* 100.

35. Cf. V, I, 3; Benjamin, *Gesammelte Schriften,* 2:601; 3:223–24; 5:K, 3, 5; and figure 13. 5, the picture puzzle from *Merkprosa. Ein Lesebuch mit Vexierbildern aus dem 19. Jahrhundert,* ed. Werner Berthel (Frankfurt am Main: Insel, 1978). "One can say of course [in reference to the picture puzzle: "rabbit-duck"] that there are certain things which fall under the category of both 'rabbit on a picture' and 'duck on a picture.' One of these things is a picture, a drawing.—But the *impression* is not simultaneously that of a duck on a picture and of a rabbit on a picture" (Ludwig Wittgenstein, *Philosophische Untersuchungen* [Frankfurt am Main: Suhrkamp, 1977], 308). Also:

> I see at once the solution to a picture puzzle. Where there were once branches, there is now a human shape. My visual impression has changed, and I now recognize that it not only has form and color, but also a very specific "organization."—My visual impression has changed;—what was it like before; what is it like now?—Do I represent it by an exact copy—and is it not a good representation?—then no change shows itself. (312)

"Whoever searches in one figure (1) for another figure (2), and then finds it, sees the first figure (1) in a new way. It is not simply that he can give a new kind of description of figure (1), but rather that his observation was a new experience of seeing" (317).

36. See the view of the lion court of Alhambra, in O. Jones and M. J. Goury, "Plans, Elevations, Sections and Details of Alhambra . . ." (London, 1842), 13–14. Rpt. in *Europa und der Orient 800–1900,* ed. Gereon Sievernich and Hendrik Budde (Munich: Gütersloh, 1989), 376.

37. The model of the "picture puzzle" [*Vexierbild*] also functions for the inter-

relation between profane and magical reading (cf. *Gesammelte Schriften*, 2:208, 2:213, 2:209, 4:432).

38. On facefulness (*Gesichtlichkeit*) and readability (in the sense of a reading that anchors meaning), the face as a fundamental pattern of identifiability, see G. Deleuze and F. Guattari, "*Das Jahr Null — Gesichtlichkeit*," in *Bildlichkeit*, ed. V. Bohn, (Frankfurt am Main: Suhrkamp, 1990), 430–68. See also the facial matrices of Wölfli noted above, Figure 13.1.

39. "Satz und Gegensatz" cites a phrase of German Romanticism and an inventive technique of the baroque: "Satz und Gegensatz," following the pattern: "Death is no dance"/"Death is a dance," designated a form of double-texts by the same author cf. *Frauenzimmer Gesprächsspiele* by Georg Philipp Harsdörffer ([Nürnberg, 1646; rpt. Tübingen: Niemeyer, 1969], 6: supplement, 49–50). I thank Erika Greber for this reference.

40. Julia Kristeva speaks of a "pulsing of its rhythm," in which "language" establishes "meanings." See "Zu einer Semiologie der Paragramme," in *Strukturalismus als interpretatives Verfahren*, ed. Helga Gallas (Darmstadt: Luchterhand, 1972), 168.

41. Derrida, *Of Grammatology*, 86.

42. "The way one reads a text whose meaning is secured not so much in the words but rather in the gaps, *between* the lines" (Samuel Weber, "Benjamin-Lektüre," *MLN* 94 [1979]: 441). In a reading that takes on the task of a critical encounter with de-contextualized words and letters (443), "strange" new "methods of combination" between them are opened up — "expressions and words" for which the reader "lies in wait" "in every act of reading." One thinks here of the play with the baroque and the mnemotechnic tradition that is the subject of one of Benjamin's emblems under the title "Brezel, Feder, Pause, Klage, Firlefanz" (*Gesammelte Schriften*, 4:432–33).

43. Cf. Benjamin, *Gesammelte Schriften*, 2:208, 212.

44. Cf. Benjamin, "Schmöker" (Potboiler), in *Berliner Kindheit* (*Gesammelte Schriften*, 4:274–75). The connection between the "flurry of letters" and "snow flurries" and the silence of both is captured in a phrase of J. Grimm (from the introduction to the *Deutsches Wörterbuch*), which Benjamin cites in the selection of letters *Deutsche Menschen* (4:217). The swirling of words/letters/flakes is encountered by that reading that "does not allow itself to be censored by 'meaning'" (4:609) and that adheres to the isolated letters and their materiality — thus the fascination with the reading box (4:267), cf. "Aussicht ins Kinderbuch" (4:609–15), and "Lesendes Kind" (4:113).

45. [Translator's Note: Several semantic fields are brought together in Benjamin's use here of the term "undicht." In addition to its more colloquial translation as "leaky" or "leaking," which relates to Benjamin's flurry-metaphoric (*das Gestöber, das Flockige*), "undicht" also signifies a type of "loose weave" within a textile-metaphoric. "Undicht" thus encompasses "das Flockige" and "das Lockere" of both metaphorical contexts that converge in the implied model of writing as *Dicht*-ung.]

46. Clouds (*Gewölke*), which as clouds of color are (in Benjamin) also opposition-

ally situated in relation to the outline (cf. Benjamin, *Gesammelte Schriften*, 4: 613ff.), dissolve self-identity, which photography demands of what it is supposed to "record." Then there is no photography, no "depiction," for the tear or rip, which is lost and self-scattering in the similarity with words and things. "The paints that I then mixed colored me. When they ran together on the palette, I drew them up into my brush as cautiously as if they were dissolving clouds [*Gewölk*]. . . . Thus was I too amid my jars and brushes at once dislocated into the picture. I resembled the porcelain into which I entered with a cloud of color" (cf. 6:261–63). "It is not that things step out from the page of the child-artist—in watching, the child himself enters into the page as a cloud [*Gewölk*] which satiates itself with the world of pictures' brilliance of color" (4:609). (1) The cloud (*Gewölk*) of colors, (2) the outline as ornament, (3) the written materiality (of the ornament), (4) the flurry (*Gestöber*) as the internal implication of the constellation—this results in a fourfold constellation, which can no longer be assimilated into an oppositional order.

47. This corresponds to the (typo)graphic development of writing in the "typeface" [*Schriftbild*] of the "Coup de dés" and the advertisement (Benjamin, *Gesammelte Schriften*, 4:479).

The writing which penetrates ever further into the graphic of its new and ex-centric visuality gains immediate possession of its adequate subject matter. . . . Poets, who will then be first and foremost *experts in writing* as they have been for ages, will only be able to take part in the writing of rebuses [*Bilderschrift*], when they open up for themselves these regions in which the latter are constructed (without producing difficulty themselves): those of the static and technical diagram. (4:104)

CHAPTER 14

1. This is also the central focus of one of the few articles to deal with Benjamin's reading of Kraus; see Josef Fürnkäs, "Zitat und Zerstörung: Karl Kraus und Walter Benjamin," in *Verabschiedung der (Post)Moderne? Eine interdisziplinäre Debatte*, ed. Jacques Le Rider and Gerard Raulet (Tübingen: Narr, 1987), 209–25.

The source of all quotations from Walter Benjamin's *Gesammelte Schriften*, ed. Rolf Tiedemann and Hermann Schweppenhäuser, 7 vols. (Frankfurt am Main: Suhrkamp, 1972–1989) is indicated in the text by volume and page number. References to English translations of Benjamin are to the following editions: *One-Way Street and Other Writings*, trans. Edmund Jephcott and Kingsley Shorter (London: Verso, 1985), abbreviated as *OWS*; and *Illuminations*, ed. Hannah Arendt, trans. Harry Zohn (New York: Schocken, 1992), abbreviated as *I*. Translations of all passages with a refererence to the German source alone are the translator's own.

2. Most essays on sexuality and the concept of gender in Benjamin's works center on the figure of the whore. On Eros, see above all Giorgio Agamben, "Walter

Benjamin und das Dämonische. Glück und geschichtliche Erlösung im Denken Benjamins," in *Walter Benjamin 1882–1940, zum 100. Geburtstag*, ed. Uwe Steiner (Bern: Lang, 1992), 189–216; Norbert Bolz, "Prostituiertes Sein," in *Antike und Moderne. Zu Walter Benjamins "Passagen*," eds. Norbert Bolz and Richard Faber (Würzburg: Königshausen und Neumann, 1986), 191–213; Jochen Hörisch, *Die Theorie der Verausgabung und die Verausgabung der Theorie. Benjamin zwischen Bataille und Sohn-Rethel* (Buchladen: Wassmann, n.d.); Sigrid Weigel, *Body- and Image-Space: Re-Reading Walter Benjamin* (London: Routledge, 1996); and Sigrid Weigel, "Reading/Writing the Feminine City: Calvino, Hessel, Benjamin," in *"With the Sharpened Axe of Reason": Approaches to Walter Benjamin*, ed. Gerhard Fischer (Oxford: Berg, 1996), 85–98.

3. [Translator's Note: Jephcott and Shorter's translation is "To convince is to conquer without conception" (*OWS* 47).]

4. See his contributions since 1911 to *Der Anfang*, which are reproduced in volume 7 of Benjamin's collected works.

5. [Translator's Note: Jephcott and Shorter's translation "It [that is, the demon] died at source" for "Er fiel am Ursprung" fails to recognize the allusion to the fall of Satan from heaven: "He fell in the beginning" is thus preferable as a translation here, and the "demon" is gendered masculine throughout, as he is in the German.]

6. It is not only the mention of the *Angelus Novus* at the conclusion of the Kraus essay but also the work on this constellation that links the Kraus essay to the "angel of history" and situates it within the prehistory of the historico-theoretical theses.

7. The connections among testimony, lament/accusation, and justice sketched out by Benjamin in this essay remain as yet undiscovered for the current debate about thought after Auschwitz, despite the fact that his reflections here are much closer to this historical problematic than the essay on "The Critique of Violence," which has been so much at the center of discussion since Derrida's reading brought it renewed prominence.

8. Among others is the motto of Thesis XIV, in "On the Concept of History," 1:701; *I* 252.

9. Benjamin is here quoting from Berthold Viertel's book on Kraus (cf. 2:1129).

10. This is a constellation similar to that of the "angel of history."

11. Written in the early 1930s. See Sigrid Weigel, *Topographien der Geschlechter. Kulturgeschichtliche Studien zur Literatur* (Reinbek b. Hamburg: Rowohlt, 1990), as well as Weigel, *Body- and Image-Space* for a fuller discussion.

Index

In this index "f" after a number indicates a separate reference on the next page, and "ff" indicates separate references on the next two pages. A continuous discussion over two or more pages is indicated by a span of numbers. *Passim* is used for a cluster of references in close but not consecutive sequence.